P9-CKB-660

Chaco & Hohokam

*The publication of this book
was made possible by generous support from
the Brown Foundation, Inc., of Houston, Texas,
and Charlotte N. Gray.*

SCHOOL OF AMERICAN RESEARCH
ADVANCED SEMINAR SERIES

Douglas W. Schwartz, General Editor

Chaco & Hohokam

CONTRIBUTORS

PATRICIA L. CROWN
Department of Anthropology
University of New Mexico, Albuquerque

DAVID E. DOYEL
Department of Anthropology
Arizona State University, Tempe

DAVID A. GREGORY
Tucson, Arizona

W. JAMES JUDGE
Department of Anthropology
Fort Lewis College
Durango, Colorado

STEPHEN H. LEKSON
Crow Canyon Archaeological Center
Denver

W. BRUCE MASSE
Department of Anthropology
University of Hawaii, Honolulu

CHARLES L. REDMAN
Department of Anthropology
Arizona State University,Tempe

LYNNE SEBASTIAN
Office of Cultural Affairs
Historic Preservation Division
State of New Mexico, Santa Fe

H. WOLCOTT TOLL
Office of Archaeological Studies
Museum of New Mexico, Santa Fe

R. GWINN VIVIAN
Arizona State Museum
University of Arizona, Tucson

DAVID R. WILCOX
Museum of Northern Arizona
Flagstaff

Chaco & Hohokam

Prehistoric Regional Systems in the American Southwest

Edited by
PATRICIA L. CROWN & W. JAMES JUDGE

SCHOOL OF AMERICAN RESEARCH PRESS
SANTA FE, NEW MEXICO

School of American Research Press
Post Office Box 2188
Santa Fe, New Mexico 87504-2188
www.sarweb.org

Director & Editor: Joan K. O'Donnell
Designer: Deborah Flynn Post
Indexer: Andrew L. Christenson
Typographer: Keystone Typesetting, Inc.
Printer: Sheridan Books

Library of Congress Cataloging-in-Publication Data:

Chaco & Hohokam : prehistoric regional systems in the American Southwest /
edited by Patricia L. Crown & W. James Judge. — 1st pbk. ed.
      p.   cm. — (School of American Research advanced seminar series)
Papers from a seminar held in Oct. 1987; sponsored by the School of American
Research. Includes bibliographical references and index.
ISBN 0-933452-75-6 (cloth) — ISBN 0-933452-76-4 (paper)
1. Hohokam culture.   2. Chaco Culture National Historical Park (N.M.)   3. Indians
of North America—Southwest, New—Antiquities.   4 Southwest, New—Antiquities.
I. Crown, Patricia L.   II. Judge, W. James (William James)   III. School of American
Research (Santa Fe, N.M.)   IV. Title: Chaco and Hohokam.   V. Series.
E99.H68C48   1991   978.9'82—dc20   90–26559   CIP

© 1991 by the School of American Research Press. All rights reserved.
Manufactured in the United States of America.
Library of Congress Catalog Card Number 90–26559.
Internation Standard Book Numbers 0-933452-75-6 (cloth),
0-933452-76-4 (paper).
Fifth paperback printing 2004.

Contents

ILLUSTRATIONS

TABLES

Acknowledgments

The editors of this volume would like to extend their deepest gratitude to the School of American Research, the United States Bureau of Reclamation, and Mrs. Peter A. Gerardi for funding this advanced seminar. We are particularly grateful to Bureau of Reclamation archaeologist James Maxon for supporting our proposal for funding from that agency. Douglas W. Schwartz and Jonathan Haas of the School of American Research provided encouragement from the inception of this seminar through the conclusion of a memorable week. We could not have asked for a more stimulating atmosphere in which to hold the seminar, or a more informed and exciting group of scholars with whom to interact. Seminar house manager Jane Barberousse and her staff made our stay in Santa Fe exceptionally pleasant and ensured that all of us left not only a little wiser, but a little heavier as well. Jane Kepp, director of publications at the School of American Research, and Joan K. O'Donnell, editor, patiently guided us through the steps of manuscript preparation. Jane Kepp and two anonymous reviewers provided thoughtful comments on the original manuscript, and Charles Sternberg drafted many of the figures.

Chapter 1

Introduction

PATRICIA L. CROWN and W. JAMES JUDGE

THE Hohokam and Chaco regional systems stand out as two of the major prehistoric developments in the American Southwest. The two systems exercised considerable influence over broad geographic areas of roughly similar size (figs. 1.1, 1.2). Although contemporaneous, they seem to have developed and functioned independently, with little interaction. Recently, extensive archaeological research projects have been completed in the two areas, yet these also have been conducted largely independently. Virtually no effort has been made to compare the adaptations and processes that characterized the two systems.

The School of American Research advanced seminar "Cultural Complexity in the Arid Southwest: The Hohokam and Chacoan Regional Systems," held in October 1987, brought together experts in both Hohokam and Chaco archaeology to review the results of recent research, to compare the initiation, growth, and decline of both systems, and to assess their importance to broader issues of anthropological relevance. We did not perceive this seminar as providing a definitive statement on the regional system as a concept; instead, we used the term as an organizing framework to facilitate discussion of prehistoric systems characterized by ongoing interaction and alliance.

At the beginning of the seminar, we defined prehistoric regional systems as consisting of a number of interacting but geographically separate communities that were dependent on each other through the exchange of goods and services (Judge 1984:8). As the seminar progressed, it rapidly became apparent that each participant brought to this definition a slightly different perspective. Although we all agreed on some aspects of these systems, we found that our understanding of their boundaries varied according to the specific analytic criteria used to examine them. For

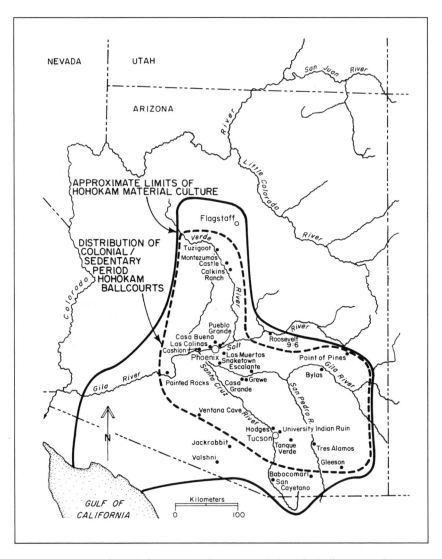

Figure 1.1. *The Hohokam regional system as defined by ballcourts and material culture.*

example, we could draw substantially different boundaries for the Chacoan regional system on the basis of ceramic exchange as opposed to the presence of "great houses." In part, our difficulty in defining a regional system in a consistent manner rested on the difficulty of identifying true economic dependency in the archaeological record.

Recognizing the frailty of the concept, we nonetheless found it a useful

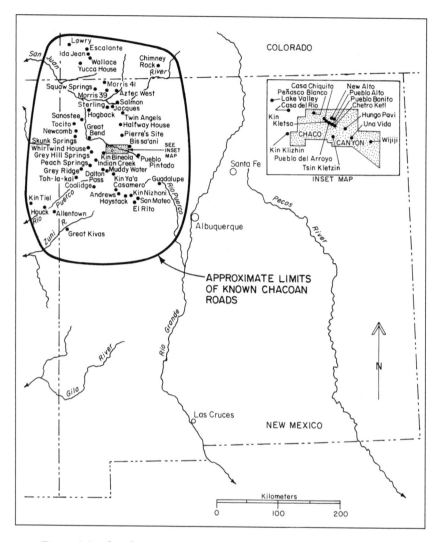

Figure 1.2. *The Chaco regional system as defined by roads and other architectural criteria.*

framework for discussing the data. And as we discovered in the seminar, regardless of how the boundaries were defined, there was more intensive interaction and exchange in goods and ideas between populations living within the defined areas than between these populations and groups outside. We retained the regional system concept, then, because it facilitated communication and because a major focus of the conference was the attempt to understand the nature of this interaction.

As organizers of the seminar, we felt that in-depth comparison of Chaco and the Hohokam offered a unique opportunity to the discipline of anthropology since it is rare that such groups can be isolated in a prehistoric context with the degree of refinement now available in Arizona and New Mexico. Not only can the two groups be identified, but their origins can be traced, their growth and interaction examined, and the truncation of each system evaluated. Furthermore, archaeologists have excellent control over paleoenvironmental variables in each of the regions. As a result, we had an unusual opportunity to analyze the archaeological record and address general, yet very important, anthropological issues relating to the development, function, and decline of cultural complexity in a known environmental context.

Although numerous questions of relevance to these issues could be defined, when we organized the seminar we focused on three main categories. First, what stimulated the origin and growth of the Hohokam and Chaco systems? Second, how were these systems bounded and how were the boundaries maintained? Third, what factors served to truncate the systems: that is, what prevented the attainment of further complexity?

With respect to the first question, the conference examined those factors that facilitated the systems' origins, as well as the reasons they developed where they did and when they did. We felt it was important to know why the Hohokam and Chaco regions experienced greater complexity than other portions of the Southwest during this early time period (A.D. 900–1100). The seminar examined system growth, both spatially and temporally, in terms of conditions in each area that may have served to facilitate or constrain such growth.

We then examined the natural and cultural factors that served to identify the systems, as well as how those delimiting boundaries were maintained, how permeable they were, and what kinds of system interaction were facilitated or constrained by the bounding methods. We also looked at possible relationships between the two systems from the standpoint of system growth. A final issue with respect to system delineation was the attempt to deal with gross population estimates for each region and to examine the relationship between population density and system size, growth, and complexity. As will become apparent to the reader, it was this portion of the discussion that engendered the greatest disagreement among the participants.

The decline in complexity of both the Hohokam and Chaco systems has been a question of interest to archaeologists for a long time. Although the Chaco region was largely abandoned after reaching maximal size in the twelfth century A.D., the Hohokam area continued to be occupied, although at a different level of complexity and influence. This situation offered us an excellent opportunity to review recent data on possible cultural and natural factors that might have initiated the demise of each system, and to evaluate hypotheses about why the decline was manifested differently in the two areas.

TOPICAL ORGANIZATION

The seminar covered four main topics within the broader problem domain of regional systems: subsistence, settlement, exchange, and social complexity. The scholars invited to participate were selected for their special expertise in these topics, their continuing commitment to the prehistory of these areas, and their involvement in recently completed major projects. Each participant addressed one topic from the standpoint of relevance to the three main anthropological issues defined earlier, and each prepared a comprehensive paper reviewing current data and models relating to that topic for one of the geographic areas.

While the other seminar participants prepared topical papers, the two of us wrote papers introducing the reader to each of the regional systems: the history of research, basic culture history, and definition of the system boundaries. Charles Redman participated in the seminar and commented on the papers. His extensive experience in the archaeology of other arid portions of the world brought a broader perspective to the discussion of questions of general anthropological significance, as is reflected in his contribution to the volume.

SYNOPSES OF VOLUME CONTRIBUTIONS

At this juncture, we offer brief synopses of the individual participants' papers in order to place the following chapters in broader perspective. We will summarize the seminar discussions and review interregional comparisons in the concluding chapter of the volume.

CHACO

In discussing the Chaco settlement system, Stephen Lekson offers a much less restrictive view of its size than have previous archaeologists. He focuses on roads (extrinsic criteria) that link communities of great houses, great kivas, and unit houses. Where road segment evidence is lacking, he uses the contextual relationships of these major architectural components to argue that a given cluster of sites is Chacoan. Employing these criteria, Lekson presents a Chaco regional system that is greatly expanded from that suggested by other scholars. He bounds the region physically by the

Rockies to the north and the Mogollon Rim to the south, and culturally by the Kayenta Anasazi to the west and the Rio Grande Anasazi to the east. At this macroscale, he sees almost uniform settlement distributed throughout most of the Colorado Plateau, with the sites formally integrated by the Chaco road system. Given his view of the region, Lekson does not consider the central area to have been abandoned in the twelfth century; instead, the center diminished in activity and its peripheries flourished.

In contrast, Gwinn Vivian questions the concept of a single Chaco system. He returns instead to Kluckhohn's early hypothesis of two contemporaneous egalitarian systems, each with its distinct roots. Vivian terms these systems Cibolan (small-house communities) and San Juan (great-house settlements), the latter developing in the core area, then spreading beyond the canyon. Addressing the topic of subsistence, he feels that the potential of the Chaco core area has been underestimated. He suggests that with the support of the Escavada area, nutrient replenishing through silting, extensive water control mechanisms, the use of wild foods, and the lack of fallow periods, the population of the area might have exceeded 5,000. This is considerably greater than other recent models, which have suggested levels of around 2,000. Vivian thus questions the vacant city and pilgrimage concepts currently in vogue. He also notes that the system developed in a relatively favorable climate and suggests that the resource-population imbalance, when it occurred, was solved by emigration from the core to the outlying areas.

In discussing Chacoan exchange, H. Wolcott Toll takes a more traditional view of the size of the system than does Lekson and does not feel that a duality of the nature suggested by Vivian existed. He notes that Pueblo Bonito is unique among Chaco sites in the frequency of exotic materials found there and suggests that most exchange in the system was utilitarian. Quantitatively, there was exaggerated movement of materials from the Chuska area to Chaco during the peak building period (A.D. 1040–1100), evidenced by the large numbers of imported ceramics, lithics, roof beams, and possibly big game. In terms of exchange, Toll suggests an early system focus to the south of Chaco, followed by one to the west, and ending with Chaco finally becoming the geographical center of the system due to increased activity to the north. He feels that the movement of subsistence goods within the region may have been an adaptation to compensate for climatic variability in the A.D. 1000s, and he emphasizes his belief that large quantities of utilitarian items were being moved when the system was functioning at its peak.

Lynne Sebastian, who deals with the issue of Chaco social complexity, disagrees with what she terms Toll's "nonadministered redistributive" economy and the presumed absence of elites. She feels the system could not have operated without some degree of institutionalized leadership and bases her own explanation on a computer simulation of surplus production in Chaco, which she correlated with great-house construction. Both land-intensive and labor-intensive strategies were used to increase production, but the latter strategy results in a higher potential increase due to the capture of "unearned" water. This led in turn to an asymmetry of power and obligations between neighbors. Would-be leaders took advantage of this situation to develop a power base and to initiate the economic system. The structure later developed to the point that it could survive variability in production, possibly because the leaders claimed access to the supernatural and thus lent a strong ritual component to their leadership. Sebastian notes that even though the Chaco and Hohokam systems evolved in quite different environments, they both seem to have developed mechanisms of integration based on institutionalized leadership, a development that may be endemic to the general process of sociopolitical evolution.

HOHOKAM

David Gregory provides in his contribution a comprehensive overview of Hohokam settlement form and variation. Using a recently developed assessment of prehistoric Salt River flow rates, he presents a model of Hohokam development closely tied to relative stability or variation in annual flow rates. He argues that evidence for economic interdependency or political unification on a regional scale is lacking for the Hohokam, and he therefore calls for further examination of the validity of the regional system concept in this case, contrasting the evidence for sustained interaction, economic interdependency, and integration in the Chacoan system with the Hohokam situation.

Bruce Masse, examining the roles played by the environment and the subsistence system in the growth of a Hohokam regional system, argues that the system developed at about A.D. 700 through interaction with other areas as a result of exchange networks, the growth of the irrigation systems, and population increase. He points out that the boundaries coincided with the limits of floodwater and irrigation agriculture in the Southwest and with the availability of mesquite and cactus products. Using the same information on Salt River flow rates used by Gregory, Masse argues that availability of water was not a problem, but flooding was. A flood in A.D. 899 caused decentralization and widespread population movement from the Salt-Gila Basin into areas where greater reliance on dry farming provided a more secure subsistence base. At the same time, more ballcourts were built to maintain control over the regional economic system through hypothesized exchange associated with the gathering of populations to witness rituals or games in the ballcourts. The eventual collapse of the regional system probably resulted from a combination of factors: flooding in the 1080s, hydrologic degradation in the early 1100s, and larger communities forcibly recruiting labor or levying tribute from surrounding populations. A major flood in 1358 ultimately destroyed the canal networks, resulting in the final depopulation of the Hohokam area.

In his discussion of Hohokam economy, David Doyel argues that the system grew in response to the need for exchange activities between areas with resource imbalances. The ballcourt system provided a mechanism for exchange, but the boundaries of the system were flexible and changed through time. The system expanded until 1050 or 1100, when it collapsed and was reorganized. Doyel reviews a variety of models for the final post-1300 collapse and depopulation of the Hohokam area.

David Wilcox believes that Hohokam population consisted of corporate kin groups crosscut by sodalities and integrated by the ceremonial exchange systems known to prehistorians through the system of ballcourts. The ballcourt network, an open system marked by "continuities of interaction" rather than by boundaries, disappeared by 1100, at which time populations in the Salt-Gila Basin faced both less predictable water supplies and greater social circumscription. Combined with increasing conflict with surrounding groups, these factors led to a need for greater coordination of effort and social control. Ultimately, the increased vertical hierarchy marked by habitation on the platform mounds after 1300 indicates that such social control was instituted.

DISCUSSANT

In his discussion of the seminar papers, Charles Redman provides two comparative examples of the growth of social complexity in other parts of the world and suggests that a major reason complex societies emerge is to manage people and resources. Since relatively low population levels characterized the Hohokam and Chaco regional systems, control of resources must have been a factor in system growth. The neighboring, more advanced Mesoamerican society might have made demands for materials from Southwestern groups, influencing the growth in complexity in the Southwest. The Hohokam situation might have parallels in Mesopotamia, where irrigation agriculture provided the potential for higher population density than existed in surrounding areas and where a redistributive economy directed by a religious-based elite produced and exchanged goods with surrounding areas. By contrast, the Chaco regional system growth was not tied to the agricultural potential of the core, or canyon, itself. Rather, Chaco was centrally located geographically with respect to moving goods and controlling exchange routes. Citing a North African example, Redman suggests that economically active communities would have to exist on the peripheries of the regional system to move goods through these networks.

The advanced seminar "Cultural Complexity in the Arid Southwest" brought together specialists from the two prehistoric cultural systems currently considered the largest, most complex, and best documented in the southwestern United States. More importantly, it served to foster productive discussion of issues relevant to archaeologists and anthropologists working in other areas and in other time periods. We hope that the papers in this volume will serve to bring a new understanding about the growth and functioning of cultural systems to the anthropological community as a whole.

Chapter 2

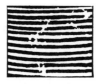

Chaco: Current Views of Prehistory and the Regional System

W. JAMES JUDGE

THE information presented in this chapter is intended to offer the reader a background in the development of Chaco archaeology up to the time the papers in this seminar were written (October 1987). Included is a review of the history of research in the Chaco area, the chronology and description of cultural stages, the definition of the Chaco regional system, and a brief synthesis of prior theories of its development.

HISTORY OF RESEARCH

This review of research in the Chaco area focuses first on the canyon itself and then on the outlying areas, the order in which research actually progressed on the "Chaco phenomenon." Prior reviews of work in the canyon have been written by Brand and others (1937), Pierson (1956), Vivian and Mathews (1965), Vivian (1970b), Hayes (1981), and Lister and Lister (1981), among others. My treatment will be brief and will emphasize the more recent research, including work done on the outlier system.

The first detailed records of Chaco Canyon were provided by Lieutenant James Simpson, a surveyor with an American military expedition to the Navajo country in 1849. Though in the canyon only a brief time, Simpson recorded 11 of the major ruins there. Richard Kern, the expedition artist, made sketches of a number of these.

William Henry Jackson, photographer with the Hayden Survey, visited the canyon in 1877, taking some 400 photographs of the sites. Unfortunately, he was testing a new technique and none of the photos turned out. Though this was a monumental loss, Jackson did name and describe several additional sites beyond those noted by Simpson.

In 1896, Richard Wetherill, well known in southwestern Colorado for his discoveries in the Mesa Verde area, homesteaded in Chaco Canyon and established a trading post there. He was instrumental in bringing the Chacoan sites to the attention of the Hyde Exploring Expedition and in obtaining funding from them to investigate Pueblo Bonito. Frederick Putnam, of the American Museum of Natural History and Harvard University, was officially the director of the Hyde project, but field supervision was assigned to George Pepper. Pepper and Wetherill shared supervision of the excavations at Pueblo Bonito for four seasons, during which approximately 190 rooms were dug at a cost of about $3,000. Though the excavations stopped in 1899, Wetherill continued to live in the canyon until June of 1910, when he was killed by a Navajo in a dispute over cattle.

A certain amount of controversy surrounded the Hyde project, and as a result, a special agent of the General Land Office, S. J. Holsinger, was assigned to investigate the situation in 1901. In addition to examining the archaeological work that had been done, Holsinger made extensive and detailed descriptions of the climate and of many ruins, irrigation systems, stairways, and segments of the prehistoric road between Pueblo Alto and Chetro Ketl. Largely as a result of Holsinger's work, in 1907 Chaco Canyon was included among the first group of sites to be given status as national monuments by President Theodore Roosevelt, following the enactment of the Antiquities Act.

In 1920, Edgar L. Hewett, known in the Southwest for his concern for antiquities and his affiliation with the School of American Research (SAR) and the Museum of New Mexico, began the excavation of Chetro Ketl, a large and very important site a few hundred feet east of Pueblo Bonito. This excavation was suspended from 1921 to 1929, while Neil Judd renewed the excavation of Pueblo Bonito. Hewett returned in 1929, this time affiliated with the University of New Mexico as well as SAR. Work continued at Chetro Ketl through 1934, and over half of the site was dug. Unfortunately, apart from a dissertation by Florence Hawley Ellis (Hawley 1934) on the Chetro Ketl dump, very little was published on the excavation of that important site. Lekson (1983) has recently provided an excellent compilation of what is known about Chetro Ketl. A number of other important sites were dug under Hewett's general supervision, including the Talus Unit behind Chetro Ketl; Tleyit Kin; and two great kivas—Casa Rinconada and Kin Nahasbas.

In 1921, Neil Judd of the Smithsonian Institution renewed work at Pueblo Bonito with financial support from the National Geographic Society. Between 1921 and 1927, Judd finished the excavation of Bonito, dug Pueblo del Arroyo, and undertook tests at several other sites (Peñasco

Blanco, Pueblo Alto trash mound). With Judd was Frank H. H. Roberts, also of the Smithsonian, who assisted with the testing and excavated a number of sites, including Shabik'eshchee Village, the type site for the Basketmaker III period on the Colorado Plateau.

Following the Judd-Hewett era—and in recognition of the need to preserve the excavated sites—the National Park Service established its Ruins Stabilization Unit in 1937. This group was based in Chaco Canyon until 1957 and undertook a considerable amount of excavation under the rubric of stabilization. Records of this activity were kept by the unit.

In 1938, the University of New Mexico field school in archaeology began work in the canyon, under the direction of Donald Brand, Paul Reiter, and Clyde Kluckhohn, among others. A total of 10 field seasons were spent in Chaco, with fieldwork focusing on small sites across the Chaco Wash from Pueblo Bonito, the "BC" sites. In 1947, the last year of the field school, Lloyd Pierson undertook the first formal archaeological survey of the canyon, recording 211 sites.

Gordon Vivian, who had excavated Casa Rinconada with Hewett and was directing the Ruins Stabilization Unit, excavated the 3-C site in 1939. Continuing his stabilization work, Vivian reconstructed Casa Rinconada and later dug the Tri-Wall complex behind Pueblo del Arroyo. In 1951 and 1953, he completed the excavation of Kin Kletso, assisted by Tom Mathews. Gordon's son Gwinn completed his master's thesis on the Navajo occupation of the Chacra Mesa in 1960, and in 1970 finished his doctoral dissertation on Chaco Canyon (Vivian 1970b). His was the first "modern" approach to the explanation of the Chaco phenomenon from the canyon perspective.

In 1969, a seminar was sponsored by the School of American Research in Santa Fe to outline the character of a long-term, multidisciplinary research project in Chaco Canyon. This project was largely the idea of John Corbett, chief archaeologist of the National Park Service at the time, and was to be funded by the Park Service in cooperation with the University of New Mexico. The seminar resulted in a research prospectus for the project, written by Will Logan and Zorro Bradley, which was approved and initiated by the Park Service in 1971. Robert Lister was selected as director of what came to be known as the "Chaco Project" or the "Chaco Center," located at the University of New Mexico. I assumed direction of the project from 1977 until 1985.

In 1971, under my direction, Dennis Stanford completed an initial 25-percent sample survey of Chaco Canyon National Monument (Judge 1972). From 1972 through 1975, Alden Hayes undertook a 100-percent inventory survey of the monument, which resulted in the identification of some 1,991 sites (Hayes 1981). The work was complemented by intensive studies in remote sensing, also funded and administered by the Park Service as part of the Chaco Project.

Beginning in 1973, the Chaco Project initiated a series of excavations of a sample of "small" Chacoan sites, including sites near Fajada Butte, in Marcia's Rincon, at the mouth of Werito's Rincon, at Atlatl Cave, and at various other places in the canyon. Publications resulting from these excavations include books by Windes (1978), McKenna (1984), and McKenna and Truell (1986). A series of Navajo hogans were excavated in 1973 and 1974 as part of the project, resulting in a monograph by David Brugge (1986), who also wrote A History of the Chaco Navajos (Brugge 1980).

The Chaco Project began testing Pueblo Alto, the major unexcavated Classic Chacoan structure on the mesa north of Pueblo Bonito, in 1976. A sampling and research design was developed for the site (Judge 1976), and work continued there for three field seasons. A three-volume final report on this work has been completed (Mathien and Windes 1987; Windes 1987a).

Also in 1976, a sample survey of several outlying Chacoan areas was initiated by the Chaco Project under the direction of Robert Powers, to complement work being carried out by the Public Service Company of New Mexico. This resulted in the publication of a synthetic report on the outliers (Powers, Gillespie, and Lekson 1983).

Other archaeological work undertaken in Chaco Canyon during the years of the Chaco Project included an extensive rock art survey under the direction of James Bain of the New Mexico Archaeological Society, various kinds of fieldwork in archaeoastronomy (e.g., Carlson and Judge 1987), testing at Una Vida and Kin Nahasbas before backfilling by the Park Service (Gillespie 1984), and inventory survey under the direction of Bob Powers to cover new areas added to the renamed Chaco Culture National Historic Park by the 1980 legislation (see below).

Turning to the research undertaken on Chaco outliers, as opposed to the core canyon area, I would note first that prior to the 1970s there was little recognition that the core area and the outlying Chaco-like sites represented an integrated whole. If anything, the sites with obvious Chaco similarities (e.g., Aztec, Pueblo Pintado, Kin Bineola, etc.) were thought to represent Chacoan occupations that followed the abandonment of the canyon. It was not until remote-sensing techniques were applied systematically to the investigation of the prehistoric roads (the existence of which, incidentally, had been known for some time; see Vivian 1983a for a review) that the concept of an integrated system began to take root. This provided the theoretical basis for a number of models of the San Juan Basin as a whole during the Classic Chaco period (Judge 1979).

As this concept began to take shape, several large-scale surveys were initiated, resulting in the publication of two major summaries of the Chaco system. One of these was funded by the Public Service Company of New Mexico and focused on all sites in the San Juan Basin that appeared to have Chacoan affinities, particularly large formal structures and great kivas (Marshall et al. 1979). In addition to describing sites in the interior basin (sometimes referred to as the Chaco Basin), the study included sites in southwestern Colorado and the Zuni area. Eighty sites in all were reported, though not all were demonstrably Chacoan and not all were contemporary with classic developments in the canyon. Primarily descriptive in nature, the study did offer a brief interpretive summary that dealt with the concept of using a combination of public architecture (public buildings, great kivas) and associated smaller sites to identify outlying communities.

A second study, funded by the Chaco Project, undertook intensive survey of three outliers (Bis sa'ani, Peach Springs, Pierre's Site), as well as a reconnaissance and literature survey of 33 more (Powers, Gillespie, and Lekson 1983). A final chapter provided an extensive interpretive summary, including chronology, community and regional settlement patterns, environmental variability, and site type variability.

Another summary (Plog and Wait 1982) followed an SAR seminar on the San Juan Basin, organized primarily to deal with the tremendous amount of archaeological contract data being compiled due to energy development in the basin. Much of the data had been computerized as part of the San Juan Basin Regional Uranium Study (the SJBRUS data base), enabling the quantification of settlement studies. Though this summary was oriented toward cultural resource management planning for all time periods and site types in the basin, it also provided valuable information on the Chaco system itself.

The final summary to emerge recently (Kincaid 1983) was the result of concern on the part of the Bureau of Land Management (BLM) about the management of Chaco roads. The publication followed extensive study of the roads and included inventory, testing, detailed verification of alignments identified through aerial photo interpretation, and an analysis of road corridors. Though focusing on the roads, it provided valuable information on the variety of associated architectural structures, as well as verification of the roads themselves and the labor investment involved in their construction and maintenance.

In the 1970s and 1980s, then, it became increasingly apparent that the so-called Chaco phenomenon involved a regional system of considerable extent (approximately 67,340 sq km, or 26,000 sq. mi.), with Chaco Canyon serving as the core area, connected by a system of formal, engineered roads linking a network of as many as 70 outlying communities, each with Chacoan public houses and great kivas. Archaeologists realized that they were dealing with a phenomenon much more complex than initially was conceived, and this, of course, has led to a great deal of speculation about the nature and function of the system.

Given this introduction to the Chaco outliers, I would like to briefly review research on them that had taken place prior to the studies noted above. I give the ownership of each site to emphasize the complex problems facing archaeologists trying to ensure that the sites are managed and interpreted in a coherent fashion. I will discuss only those sites that have been the subject of investigation (formal or informal) or preservation measures. Figure 2.1 shows the location of these sites.

Village of the Great Kivas. Currently owned by the Zuni tribe, the site was excavated by Frank H. H. Roberts in the 1920s. His report was published as a Bureau of American Ethnology *Bulletin* (Roberts 1932).

Casamero. The Chacoan structure and great kiva are under BLM ownership, and the structure was dug in the 1960s by the Cottonwood Gulch Foundation. Ann Sigleo, who directed the fieldwork, submitted a report to the Chaco Project on the excavation. The site was later (1970s) stabilized by the BLM under the direction of Earl Neller. Finally, extensive survey and test excavations were carried out on the surrounding site community (under private ownership) by the School of American Research's archaeology division. This was done prior to the construction of the Prewitt power plant, and the work was directed by John Beal.

Candelaria (formerly Las Ventanas). Under private ownership, the tower kiva and a portion of the room block at the Candelaria Site were looted extensively until the site was purchased, and renamed, by the Archaeological Conservancy. It was backfilled by volunteers in the late 1970s. No reports have been published on this large site, although it was initially described by Bandelier (1892). Marshall and his colleagues (1979) provide further description.

Kin Ya'a, Kin Klizhin, Kin Bineola, Pueblo Pintado. Though geographically dispersed, all of these sites are owned and administered by Chaco Culture National Historic Park. All are fenced, stabilized, and periodically

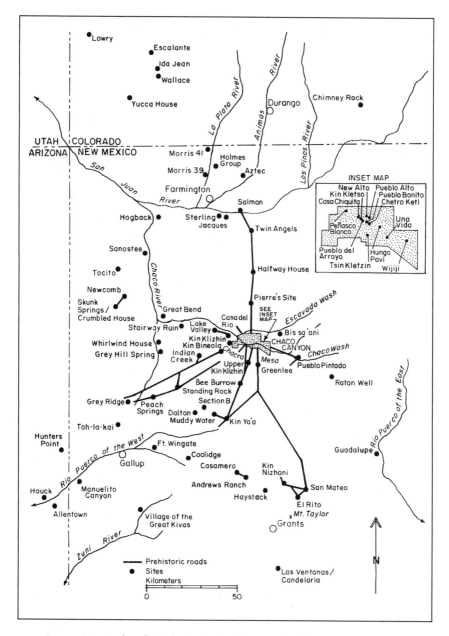

Figure 2.1. *Archaeological sites in the Chaco regional system, geographically defined.*

monitored by the Park Service. None has been excavated, but the Park Service does have stabilization records of work done at each site.

Guadalupe. The easternmost of the outliers in the San Juan Basin area, the Guadalupe Ruin is owned and managed by the BLM. The Chacoan structure was excavated in the mid-1970s by the Rio Puerco Project under the general direction of Cynthia Irwin-Williams. A full report on the excavation is available as the unpublished doctoral dissertation of Lonnie Pippin (1979). The BLM has prepared an extensive management plan for the site.

Bis sa'ani. This site is owned by the Navajo Tribe. Due to its proximity to Chaco Canyon and the fact that the land surrounding it was leased for coal development, Bis sa'ani has been the focus of extensive archaeological investigation. As a result, it is undoubtedly the most completely documented of the Chaco outliers and, due to its precarious location on top of an eroding shale ridge, it presents one of the most challenging stabilization/preservation problems of the known outliers. The site and its associated community were noted in an inventory survey of the area (Wilson 1979), and later were the subject of further documentation by the Chaco Project's outlier survey (Powers, Gillespie, and Lekson 1983). The Chacoan structure and a sample of the community sites were excavated by the Navajo Nation Cultural Resources Management Program, and a detailed, four-volume report has been published (Breternitz, Doyel, and Marshall 1982).

Aztec. Owned and maintained by the National Park Service as Aztec Ruins National Monument, the west ruin at Aztec was excavated and reported by Earl Morris (1919), who also excavated and restored the great kiva (Morris 1921). Park Service work at the Hubbard Site, the tri-wall structure in back of the west ruin, was reported by Gordon Vivian (1959). The east ruin remains uninvestigated.

Salmon Ruins. Currently owned and maintained by the San Juan County Museum Association, much of the north and east portion of the site was excavated in the 1970s by Cynthia Irwin-Williams's San Juan Valley Archaeological Project (Irwin-Williams and Shelley 1980). The museum association has completed stabilization of a considerable portion of the excavated structures.

Sterling. The site is under private ownership. Much of the room block and kiva was severely eroded by an arroyo. A portion of the remainder of the site was excavated by members of the New Mexico Archaeological Society, under the general direction of the San Juan Valley Archaeological Project. An initial report has been published (Bice 1983).

Morris 41. Under private ownership, Morris 41 represents a tragedy for those interested in archaeological site preservation. The Chacoan structure at the site was initially recorded (but not excavated) by Earl Morris (1939). It was protected for a long time by sympathetic owners, but was put up for sale in the mid-1970s. An attempt to purchase it by the precursor of the Archaeological Conservancy was unsuccessful due to an inadequate amount of time to raise necessary funds. The site was eventually purchased by an individual who claimed to be an archaeologist, but who zoned it for commercial development and then systematically looted it for a number of years. As of this writing, what is left of the site is up for sale.

Chimney Rock. Owned and maintained by the National Forest Service, this is the only federally owned Chacoan outlier not under the administrative jurisdiction of the Department of the Interior. Some excavations at the site were undertaken in the 1920s by Jeançon and Roberts (1923, 1924), and University of Colorado investigations of the Chacoan structure and the associated great kiva were published by Frank Eddy (1977). The site has been stabilized by the Forest Service.

Yucca House. Managed by the Park Service as a component of Mesa Verde National Park, the site has not been excavated. Records of stabilization undertaken by the Park Service are on file at Mesa Verde.

Wallace Ruin and Ida Jean Site. Both of these sites are privately owned. Investigations by Bruce Bradley at the Wallace Ruin have been underway for some time, and both preliminary and interim reports have been published (Bradley 1974, 1988). Salvage work by the Brisbins at the Ida Jean Site was reported in manuscript form in 1973. The site has since been bulldozed in its entirety and is effectively destroyed.

Escalante. The site is owned and managed by the BLM. The Chacoan structure and one of the associated sites (Dominguez Ruin) were excavated and stabilized by the University of Colorado. A report has been published on these investigations (Hallasi 1979). A status burial found at the Dominguez Ruin was reported by Reed (1979).

Lowry. The Lowry Ruin, perhaps the northernmost Chacoan outlier, is owned, stabilized, and interpreted by the BLM. It was excavated and reported by Paul Martin (1936). A feature at the site interpreted by Martin as a ditch may in fact be a segment of a prehistoric road (Vivian 1983a).

The sites reviewed above do not, by any means, represent all of the known Chacoan outliers. Since this is a review of Chaco research, I have discussed only those sites that have been investigated or stabilized, formally or informally, and about which reports have been compiled and in some cases published. It is apparent from this review that of the total number of outliers known at this time, probably on the order of 70 or 80, only a few have been investigated, fewer have been reported, and even fewer still have had reports published. There has certainly been no systematic, problem-oriented research undertaken on a representative sample of the Chaco outliers.

Another point brought out by the review is the magnitude of the Chaco system. From the Lowry Site at the north to Candelaria at the south, and from Village of the Great Kivas at the west to Guadalupe at the east, the area covers roughly 67,340 square kilometers. Few living human beings have set foot on all of the outliers, and I doubt that anyone in the past did either, given the transport technology of A.D. 1100. Assuming that all the outliers were occupied contemporaneously, one wonders how a regional system too large to be physically appreciated by any single individual could be effectively administered. Perhaps the regional system we define today is more an artifact of our own analyses than a reality of the past.

CHRONOLOGY

The Chaco chronological sequence differs from that of the Hohokam area in being well established and backed by numerous absolute dates (Bannister 1965; Lekson 1983). Chetro Ketl is one of the best-dated sites in the Southwest, with over 500 tree-ring dates compiled at present. These data, with the addition of dates from other Chacoan structures, have allowed us to recognize major building sequences in the canyon area during the Bonito phase (Lekson 1983, 1986).

Numerous discussions of Chaco chronology occur in the literature (e.g., Vivian and Mathews 1965; Hayes 1981; Judge et al. 1981; Judge 1982; Cordell 1982), most of which mirror the early frameworks presented by Kidder (1927) and Roberts (1935), with the addition of the Bonito phase (Gladwin 1945) to represent the Classic architectural developments in the canyon.

Hayes (1981) retained the Pecos classification in his inventory survey of the canyon. Windes (Toll, Windes, and McKenna 1980) modified and refined Gladwin's Bonito phase, based on information gained from Chaco Project investigations. A comparison of Windes's chronology with that of Hayes is presented in Judge and others (1981). The chronology used here (fig. 2.2) is roughly the same as that of Windes, with slight modifications based on recent information (Thomas C. Windes, personal communication, 1987). The corresponding cultural stages are discussed in the next section. Diagnostic ceramic types used as criteria for cultural stage definition will be referred to in general terms only. For more complete descriptions of Chacoan ceramic types, forms, characteristics, and sequences, see Windes (1984a) and Toll (1986).

I should add at this point that the absolute chronology established for Chaco is not based solely on dendrochronology, though tree-ring dating is certainly the primary method. A large number of archaeomagnetic dates and a substantial number of radiocarbon dates have been obtained from Chaco, both serving to supplement the excellent ceramic cross-dating techniques available.

PALEO-INDIAN, ARCHAIC, AND BASKETMAKER II

Although included in the chronology, the Paleo-Indian, Archaic, and Basketmaker II periods (10,000 B.C.–A.D. 500) are less relevant to the formation and development of the Chacoan regional system than are the later periods. Judge (1982) discusses these stages in some detail for the San Juan Basin in general. Further discussions of early time periods have been presented by Vierra (1980), and Eschman (1983) has reported on the Archaic chronology of the basin in light of recent radiocarbon dates.

Suffice it to note here that the roots of the regional system go back some 9,000 years, with little major climatic change for the last 3,000 to 4,000 years. Thus, the population was well settled and adapted to the climate of the basin prior to the emergence of the Chacoan system.

BASKETMAKER III

Basketmaker III (A.D. 500–ca. 700) is well known in Chaco. Shabik'eshchee Village (Roberts 1929), located at the east end of the canyon, has long been regarded as the Southwestern type site for this time period. The Chaco Project identified 134 additional Basketmaker III sites in the inventory survey (Hayes 1981), and a number of excavated sites yielded evidence of Basketmaker III occupation beneath later structures (McKenna and Truell 1986). Basketmaker III ceramics consist primarily of Lino Gray and La Plata and White Mound Black-on-white. Pit houses were shallow with antechambers, and they frequently incorporated upright stone slabs.

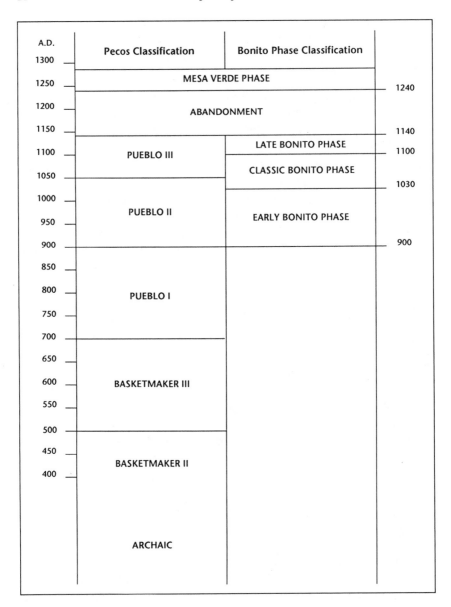

Figure 2.2. *Pecos and Bonito phase chronologies.*

Storage cists were found inside and outside the structures. Clusters of pit houses often formed small villages, some of which contained great kivas (e.g., Shabik'eshchee).

In all probability there was a substantial, though dispersed, Basketmaker III settlement in the San Juan Basin. Undoubtedly, sites were clustered in those areas that had proven throughout the Archaic occupation to be environmentally favorable and reliable. Chaco was evidently one such place.

PUEBLO I

As elsewhere on the Colorado Plateau, Pueblo I (A.D. 700–ca. 900) in Chaco marked the transition to surface habitation. Sites there show evidence of storage rooms (not cists) forming an arc behind the pit structure, with *ramada* areas, or open porches, in front of them. Presumably, most of the daily domestic activities took place in these ramada-storage areas. Pit structures were evidently still lived in, perhaps especially in the winter, but they were much deeper than the Basketmaker III structures, had a ventilator instead of an antechamber, and in some cases had a *sipapu*, or entrance to the spiritual world. Sometimes termed "protokivas," these structures indicate a gradual change in function away from purely domestic activities. Ceramics marking this period in Chaco are those continuing from the Basketmaker III period, along with Kana'a Gray (neck-banded) and Kiatuthlanna Black-on-white. There may be less evidence of aggregation into villages during Pueblo I than in the prior period, although this is difficult to determine given the multicomponent nature of the majority of the Chacoan sites.

PUEBLO II

Hayes (1981) initially split Pueblo II (A.D. 900–1050) into early and late phases, with the first marked by Red Mesa Black-on-white ceramics and the second by the introduction of Escavada Black-on-white and Gallup Black-on-white. Following his field survey, however, Hayes noted that the "attempt to separate Pueblo II into two phases was only partly successful" (Hayes 1981:28). Architecturally, there seems to be little difference between the two phases, and both are typical with respect to other Pueblo II sites on the Colorado Plateau. The transition to surface habitation was completed, and the pit house of Basketmaker times had become a kiva in Pueblo II. Room blocks were single-story and linear, typically standing in two tiers behind the kiva with habitation rooms in front and storage rooms in back. The primary difference between Chaco Canyon and the rest of the plateau at this time lies in the emergence in Chaco of the first large Bonito phase structures. These will be described below.

PUEBLO III

The small sites representing Pueblo III (A.D. 1050–1300) in Chaco must be viewed in contrast to the large Bonito phase structures found nearby. Gladwin (1945) coined the term "Hosta Butte Phase" for these small sites, considering them earlier than the large structures. Even today there is no firm agreement on the contemporaneity of occupations of the two types of sites (see discussion of the Classic Bonito phase, below).

The primary difference between Pueblo III sites in the canyon and those elsewhere is in site size. Whereas in much of the plateau this time period is marked by aggregation into quite large sites, in the canyon the Pueblo III site averaged only 10 rooms (Hayes 1981:51). Again, these sites must be considered in the context of possible contemporaneity with the Bonito phase sites. The dominant ceramic type early in this period is Gallup Black-on-white. Later, particularly after A.D. 1100, a new type is introduced in the form of Chaco-McElmo Black-on-white, whose organic paints contrast markedly with the mineral-based paints used up to that time. Finally, following the collapse of the Bonito phase, an apparent late reoccupation in the 1200s brought Mesa Verde Black-on-white ceramics to the canyon.

EARLY BONITO PHASE

In the early 900s—or possibly even the late 800s—Chaco Canyon was the setting for a new cultural trajectory termed the Bonito phase (after Gladwin 1945). The ceramic marker for the introduction of this phase, the early Bonito phase (ca. A.D. 900–1020/1040), is Gallup Black-on-white, but the most significant changes made were architectural. Although the morphology of sites did not alter drastically (the arc-shaped room layout located northwest of the pit structure continued from Pueblo I), the size of both rooms and pit structures increased greatly. Furthermore, early Bonito phase structures were multistory, at least in the back tier of rooms. This back tier evidently was used for storage and was fronted by a tier of featureless rooms, which in turn was bordered by a tier of ramadas or domestic areas. Thus, the architectural changes that initiated the Bonito phase featured much larger, multistory rooms, much larger pit structures, and a more formalized building style. These sites also manifest a much more disciplined use of the ubiquitous tabular sandstone for masonry.

At least three sites in Chaco Canyon reveal evidence of this early architectural change: Peñasco Blanco, Pueblo Bonito, and Una Vida. Recent work at Pueblo Bonito suggests that the changes may have started there as early as the late 800s (T. C. Windes, personal communication, 1987). There is agreement (due to the occurrence of Red Mesa Black-on-white) that the small Pueblo II sites were occupied contemporaneously with these new structures.

CLASSIC BONITO PHASE

Although there is little evidence (from tree rings) of much construction during the latter half of the tenth century, in the early 1000s the Classic Bonito phase (A.D. 1020/1040–1100) brought both additional construction and the dominance of Gallup Black-on-white pottery.

Lekson (1986) has documented the Classic Bonito phase building events, which are summarized here. By A.D. 1020, additional construction is seen at Pueblo Bonito, and new construction occurs at Pueblo Alto and Chetro Ketl. This new construction mirrored that of the early 900s, but it displayed linear, rather than arced, tiers. Pit structures became true Chacoan kivas (i.e., definite kivas with considerable stylistic variability, but much larger than the average kiva in the Southwest). After 1050 there was additional construction on existing structures, and new building occurred at Pueblo del Arroyo.

It was during the period from 1075 to 1115 that Chaco Canyon experienced its peak development. The construction labor investment doubled, major construction events took place at most of the large sites, and new sites were constructed. Building, much of it devoted to the construction of storage rooms, seemed to reach a frenzy in the latter part of the eleventh century.

The Classic Bonito phase also witnessed the construction of isolated great kivas (Casa Rinconada, Kin Nahasbas), the "construction" of formal trash mounds associated with some of the large sites, increased construction activity at the outliers, and the emergence of the road system. There is some debate about the contemporaneity of the small sites (i.e., Hosta Butte phase sites) during this period. Tom Windes feels they generally were abandoned during the Classic Bonito phase, but were occupied contemporaneously with the large structures both before and after this period. He bases this conclusion on the results of ceramic transects carried out at most of the small sites in the late 1970s and early 1980s by the Chaco Project (T. C. Windes, personal communication, 1987). The "traditional" view is that the small sites were occupied throughout the entire Bonito phase.

There is little question that this was a critical period in the development and operation of the Chaco regional system. During this time, the material correlates of the system attained much of the configuration we see today, resulting in the archaeological evidence that has fascinated researchers and the public for so long.

LATE BONITO PHASE

The Late Bonito phase (A.D. 1100–ca. 1140) witnessed significant changes in ceramics, in architecture, and, presumably, in the character of the regional system. Ceramic changes involved the introduction of carbon-painted wares, predominantly Chaco-McElmo Black-on-white. New sites were constructed (e.g., New Alto, Casa Chiquita, Kin Kletso) using a different masonry style that relied on large, shaped blocks, reminiscent of the masonry of the Mesa Verde area. Furthermore, the layout of these sites was quite different. The U or E shape gave way to enclosed rectangles, with kivas completely enclosed by the room blocks. Existing sites were also remodeled: large rooms were subdivided, and some large Chacoan kivas were abandoned and filled with domestic trash.

Outlier construction continued during the Late Bonito phase, but was focused on the area of the San Juan River and north of it. There is disagreement about what these early twelfth-century developments meant in Chaco Canyon. Windes (personal communication, 1987) sees strong San Juan/Mesa Verde influence at this time, perhaps even an influx of people from those areas. Lekson (1984) feels that the evidence reflects changes in the development of the system in the canyon. He would consider this period, rather than the preceding one, to represent the peak of activity there. It is my feeling (Judge 1989) that the changes indicate a shift in administration of the system from Chaco Canyon to the north, with Chaco becoming more residential and less ritual in nature—itself effectively becoming an outlier to a more northern center.

On one thing there seems to be general agreement: Chaco Canyon was largely "abandoned" by A.D. 1140. This interpretation is based on the virtual absence of tree-ring construction dates after this time (1132 is the last known cutting date). If people continued to live in the canyon, there is very little evidence for it. This qualitative reduction in activity is taken to imply the collapse of the Chacoan system, at least as it was known in the Classic Bonito phase.

MESA VERDE PHASE

Following the abandonment of Chaco for about 100 years, there was a Mesa Verdean "intrusion" into the canyon (ca. A.D. 1240–1300). From all appearances this was an actual influx of people who reoccupied some Chacoan sites, constructed others (some of which were cliff dwellings), and used pottery of the classic Mesa Verde Black-on-white type. Site types are not atypical of the period elsewhere on the Colorado Plateau. No detailed investigation of this late and relatively brief occupation of the canyon has been undertaken; thus, its extent and character are largely unknown. A considerable number of "Mesa Verde" sites have been found on Chacra Mesa, however, suggesting a possible gradual migration to the east.

THE NAVAJO PERIOD

The Navajo occupation of Chaco Canyon was extensive, lasting from the early 1700s until 1947, when Chaco Canyon National Monument was fenced by the Park Service. Forked stick hogans, refugee sites, and stone hogans are found throughout the canyon. They have little to do with the Chaco regional system, however, and will not be discussed in detail here. For a full treatment of the Navajo in Chaco Canyon, see Brugge (1980, 1986).

DEFINING THE CHACO REGIONAL SYSTEM

A number of criteria have been used to define the Chaco regional system or—more frequently, perhaps—to describe the "Chaco phenomenon" rather than to identify a formal system. Topography has been used considerably, and topographic criteria tend to conform to the structural unit known geologically as the San Juan Basin. This area, shown in figure 2.1, consists of a relatively flat and homogeneous interior basin with low ecological diversity, surrounded by mountainous areas of relatively high diversity. Chaco Canyon lies roughly in the center of the basin; thus, the topographical criteria for regional definition have been favored by those seeking environmentally based explanations of how the system functioned.

Architecturally, a given cluster of characteristics has been used frequently enough for system definition to gain credence with most archaeologists, particularly those who have spent time in the San Juan Basin trying to locate and identify the outlying site areas. These criteria are much the same as those used in the canyon to define and distinguish the Bonito phase sites there, and to contrast them with the surrounding small sites. The criteria are discussed in detail by Marshall and others (1979:15–18) and by Powers, Gillespie, and Lekson (1983:14–18), among others. They are used to distinguish Chacoan outlying communities, the geographical extent of which defines the regional system as shown in figure 2.1. They can be summarized as follows:

1. Presence of a central, relatively large masonry structure. These structures have been called everything from "public houses" to "great houses" to "Chacoan structures," and numerous other terms. They are more or less centrally located within a cluster of smaller sites, or small-

house sites, to form a "community," and they stand out as much larger than the average surrounding sites. Actual structure size and room frequency vary considerably throughout the system; the key to distinguishing these structures is their large size relative to surrounding sites.

2. Large rooms. Where discernible without excavation, rooms within the large structure are noticeably larger than those of the associated small-house sites.

3. Large kivas. As noted above, there is considerable stylistic variability of features within Chacoan kivas. What is common, however, is the large size of these kivas vis-à-vis those seen in small-house sites.

4. Site layout. The key to describing this criterion is the concept of "formality." There is a planned appearance to the structures and kivas that distinguishes them from growth by accretion common to the smaller sites. This gives the Chacoan structure a "formality" not noticed elsewhere in the communities.

5. Great kivas. One or more great kivas usually (not always) are found in association with the large structure, frequently located less than 100 meters away.

6. Prehistoric roads. Frequently (again, not always), evidence of a pre-historic road is found in the community area, usually leading to, or past, the large structure. The lack of evidence of a road today may result from erosion, deposition, disturbance, or lack of adequate aerial imagery to permit interpretation—or it may simply mean there never was a road. Where identified and studied (see Kincaid 1983), road systems are quite complex and possess their own features and associated structures. Some of these structures may well comprise a visual communication network operative throughout the regional system (Hayes and Windes 1975).

7. Other. The presence of ceramics typical to Chaco Canyon (e.g., Gallup Black-on-white) is common to many outliers but does not constitute a necessary criterion if contemporaneity with the Classic Bonito phase can be demonstrated in another way. The farther one gets from the canyon, the more variable the ceramic assemblages become and the more unreliable ceramic types are for regional system definition. Much the same is true with masonry styles. Though core-and-veneer masonry is common to many Chaco outliers, it is not necessary to their definition. As is well known, masonry varies considerably with respect to the availability of local source materials.

Even given agreement on these criteria, the extent of the Chaco regional system is difficult to define precisely, and there is a considerable amount of debate among archaeologists as to how big (or small) it really was. This is due largely to the subjective interpretations of the criteria, the frequent need to rely on surface evidence, the question of how much to rely on masonry and ceramic data, and disagreement as to the number of criteria that need to be present to be considered conclusive.

Regardless of the inherent difficulties, an attempt at defining and bounding the system was made by the Chaco Project in support of the legislation passed by Congress to protect the outlying sites. Figure 1.2 shows these boundaries, which encompass the core canyon area with an associated 33 outliers (or "archaeological protection sites," as they were termed in the legislation) and the extent of the road system as it was known when the legislation was passed in 1979. These 33 sites do not comprise the total number of outliers in the system as defined geographically; instead, they were those known at the time that were still intact enough to yield archaeological information of value to future interpretation of the system. It also should be noted that the system as seen in figure 2.1 is a diachronic composite. Its extent, morphology, and character changed considerably as it developed, with outlier site density focused to the south and southwest at first, and gradually moving north through time.

Having defined a system, our challenge now is to explain it—certainly one of the tasks of the seminar—and it might be appropriate here to at least list those researchers who have attempted to do so. More detailed reviews of approaches to understanding the Chaco phenomenon have been presented by Vivian (1970b), Hayes (1981), Breternitz (1982), and Schelberg (1982). Attempts at explanation have been made by two general categories of researchers: those who feel the system could not have developed without extensive stimulation from Mexico (the "Mexicanists"), and those who feel it developed independently of any major influence from outside the Southwest (the "indigenists"). Vivian (this volume) offers a valuable review and critique of a number of these explanations.

The first category of scholars includes the following (listed chronologically): Ferdon (1955), Di Peso (1974), Kelley and Kelley (1975), Lister (1978), Frisbie (1980), Reyman (1980), Washburn (1980), Hayes (1981), and Schroeder (1981). The explanations of these researchers all differ to a certain extent, but seem to stem from two common assumptions. The first assumption suggests that the Mexican trade items and traits found in Chaco (copper bells, vase forms, macaws, colonnades, etc.) are evidence of close personal contact with the south: contact that involved actual people rather than down-the-line trade. The second assumption is that there is such a disparity between the material remains of the Chaco structures and contemporaneous sites elsewhere that the system simply could not have

evolved independently of outside influence. In recent years, partially because of the increased amount of fieldwork and interpretation done in the
San Juan Basin and partially because of increasing awareness of the vast
extent of the Chaco region, models based on strictly Mexican origins of the
Chaco system have not been widely endorsed.

The second, and larger, category includes these contributions (again
listed chronologically): Judd (1964), Vivian and Mathews (1965), Vivian
(1970a, 1970b), Grebinger (1973, 1978), Judge (1977, 1979), Altschul
(1978), Cordell (1979, 1982), Cordell and Plog (1979), Marshall and
others (1979), Tainter and Gillio (1980), Winter (1980), Judge and others
(1981), Schelberg (1982), Breternitz (1982), Powers, Gillespie, and Lekson
(1983), Irwin-Williams (1983), LeBlanc (1983), Vivian (1983b), Doyel,
Breternitz, and Marshall (1984), Lekson (1986), Sebastian (1988), H. Toll
(1985), and Judge (1989). Many of the views of these scholars are presented partly in reaction to the Mexicanists. Among the questions they
have raised are these: Why did the Mexicans not establish "Chaco" in the
Rio Grande valley, closer to the source of turquoise, if that was the desirable
commodity? If not turquoise, what exactly were the Mexicans getting in
return for their efforts in Chaco? Many researchers do not see the Mexican
influence in Chaco as being strong enough to represent anything more
than long-distance trade. And finally, most feel that a culture can reach a
high degree of complexity in its past, yet emerge in the ethnographic
present as less complex and qualitatively different.

Archaeologist and layman alike have been intrigued by the Chaco phenomenon for years, viewing it and attempting to understand it from the
spectacular ruins displayed in the core area. Chaco Canyon and the ruins
therein hold an air of mystery and fascination difficult to describe, and
equally difficult to ignore, in searching for archaeological answers. Yet we
know now that it is the regional perspective, that which is gained by
looking far beyond the canyon, that in the end will reveal the true nature of
the thing we call Chaco. The chapters that follow look beyond the canyon,
each from a different viewpoint, and each interpretation offers a different
perspective on the phenomenon. It is hoped that together these contributions will lead to a more complete understanding of how such systems
develop, how they function, and why they ultimately cease to exist.

Chapter 3

Settlement Pattern and the Chaco Region

STEPHEN H. LEKSON

SETTLEMENT pattern is architecture writ large. This is particularly true for Chaco, an archaeological entity defined first by its architecture and finally, as I will argue here, by its settlement pattern. Pueblo Bonito and its kindred great houses at Chaco Canyon are spectacular buildings, world famous architectural monuments. But if the Chaco Canyon great houses are the apex of Chacoan architecture, what about less spectacular Chacoan buildings? To understand the *range* of Chacoan building, we must look at architecture not just in Chaco Canyon but within the whole of the Chaco region—and the region will be defined by a particular settlement pattern, the community.

In early Southwestern archaeology, regions were defined by architecture and pottery, with primary emphasis on pottery. Pottery was (and is) the medium of choice for measuring cultural interaction over space. Judge (this volume) defined regional systems in behavioral terms of mutual dependence through the exchange of goods and services. The goods most amenable to archaeological observation are ceramics, but because pottery moved through the region in astonishingly high volumes, it may not be the most useful marker of the Chaco region. Recent studies have shown that much (and during some periods, most) of the pottery found at Chaco Canyon was not made there, but was imported from other areas within and beyond the textbook Chaco district (H. Toll 1985). And the particular pottery found at Chaco Canyon, whatever its origins, is rare or absent at several sites traditionally considered Chaco outliers. Given these intriguing (if slightly disconcerting) dynamics, the use of pottery as a calling-card criterion for regional definition becomes problematic.

Does ceramic exchange map all aspects of regional systems? If not, behavioral models of regional systems based on ceramic distributions will be framed within inappropriate regions. A regional system might be better defined by complementary lines of evidence, combining portable artifacts, architecture, and setting. Such a strategy runs the risk of simply redefining traditional culture areas, but new approaches to the empirical patterning of archaeological remains can avoid that pitfall. Specifically, relational or contextual approaches to key features, such as ballcourts or great houses, allow us to use those long-recognized traits to redefine regions of significantly different dimension than realms of ceramic exchange. Are architecturally defined regions preferable to ceramically defined regions? The answer to this question depends on the type of inquiry being pursued. Ceramics may be more appropriate for some issues, architecture for others. I find it interesting that the two classes of data delimit rather different geographic areas. This chapter defines a Chaco region architecturally, but I do not mean to suggest that this is *the* Chaco region. The architectural region is simply one geographic scale within which models of exchange or adaptation should be evaluated.

Architecture is one key to the Chaco region. In recent studies, the region has been defined by Chaco "outliers": great houses found outside the confines of Chaco Canyon proper (Lekson et al. 1988; Fowler, Stein, and Anyon 1987; Marshall et al. 1979; Powers, Gillespie, and Lekson 1983). Thus, the main problem in defining the Chaco region lies in defining what is and what is not an outlying Chaco great house. The circularity of defining, by architectural criteria, a region in which to study a range of architectural settlement patterns is a critical issue in contemporary Chaco studies—and is the topic of this paper. To examine this question, we must first review the architectural variety present in Chacoan settlement.

ELEMENTS OF CHACOAN SETTLEMENT

Chaco Canyon contains a surprising variety of architectural forms (Lekson 1986; McKenna and Truell 1986; Vivian and Mathews 1965). Only a few of those building types will be discussed here: great houses, great kivas, and unit houses—the three basic elements of the Chaco community.

GREAT HOUSES

Great houses, the sine qua non of Chaco archaeology, are typified by the huge ruins of Chaco Canyon, such as Pueblo Bonito. The massiveness of these ruins (fig. 3.1), their regular and symmetrical layouts, and (perhaps most of all) the banded "core-and-veneer" masonry were taken,

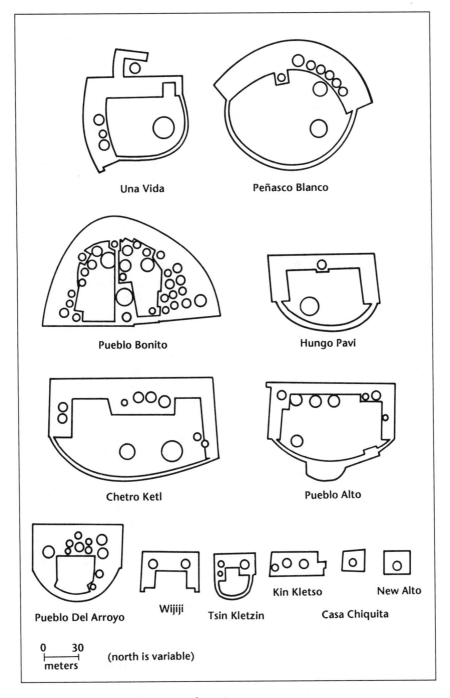

Figure 3.1. *Great houses at Chaco Canyon.*

traditionally, as definitive; details such as enclosed above-ground kivas, tower kivas, large room size, and so on, constituted additional Chacoan criteria (e.g., Vivian and Mathews 1965).

These criteria were derived, for the most part, from the combined architectures of Pueblo Bonito, Chetro Ketl, and Pueblo del Arroyo—the three largest excavated Chaco great houses (Judd 1959, 1964; Lekson 1983). However, those three structures changed dramatically over the many decades during which they were built and used (fig. 3.2). Pueblo Bonito, for example, is the composite of at least seven distinct stages of construction spanning two centuries (Lekson 1986). Which Pueblo Bonito are we supposed to be looking at? And were any of the Pueblo Bonitos typical of the full range of Chacoan building?

Vivian and Mathews (1965) concluded that several of the great houses at Chaco (Tsin Kletzin, Kin Kletso, Casa Chiquita, and New Alto) were actually intrusive units built by immigrants from the San Juan area. I have argued that these supposedly intrusive sites are as much a part of Chacoan building as Pueblo Bonito itself (Lekson 1986). Truell (in McKenna and Truell 1986) has identified 60 smaller, unnamed structures at Chaco Canyon built with the core-and-veneer masonry that is the putative hallmark of great-house construction. What group of attributes, common to which group of sites at Chaco, should define Chaco architecture? The architectural criteria of "Chacoan-ness" are by no means clear, even in Chaco Canyon, and the definition becomes even murkier when considering outlying great houses.

Chaco Canyon has long been recognized as a unique architectural development in the Anasazi world. Criteria generated from only the most unusual and spectacular sites (i.e., those at Chaco Canyon) will almost certainly mask or eliminate variability within the range of great-house building. How can we hope to know the range of great-house architecture with criteria defined from only the extreme "right tail," as it were, of the distribution? An array of Chaco sites defined independently of architectural criteria would certainly help. Fortunately, we have the means for independent definition in the Chaco road network (Stein 1989).

Chaco's roads allow us to see the variation in great houses, if we assume that large sites associated with Chacoan roads are themselves "Chacoan"—an assumption seldom challenged, at least within the San Juan Basin. Great houses associated with the major San Juan Basin roads show a much greater variety of plans, configurations, and other details than do the great houses in Chaco Canyon (Fowler, Stein, and Anyon 1987; Kincaid 1983; Marshall et al. 1979; Nials, Stein, and Roney 1987; Powers, Gillespie, and

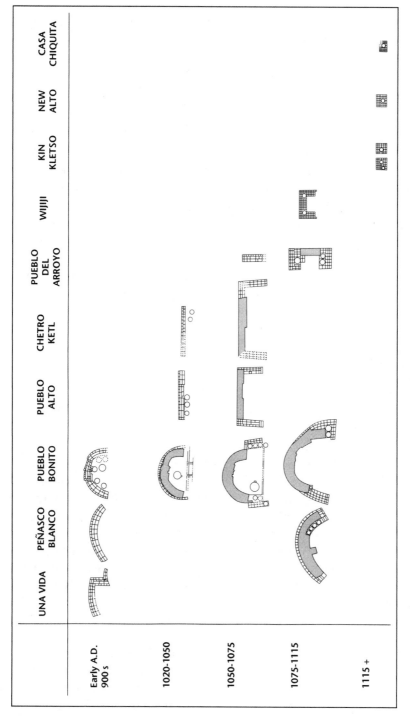

Figure 3.2. *Architectural development over time of Chaco Canyon great houses.*

Lekson 1983). Examples of San Juan Basin great houses, drawn from these sources and my own data, are shown in figure 3.3.

Very few outlying great houses have been excavated, but those that have show many of the architectural details of the Chaco Canyon sites (core-and-veneer walls, coursed masonry facings, elevated kivas, and so forth). But excavated data are rare and will remain so for the foreseeable future; therefore, the criteria generated from the road-defined array of great houses must refer to surface characteristics. Based on this road-defined array, the criteria of massive construction, a compact formal groundplan, and—most importantly—the structure's architectural context have come to be used as standard common denominators. Powers, Gillespie, and Lekson (1983:308) note that "generally, if the layout and architectural features of a site are unclear or unknown, its recognition as a Chacoan structure is based on *its greater size relative to contemporary sites*" (emphasis added).

Thus, to a very large extent, great house criteria have shifted from intrinsic *traits* to extrinsic *contexts*. Given the appropriate time period, evidence of a compact plan, and massive construction, the deciding criterion is this: Is the candidate great house a significantly bigger "bump" than other contemporaneous bumps in its vicinity? (The smaller bumps will be discussed below.) Examples of sites identified as great houses based on these criteria (drawn from the sources cited above) are shown in figures 3.4 and 3.5.

Comparison of outlying great houses (figs. 3.3, 3.4, and 3.5) to the Chaco Canyon great houses (fig. 3.1) shows that most outlying great houses are rather small. Discounting the structures in Chaco Culture National Historic Park and the "Big Four" (Kin Bineola, Pueblo Pintado, Aztec Ruins, and Salmon Ruins), almost all of the great houses listed by Powers, Gillespie, and Lekson (1983:table 41) range in floor area from only about 2,000 square meters down to a paltry 200 square meters. In fact, most are under 1,000 square meters: that is, one-fifteenth to one-twentieth the size of buildings like Pueblo Bonito and Chetro Ketl. Outlying great houses are not large sites by either Chaco or later Anasazi standards (compare figs. 3.3, 3.4, and 3.5 to the contemporary and later non-Chacoan sites shown in figs. 3.6 and 3.7).

GREAT KIVAS

A second element of Chacoan building, which rivals great houses in its archaeological interest, is the great kiva. Great kivas are round, masonry-lined pit structures that are remarkable for their large size: during the A.D. 1000s and 1100s, they generally were greater than about 10 meters in

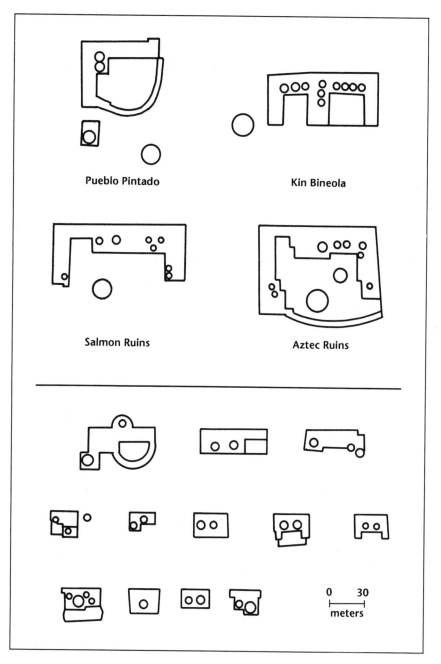

Figure 3.3. *Great houses: the "Big Four" (Pueblo Pintado, Kin Bineola, Salmon Ruins, and Aztec Ruins) and selected great houses from areas north of the Chaco drainage.*

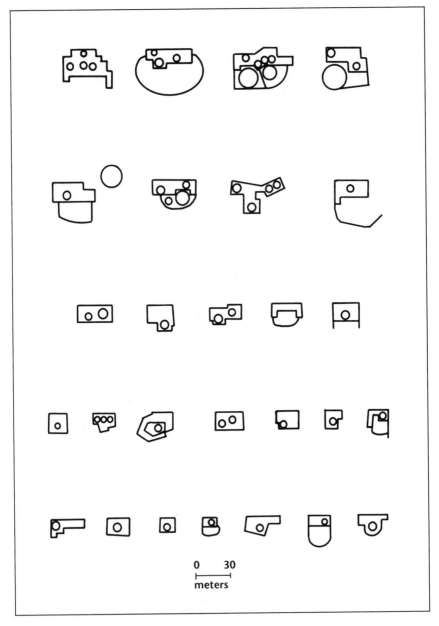

Figure 3.4. *Great houses: selected examples from the Chaco drainage.*

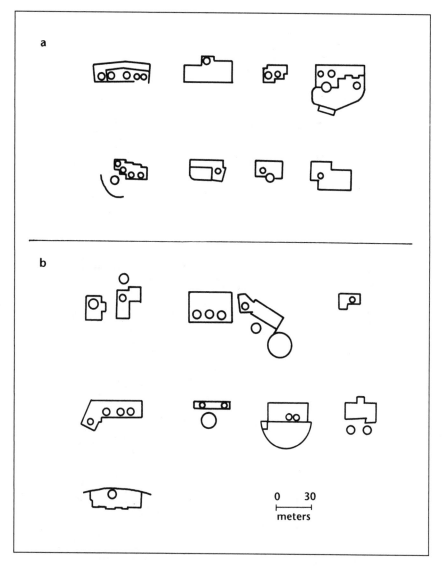

Figure 3.5. *Great houses:* a, *selected examples from areas east of the Chaco drainage;* b, *selected examples from areas south and west of the Chaco drainage.*

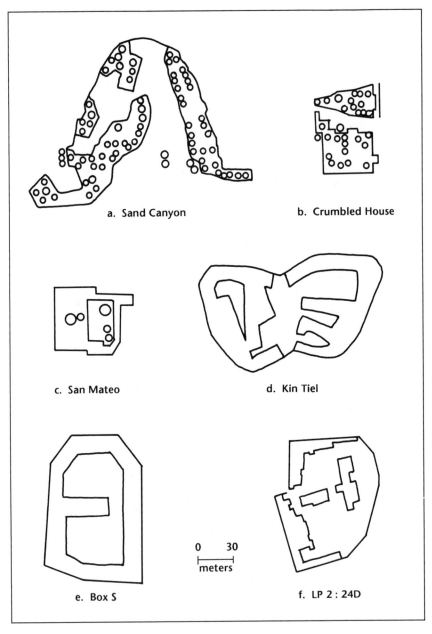

a. Sand Canyon

b. Crumbled House

c. San Mateo

d. Kin Tiel

e. Box S

0   30
meters

f. LP 2 : 24D

Figure 3.6. *Selected thirteenth- and early fourteenth-century Anasazi sites, for comparison with eleventh- and twelfth-century Chacoan sites shown in figures 3.1 through 3.5. a, Sand Canyon near Cortez, Colorado; b, Crumbled House; c, San Mateo; d, Kin Tiel; e, Box S Site, near El Morro, New Mexico; f, LP 2:24D, near Acoma, New Mexico.*

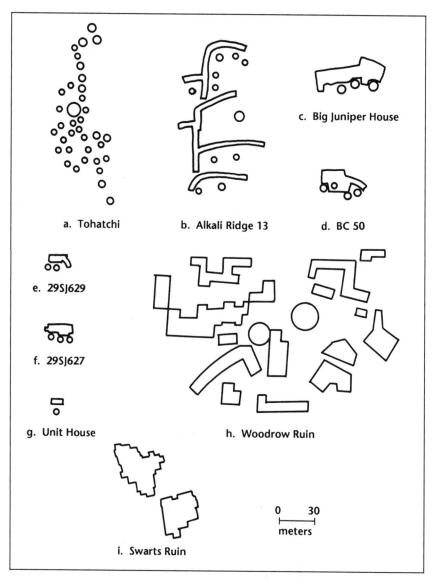

Figure 3.7. *Selected pre-thirteenth-century sites, for comparison with eleventh- and twelfth-century Chacoan sites shown in figures 3.1 through 3.5. a, Tohatchi Basketmaker III village, near Tohatchi, New Mexico; b, Alkali Ridge Pueblo I site, near Blanding, Utah; c, Big Juniper House, Pueblo II site at Mesa Verde, Colorado; d, BC 50, Pueblo II–III site at Chaco Canyon; e, 29SJ629, Pueblo II–III site at Chaco Canyon; f, 29SJ627, Pueblo II–III site at Chaco Canyon; g, Prudden (1918) "unit house"; h, Woodrow Ruin, Mimbres site near Cliff, New Mexico; i, Swarts Ruin, Mimbres site near Silver City, New Mexico.*

diameter (McLellen 1969; Vivian and Reiter 1960; Marshall et al. 1979), compared to contemporaneous pit structures and small kivas which averaged about 4 meters in diameter (McKenna and Truell 1986).

Great kivas are often thought to be synonymous with Chaco (Roberts 1932; Vivian and Reiter 1960:106). Indeed, LeBlanc (1986:108) argues that "all, or almost all, of the masonry-lined great kivas known archaeologically in the Anasazi area are associated with Chaco big [great] houses." I would amend this statement to refer to all great kivas built from A.D. 900 to 1200.

UNIT HOUSES

Unit houses, or unit pueblos, are small masonry pueblos of seven to ten rooms and one or two pit structures or kivas. They are the basic building blocks of Chaco (and probably general Anasazi) domestic architecture. There are, of course, many exceptions to the preceding statement (Gorman and Childs 1981), but the unit house (fig. 3.7g) is a proven and useful concept for the analysis of Anasazi settlement.

The unit house is the point of reference for Chacoan building; these are the "small bumps" to which the "big bumps" of great houses are compared. Just as Pueblo Bonito and the other great houses at Chaco shared the canyon with hundreds of smaller structures, so also do outlying great houses stand amid clusters of unit houses, or "communities."

COMMUNITIES

A "community" is a cluster of unit houses around a great house, a great kiva, and other central features (Breternitz, Doyel, and Marshall 1982; Marshall et al. 1979; Powers, Gillespie, and Lekson 1983). If the unit house is the fundamental element of Anasazi architecture, the community is the fundamental element of Anasazi settlement.

Because unit houses are freestanding buildings, they have usually received separate site names or numbers and have been seen as separate settlements (e.g., Morris 1939:39). However, many (and, I believe, most) unit houses of the 1000s and 1100s were spatially clustered in communities (as suggested in Rohn 1977). Several such communities are illustrated in figure 3.8. Chaco Canyon, shown in figure 3.9, is itself a densely clustered community (Lekson 1986).

There is considerable variation within Chacoan communities, but little of this variation can be usefully quantified. During the great "outlier hunts" of the 1970s, communities were surveyed in the immediate vicinity of several outliers (Marshall et al. 1979; Powers, Gillespie, and Lekson 1983), but of the hundreds of communities that we know to exist, only a handful have in fact been fully defined and described.

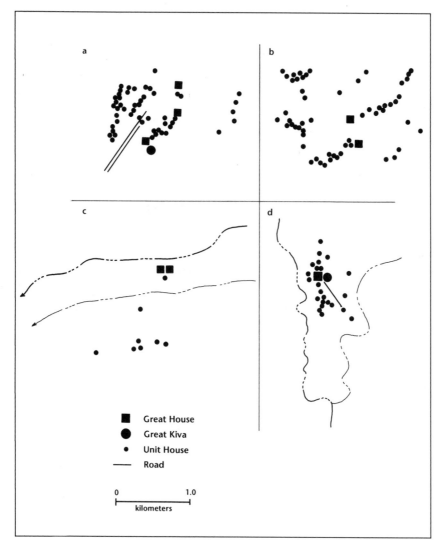

Figure 3.8. *Examples of communities:* a, *Muddy Water;* b, *Kin Nizhoni;*
c, *Bis sa'ani;* d, *the Holmes Group.*

There is no clear association of great-house size and community size,
although incomplete community definition and unresolved problems of
contemporaneity make examination of this relationship difficult. For example, the Bis sa'ani great house is of approximately the same floor area as
the combined floor areas of the unit houses in its surrounding community;
the Skunk Springs great house, although only twice as big as Bis sa'ani, sits

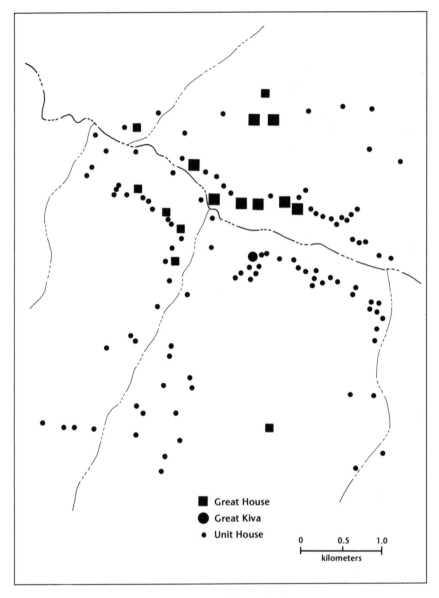

Figure 3.9. *Community organization of central Chaco Canyon.*

amid a community 30 to 40 times larger, of which an unknown portion is contemporary with the great house.

At the largest sites in Chaco Canyon, it appears that the number of great kivas may be indexed to great-house size (Lekson 1986:51). A ratio of total community size to number of great kivas may also exist at outliers (Breternitz, Doyel, and Marshall 1982:1233; Stein and McKenna 1988). Although the smallest communities, such as Bis sa'ani, have no great kivas, there are at least three great kivas at Skunk Springs. Thus, if contemporaneity can be established, the number of great kivas may be an index to the size of the community or the "service area" of outlying great houses. However, as figure 3.8 indicates, some large communities have no known great kivas, and this relationship is, therefore, not well established.

Almost all outlying great house–great kiva combinations have associated communities. But do all communities have either great houses, great kivas, or both? The major outlier surveys have focused on great houses, and therefore may have systematically excluded communities without these types of buildings. In my opinion, most and perhaps all large clusters of eleventh- through twelfth-century unit houses in the Chaco region (defined below) will be found to have a great house, a great kiva, or both.

THE LOGIC OF THE CHACO REGION

The Chaco region is usually mapped as the distribution of great houses, or outliers. As discussed above, outlying great houses were first defined by intrinsic criteria: technological features and formal elements that characterize the large sites in Chaco Canyon. Using intrinsic criteria, one could argue that only the so-called Big Four were really outliers: that is, only they were identical to Pueblo Bonito and Chetro Ketl. The taxonomic fate of scores of other Chaco-like sites has been largely a matter of the archaeologist's predilections and taste. In the absence of a scientific method for determining what agreement of which criteria was sufficient for taxonomic identity, determinations of the "Chacoan-ness" of candidate outliers was necessarily arbitrary, a matter for debate between Chaco enthusiasts and more moderate Anasazi archaeologists.

Chacoan roads offer an extrinsic, relational framework for defining great houses. Roads demonstrate an unambiguous physical relation between Chaco Canyon and outlying great houses. As discussed above, many of the great houses at the farthest ends of roads do not look very much like Pueblo Bonito or Chetro Ketl, giving us good reason to question and probably reject the most rigid intrinsic criteria. Unfortunately, our knowledge of roads is fragmentary. Roads themselves are not a panacea for regional definition, but the relational criteria developed from the roads are a critical point of entry into the taxonomy of regional settlement patterning.

Roads demonstrate not only the variability of outlying great houses, but, more importantly, the patterned architectural context of great houses in communities. Contextual criteria can be defined from the community pattern to recognize outlying great houses for which associated roads are not evident. The community context defines great houses without reference to intrinsic architectural or formal criteria specific to the great house itself, or its relation to roads. Recall, moreover, that many outlying "big bumps" *do* display Chacoan architectural traits and features, and some of the big bumps farthest from Chaco have clearly associated road segments.

Contextual criteria are, of course, simply intrinsic criteria of the community (rather than of the great house), and they are subject to the same logical conundrums and taxonomic difficulties of any intrinsic definitional approach (some of these difficulties will be discussed below). Despite these problems, the community contextual approach offers a perspective that is startlingly different from previous approaches to defining the Chaco region.

Judge (this volume) describes the Chaco region as it was understood in the mid-1980s, defined by a combination of architectural and artifactual criteria, and by roads. The area he delimits is rather larger than the Chaco region as it was understood in the mid-1970s (Marshall et al. 1979; Powers, Gillespie, and Lekson 1983), but still smaller than the Chaco region suggested by LeBlanc (1986:112–13; Lekson et al. 1988). The Chaco region has grown enormously over the last 15 years, and its ultimate limits may not have been reached.

If the community pattern—great house, great kiva, unit houses, and (often) road segments—is used to define the Chaco region (fig. 3.10), the area included is very much larger than the San Juan Basin, and much larger than Judge's region. Figure 3.10 is a very approximate map; the communities and great houses indicated are by no means all that are currently known or suspected, nor all that we may with confidence expect eventually to find. This is not the ultimate outlier map; it was prepared simply to show the probable extent of the Chacoan system, not the distribution and density of all communities within it. Indeed, voids on figure 3.10 within the Chaco region correspond largely to under-surveyed areas.

THE NEW MODEL CHACO

The Chaco region shown in figure 3.10 is about eight times larger than that defined in the 1970s and early 1980s; it is larger, even, than the large area perceptively suggested by LeBlanc (1986). The Chaco region has expanded

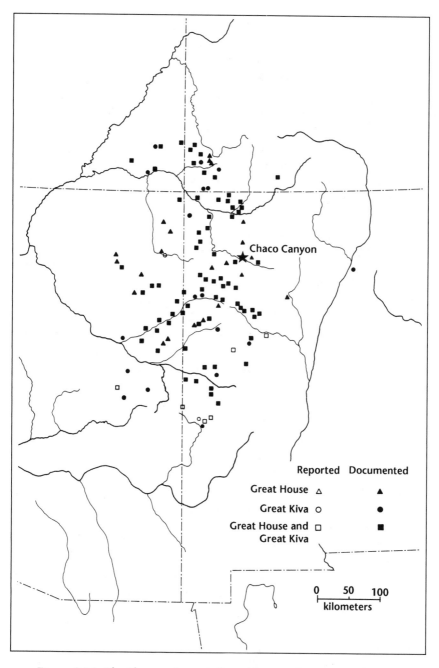

Figure 3.10. *The Chaco region as indicated by great houses, great kivas, and the Chacoan community settlement pattern.*

beyond Chaco Canyon, beyond the San Juan Basin, and almost beyond the limits of the Anasazi. This new scale is simply too large for the economic-ecologic underpinnings of existing Chaco scenarios—ecological models developed for the San Juan Basin scale (Lekson et al. 1988).

"Chacoan" is defined here by a distinctive settlement pattern of the eleventh through twelfth centuries: a community of unit houses focused on a great house and a great kiva. Does this usage of "Chacoan" have ethnic or sociopolitical implications? In the past, we assumed that Chaco Canyon was the center of a regional system and therefore the term "Chacoan" was intended to imply social or political connection to that center. If this assumption is still correct, then the expanded Chacoan, or Chaco, region shown in figure 3.10 suggests the existence of a sociopolitical entity on a scale previously unsuspected in the Anasazi Southwest.

The community pattern is so very widespread, however, that one may well wonder if this Chacoan community is in fact indicative of a sociopolit-ical entity. The community structure, identified here as Chacoan, could instead have been a nonspecific, pan-Anasazi pattern. Every village may have had a great house and a great kiva; those structures may have been a necessary part of any Anasazi settlement in the 1000s and 1100s (cf. Wheat 1983). If this were the case, Chaco Canyon was an unusual development within a widespread, pan-Anasazi distribution of great house–great kiva settlements.

Has the Chaco region become so large, then, that it is essentially mean-ingless? Arguing strongly against this dismal conclusion are the roads. Roads in the San Juan Basin trace the skeleton of a regional system centered on Chaco Canyon; indeed, roads are the least ambiguous archaeological evidence of a regional system we have ever found in the Anasazi Southwest. Several of the farthest outlying great houses also have evident road seg-ments. If those roads connect the outlying great houses to Chaco (and if all the roads date to the eleventh and twelfth centuries), then the very large Chaco region (fig. 3.10) may indeed be real, however difficult it may be to explain. However, the physical connection of outermost roads with the Chaco center has not yet been made (with the exception of the Rio Puerco of the West outlier group). We do not know enough about roads—we may never know enough about roads—to resolve this problem.

There are alternate lines of inquiry that we can follow. Although the Chaco region as shown in figure 3.10 includes most of the Anasazi area, two important areas are excluded: the Kayenta and upper Rio Grande regions. The Kayenta area was, of course, as much Anasazi as Chaco, but had neither great kivas nor great houses in the 1000s and 1100s (Jeffrey S. Dean, personal communication, 1987; Alexander J. Lindsay, personal communication, 1987; Jonathan Haas, personal communication, 1987). Nor, evidently, did the upper Rio Grande, although a single great kiva has been reported at the Pojoaque Grant Site (Peckham 1979) and an anomalous unit house community has been found near the Cerrillos turquoise mines (Wiseman and Darling 1986). Since the Kayenta and upper Rio Grande areas, presumably comprising the same Anasazi base population as the Chacoan, did not share this settlement organization, then these two notable exceptions may prove the Chacoan rule. If the great house–great kiva community pattern is not pan-Anasazi, then it represents a spatial division of the Anasazi and, arguably, a regional system.

ISSUES IN CHACOAN REGIONAL DEVELOPMENT

The topics suggested for the seminar that produced these papers structure my concluding remarks on Chacoan settlement patterns. On the most general level, three themes were addressed by the seminar: origins and growth, boundaries, and truncation. Topics specific to the analysis of Chaco and Hohokam settlement included hierarchies, aggregation, and internal regionalization.

ORIGINS AND GROWTH

This analysis of the Chaco region is based largely on surface data from various surveys. We know very little about the time depth of the sites and communities shown in figure 3.10; or rather, we know about time depth at only a few of those sites.

Many Chacoan communities were occupied from the Basketmaker III through Pueblo III periods. Others, such as Bis sa'ani (Breternitz, Doyel, and Marshall 1982), were occupied for only a short period during the last decades of the Chaco system. Breternitz, Doyel, and Marshall (1982) offer a good general discussion of great-house communities with both short and long time depth, but it is difficult to extend their ideas about differing occupation lengths to the many unexcavated sites of the entire Chaco system. Surface ceramics at great houses often fail to represent earlier (and sometimes later) occupations. For example, ceramics on the surface of Aztec and Salmon ruins evidence only the final, mid- to late-thirteenth-century use of these buildings, and they offer few if any hints that they were constructed in the late eleventh and early twelfth centuries. Conversely, sherds from the surface of middens at several outliers represent the eleventh-century occupations, and fail to reflect the later, thirteenth-century use of the structures (Windes 1982b).

Surface ceramics indicate that great houses were in use during the eleventh and early twelfth centuries, but we cannot tell with certainty when many of those structures were originally built (and when they were finally abandoned); thus, settlement patterns, at this time, tell us surprisingly little about the history and dynamics of the Chaco regional system. The sites mapped in figure 3.10 represent the system at its peak, but the chronology, origins, and growth of that system will require much more extensive excavated data than are currently available.

BOUNDARIES

The boundaries of the Chaco region are perilously close to those of the Anasazi in the 1000s and 1100s, with the notable exceptions of the Kayenta and Rio Grande areas. The northern boundary is the Rockies; the southern boundary is the Mogollon Rim and the Mogollon Mountains. East and west, the boundaries are defined not by physiography but by archaeological units we are accustomed to thinking of as cultural: the Kayenta and the upper Rio Grande Anasazi.

The northern boundary is, in a real sense, absolute: the Rockies create a nearly impermeable border, beyond which there is little of interest, archaeologically, to the present study. To the south, however, was a "boundary" both permeable and interesting. The Mogollon Rim was no *Ultima Thule*; both the Mogollons and the land to their south were densely occupied by dynamic societies that may or may not have been impressed by things like Chacoan great houses.

Along corridors such as the San Francisco, upper Gila, and Mimbres rivers, some very large sites were contemporaneous with Chaco. Other than the huge buildings at Chaco Canyon, there are no contemporaneous Anasazi rivals to the size of 150-room (and larger) classic Mimbres sites like Swarts and Woodrow ruins (see fig. 3.7). A community organization, with small pueblos grouped around great kivas (rectangular, and therefore ignored in Chacoan studies), is also present in the Mogollon areas (Lekson 1988). The relationship of the Mogollon to Chaco and its implications for the Chaco region are currently far from clear, but future thinking should include this southern community pattern.

The boundary to the southwest, between Chaco and the Hohokam, seems clear and abrupt. That is, there appears to be very little architectural communication across the rugged Mogollon Rim of Arizona—an area of remarkably little recent work. Beyond a few very specialized forms, such as platform mounds (Lekson 1986), there are almost no architectural parallels between the two areas. Nor does Hohokam settlement (e.g., Wilcox, McGuire, and Sternberg 1981; Doyel ed. 1987) appear to resemble the Chaco community pattern. From existing architectural and settlement data, it appears that Chaco was Chaco and Hohokam was Hohokam, and never the twain did meet.

ABANDONMENT AND TRUNCATION

Major building at Chaco Canyon ceased at about A.D. 1150, but neither the canyon nor the Chaco region was abandoned at that time. Truncation, in the sense of decapitation, might be the appropriate metaphor for this collapse. Indeed, the outer margins of the Chaco region, as defined in figure 3.10, experienced a spectacular florescence in the late 1100s and 1200s, immediately after construction ceased at Chaco Canyon. The Mesa Verde phase to the north and the Tularosa phase (and related phases at Zuni) to the south were periods that eclipsed the earlier Chaco period in these areas. Remarkable developments also occurred to both the east (upper Rio Grande) and to the west (Kayenta) of the old Chaco region. The peripheries of the region were quite healthy; only the central San Juan Basin was diminished.

Diminished, but not abandoned. The "horizon marker" for the San Juan Basin post-Chaco is Mesa Verde Black-on-white pottery (and local varieties of this type). Mesa Verde Black-on-white is found *beneath* the final floors of great kivas at several Chaco Canyon great houses. Presumably, small hunting parties do not re-floor great kivas, so in some way the old center was being maintained.

Great houses in Chaco Canyon were built to last; indeed, large sections of several great houses were intact as late as the 1880s, so we can be sure that great houses remained useful structures through the 1200s and 1300s. Although major construction in Chaco ceased in the mid-1100s, Chaco and its great houses probably continued to function in some fashion—for example, as a ceremonial center—for long beyond that date. Our problem is to define that function without Western preconceptions about building, growth, and entropy. If Chaco had been a city in 1150, it almost certainly was not one in 1250; but it may still have been a center.

HIERARCHIES

Were there hierarchies within the Chaco region? On one level, the answer is obviously yes: Chaco Canyon itself was orders of magnitude larger than any other community in the region, and it incorporated a larger variety of building types and facilities. The only possible exception would be the Animas Valley complex, developed at the very end of the great-house building period (Stein and McKenna 1988). For most of the two and a half centuries of great-house building, Chaco was almost certainly preeminent in some sense.

Were there hierarchies among or between the other communities of the region? On this level, the answer is much less clear. As noted above, there are few data for useful analysis of communities. There is a range of sizes of Chacoan communities, but there do not appear to be marked *structural* differences between communities. The set of facilities that define communities—great houses, great kivas, and so forth—is shared by all communities. But of course, this is a circular argument, since those intrinsic features define Chacoan communities.

AGGREGATION

Over most of the Anasazi area, settlement was always characterized by communities: that is, clustered sites and settlements (e.g., Tohatchi and Alkali Ridge 13; fig. 3.7). Great houses were, presumably, a Chacoan addition to what was a long-standing settlement pattern. The notion of a "Pueblo II dispersion," with unit houses scattered over the Southwest like corn-belt farmsteads, is almost certainly inaccurate. Thus on the regional scale, questions of aggregation and dispersion probably do not apply—unless Chaco itself is evidence of significant aggregation.

The question of aggregation at Chaco is complex. Blake, LeBlanc, and Minnis (1986:463) argue that Chaco Canyon had a population growth rate of 0.78 percent, too high to be accounted for by simple biological increase. They argue that immigration would have been necessary to attain the 5,652-person population peak suggested by Hayes (1981). However, Hayes's population figures have since been questioned and reduced (Lekson 1986; Windes 1982a, 1984b, 1987b; Windes and Doleman 1985). Using lowered peak population estimates of 2,100 to 2,700 people (Lekson 1986:272), the annual growth rate need only have been 0.3 percent, which falls within the published ranges for Neolithic-level societies (Hassan 1981). The question may well be moot: population and population growth at Chaco Canyon are central to Chaco studies, but neither architecture nor settlement pattern provides unambiguous answers (Lekson 1986: 269–72).

Within individual outlier communities, the problems of determining contemporaneity between unit houses and between unit houses and great houses is acute. Early thinking about great houses envisioned them as housing the aggregated population of earlier unit houses (e.g., Gladwin 1945). At most known communities, the large numbers of unit houses and the relatively small floor area of great houses suggests that this scenario is unlikely—unless unit houses were not all contemporaneous.

That not all unit houses in a community are contemporaneous seems likely. The question then becomes what *proportion* of unit houses are contemporaneous, and to this we have no answer. The only excavated Chaco community is Bis sa'ani, a late, very small settlement. Breternitz, Doyel, and Marshall (1982) argued that Bis sa'ani and the unit houses of its community were contemporaneous.

Bis sa'ani provides a very interesting opportunity to study a "single component" Chaco community. There are a number of striking parallels between the total floor areas, total number of kivas, hearths, and so forth, between the great house and the combined unit houses of its community (Breternitz, Doyel, and Marshall 1982; Lekson 1985). These parallels could be interpreted as the unit-house organization being reflected, one-to-one, in the great-house architecture; or, intriguingly, they could also be interpreted as the aggregation of the unit-house population into the great house itself. The degree of chronological resolution at Bis sa'ani—or any Southwestern site—is almost certainly too coarse to detect aggregation over a very short term, say a decade or so. Could the apparently small size of the Bis sa'ani Community represent the proportion of unit houses at larger communities that were actually occupied at one time? That is, of scores of unit houses at a large outlier community like Muddy Water, were only five or so actually occupied at any one time? If so, then outlier communities could indeed represent local aggregation into great houses, albeit within a very small area. Communities, by definition, are aggregates, but a great house would be a quantum leap in neighborly crowding over the older, more dispersed, Anasazi community pattern. Intracommunity aggregation into great houses is a possibility (and not one that I favor) that must be considered—a possibility that our crude chronological controls will not allow us to dismiss.

INTERNAL REGIONALIZATION

After A.D. 1150, the peripheries of the Chaco region were markedly regionalized by the comparative void of the San Juan Basin itself. The Mesa Verde, Kayenta, upper Rio Grande, and Tularosa areas were separated by the greatly diminished center, and this void fostered increasing differentiation in their archaeologies. But what of Chaco at its peak? Was there marked regionalization within the Chaco region in the 1000s and 1100s?

I have argued, from the perspective of settlement patterns, that there was homogeneity within the Chaco region. With the region potentially expanded to the point of identity with Anasazi, it is the center—the unique developments at Chaco Canyon—that gives the concept of a Chaco region whatever validity it may enjoy. Thus, the primary internal regionalization of the Chaco region was the differentiation of Chaco Canyon itself from the overwhelming homogeneity of the Anasazi world around it.

THE CHACO REGION AND THE HOHOKAM REGION

Chaco and Hohokam regional settlement patterns reflect the larger ecology of the Southwest. The Chaco system was a spatially extensive adaptation to the broad grasslands and piñon-juniper scrub forests of the Colorado Plateau; one conclusion of this paper is that Chacoan sites are found over almost all of this biotic region. In contrast, the central Hohokam region was tightly focused on the riverine oases of the Sonoran desert, and Hohokam settlement extended in a strongly linear pattern along rivers and canals. The different settlement patterns directly represent agricultural adaptations to the very different biotic settings of the two systems.

With sufficient moisture, most southwestern soils will support corn agriculture; water is the critical and controlling variable. On the Colorado Plateau, water for prehistoric farming came mainly from rainfall. Direct rainfall ("dry farming") was the main source for agricultural water over most of the Anasazi area. Scattered over the region, thousands of small, very localized landforms might concentrate rainfall runoff, to create locally favorable farming areas. Very rarely, small creeks might be diverted by canal or ditch irrigation, but in the Anasazi world of the tenth and eleventh centuries, there appears to have been little or no use of major streams or rivers for farming water.

Topography affects the amount and distribution of rainfall, but within the broad plains of the Colorado Plateau, rainfall is effectively, if not statistically, random. This randomness led to a very widespread, seemingly uniform archaeology over the Colorado Plateau, mirrored today in the extensive Navajo settlement. Over the vast sameness of the plateau, anywhere and everywhere a wrinkle of terrain or hydrology concentrates rainfall, Navajos settle and the Anasazi settled before them. The terrain and climate of the plateau virtually predict a broad, even, extensive pattern of archaeological settlement—much like the Chaco pattern seen in figure 3.10.

The Hohokam adaptation to the Sonoran desert was quite different. Some upland Sonoran regions can support rainfall runoff farming, but in the Phoenix Basin and other central areas of Hohokam settlement, the scant rainfall is insufficient for dry farming and irrigation is necessary for successful agriculture. Irrigation must come from live water drainages, such as the Salt and the Gila rivers. The large size of the Sonoran streams required the major technological development of the canal systems that characterize the Hohokam. Settlement was tethered to the river courses and the canals that diverted water from those rivers. Thus, the strongly linear pattern of Hohokam settlement is predicted by the hydrology of the canals that fed Hohokam fields, themselves necessitated by the extreme aridity of the Sonoran desert.

This basic ecological difference between Chaco Anasazi and Hohokam is reflected in the two systems' most extraordinary achievements: Chacoan roads and Hohokam canals. The Hohokam canal systems were starkly functional. They were required for farming, and their form and extent were dictated by hydrology. Canal systems dictated the pattern of Hohokam settlement, and they clearly demonstrate the economic interdependence of communities located along individual canal systems. Chaco roads, on the other hand, appear to be almost bewilderingly symbolic. In many instances, roads connected existing communities of considerable temporal depth (that is, the alignment of the roads was determined by the locations of sites). The Chacoans had no wheeled vehicles or domestic animals for pack trains. Since there were no transportation requirements for the large scale of Chacoan roads, it can reasonably be assumed that the scale and elaboration of the Chaco road network was not motivated by simple economic function. Indeed, certain roads have been suggested to be visible expressions of prehistoric cosmology (Sofaer, Marshall, and Sinclair 1989). It seems likely that the labor and effort that went into Chaco roads cemented intercommunity relationships between settlements at the ends of each road segment. Roads symbolically expressed the cohesiveness of the extensive Chaco regional system—a reading very different from the clear, unambiguous archaeological message of the Hohokam canal systems. Canals were the spine of Hohokam subsistence and settlement; roads were filaments in a larger yet looser web, at the center of which was Chaco Canyon.

——————— *Acknowledgments* ———————

I would like to thank the following people for their generous assistance: at the University of Arizona, Ken Kvamme, Gwinn Vivian, Sharon Urban, Chris Downum, J. Jefferson Reid, Alexander Lindsay, and Jeffrey Dean; at Crow Canyon Archaeological Center in Cortez, Colorado, William Lipe and Bruce Bradley; at the Laboratory of Anthropology in Santa Fe, Stanley Grochowski, Rosemary Talley, Marsha Jackson, Curtis Shaafsma, and Regge Wiseman; and at various locations, Peter McKenna, Winston Hurst, William Lucius, Dennis Gilpin, and Jonathan Haas. John Stein and Andrew Fowler were extremely kind about sharing their data, and John Stein in particular contributed materially to the site distribution shown in figure 3.10. I owe a great debt to John's years of research inside and (more recently) outside the San Juan Basin.

Chapter 4

Chacoan Subsistence

R. GWINN VIVIAN

THE concept of a Chaco regional system has emerged, I believe, largely as a means to account for the distribution of a distinctive community type characterized by great-house architecture (see Lekson, this volume) that occurs in much of the greater San Juan Basin. In most models, the system functioned as a mechanism for redistributing materials within the basin. In particular, it involved the transport of raw materials, processed goods, and foodstuffs from small-house communities ("unit pueblos") situated on the margins of the basin to a resource-poor but densely populated zone that included Chaco Canyon in the interior basin. Collection and transport of goods to great-house communities in Chaco Canyon were controlled by a "managerial elite" that operated small-scale great houses ("outliers") that were established in production settlements. This process evolved over a period of two to three centuries (ca. A.D. 800–1100) and was marked late in Chaco's prehistory by roads linking outliers to Chaco Canyon. The system is frequently characterized as being somewhat symbiotic in nature, though it is usually proposed that the system was controlled by various great houses in Chaco Canyon.

I question the existence of a Chaco regional system as defined in most models and base my dissent on two arguments. First, I do not believe that the great-house community type was widespread in the San Juan Basin until late in Chaco prehistory. Second, I do not believe that it was ever necessary to bring foodstuffs in any quantity into Chaco Canyon to sustain the local population, even though some raw materials (e.g., timbers, lithics) and processed goods (ceramics) were imported. In this paper I limit myself to arguing the second point as it pertains to the general subject of Chacoan subsistence. In doing so, I will review environmental data relevant to subsistence in the San Juan Basin, summarize and evaluate redistributive models, consider population estimates and production potential in the greater Chaco Canyon area, and present an alternative subsistence scenario for that zone.

I have proposed elsewhere (Vivian 1989) that cultural manifestations in the San Juan Basin during the prehistoric "Puebloan period" do not represent a single Chaco system but instead two essentially egalitarian sociopolitical systems with roots in two cultural traditions, the Cibola and the San Juan. System variability was expressed most visibly in settlement pattern and architecture, though distinctiveness blurred over time within the interior basin. The Cibola tradition was represented by small-house communities with social relationships embedded in the lineage, and settlements functioned through the lineage for the duration of Cibolan cultural development in the basin. Cibola small-house settlements were common in Chaco Canyon and throughout most of the San Juan Basin, particularly south of the San Juan River. Cibola communities can be identified by the eighth century, and they functioned until the general depopulation of the interior basin in the second half of the twelfth century. Their architecture and settlement plan changed little over time. Small-house communities practiced mixed subsistence strategies, and farming was largely dependent on ak-chin and dry-farming techniques as defined for the Hohokam by Masse in this volume.

The great-house architectural and settlement type, which is associated with the Chaco regional system by most archaeologists, was a variant of the San Juan tradition. The Chaco–San Juan community type had its origins in Chaco Canyon during the ninth century. Throughout the tenth and most of the eleventh centuries great-house communities crystalized structurally in the Chaco core. The core encompasses a strip of land approximately 16 kilometers wide and 65 kilometers long that extends along the Chaco Wash and includes Chaco Canyon, a large portion of the Chacra Mesa, the lower Escavada drainage, and the Lake Valley area near the confluence of the Kin Bineola and Chaco washes. The Chaco–San Juan tradition functioned sociopolitically through a specialized sequential hierarchy founded on the principle of dualism (Vivian 1989). Chaco–San Juan communities were also dependent on mixed subsistence strategies, but farming in the Chaco core, and possibly elsewhere, involved considerable use of water control facilities utilizing runoff.

ENVIRONMENTAL MARGINALITY AND SUBSISTENCE

Prehistoric farming strategies in the San Juan Basin were conditioned by edaphic, climatic, and hydrologic patterns. The basin is characterized by relatively poor soils, a frequently short growing season, and limited annual precipitation that can fluctuate markedly both spatially and temporally during periods when effective moisture is most critical for crops. Paleo-climatic investigations in the San Juan Basin indicate that no major change in climate has occurred over the past 5,000 years, though the same data suggest that short-term and long-term fluctuations in precipitation and presumably temperature were common. All of these conditions contributed to the marginal nature of the area for successful agriculture, particularly from about A.D. 500 to 1200, which coincided with the major period of Puebloan occupation.

The most significant climatic feature of this period was a pronounced decline in total annual moisture that began at about A.D. 725 to 750 and bottomed out at approximately 875. Moisture then increased and reached the 750 levels around A.D. 1050. Superimposed on these precipitation peaks and troughs were cycles of rainfall periodicity (expected frequency of moisture events) and variance (overall quantity that could be expected in a rainfall event). Jorde's (1977) research shows close correspondence between changes in rainfall periodicity, variance, and total moisture values. For the period from 750 to 1050, rainfall was characterized by shorter periodicity and an increase in variance. However, for the period from 1050 to 1350 there is longer periodicity and a decrease in rainfall variance.

Climatologically, Puebloan occupation in the San Juan Basin between 500 and 1200 spanned two periods of high moisture values and one period of low moisture. The most critical periods for agriculturalists were the major drought from 850 to 900 and cyclical shifts in periodicity and variance at about 750 and 1050.

Although edaphic and climatic conditions basinwide contributed to low agricultural productivity, zones bordering the interior basin received slightly greater amounts of precipitation, and soils in the southern margins of the basin were more suited for irrigated or floodwater farming. However, survey data indicate that the only area in the basin that showed a consistent pattern of continued population increase and site packing, or extreme site density, was the Chaco core. In contrast, Gillespie and Powers (1983) observed that although some areas, such as the Chuska Valley and the Chaco Slope, always maintained a fairly dense settlement pattern, density did vary through time, presumably as a result of adjustments to cyclical shifts in moisture.

Continued population increase in the Chaco core was not only inconsistent with the settlement record in other basin zones but was incongruous considering the nature of soils and temperature in Chaco Canyon where most of the core population was concentrated. Studies conducted by Judd

(1954) and Bradfield (1971) revealed that canyon soils were low in soluble calcium and largely impervious to water. Bradfield (1971:58–59) also determined that they were at least 30 times more saline than the worst Hopi fields. Love (1977), however, determined that canyon soils were not uniform. Those within the main canyon had greater quantities of clay, whereas those located in side canyons and near the mouths of side canyons were more sandy.

Temperatures in Chaco Canyon are colder than in many locales in the basin, including a number at higher elevations, because of cold air drainage into the canyon. Canyon temperatures from 1952 to 1982 ranged from a high of 102 degrees Fahrenheit (39° C) to a low of −38 degrees Fahrenheit (−38° C), but Gillespie and Powers (1983) observed that fewer than half of the years between 1960 and 1982 had 100 frost-free days, and no years had as many as 150. Agricultural production on an annual basis would be severely curtailed in the canyon if Hack's (1942) optimum agricultural conditions of 120 frost-free days for the Hopi area were applied to Chaco Canyon. Though average annual moisture for Chaco Canyon (22 cm) is lower than that of a number of other interior basin zones, the reliability of precipitation was essentially constant basinwide, leading Schelberg (1983:8) to comment that "from the point of view of the Anasazi, no area was predictably better than any other area."

In addition to poor and deteriorating soils, unpredictable moisture patterns, and shorter frost-free periods, populations in the Chaco core had to contend with limited subsistence diversity resulting from minimal topographic relief. Moreover, although subsistence within the core was marked by increasing reliance on horticulture, climatic perturbations tempered total dependence on cultigens. As a result, use of game and wild plant foods, which themselves were not unaffected by changes in climate, fluctuated in importance over time. The ultimate consequence was periods of subsistence stress.

COPING WITH SUBSISTENCE STRESS: PREVIOUS MODELS

Models presenting hypothetical solutions to population-resource imbalance in the San Juan Basin were developed by Judge (1979), Marshall and colleagues (1979), and Irwin-Williams and Shelley (1980). In general, they presented three options for reducing subsistence stress in the interior basin: agricultural intensification, exchange, and out-migration. The model developed by Irwin-Williams and Shelley (1980) was the only one that included hypothetical mechanisms for implementing and maintaining these options.

Agricultural intensification in these models involved increasing total area under cultivation or increasing yields in each unit under cultivation. The latter process was presumed to have involved some form of water control, and both solutions implied a need for increased labor and, in the case of water control, coordinated labor. Facilities for water control were identified and technological processes postulated, but social mechanisms for ensuring the presence of massed labor or the means for manipulating its members were not specifically defined.

Exchange generally was presented as a process initiated through simple reciprocity between kin or ritually linked groups that evolved into more ordered and complex redistribution as population increased and climatic variability stimulated periodic localized shortages or surpluses. Though reference was made in some models to "alliance networks" (e.g., Cordell and Plog 1979; S. Plog 1980b), mechanisms for instituting and then maintaining control of a redistributive system were not explicated. Judge suggested that turquoise served as a medium of exchange and eventually assumed more ritual than economic importance, but he did not propose the processes that established "elite" control over this commodity. Authors of these models were hesitant to suggest the presence of true markets (see Toll 1981 for a consideration of markets).

Mobility was thought by some to have been restricted by the availability of exploitable niches in the basin, but when out-migration was possible it was assumed that the founding of new settlements was facilitated by previously established social ties forged through marriage or exchange.

These models gained greater credence as the extent of the Chaco outlier and road networks was established. Outliers for the most part were located in zones with better soils, more dependable rainfall, and in some cases highly localized resources. Although interpretive differences existed and there was less dependence on the direct application of geographers' transport and marketing models (e.g., Ebert and Hitchcock 1973) to explain the roads and outliers, most of the models were characterized by a basic tenet: outliers were established as centers outside the Chaco core for production of goods, including foodstuffs, that were cycled to Chaco Canyon on roads.

A need to modify these models arose when evidence for massive great-house construction projects during the second half of the eleventh century (Lekson 1986) contrasted sharply with extremely limited evidence for large-scale importation of foodstuffs into the canyon during this period. The principal reaction was to question the residential function of great houses in the eleventh and twelfth centuries. Judge (1979:903), for example, hypothesized in 1976 that large-scale additions to great houses and new great houses erected during the late eleventh century functioned in part as storage units for "formal redistributive events." However, with increasing negative evidence for redistribution through canyon great houses, he advanced a concept in 1984 of consumption rather than redistribution. This permitted him to reduce significantly the permanent population levels in great houses.

Judge then suggested that these buildings served to accommodate periodic influxes of pilgrims from outlying areas who were drawn to Chaco Canyon to participate in organized ritual that involved central consumption of goods and services. Moreover, these festivals functioned "as a forum in which leaders from the various outliers administered the alliances that regulated exchange . . . to help compensate for any variability occurring in crop production" (Judge 1984:10). The implication was that although foodstuffs may not have been transported to the canyon for redistribution, plans for redistribution on a subregional basis were made at these gatherings. Judge proposed that increased great-house construction during this period represented compensation paid in the form of labor for ritual services. Reduced summer moisture in the 1080s and 1090s challenged the economic and ritual dominance of Chaco Canyon in the region, and Judge proposed that a shift of "power" occurred in the early twelfth century (ca. 1115–1120) to a new regional center at the confluence of the Animas and San Juan rivers. This shift became permanent when a significant decrease in regional moisture began at about A.D. 1130. Construction in Chaco Canyon declined rapidly thereafter, and most existing buildings were used for residential rather than ritual purposes.

Truell (1986) modified Judge's model by suggesting that much of the great-house construction was done by persons living in small-house settlements in the canyon. She cited the lack of chronological data for construction of small houses during much of the eleventh century and proposed that "if extensive large site construction was undertaken during this period and small site occupants were involved in this building, as some have suggested . . . there may have been neither the time nor the resources to expend on small site construction" (Truell 1986:143). Truell did not propose great-house population figures but implied at least some residential use of these structures. Most importantly, she drew attention to the presence of small-house sites in the canyon and the need to consider them in resource-population models.

Marshall also reevaluated the relationship of outlier communities with great houses in Chaco Canyon. His work at the Bis sa'ani outlier complex fostered the concept of a "Chaco Halo" (Marshall, Doyel, and Breternitz 1982) which had implications for subsistence requirements and production in Chaco Canyon. Marshall continued to believe that Chaco Canyon was the center of development in the San Juan Basin over a long period of time, that great houses served specialized functions (including storage), and that they provided services to and in turn were serviced by outlier communities. However, the Chaco Halo model reduced the outlier contributor zone for foodstuffs to a constellation of sites distributed discontinuously around Chaco Canyon in an area of approximately 360 square kilometers. These sites served as agricultural production support centers for a Chaco Canyon "megacommunity," thereby drastically reducing if not eliminating the need for long-distance transport of food from other sectors of the basin.

Marshall recognized that agricultural intensification, which was critical for the maintenance of the Chacoan system, may have been even more important in areas peripheral to the canyon than within it. The Chaco Halo concept allowed Marshall to reconsider population size and organizational structure of great houses in Chaco Canyon. Following the trend toward seeing a much-reduced population in these structures, he suggested that small-house sites in the Chaco Halo housed a portion of the canyon population that dispersed seasonally for agricultural tasks and returned to great houses only for ceremonial events.

PREVIOUS SUBSISTENCE STRESS MODELS: A CRITIQUE

To reiterate briefly, agriculturally based Puebloan communities in much of the San Juan Basin faced frequent subsistence stress from approximately A.D. 500 to 1200 as a result of population-resource imbalance created by the marginality of the region for maize farming. This was a major problem in the interior basin, and in the Chaco core in particular, where soils were poor, cold-air drainage in Chaco Canyon shortened the growing season, and moisture was frequently insufficient for plant growth.

Yet Chaco Canyon and the slightly larger Chaco core were distinguished from other basin zones by small-house site packing and numerous great houses, which suggested population growth. Population density, the presence of roads radiating from Chaco Canyon to surrounding outlier settlements, and the central location of the Chaco core in the basin prompted the identification of great-house communities in Chaco Canyon as central nodes of a regional exchange system. The "primacy" of these canyon communities within the basin was thought to have been established early, and activities in outlier communities were presumed to have been directed by canyon great houses.

Models explaining population-resource imbalance were focused on the Chaco core, where stress levels were presumed to have been greatest. Proposed responses included group fissioning and dispersal, transport of goods to the Chaco core from more productive zones on the basin peripheries, and agricultural intensification. When evidence for large-scale import of foodstuffs into the core was not supported by field data, explanations shifted from redistribution to revising the function of great houses. In this process, great-house population figures were reduced.

The "vacant city" model is weakened, however, by the fact that the sociopolitical processes and mechanisms that generated and maintained the system are not postulated. This factor is critical if one is to interpret the presence of numerous small-house settlements in the Chaco core and define the hierarchical structuring of great- and small-house communities. Although such a task is possible, it may not be necessary to reduce population as an explanatory device for resolving subsistence stress in the Chaco core if agricultural intensification could achieve the same result.

Cordell (1982) observed that three modes of intensification were possible in the San Juan Basin: (1) a labor-intensive mode dependent on the employment of soil and water control devices; (2) a land-intensive mode involving multiple planting and overplanting; and (3) a time-intensive mode involving shifting cultivation. She noted that markedly different population densities should result from whichever mode was selected. Land- and time-intensive modes should produce smaller, more dispersed populations, whereas labor-intensive systems should require larger and more concentrated groups. Judge (1979; Judge et al. 1981) proposed that intensification in Chaco Canyon initially was land intensive but ultimately became more labor intensive as water control systems were introduced. I have argued (Vivian 1984) that great-house farming in the canyon began as a labor-intensive system and changed to a land-intensive mode only late in the eleventh century in conjunction with out-migration from the canyon.

POPULATION ESTIMATES AND PRODUCTION POTENTIAL

If the Chaco core supported a resident great-house and small-house population in the tenth and eleventh centuries, the alternatives for explaining community structure and function in the Chaco core are increased. To do so requires an evaluation of population estimates and production potential in Chaco Canyon and the Chaco core.

CHACO CANYON: POPULATION ESTIMATES

Drager (1976) utilized Stubbs's (1950) population data and aerial photographs of 25 modern pueblos to establish significant correlations between population and several space-related variables (e.g., total number of rooms, total structure area, total floor space). He concluded that "the gross area within the walls of a pueblo minus the areas which can be identified as kivas, plazas, and non-roofed spaces is the best indicator of population" (Drager 1976:162). When the total floor area of all 25 pueblos was divided by the total population of all pueblos the ratio was 10.73, which was very close to Naroll's (1962) ratio of F (floor area) $= 10\ P$ (persons). Using his own equation, Drager determined that great houses in Chaco Canyon had a population of 2,947. When this figure is combined with Hayes's (1981) estimate of 2,889 for contemporaneous small-house sites, a maximum population for Chaco Canyon in the eleventh century is 5,836.

Hayes's estimates for canyon great- and small-house populations were based on an assumed family size of 4.5 individuals and a three-room living unit per family. Using room counts for Early Pueblo III (A.D. 1050–1175) structures, he derived a figure of 2,889 persons for small-house sites and 2,763 for great houses, with a canyon total of 5,652. Lekson (1986) arrived at a similar figure (5,211) through a comparison of postulated construction labor at canyon great houses (a conjectured average annual expenditure of 55,645 person hours, representing 2,762 workers) with Ford's (1968) projected yearly labor requirements at San Juan Pueblo in 1890. Ford's estimate was based on an assumed work force of 212 persons in a total population of 400. Although he did not so specify, Lekson apparently assumed that both great-house and small-house groups were involved in great-house construction; otherwise, his figure would be increased by approximately 3,000 small-house inhabitants, giving a total canyon population that he surely would find objectionable.

Windes (1984b:84) computed a "greatly reduced population in the canyon, perhaps 2000 or less in the late A.D. 1000s," based on equating firepit rooms with single households. Proceeding from the assumption that there was minimal habitation of upper-story rooms in great houses, he estimated the number of firepits that may have been in use during the last half of the eleventh century at Pueblo Bonito, Pueblo del Arroyo, and Pueblo Alto. Using an index of six persons per household, he concluded that "Bonito might have contained roughly 100 people at its height . . . about 40 to 60 people are predicted for del Arroyo . . . [and] at Alto, a high of about 100 and a low of about 50" (Windes 1984b:83–84).

To derive an estimate of the population that could be supported by agriculture in Chaco Canyon, Loose and Lyons (1976) summarized data on recent Puebloan per capita dietary requirements supplied by cultigens. White (1962) reported 1.09 acres per capita for Zia in 1936, and Tyler (1964) listed 1.06 acres for Zuni and 1.39 acres for Acoma, Laguna, and Santa Ana; the mean for the five pueblos is 1.18 acres (0.48 hectares) per capita. Acknowledging the implications of modern dietary supplements, Loose and Lyons reported Bradfield's (1971) estimates of 2.5 acres per person for the Hopi of the Oraibi Valley between 1851 and 1865. They also cited an unpublished study of maize agriculture by Jorde which concluded "that at least 0.89 acres per person were necessary for typical Pueblo corn, bean, and squash subsistence," and they pointed out that his study "took into account Puebloan metabolic rates, age and sex structure of populations, Puebloan stature, prehistoric cultigen productivity, surplus and seed storage, and the total portion of the Puebloan diet that corn, beans, and squash provided" (Loose and Lyons 1976:149).

The per capita figures were then applied to various appraisals of land under cultivation in Chaco Canyon. These estimates varied widely, though most calculations were confined to a zone extending from Shabik'eshchee Village to the confluence of the Chaco and Escavada washes—a distance of about 20 kilometers. Hayes equated viable cropland with canyon floor alluvium, an area of approximately 3,200 acres (1,295 hectares). Loose and Lyons (1976) produced a similar figure (3,584 acres; 1,451 hectares) calculated from the total area covered by two vegetative zones that they assumed were associated with old field areas. I (Vivian 1974) estimated 2,000 acres (810 hectares) of farmland for a smaller portion of the canyon (Gallo Canyon to the Chaco-Escavada confluence), based on zones in the main canyon that derived floodwater from side canyon drainages. If some regularity in canyon drainages is assumed, an additional 667 acres (270 hectares) may be added to my figures for the area from Gallo Canyon to Shabik'eshchee Village, thereby increasing my canyon estimate to 2,667 acres (1,080 hectares).

When Loose and Lyons's population data are correlated with estimated land under cultivation, population figures range from a low of 1,067 to a high of 4,027 (table 4.1). The Loose and Lyons estimates derive from the assumption that cultigens constituted the major portion of the Chacoan diet during the Puebloan period. This assumption is based in large part on the lack of good data relative to percentages of wild plant and animal foods that contributed to Puebloan diet.

We do know that the same basic foods, including fauna and non-cultigens, were consumed by both great- and small-house populations. Mollie Toll (1984:249) found that subsistence resources at all sites were

TABLE 4.1. *Population estimates for Chaco Canyon, based on acres under cultivation and cultivated acres per capita*

Acres under Cultivation	Acres per Capita		
	0.89	1.18	2.5
3,584 (total canyon)[a]	4,027	3,037	1,434
3,200 (canyon alluvium)[b]	3,595	2,712	1,280
2,667 (canyon drainage zones)[c]	2,997	2,260	1,067

[a]Source: Loose and Lyons 1976.
[b]Source: Hayes 1981.
[c]Source: Vivian 1974.

fundamentally the same "both in [the populations'] dependence on locally available wild species and on corn agriculture," and Palkovich (1984:111) concluded that all groups in Chaco Canyon "suffered as a result of their nutritionally marginal agrarian existence." Faunal resource studies showed that assemblages differed more over time at all sites than between contemporaneous components at great and small houses. Though Akins's (1984) analysis of economic species from great- and small-house sites showed greater quantities of faunal resources at one great house (Pueblo Alto), the consumable meat represented by the bone was not high.

Akins (1984:234) did estimate population at Pueblo Alto based on a projected "daily intake of 200 calories of meat, which is equivalent to approximately 40% of a cottontail rabbit." Though an average daily intake of 200 calories of meat per individual in Chaco Canyon may be too high, meat resources available almost certainly included several species not present in great numbers in the bone counts. Akins's data, for example, listed high percentages of unidentified small mammals but minimal numbers of "economic rodents" and birds. Clary's (1984) analysis of human coprolites from Pueblo Alto and Pueblo Bonito, on the other hand, showed that 71 percent of the samples contained small fragments of not only cottontail and prairie dog but deer mouse and small birds.

Though only cottontail was represented by large percentages in the bone counts from the Pueblo Alto refuse mound, Clary (1984:267) concluded that "the abundance of bone from small mammals and birds in these samples suggested that protein requirements were to a large extent fulfilled by the consumption of those species." Bone parts for all species represented, including cottontail, further suggested that the entire animal was eaten. If bone of small mammals and birds was consumed with the fleshy parts, bone size would be reduced considerably, thereby making its archaeological recovery more difficult. Moreover, eventual deposition of this bone in refuse mounds was not necessarily ensured. All of the Pueblo Bonito coprolite samples were from rooms, and only 36 percent of the Pueblo Alto specimens were from the refuse mound. If animal protein in Chacoan diet included a high percentage of small animals and birds whose bones are underrepresented in refuse deposits, Jorde's acreage-per-capita figure of 0.89 (Loose and Lyons 1976:149) may be the most representative, thereby increasing the argument for subsistence self-sufficiency in Chaco Canyon.

CHACO CANYON: CROP PRODUCTION

Subsistence self-sufficiency of Chaco Canyon's population based on the contributions of wild plant and animal foods to the Chacoan diet can be countered, however, by the argument that production estimates must take into account the fallacies of assuming that all land in Chaco Canyon that could have been farmed was always under cultivation, that climatic conditions were constant, and that precipitation was equally distributed throughout the area. Schelberg (1983) has pointed out that past studies of Chacoan agricultural production not only assumed equal productivity of all land but failed to consider the need for fallow. Citing Hastorf's (1980) study of Precolumbian agricultural techniques in the Southwest, Schelberg presumed a 40-percent fallow for agricultural land in Chaco Canyon, a factor that could reduce the population figures listed above by almost half.

Though I have considered the basic mechanics of water control in Chaco Canyon (Vivian 1974, 1984), neither I nor Judge has determined whether the temperature, moisture, and soil conditions cited as restrictive to farming (e.g., Loose and Lyons 1976; Gillespie and Powers 1983; Schelberg 1983) uniformly affected all crop production or varied within the canyon or between the canyon and other zones in the Chaco core. Accordingly, the productive potential of lands within Chaco Canyon and the Chaco core should be reevaluated with respect to growing season, water availability, and fallowing.

Growing Season. Gillespie and Powers (1983) observed that the frost-free season in Chaco Canyon was considerably shorter than has often been reported (e.g., Cordell 1982; Hayes 1981), averaging little more than 100 days since 1960. This was below the 110 to 130 days accepted as necessary for maize, thereby making maize agriculture extremely risky in the canyon. Gillespie's (1985) subsequent analyses suggested, however, that although temperature was a critical variable, the canyon may not have been the high-risk area it previously was thought to be. His conclusions were based on several factors, the most important of which were a current regional climatic trend toward shorter frost-free periods and the need to make a distinction between "frost-free season" and "growing-season." He noted that in the 1940s the U.S. Weather Bureau had changed from recording "growing season" (defined by "killing frosts" which generally begin at 30° F) to recording time spans between 32-degree-Fahrenheit (0° C) minima ("frost-free" periods).

Gillespie's analysis of 250 weather records from New Mexico indicated that this change resulted in an average difference of 13 days. This would extend the growing season by almost two weeks, which is of considerable significance for maize because it usually is not damaged until temperatures drop below 30 degrees Fahrenheit. Gillespie (1985:19) concluded that "the possibilities that fast-maturing strains of corn were used and that recent frost-free periods are not indicative of effective growing season suggest that periods less than 110–130 days are not necessarily prohibitive. These low figures would perhaps be better considered as a potential limitation rather than a barrier to maize agriculture."

Available Water. Based on their evaluation of available water for intensive agriculture in Chaco Canyon, Loose and Lyons (1976) drastically reduced their estimates of land suitable for intensive farming in the canyon to 75 acres (30 hectares). Though other estimates have not been cut as severely, limited moisture is often cited as a major deterrent to plant growth and a critical factor in crop yields. Kirkby's (1973) study of land and water resources in the Oaxaca Valley provides a measure of the significance of water in crop yields. She showed that given sufficient water, similar maize yields could be obtained from any physiographic zone, slope (up to 16 degrees), and soil texture in the valley. This point was emphasized by her observation that even with furrow irrigation, "differences in corn yield from 150 to 300 kilos per hectare down to 0 kilos per hectare can be found within 10 meters distance along a single furrow" (Kirkby 1973:44). Success was largely dependent on the reliability, frequency, and magnitude of flow. "Good" floodwater farming was always associated with distribution canals drawing water from sources that would provide at least one watering every growing season. "Poor" floodwater systems had much less dependable sources and usually only employed "simple trinchera-type walls to slow down and spread floodwater" (Kirkby 1973:49).

Though precipitation in Chaco Canyon was controlled by factors common to much of the interior basin, the unique conditions for the collection of runoff in the canyon made it highly suitable for more intensive farming. Runoff comes primarily from bordering mesas, but the distribution of flow differs from many other areas in the basin because of the canyon topography. Catchment areas for runoff are dendritic, but they tend to be narrow, so that water reaches the canyon floor via many short, usually small, closely spaced drainages. This distributes runoff more evenly throughout the canyon and reduces the velocity in all but the largest drainages. Volume and velocity of runoff do vary, however, on the north and south sides of the canyon as a result of landform differences. In general, volume and velocity are greater on the north because of fewer obstructions to flow, less absorbent surfaces, and tributary canyons that are not cut to the level of the main canyon.

Accordingly, floodwater farming in the canyon was largely determined by the nature of runoff. Most of the southern side canyons were suitable for ak-chin planting that took advantage of restricted runoff, although much of the cultivation in these zones probably merged into dry farming. Greater water velocity and volume in northern drainages, however, called for more elaborate water and soil control, and I have presented (Vivian 1974) evidence for such a system. I proposed that all drainage zones on the north side of Chaco Canyon between the Gallo tributary and the confluence of the Escavada and Chaco washes were tapped for runoff, but Lagasse, Gillespie, and Eggert (1984:207) thought that most tributary systems "were probably not capable of handling runoff from the major lateral drainages as suggested by Vivian (1974)." They predicted that if water was taken from these sources other features should be present. In fact, major diversion and collection systems have been documented for both the Gallo and Cly canyon drainages, and smaller but equally complex features are known from most smaller lateral drainages. There is little doubt that most water flowing into the canyon via northern drainages was collected and used.

Floodwater farming on the north side of the Chaco Wash was made even more effective by the method of distribution to fields. Kirkby (1973) observed that many floodwater systems utilizing canals allow water to flow from ditches unchecked over field areas, or use "furrow irrigation," which tends to water crops unevenly. The effects of uneven distribution are dramatically reflected in crop yields. More equal distribution of floodwater to Chaco's fields was insured by dividing farming areas into major bordered plots that were further subdivided into small, gridded gardens of a standard shape and size.

The best-known field area in Chaco Canyon, the Chetro Ketl gridded gardens, is estimated to have been about 9 hectares in extent. The visible field zone was divided into two rectangular, bordered plots separated by a canal. Each plot was gridded into individual gardens that averaged 308 square meters (approximately 22.5 by 13.5 m), for a total of about 100 gardens per hectare (in contrast, field areas watered by single ditches in the Oaxaca Valley ranged in size from 0.27 to 2.8 hectares). Masonry gates channeled water from the bordering canal into the large rectangular plots, where watering of individual gardens was done through smaller gates or temporary openings in low earth ridges separating each plot. Tests in the Chetro Ketl gardens indicated that "extensive land leveling was carried out on an area of at least 2.4 hectares and possibly as much as 4.8 hectares . . . [and] modern gradients measured across the prehistoric field were 1.17 percent while gradients just off the field were 1.98 percent" (Loose and Lyons 1976:142).

Fallowing. Schelberg (1983), among others, has pointed out that the high clay content of soils in Chaco Canyon restricts absorption of water and leads to accumulation of salts that ultimately make the soil virtually unproductive even with fallowing. The even distribution of runoff on gridded fields presumably would accelerate this process, thereby canceling out any advantages gained through water control.

This almost certainly was *not* the case, however, because canals delivered not only water to field areas but large quantities of sand, silt, and organic detritus. Replenishment of field nutrients through floodwater is well known. Boserup (1965) pointed out that fields with short fallow or no fallow at all could be replenished through various fertilization measures, including silt deposits from canals. Bradfield (1971:18) reported that among the Hopi, "the fertility of *ak-chin* fields is annually renewed by the silt carried down in the flood-water," and he observed that the sand layer also acted as a mulch to minimize evaporation of soil moisture retained above the underlying clayey soil. This was particularly important for spring germination that was dependent on residual moisture from winter and early spring snowmelt. Within the Chaco core, Powers, Gillespie, and Lekson (1983:24) found that the best farming locales in the Bis sa'ani area on the northern edge of Chaco Canyon were those "where there is a thin sand cover over the finer clayey alluvium." Today, virtually all northern side canyons in Chaco Canyon have wide sandy deposits at their mouths that presumably were laid down prior to the arroyo cutting that presently characterizes many of these tributaries.

The division of fields into standard-sized units also insured equal distribution of sediments to all plots. Profiles made by Loose and Lyons (1976) in the Chetro Ketl gridded gardens indicated that sand was being deposited on fields prehistorically. Though there are no studies of the rate of sediment deposition in Chaco gridded fields, Lagasse, Gillespie, and

Eggert (1984) calculated the quantity of sediment collected in a masonry damned reservoir near Tsin Kletzin on the Chacra Mesa. They determined that during a 20-minute storm, a 16-hectare area would produce 481 cubic meters of water and approximately 6.3 cubic meters of sediment. A 60-minute storm would yield 1,470 cubic meters of water and 18.6 cubic meters of sediment.

The sediment-transport power of these small, intense rainfall events was reflected by the fact that most sediment carried was sand. Sediment source areas for the Tsin Kletzin reservoir and the Chetro Ketl fields were not dissimilar, reemphasizing the fact that heavy accumulations of sand might be expected in the Chetro Ketl fields. Presumably, the gradual reduction of ground cover on the mesa above Chetro Ketl through prehistoric fuel collection could have contributed to even greater sediment removal and transport. Excavated ditches and gates in canyon water control systems provided evidence for the continuing deposition of silt on gridded fields. Ditch cleaning appeared to have been minimal. Instead, profiles showed constantly rising levels in ditches that necessitated the raising of gates, which indicates that field levels were gradually rising.

Given a slightly longer growing season, controlled watering of sizeable field areas on the north side of the canyon, and possible elimination or shortening of fallowing through regular deposition of sand and silt on gridded fields, cultigen yields in the Chaco Canyon may have been greater than expected. Moreover, there is some evidence that gridded, ditch-watered fields were developed in a few small areas on the south side of the canyon in zones with suitable water sources and tracts of canyon bottom alluvium that could be replenished with sand and silt deposited in runoff. Other zones on the south side of the canyon were more highly suited for ak-chin or dune farming, both of which were less affected by clay build-up and salinization.

If approximately half of the acreage that I estimated was under cultivation in the canyon (ca. 3,000 acres; 1,215 hectares) in the eleventh century (Vivian 1974) was in fallow, the cultigen-supported population estimates (based on several different acreage requirements per capita) would be as shown on the first line of table 4.2. On the other hand, if 60 percent of the acreage was not fallowed because of field nutrient enrichment through silt deposition, supportable farmland would increase to 2,400 acres (972 hectares), and the cultigen-supported population estimates would increase as shown on the second line of table 4.2.

The highest figure thus obtained—2,696—is still almost exactly half the lowest estimated population figure based on communal labor (5,211;

TABLE 4.2. *Population supported in Chaco Canyon on 1,500 and 2,400 acres, based on three acreage-per-capita estimates*

	Acres per Capita		
Acres under Cultivation	0.89	1.18	2.5
1,500	1,685	1,271	600
2,400	2,629	2,034	960

Lekson 1986), and less than half of figures based on occupied space (5,836; Drager 1976) and room counts (5,652; Hayes 1981).

THE CHACO CORE

Schelberg (1983) has suggested that areas bordering Chaco Canyon could have provided additional cropping zones for canyon residents. This concept was also presented in Marshall, Doyel, and Breternitz's (1982) Chaco Halo model and has merit in that it does not require elaborate exchange systems for maintenance of canyon populations. Chacoan farmers simply exploited more distant zones, but zones that were within their transport capabilities.

Data relevant to agricultural intensification outside Chaco Canyon but within the Chaco core are more limited but basically support Schelberg's premise. A variant of the canyon water control system was developed in the Kin Klizhin and Kin Bineola drainages southwest of the canyon. In both cases, water was diverted from the main watercourse by masonry and earthen dams and carried via large canals to smaller feeder ditches that channeled the flow to gridded gardens. Great houses are present in both valleys. It is unclear how much surplus food could have been produced in these outlying areas for use in Chaco Canyon, but the Kin Klizhin great house is small (an estimated 14 rooms), and the valley farming area is large, which suggests that some food may have been transported to the canyon.

An equally suitable zone along the Escavada Wash north of Chaco Canyon was close by (4 to 8 km) and had attributes conducive to land-intensive if not labor-intensive farming. The Escavada is much wider than the Chaco Wash (ranging from 100 to 300 m in width), and though it runs only sporadically during the summer and fall, its flow is much slower than that of the Chaco Wash. In addition, groundwater levels are higher along the Escavada, and soil bordering the drainage has a high percentage of sand that absorbs water following runoff. Cold-air drainage here does not present the same problems as in Chaco Canyon, and a slightly longer growing season can be expected most years. Though a number of small-house communities were present in this zone, there was only one great-house community (Bis sa'ani) on the drainage, and it was small and established late.

Schelberg (1983) estimated the potential productive capacity of a 37-kilometer section of the Escavada drainage. He computed farming acreage on the basis of three average widths (1,000, 500, and 250 ft.) along the wash, which gave respective totals of 2,788, 1,394, and 697 acres (or 1,129, 564, and 282 hectares). He then determined population that could be supported by cultigens harvested from the Escavada fields using 0.89 and 2.5 acres per capita (the 1.18 acres-per-capita figure used in previous estimates has been included). Next, supportable population figures based on 40-percent and 50-percent fallow were derived. His figures are shown in table 4.3; only the 40-percent-fallow estimates are given.

Schelberg increased the total population figures supported by Chaco-Escavada cultivation by 331 persons to account for small-house residents on the Escavada drainage. Using Windes's (1981) great-house count of 780 and Hayes's (1981) small-house count of 2,889, he arrived at a total Chaco-Escavada population of 4,000 (the 331 Escavada population figure apparently represents the remainder of a rounded, assumed total population of 4,000).

Using the Loose and Lyons (1976) figure for land under cultivation in Chaco Canyon (3,584 acres), Schelberg (1983:17) concluded, "with 40% in fallow and .89 acres per person, the combined Chaco-Escavada area could have supported from 2885 to 3355 people. This still leaves at least 600 persons without local support and the figure would be even larger if the acres per person were increased." However, Schelberg used only the 250- and 500-foot-width figures for the Escavada drainage. If the 1,000-foot figure is used, the supportable population ranges increase from 2,885 to 4,296. Furthermore, if gridded fields that received annual silting in Chaco Canyon were not fallowed, the maximum population figure could rise to 4,576. This is only 664 to 1,074 fewer than estimates developed by Lekson (1986) and Hayes (1981), respectively. More limited fallowing in the canyon and surplus production in the Kin Klizhin and Kin Bineola valleys could raise the figure even closer to the 5,000 to 5,500 population figure that occurs repeatedly in many population estimate exercises.

All of the production and population estimates cited have been based on an assumed "average good year" for agriculture in the Chaco core. Obviously, there were some better years and many worse years. But overall, much of the eleventh century seems to have been favorable for agriculture.

TABLE 4.3. *Population estimates for the Escavada drainage, based on no-fallow and 40-percent-fallow factors and three average cultivation zone widths*

Acres per Capita	Zone Width in Feet		
	1,000	500	250
No Fallow:			
0.89	3,133	1,566	783
1.18	2,363	1,181	590
2.5	1,115	557	278
40% Fallow:			
0.89	1,880	940	469
1.18	1,418	708	354
2.5	669	334	166

Source: Schelberg 1983.

During this period, population apparently increased in the Chaco core, and construction, particularly of great houses, surged dramatically.

Explanations for these changes have taken an interesting twist in recent models or, more commonly, in revisions of existing models, because it has been assumed that climatic and edaphic conditions in the Chaco core curtailed population growth at levels below estimates based on room counts, labor requirements, and living space. As a result, it is now fashionable to construct theories based on vacant cities, festive pilgrims, and wholesale consumption of goods in brief but periodic events at canyon great houses. A preliminary reexamination of critical climatic and edaphic conditions in Chaco Canyon suggests that the Chaco core may have supported the levels of population previously estimated. If this is the case, explanatory models based on a much-reduced population must be reexamined.

Chapter 5

Material Distributions and Exchange in the Chaco System

H. WOLCOTT TOLL

UNTIL the advent of regional perspectives in the 1960s, Chaco and other areas of the prehistoric Southwest were generally perceived by archaeologists as collections of self-sufficient villages, or perhaps even self-sufficient households. Thus, respectful disbelief was Judd's (1954:234–38) reaction to Anna Shepard's precocious contention that considerable quantities of the ceramics found at Pueblo Bonito were from the relatively distant Chuska and La Plata valleys. In a similar vein, when new styles of ceramic decoration appeared in the later part of the Chaco sequence, the prevailing interpretation was that there had been a wave of immigration from north of the San Juan River—a view shared by Roberts (1927), Judd (1954), and Vivian and Mathews (1965)—rather than a succession of temporal and economic shifts. This is not to say that archaeologists of the first 80 years or so of Chaco studies considered Chaco to have existed in grand isolation. George Pepper (1920) of the Hyde Exploring Expedition and Neil Judd (1954) recognized that a number of materials were likely to have come from as far away as Mexico. A standard feature of reports of all vintages was a section on "trade wares," which would enumerate ceramics recognized to be from Arizona or the Mogollon, though the numbers of such specimens were always small.

The "local assumption" (S. Plog 1980a) was followed by a series of quite different explanations, in which varying forms of exchange are seen as prime movers in developments in Chaco. The first of these explanations, that of the "Mexicanists" (see Judge, this volume), explains the development of large sites in Chaco as resulting from economic imperialism from Mesoamerica. The goods most often cited in these formulations are turquoise and slaves (Kelley and Kelley 1975). In terms of material goods the evidence cited consists, on the whole, of low-frequency exotics, especially copper bells and parrots. Much of the other evidence is given in terms of similarity of architecture (see Lekson 1986) and symbols (Reyman 1971).

Exchange is also crucial to many "indigenist" formulations, most of which involve regional systems. The goods seen as primary vary, but can be divided into prestige items and subsistence goods. Judge (1979) suggested that Chaco served as a redistribution point, functioning to even out the frequent patchiness of precipitation, and hence crop production, of the San Juan Basin. Both before and since the redistribution model was put forward, other models have emphasized the exchange of nonsubsistence goods, including religious knowledge and symbols of status that served to maintain links among controlling entities of communities within the Chaco system.

EXCHANGE AND THE ORIGINS OF THE CHACO SYSTEM

Perhaps in accordance with the actual system's "trajectory" between A.D. 900 and 1125, for the last decade or more the Chaco system has been getting steadily larger in the archaeological view. Based on recent reconnaissance, Stein (in Fowler, Stein, and Anyon 1987) suggests that the Chaco phenomenon extends well into Arizona and well south of the Red Mesa Valley, which runs between Grants and Gallup, New Mexico. Fowler (Fowler, Stein, and Anyon 1987:3), in discussing the expansion of sites identified as "Chaco," asks the question, "How far can one extend the boundaries of the 'Chaco System' before it becomes the 'Anasazi System'?" Lekson (this volume) in essence proposes that Chaco is Eastern Anasazi Pueblo II. My view is that calling the Anasazi east of the Kayenta "Chaco" is not useful. The extent to which Chaco, the place, both drove and epitomized community structures elsewhere—as opposed to epitomizing "big bump–little bump" organization only—is a critical, but presently unanswerable, question.

In terms of a material exchange system, what we know about sources of materials found in Chaco shows that although central Chaco had a broad-based supply area, it was not as large as the huge area suggested by Stein and Lekson. Certainly we do not know enough about sources of all classes of items, but the San Juan Basin does account for the vast majority of materials found in Chaco. Thus, a more traditional view of the Chaco region is adopted here, to include the area from just north of the San Juan River south to the Red Mesa Valley, and from the Chuska Valley east to Guadalupe Ruin in the valley of the Rio Puerco of the East.

The fact that relationships cross regional bounds shows much about the nature of boundaries, at least as they are discernible archaeologically. Quite clearly they were permeable, flexible, and perhaps not even recognized beyond their topographic definition. Distance ultimately limits any prehistoric subsystem, and it obviously affects different subsystems in very different ways (see, for example, the historical Zuni acquisition areas in Ferguson and Hart 1985:34–55). Based on material frequency distributions, we can define practical (as opposed to absolute) boundaries of acquisition for various items. Determining whether these practical boundaries are functions of distance or of politics is another, and far more speculative, endeavor. "Regional system" is used here as a convenient means of referring to a phenomenon so complexly multileveled and interconnected that we can only begin to understand and study it. The concept is a recognition of the fact that complex interactions take place at a higher level of intensity in geographically defined areas. The interactions involved are what really merit study, if we aspire to making meaningful contributions to how and why human societies develop and change.

Models for the origins of the Chaco system give varying weight to the importance and scale of exchange. Thus, Mesoamericanist models attribute the system to long-distance trade in exotic items; hierarchical power models find short-range exchange of labor for food and regional exchange among elites important, with the former the basis for inequalities; more ecologically oriented models argue for a causal stimulus involved with regional movement of subsistence goods and people to compensate for local production shortfalls. Although the nature of the exchange varies, it can be said that exchange plays a fundamental role in all of the models for the origin of the Chaco system. This recognizes the presence of large quantities of nonlocal goods in sites of all types and ages, and, in most cases, the precariousness of the subsistence base.

To even begin to understand the cultural meaning of an exchange, one has to know the involved parties and their relationships and understand the contexts of the transfer of goods or labor. Because these aspects of exchange require direct observation, archaeological exchange is something quite different. In archaeology, exchange means goods that are found someplace other than where they were made or extracted. The common assumption is that those materials are most likely to have gotten away from home through some transfer of goods between residents of the two locales. Recently, however, the importance of movement of people within regions in the Southwest (e.g., Vivian 1981; Marshall et al. 1979) has been increasingly recognized, as has the fact that people without vehicles are capable of traveling long distances with substantial quantities of goods.

Both of these types of mobility provide mechanisms for acquisition and transport of goods without those goods ever having been "exchanged." The anthropological implications of getting or bringing your own are very different from getting it through some form of social relationship, whether friendly or hostile. Transfers of goods between people may come about through barter, gift, or violence (Ford 1972a), or, in more "civilized" organizations, through tribute, tax, or extortion, but the baseline for any discussion is distribution of materials of known source.

Under optimal conditions, a discussion of exchange would be based on a series of perfectly controlled synchronic maps of the entire Southwest formulated from entirely consistent information showing distribution contours for each of a large number of confidently sourced items, with all quantities carefully controlled by excavation volume. We are, however, at quite the opposite end of the spectrum from that blissful state, and are forced to rely on limited and usually unequal samples placed in broad time spans, primarily from Chaco Project excavations in the central canyon itself. This viewpoint means that items for which large samples exist are emphasized, and it means that exchanges in the more abstract realm—which are very important exchanges—are underemphasized. Although these samples are a poor proxy for the Truth, they do allow discussion of material movement and provide some inkling of volumes.

Another glaring lack in the information presently available concerns what went out of Chaco in exchange for the items found there. Of course, what the residents of the central canyon had to offer may have been nonmaterial (e.g., labor, knowledge) or perishable (food, craft items), or high value–low volume and frequency (e.g., turquoise, jet ornaments). Unfortunately, there are no durable goods that can be identified specifically as having come from central Chaco Canyon. Both ceramic and lithic raw materials found within usual production distances are so widely distributed that items produced 50 kilometers or more from the central canyon cannot be confidently distinguished from items made in the central canyon until much more precise sourcing techniques are available. This fact greatly compounds the problems in studying the types—and in some cases the existence—of true exchange in the system.

EXOTICS: EXTRAREGIONAL ITEMS

"Exotic" is used here in a combination of its normal senses: it refers both to importedness and to unusualness and romance. The primary items considered under this category are considered ornaments. Ornaments from Chaco Project excavations and the Chaco region in general have been

TABLE 5.1.   Occurrence of turquoise, copper, and shell at Chaco Project
Anasazi sites, by time period and site type

Time Period and Artifact Type	Turquoise		Copper		Shell	
	Large Site	Small Site	Large Site	Small Site	Large Site	Small Site
A.D. 500–920						
Artifacts, beads	–	17	–	0	–	17
Modified, other	–	10	–	0	–	3
A.D. 920–1040[a]						
Artifacts, beads	3	165	0	0	8	25
Modified, other	37	287[c]	0	1[b]	25	58
A.D. 1040–1120						
Artifacts, beads	23	228[d]	2	0	12	3
Modified, other	13	69	0	0	17	6
A.D. 1120–1200						
Artifacts, beads	6	2	0	0	1	2
Modified, other	3	0	0	0	10	2
Post–A.D. 1200 (Mesa Verde)						
Artifacts, beads	0	2	0	1	0	0
Modified, other	0	4	0	0	10	4
Totals	85	784	2	2	83	120

Source: Data compiled from Mathien 1985:527–29, 552–56, 565–67, 571–72, 602–3.
[a]Data include site 29SJ627, from the time period 1000–1050.
[b]Unmodified copper.
[c]In addition, more than 2,000 pieces of turquoise debitage came from small sites of this period.
[d]From the 29SJ423 shrine cache.

exhaustively cataloged by Joan Mathien (1985), and the following discussion is based on distillations of her work. There are three main types of unquestionable exotics found in Chaco: turquoise, shell, and worked copper. Turquoise and shell are found in far greater abundance and in a wider variety of locations than is worked copper. Table 5.1 shows the occurrence of these three materials at sites excavated by the Chaco Project; their occurrence is broken down by time period, with some crude adjustments. Particularly after the early A.D. 1000s, dating of periods in Chaco relies mostly on ceramic dates. One of the least-known periods in central

TABLE 5.2. Collection sizes of bulk common materials from Chaco Project sites, by site type and time period

Site Type	Time Period (A.D.)	Sherds	Lithics	Bone
Large Sites:				
Pueblo Alto	920–1120[a]	90,139	12,339	55,000
Una Vida	920–1220	1,248	103	3,374
Totals		91,387	12,442	58,374
Small Sites:				
6 sites[b]	pre-920	17,114	5,540	8,114
29SJ629[c] and 1360	920–1040	45,606	8,072	3,526
29SJ627	920–1120	84,473	7,145	6,752
29SJ633	1040–1220	7,686	632	3,904
Totals		154,879	21,389	22,296

Source: Adapted from Akins 1985:402 and McKenna n.d.
[a]The A.D. 1040–1120 shrine contains little material.
[b]Sites include Shabik'eshchee, 29SJ423, 29SJ628, 29SJ299, 29SJ721, and 29SJ724.
[c]Also contains a small post-1100 component.

Chaco is the Mesa Verde phase, or terminal Anasazi occupation. Current indications are that a fair number of people lived in Chaco between A.D. 1200 and 1250, or perhaps 1275. Although archaeomagnetic dates centering on A.D. 1300 have been returned, 1300 is likely to postdate the Anasazi occupation of Chaco (see McKenna in Truell et al. 1990).

Table 5.1 represents a somewhat futile attempt at quantification, since, except for copper bells, the units are not comparable (how many beads does one shell bracelet equal?), and since there is no standard item by which to gauge quantities (total sherd, lithic, and bone counts by time period are given in table 5.2 as crude indices). The table also is not as complete as one could wish, since comparable information for Pueblo Bonito is not available.

Turquoise. Turquoise and Chaco are sufficiently closely associated that Judge (e.g., 1983) has suggested that Chaco gained its status through production and control of turquoise. Frisbie (1975, 1983) and the Kelleys (1975) are also strong proponents for the motivating power of turquoise, though they see the material primarily as a bond with Mesoamerica.

Known turquoise sources are located in the San Luis Valley in Colorado (Villa Grove), in northwestern Arizona (Kingman), in southern New Mexico (south of the Mogollon Rim, Jarilla Mountains), and in north-central New Mexico east of the Rio Grande (Cerrillos) (Mathien 1985; Weigand, Harbottle, and Sayre 1977:17; Jernigan 1978:214). There may be a turquoise source in the Zuni Mountains, closer to Chaco, but this source is only rumored (Mathien 1985).

The Cerrillos mines south of Santa Fe are considered to be the probable source for most of the turquoise found in Chaco, though only preliminary chemical sourcing has been performed. Sites dating ceramically to the same period as major building in Chaco, and containing pottery likely to be from the Chaco area, are present near the source (Wiseman and Darling 1986). As can be seen from table 5.1, and from Jernigan's (1978) more general work, turquoise occurs throughout the Anasazi record. Its frequency in finished form in Chaco Project sites is quite low, though evidence for working turquoise, such as tiny drills and many very small pieces of waste, is present at several sites, a number of which date to the tenth, rather than the eleventh, century (Mathien 1984:177; Thomas C. Windes, personal communication, 1989). The occurrence of turquoise in Chaco does increase greatly in eleventh-century contexts in Pueblo Bonito, where finished pieces include bird effigies, pendants, long strings of turquoise beads, and a number of striking mosaics and inlaid pieces. Large finds are rumored from Peñasco Blanco, and turquoise is frequently found in shrine locations (most of the Chaco Project's finished turquoise artifacts come from an eleventh-century shrine placed on top of a Basketmaker III village: 29SJ423).

Especially if one includes the material from Pueblo Bonito, the quantity of turquoise in Chaco is considerable. In terms of volume, however, there is little doubt that the population would have been quite capable of acquiring and transporting all the turquoise in Chaco themselves, probably with a great deal less energy expenditure than was invested in the import of ceramics or construction timbers. The likelihood that turquoise was acquired directly by members of the Chaco system is increased by the apparently low population of the Rio Grande area in the vicinity of Cerrillos at this time. Combining both transport and working of turquoise, then, it seems likely that any specialization in turquoise production was part-time (Drennan 1984a; Mathien 1984).

Shell. Shell found in Anasazi sites comes primarily from the Gulf of California, quite possibly via the Hohokam (Jernigan 1978:211–14), though examples of Hohokam shell etching are lacking in the Chaco assemblage. Although there are some shell pendants similar in shape to those from the Hohokam area (compare, for example, Haury 1976:312–16 with Judd 1954:94), distinctive Hohokam zoomorphs are also absent. Shell is present throughout the Anasazi time span and area. Burials of individuals of various ages dating to both before and after the heyday of the Chaco system have been found with abundant shell accompaniments (Mathien 1985:515–23). This indicates that Chaco participated in an established shell acquisition and movement network. Shell materials were concentrated at Pueblo Bonito, but they are present at other types of sites, and access to them does not appear to have been restricted.

Copper Bells. Copper bells found in the Southwest are almost certainly imports from Mesoamerica, though exactly where in Mesoamerica is unknown (see Judd 1954:109–15). The total number of copper bells recovered and recorded from sites within the Chaco system is probably less than 50, with most sites producing 1 or 2 and Pueblo Bonito 32 (Reyman 1971). Judd (1954:109) notes no particular pattern in provenience of those he recovered, and concludes that they were not connected with rituals. The quantity of copper bells in Chaco fits with Jernigan's (1978:224) conclusion that

> there seems to have been a trickle of metal bells into the Southwest over a period of five centuries beginning in the Sedentary Period of the Hohokam [A.D. 900–1100] . . . This slow and modest influx of Mexican copper products suggests the kind of trade that involves village-to-village exchange passing through many hands rather than long distance, organized, well-stocked trading ventures. The largest lots of bells in the Southwest come from Sedentary Hohokam sites.

Both copper and shell, then, may evidence exchange of some kind with the Hohokam, though the nature and locus of this exchange is unclear. It is well within the realm of possibility that people from either region traveled to the other on occasion (Ferguson and Hart 1985).

Macaws and Parrots. Skeletal remains of a total of 36 macaws and 3 or 6 parrots have been reported from Chaco sites (Akins 1985:327–28). Thirty-one of the macaws and all of the parrots are from Pueblo Bonito, and only one macaw is from a small site (29SJ1360). Macaw feathers are also reported from Pueblo Bonito and Chetro Ketl (Akins 1985:327–28; Judd 1954:265). Judd (1954:264) makes a convincing case that live macaws were being kept at Pueblo Bonito, and, significantly, McKenna (1984:50, 321) cites suggestive but less conclusive evidence that the macaw remains at 29SJ1360 resulted from macaw keeping there as well. The presence of these clearly Mesoamerican birds alive in Chaco sites strongly suggests that journeys of relatively short duration may have taken place over quite long distances. That a number of the individuals represented were young birds (several less than a year old) could indicate either how short in duration such journeys were, or that someone at or near Chaco was successfully breeding the birds. Their small numbers, as with those of copper bells, would have necessitated very few trips by very few people over a span of a number of years to have delivered them.

The Bonito Factor. As Reyman (e.g., 1987) is fond of pointing out, the Chaco Project analyses do not treat the materials from Pueblo Bonito in exhaustive detail. This is not due entirely to ignorance—in a large number of cases, the earlier reports do not have the same type of information that results from later excavation and analysis. Thus far this discussion would seem to prove Reyman right: Bonito has been bypassed again. In this case, however, it is because in terms of what is currently known about materials from Chaco sites, Pueblo Bonito is quite clearly in a class entirely its own. Whereas the total number of finished turquoise items from all sites represented in table 5.1 is slightly less than 1,000, Mathien (1985:783) notes that over 56,000 pieces of turquoise are known from Bonito alone. Reyman (1971:279) speculates that over half a million pieces of turquoise were present in Pueblo Bonito, and notes that Pepper recovered more than 2,000 pieces of shell and four shell trumpets in his 1897–1900 excavations. These counts are far in excess of the total of these items from all other sites of all types. Counting occurrences of feathers, at least 35 macaws and parrots were recovered from Pueblo Bonito, while all other sites in the canyon have produced only 7 instances of these species (Akins 1985:327–28). Although table 5.1 attempts to exclude debitage from turquoise working and some of the Bonito total (not shown on table 5.1) may include such detritus, there is no doubt that Bonito has produced a quantity and variety of turquoise artifacts in great disproportion even to the volume of materials excavated and the size of the site—particularly when compared to the aggregate of excavation for all great-house sites other than Pueblo Bonito.

The same may be said for shell artifacts and copper bells at Bonito. Rumored finds at Peñasco Blanco (see Akins 1986; Mathien 1985) and poorly quantified materials from Chetro Ketl (e.g., Lister and Lister 1981: 97–104), as well as further excavation of other great houses, would lessen the disparity in quantity and variety of materials, but it is likely that Pueblo Bonito will remain unique, especially if the none-too-radical step of considering Chetro Ketl, Pueblo del Arroyo, and Pueblo Bonito as a single entity were to be taken. (Considering them to be separate is inconsistent with the practice of considering complexes of similar area, such as Yellow Jacket, Aztec, Morris 39 and 41, and the Holmes Group to be single "sites.")

The list of things thus far found only or mostly at Bonito could be greatly expanded; burials, some of them very elaborate, receive the most archaeological attention (see Akins 1986). This uniqueness is extremely significant to the exchange system. In terms of archaeological perception, it is often thought that all the large sites must contain similar deposits. It should be noted that Gwinn Vivian feels strongly that "the Bonito Factor" is the result of excavation sampling error: the rooms containing great quantities of material are relatively few, and Pueblo Bonito has had the largest number of rooms excavated. Vivian's argument notwithstanding, excavations of various sizes reported in varying levels of detail at Pueblo Alto, Pueblo del Arroyo, Una Vida, and Chetro Ketl have not produced comparable finds in any category. If Bonito was in fact a structure with a very special use—a system repository of sorts (Toll 1990)—then the size of the "elite" burial population is indeed quite small, and the possibilities for personal hierarchies are considerably reduced.

Table 5.1 makes two things about unquestionable exotics quite clear: they occur both at great houses and at small sites (for definitions of Chaco site types, see Truell 1986), and they occur in extremely small quantities relative to other materials. Pueblo Bonito contains a far larger assemblage of exotics than do the other sites; still, were the numbers of more mundane items from Pepper's and Judd's excavations available, they would be enormous. Exotics would constitute a greater percentage than at Pueblo Alto, for example, but the number would still be a minuscule one.

UTILITARIAN ITEMS: INTRAREGIONAL GOODS MOVEMENT

The "exotics" thus far discussed are sufficiently rare and come from sufficiently great distances to be quite clearly not everyday items. Materials from locales within the Anasazi area and within the Chaco region, but at some distance from Chaco Canyon itself, are found in far greater numbers. The most readily identified and archaeologically most numerous of these are ceramics and lithics, but there are a number of indications that biological items were also brought to the canyon from well outside of it.

LITHICS

The vast majority of the following information is drawn directly from the extensive work on Chaco lithics done by Catherine Cameron (1982, 1984; Cameron and Sappington 1984; Cameron and Young 1986). Lithic import data are summarized in table 5.3. They are drawn from data sets at different stages of refinement, which accounts for some discrepancies in the numbers.

Obsidian. Of the materials found at Chaco, obsidian is potentially one of the most precisely traceable as to source, and Cameron and Sappington (1984) have conducted source analyses on a sizable sample. Though the accuracy of some of the techniques and equipment used by Sappington in other studies has been questioned (Hughes 1984), it is assumed here that sources have been correctly identified. Except for the Grants source on Mount Taylor in the extreme southeastern portion of the area, obsidian does not occur in the Chaco region as defined above (see Cameron and Sappington 1984:155). The principal sources of the obsidian found in Chaco are the Jemez Mountains (including the Jemez and Polvadera sources) to the east, and Red Hill to the south. Other than the Grants source, which seems very little used even at sites near Grants (e.g., Kin Nizhoni), the Jemez sources are the closest known to Chaco.

The temporal distribution of obsidian shows very nicely that the shape and content of the regional exchange system was dynamic. Red Hill obsidian is prevalent in very early contexts (pre-700). From A.D. 900 to 1000, Red Hill and Jemez obsidians occur in similar frequencies, and after 1000 the Jemez area sources are by far the most abundant (Cameron and Sappington 1984:164–65) (table 5.3). The shift from southern to eastern obsidian may have occurred during the early occupation of Pueblo Alto (ca. 1000–1040), though the sample is very small. During the eleventh century, obsidian occurs at its lowest relative frequency, although it is during this period that imports of other materials reach their highest frequency. The 25 obsidian specimens from 1050–1100 Pueblo Alto contexts are predominantly (84 percent) from the Jemez, though they are somewhat more evenly distributed among sources than during the following time segment, when obsidian becomes a considerable portion of the lithic assemblage. The absence of obsidian in areas to the west of Chaco (except at great distance in the San Francisco Mountains) seems likely to bear on this low occurrence, given the apparent intensity of interaction with the Chuska Valley area during the eleventh century.

TABLE 5.3. *Lithic materials recovered from Chaco Project sites, by time period and site type*

Material[a]	Pre-A.D. 900	A.D. 920–1020 Large Site	A.D. 920–1020 Small Site	A.D. 1020–1120 Large Site	A.D. 1020–1120 Small Site	A.D. 1120–1220 Large Site	A.D. 1120–1220 Small Site	Post-A.D. 1200
Morrison Formation	31	8	32	319	8	59	0	4
Washington Pass Chert	34	95	117	1,525	64	424	5	31
Yellow-Brown Spotted Chert	24	1	30	36	31	65	3	11
Zuni Wood	4	8	7	208	2	27	0	0
Obsidian	137	12	74	14	15	167	0	9
Local Materials	4,889	1,263	8,508	3,759	1,538	1,460	66	395
Totals	5,119	1,387	8,768	5,861	1,658	2,202	74	450

Sourced Obsidian:[b]

	Pre-A.D. 900	A.D. 920–1020	A.D. 1020–1120	A.D. 1120–1220	Post-A.D. 1200
Jemez/Polvadera	29	48	22	156	7
Grants/Red Hill	86	32	3	3	2
Arizona/Utah[c]	21	5	4	7	0

Pueblo Alto Obsidian:[d]

	A.D. 1000–1050	A.D. 1050–1100	A.D. 1100–1150
Jemez/Polvadera	2	21	256
Grants/Red Hill	7	0	5
Arizona/Utah	1	4	20
Cochetopa/San Antonio	0	0	3
Totals	10	25	284

[a]Source: Cameron 1984.   [b]Source: Cameron and Sappington 1984, showing counts of all site types combined.
[c]Includes San Francisco, Superior, Modena, and Mule Creek (NM/AZ border) obsidians.   [d]Source: Cameron 1985:tables 52–54.

The twelfth century saw a marked shift in the use of obsidian. Cameron (1982, 1984) notes that obsidian peaks in frequency in Chaco Project assemblages in the 1120 to 1220 time segment, at around 7 percent of the total chipped-stone assemblage. This is reflected to a remarkable degree at several pueblos thought to relate to the Chaco system in the 1100s. At Kin Kletso a third of the recovered "flake tools" and debitage (but apparently far less of the formal tools) were obsidian (Vivian and Mathews 1965:90–91); at Bis sa'ani, a nearby "outlier," 17 percent of the lithic material was imported, and obsidian was the most abundant material in that group (Simmons 1982:1000, 1009); and at the Escalante Ruin, a possible outlier in southwestern Colorado, obsidian makes up 10 percent of the chipped stone (Hallasi 1979:264). Although 90 percent of the obsidian is from the Jemez Mountains, eight sources in all were identified in this late period at Pueblo Alto (Cameron 1985). Thus, the primary locations for acquiring obsidian changed, and the material became more commonly used.

Washington Pass Chert. This distinctive, high-quality chert outcrops in a single location in the Chuska Mountains, approximately 80 kilometers from central Chaco Canyon. It follows a clear trend of increase in Chaco contexts, becoming by far the most abundant import in the 1000s and 1100s (table 5.3). Throughout the sequence, Washington Pass chert occurs mostly as debitage rather than formal tools, though of course the great majority of all Anasazi tools are expedient rather than formal. Washington Pass debitage is especially common in the high-frequency period. The higher frequency of Washington Pass found at large sites than at smaller ones may result in part from sample deposition dates, though a similar occurrence was found in surface materials around the nearby late eleventh-century outlier of Kin Klizhin, where it reaches a frequency of 12 percent (Cameron and Young 1986). The majority of the project sample from the 1000s comes from the Pueblo Alto Trash Mound, which contains an inordinate quantity of this material. Its high frequencies in Chaco are especially striking given the small quantities recovered at eleventh-century small sites in the Navajo Mine area, much closer to the source, where Washington Pass chert reaches a maximum of 7 percent in site assemblages (Kerley and Hogan 1983).

Yellow-Brown Spotted Chert. This material is also readily identified, and its source is thought to be south of Chaco and east of the Zuni Mountains, though the exact location and extent of its availability are presently unknown. A southern source is further suggested by the high frequencies of this material found on the surface of a number of southern outliers

(Marshall et al. 1979:262a) and at the Peach Springs Community, an outlier around 60 kilometers southwest of the central canyon (Powers, Gillespie, and Lekson 1983:90). In the sample from the central canyon, this material was found to increase slightly through time, reaching at most 3 percent of the overall assemblage for any given time segment. In contrast to other imported materials, Cameron found that this material was slightly more abundant at small-house sites than at great houses. While Washington Pass chert was the most abundant nonlocal material in canyon sites and at Kin Klizhin, yellow-brown spotted chert was the most frequent in the Kin Bineola area (Cameron and Young 1986).

Imported materials constitute 17.5 percent of the Bis sa'ani Pueblo total chipped stone, but only 1.7 percent of the lithics from smaller structural sites in its community (Simmons 1982:1001). This occurrence is of special significance because there is little doubt that the smaller sites are contemporaneous with the Bis sa'ani great house; contemporaneity of small Chaco Project sites with larger ones is, on the other hand, continually in question. Simmons (1982:1012) points out, however, that the assemblages from the several types of sites in the community are basically similar, reflecting mostly functional differences. The results of survey in the Kin Bineola and Kin Klizhin areas also show a higher percentage of nonlocal materials at the great houses, but indicate that the difference from other sites in the area is not of great magnitude (Cameron and Young 1986:24–25).

CERAMICS

Nonlocal ceramics in Chaco are recognized through two primary means: surface appearance and temper composition. The surface appearance approach relies on known decorative distributions on a large scale across the entire Anasazi area. It is useful primarily for identifying products from other regions. Temper identifications are in some cases useful for identifying ceramics from various parts of a specific region. As is apparently true of lithics, ceramics from distances equivalent to those for shell and copper bells are not present. Hohokam and Mesoamerican ceramics are for all practical purposes absent; classic Mimbres Mogollon ceramics are extremely rare, but polished smudged Mogollon ceramics occur in regular, if small, percentages.

Typological Imports. Items considered imported to Chaco based on surface characteristics fall into three main ware groups: red wares (including orange wares), polished smudged brown wares, and distinctive white wares (fig. 5.1). With the possible exception of some very early examples, all vessels in the first two categories were made at some distance from

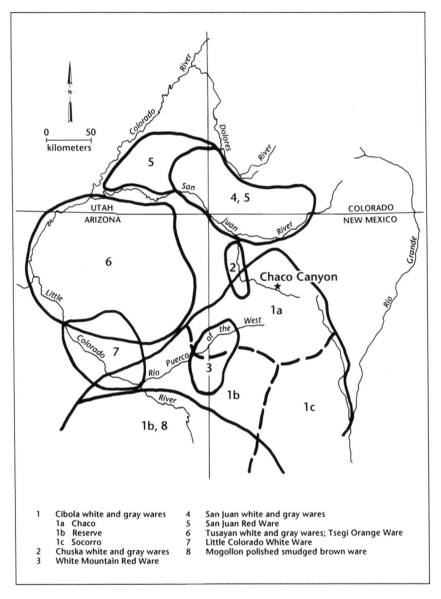

Figure 5.1. *Approximate areas of production of ceramics found in eleventh- and twelfth-century sites in central Chaco. Sharp boundaries do not, of course, exist, but areas of high frequency can be estimated. (Map is based on data compiled from several sources; see H. Toll 1985.)*

Chaco. The polished smudged brown wares are generally attributed to the Mogollon borderlands in west-central New Mexico and east-central Arizona. Red wares were made in a number of areas: for a short time early in the sequence in the Chuska Valley (Chuska); for a long period in eastern Utah and western Colorado (San Juan); through time in northeastern Arizona (Tsegi and Tusayan), though the occurrence of these wares is mostly late in Chaco; and, again later for Chaco, in west-central New Mexico and east-central Arizona (White Mountain). Imported white wares are identified by carbon paint and design (Chuska, Tusayan, Little Colorado); design, slip, and paste (Mesa Verde); or design and paste (Socorro, Cebolleta).

Temper. Most vessels in Chaco are tempered with sand, sandstone, and crushed sherd (Toll 1986). With some rare exceptions, unless it has distinctive surface treatments pottery so tempered cannot be placed as to intraregional source given the analytical techniques used by the Chaco Project. It is certain that some of the vessels that contain these indistinct tempers came from distances as great as those that could be identified, but it is conservatively assumed that they are local, though production locations for Anasazi pottery are little known (H. Toll 1985:233–45; Sullivan 1988). Among the other tempers that can be identified in central Chaco assemblages, three are of numerical importance.

Trachyte, a distinctive igneous rock that outcrops in the Chuska Mountains, has three important archaeological characteristics: its source is quite localized, it is readily identified, and it was heavily used. Combinations of distance, associated ceramic materials, artifact distribution, and technology make it certain that vessels, rather than materials, were being imported to Chaco from the Chuska Valley (Warren 1977; Toll, Windes, and McKenna 1980; Toll and McKenna 1987; Arnold 1980, 1985; Toll 1986). In the results reported here, items judged to contain more trachyte than other mixed materials were counted as imported.

The tributaries of the San Juan River that originate in the mountains of southwestern Colorado and in the San Juan Valley itself have extensive igneous cobble deposits which provided the large Anasazi populations of the area with most of their tempering material. Although this temper represents a larger, less specific area than does trachyte, it is with little doubt imported when found in Chaco Canyon. It is important to note that the majority of the area where the igneous cobbles occur is composed of sedimentary formations similar to those south of the San Juan, and that ceramics not containing crushed igneous rock are also frequent in the region, reiterating the sandstone identification problem.

Chalcedonic sandstone temper was assumed by the Chaco Project to indicate origin in the area south of Chaco, based on observations by Warren (1977). Stephen Post (personal communication, 1987), who has analyzed ceramics from a number of Anasazi sites along the Rio Puerco of the West, notes that at one site near Thoreau this temper was present in a large percentage of the gray wares at the site, even though it was infrequent at other sites farther to the east.

MOVEMENT OF CERAMICS TO CHACO THROUGH TIME

The earliest ceramics in Chaco include members from the three main nonlocal temper groups, though all are present in quantities representing less than 5 percent of the total (fig. 5.2). San Juan white wares are relatively more abundant in the pre-800 time segment than at any other time until the thirteenth century. Early brown and red wares from the Mogollon area are the primary contributors to imported ceramics in this period. The majority of white and gray wares are tempered with coarse sand or sandstone. Warren (1977) maintains that all coarse sand tempers are nonlocal in Chaco because of the composition of the local sandstone formations. Using this criterion, a much higher percentage of ceramics in the early period would be considered imported, as would gray wares of all subsequent periods. Although some of these ceramics probably were made elsewhere, the use of Warren's basic criterion—about which I have certain reservations—seems likely to result in an overestimation of import (see H. Toll 1985:141–44, 1986).

The existing sample of ceramics from the period A.D. 800 to 920 is very small, and it suggests a great increase in chalcedonic cement sandstone temper, an increase in trachyte, and an overall increase in import. The relative amounts of red wares, brown wares, and polished smudged brown wares brought to Chaco decreased, and more gray wares were imported. The much better represented segment from 920 to 1040 shows about the same level of overall import, but Chuskan pottery—primarily gray ware— became the most abundant import.

The period of maximum building in central Chaco shows Chuskan gray wares to constitute half of all utility pottery, and Chuskan imports to make up about a third of the entire ceramic assemblage. If projections from the Trash Mound at Alto are correct (H. Toll 1984, 1985), and if they can be generalized to other large sites in central Chaco, the volume of ceramic import reached almost unbelievable quantities, and again came predominantly from the Chuska area. As in the preceding period, 80 percent of red wares are from the San Juan series, but other San Juan pottery is very scarce (less than 2 percent of the respective ware categories). By 1100, San Juan

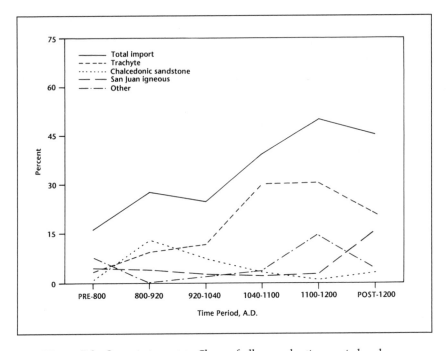

Figure 5.2. *Ceramic import to Chaco of all wares by time period and temper group. "Other" ceramics include imports identified typologically, such as red wares from the Tsegi and White Mountain series, some white wares from the San Juan and Kayenta series, and Mogollon polished smudged brown wares.*

Red Ware has been replaced as the dominant red ware by White Mountain Red Ware. Toward 1100 there appears to be an increase in ceramics from northeastern Arizona, including both red wares and black-on-white pottery (movement of Tusayan gray wares is not documented, but, given the Chuskan example, is certainly possible). This increase, suggested only by the ceramics from Pueblo Alto (Toll and McKenna 1987), comes after the cessation of deposition in the trash mound there and may even postdate the full operation of the system.

In the 1100s, import from the Chuska Valley continues at similar percentage levels, though it appears that the overall volume may be less than in the later 1000s. While Chuskan pottery is present in the latest deposits (ca. 1200) analyzed by the Chaco Project, identified San Juan white wares are more abundant than in preceding periods except for the very early ones. It appears, then, that the relatively small remnant population of the central Chaco area had more to do with the area north of the San Juan River than in earlier periods (Toll, Windes, and McKenna 1980); a large Anasazi population with large structures was present during this time. Though much of this area is clearly occupied at all periods that Chaco Canyon was, structures with Chacoan architectural traits proliferated in the late 1000s, and other major pueblos were in use well after construction in Chaco ceased.

CORRESPONDENCES BETWEEN CERAMIC AND LITHIC IMPORT

The degree to which ceramic and lithic sources correspond is relevant to understanding the operation of the system. For example, if the majority of these two technologically distinct materials come from the same part of the region, it may be that the inhabitants of that part of the region made direct use of the central canyon. If, on the other hand, a greater diversity of sources is indicated, integration of a larger area may be suggested. Lithics from an area not represented by ceramics might indicate use of that area by canyon inhabitants for other purposes (e.g., hunting in the Jemez Mountains), directed acquisition, or interaction with inhabitants of that area.

Prior to A.D. 900 the level of import of lithic materials was very low. Within that relatively small group there is a relatively high frequency of Red Hill obsidian from very far south; other materials are from the Chuska Valley, perhaps from the Four Corners, and perhaps from the Red Mesa Valley area. In this early period the ceramics also show a relatively low level of import, though a higher percentage of ceramics is imported than of lithics. The regional emphasis is southern and southwestern, seen in brown wares and smudged wares from the Mogollon area, perhaps bearing some relationship to the Red Hill obsidian. A second ceramic emphasis is the area north of the San Juan River; there appears to be no lithic material counterpart for these San Juan ceramics. Toward the end of this early time period, there is an increase in Chuska Valley materials, both ceramic and lithic, but there is a much more marked peak in ceramics thought likely to come from the Red Mesa Valley; again, there seems to be no co-occurring increase in lithic materials (yellow-brown spotted chert) from the same area.

The Chaco Project sample shows moderate increase in all imported lithic materials in the 900s, with very little difference among the various areas represented, but with more from the Chuska area than the others. The ceramics show overall levels of import similar to the limited sample from the preceding period, but pottery from the Chuska area, especially gray ware, becomes the most abundant identifiable import. During the subsequent period (ca. 1040–1100), both ceramics and lithics from the Chuska Valley reach their highest frequencies in the central canyon, both constituting 25 to 30 percent of their respective total assemblages. There is also a peak of Four Corners chert at this time, but a relative dearth of San Juan ceramics, except for San Juan Red Ware. There is little doubt that there was a substantial occupation in the Chuska Valley at this time (Wiseman 1982), but we have surprisingly little idea of the population of the well-watered San Juan, Animas, and La Plata valleys during this period. Anasazi were certainly living there, but at the scale of the twelfth and thirteenth centuries? Although Lucius (1984) has suggested that the Morrison Formation is a likely source for the clays used in the San Juan red wares, Brushy Basin (a Morrison Formation member) chert and San Juan Red Ware do not seem to constitute similar percentages of their assemblages in Chaco in any meaningful way. Given the probable area of production of San Juan Red Ware (see fig. 5.1) and its very low incidence in contemporary deposits from the Animas–La Plata–San Juan confluence, it is likely that not even the red wares represent material exchange between this area and central Chaco in the eleventh century. The intraregional western orientation seen in the ceramics and lithics is enhanced by the fact that obsidian (generally from the south or the east) reaches its lowest relative frequency during this period.

Chuskan ceramics occur in high frequencies in a sector of the region that includes the Chuska Valley and central Chaco Canyon, with an apparent corridor connecting the two areas. South of this sector trachyte temper counts are markedly lower than within it. Matching this distribution in some imprecise way are sites that have higher frequencies of yellow-brown spotted chert than of Washington Pass chert (see Marshall et al. 1979: 262a). This fact (based only on surface materials) surely says something relevant about the functioning system, even if it fails to enunciate it clearly. It indicates that ceramics and lithics probably were not regularly routed through the central canyon from the Chuskas and that direct exchange between the Chuska Valley and the Red Mesa Valley/south Chaco slope area was also relatively uncommon.

Cameron (1984:144, 147) provides figures on quantities of chipped stone consumed at Chaco Project sites. Using projections from excavation percentages for Washington Pass chert (the most abundant chipped-stone import), she estimates that a total of 130 kilograms of this material would have been imported to Pueblo Alto between 1050 and 1100. Similar projections for pottery (H. Toll 1984:131) indicate more ceramics—perhaps 49,000 vessels—were being brought to Chaco from the Chuska area during the same time. The distances for both regional and interregional movement of ceramics are at least as great as they are for lithics. Indications are, then, that considerably more effort was expended in importing ceramics than in importing lithics.

The final period for which the Chaco Project has a reasonable sample is A.D. 1100 to 1200. Chuskan materials remain the most abundant for both ceramics and lithics, but other trends seem to be largely independent. Morrison Formation materials decline, but there is an increase in ceramics, primarily white wares, from the San Juan area. Although Jemez obsidian becomes the second most abundant imported lithic material, there is apparently no corresponding ceramic import. The increase in obsidian at several sites in central Chaco is part of many substantial changes in the material acquisition system. The early 1100s were generally a time of change: the building form and volume of great houses was altered (Lekson 1986); carbon paint replaced mineral paint as the dominant ceramic decoration, and design styles shifted as well; there was probably a population increase in the long-inhabited San Juan River valley system. Yet, in Chaco, the sources of materials that relate to these changes do not seem to be in concert in the way in which Chuskan materials are in the preceding century. That is, there are very few ceramics from Anasazi Arizona, long an area producing carbon-painted wares, and there is very little Arizona obsidian. What ceramics there are from a generally eastward direction— mainly Socorro Black-on-white—are likely to be from farther south than the primary obsidian sources. There is an increase in San Juan ceramics, and design affinities continue between San Juan and Chaco ceramics, but increases in obsidian do not seem to occur in the San Juan area (based on a small and imperfect sample). White Mountain Red Ware becomes relatively common, but other ceramics and identifiable materials from well south of Chaco do not seem to appear. These events might indicate an expanded exchange system; since, however, the next development was increased population and energy investment in areas exterior to the core Chaco settlement and system (Toll, Windes, and McKenna 1980), they probably indicate a state of flux and disarray.

At least in terms of imported materials and probably architecture, an important point to be gathered from the various sequences is that the shape of the regional system varied considerably during the period 900 to 1150 (see H. Toll 1985). In essence, the overall trend in system development seems to be as follows: When the first large structures were being built in Chaco in the 900s or the late 800s, the focus of the system seems to have been southern and western. That is, rather than being at the center of a large region, Chaco Canyon during this period may have been at the northern edge of the area with which it was most closely affiliated. This association is indicated by the numbers of outliers and of materials imported to central Chaco. The configuration continued well into the 1000s, with increasingly strong bonds to the west (Chuska) and slight increases to the north. After about 1080, with an apparent florescence of sites in the north, central Chaco finally attained a geographically central position. By the late twelfth century, activity seemed to concentrate in the San Juan River area, and perhaps south of the Chaco region as materially defined, with an attenuation of population in the vicinity of Chaco Canyon.

BIOLOGICAL MATERIALS

Macaws and parrots, almost necessarily imported from Mexico, have been discussed above under exotics. The few pieces of cotton fabric found in Chaco are likely to have been imported, perhaps from the Hopi area or even from the Hohokam (Judd 1954:70–72, 1959:11). Other materials coming from distances analogous to those indicated for ceramics and lithics—and, again, in much greater quantities—include construction timbers and possibly both faunal and floral foodstuffs. Because of the unavailability in Chaco itself of construction beams for the major building episodes in the eleventh century, as many as 200,000 trees may have been brought into Chaco for construction of great houses alone (Dean and Warren 1983:202–7). Likely sources for this wood are the highlands on the southern and western flanks of the San Juan Basin: the mesas south of Crownpoint, and, once again, the Chuska Mountains. Because beams were used in construction, it seems to be generally assumed that they were acquired by residents of the central canyon directly rather than through exchange (see Lekson 1986; Dean and Warren 1983). Ceramics from the same area, however, are more generally assumed (correctly or otherwise) to have been exchanged. Either assumption should probably temper the other, or at least remind us that we do not have good control over mechanisms of movement and transfer. Once again, however, large quantities of materials and major investment in transport are indicated.

Especially to those who are impressed by the difficulties of subsistence in the Chaco region, exchanges involving food are of great interest. They are also very difficult to study. There are two lines of evidence that at least suggest food movement. First, using projected animal and human populations and faunal element distributions, Akins (1982) has suggested that much meat was imported to Chaco. Because of an increase in relative and absolute frequencies of large game in the Pueblo Alto Trash Mound, the Chuska Mountains are suggested as a likely source for much of the game. Second, great-house sites quite consistently contain a greater variety of nonlocal botanical resources such as piñon nuts and cactus seeds (M. Toll 1985). This could fit either with gatherings of people from other areas, consumption of special items at these locations, or acquisition of nonlocal resources through greater wealth. In most Chaco contexts, including

Pueblo Alto and Bis sa'ani, the corn cobs are small, but cobs recovered from Pueblo Bonito are very much larger and are similar to those from the Salmon Ruin, suggesting some import to central Chaco from wetter areas (M. Toll 1985:261–63, 268–70). Although it is possible that only the largest and best-preserved examples made it into the collections, it is also possible that corn cobs are another facet of the Bonito Factor.

Though their relevance to "exchange" is unknown, wooden artifacts and uncommon basket forms constitute another class of material culture found in central Chaco great houses in forms and abundance unusual for Anasazi sites. Elaborately painted wood, large wooden flutes, and baskets encrusted with turquoise have all been found at great houses, mostly Pueblo Bonito (Vivian, Dodgen, and Hartmann 1978; Judd 1954). A few exotic species are represented in these artifacts, but most are made from wood available within the region.

TYPES OF INTERACTION, EXCHANGE, AND ORGANIZATION

Critical to either placing Chaco into a defined type of archaeological exchange, or, more fundamentally, determining how the system functioned, is the question of how highly centralized the system was. If, for example, we could determine what quantity of goods passed through the central canyon architectural cluster, we would be in a position to speculate about central control and the degree of integration of the system. For a portion of the period during which the maximum investment in the system was being made—perhaps from 1090 to 1110—the central canyon was probably geographically central to its region. Whether or not Chaco Canyon was ever the focus for exchange of *material* goods is considerably more in doubt. Although goods came into the canyon from the region, they were imported in very different quantities and there is little evidence that they passed back out in significant quantities. There is little doubt that information flow was regular and effective, however. Given the imminence of local food shortages, the regional flow of information must have functioned as a means of staying apprised of food availability and of maintaining open channels for obtaining sustenance when necessary.

The Chuska Valley, foothills, and mountains are likely sources for nearly every basic resource imported 60 kilometers or more to central Chaco in large quantity. This could mean that there was an active exchange between populations in the Chuska area and Chaco Canyon. There are other possibilities as well: (1) that central Chaco was frequently visited by people living in the Chuska area in order to maintain contact with Anasazi from throughout the region; (2) that central Chaco was used by the regional population as a center (as above), and that the Chuska Mountains, a major natural resource area, were exploited by Anasazi from throughout the region; and (3) that the population of the two areas was the same, living and being in one area or the other as need and custom dictated.

In focusing on the Chuska connection, it is easy to lose sight of the fact that a number of other productive areas are indicated by ceramics and to a lesser extent by lithics, as well as by outlier and road locations. The Chuska material is convenient for its ease of identification and for the demonstration it gives that volumes of material were moved within the system. It is probable that areas to the south of the canyon also supplied large quantities of ceramics (and probably other goods), though they are less verifiable. Likewise, the valleys of the San Juan River and its major tributaries were inhabited throughout the occupation of central Chaco, and materials attributable to that area seem to be especially abundant very early and toward the end of the Chaco sequence. Surely it would have been advantageous to have had ties with this heavily populated and probably more reliably productive area. The perceived paucity of material from the San Juan area during the 1000s may again have resulted from different causes: perhaps goods other than San Juan Red Ware were not archaeologically durable, or perhaps the San Juan River did delineate an economic interaction boundary in the 1000s.

REDISTRIBUTION

Judge (1979) proposed that the Chaco system evolved to buffer the regular areal productive shortages likely in the San Juan Basin. Ceramic and lithic studies, however, suggested that Chaco was more an end point than a distribution point, and the thermodynamic limits on food distribution proposed by Lightfoot (1979) were part of a trend toward dismissal of redistribution (e.g., Sebastian 1983, 1988; Judge 1983). Sebastian, who identifies herself as "one of the most determined debunkers of the notion that Chaco was a redistributive system" (1988:178), argues that there are few ethnographic examples of redistribution of food, especially in times of stress, and that redistribution has been found to have been falsely associated with chiefdoms. Rather than movement and exchange of food, Sebastian (1983, 1988) suggests that areal populations maintained connections and the possibility of relocation through relationships among elites symbolized by prestige exchanges. Social differentiation in her model *is* based on subsistence goods, however, in that it projects differences among social groups in the San Juan Basin in quantity and reliability of food production resulting from the use of irrigation agriculture. The evidence is clear that large quantities of nonprestige goods were moved by the system. Although this movement may not have been redistribution in the social evolutionary sense or the main cause for the development of the system, there can be little doubt that it was an important element in the functioning of the system.

The evidence for prestige exchange is at best thin: turquoise, shell, and other exotics occur at outliers and smaller structures within the system, but not in exceptional quantities, much as they are presently lacking from most pueblos other than Pueblo Bonito in central Chaco. Also lacking are good candidates for elite individuals outside Bonito. What kind of system is it that would concentrate on exchanges of everyday items and perhaps labor investments rather than lavish items? Stark (1986:280–81) cites the Yanamamo use of "everyday items to symbolize political links." Possible implications include the de-emphasis of individual wealth and the inclusion of as wide a segment of the groups involved as possible. Use of similar yet identifiable products from elsewhere could serve to symbolize sameness and interrelationship in the face of other more centrifugal forces (see S. Plog 1980b; H. Toll 1985). The existence of stylistic similarities on spatial and temporal scales far beyond any conceivable Anasazi political system shows that such maintenance of relationships was important.

Thermodynamic studies of food transport have appeal because they seem to provide quantifiable limits to system size. The point at which engaging in "inefficient" behavior catches up with a system depends on how often the behavior occurs. Even during periods of reduced moisture, not every year is prohibitive to a successful crop. If every participating community did not engage in transport every year, the inefficiency of food transport would be distributed over a greater period and the impact reduced. Only if inefficient transports were required with great frequency or over extended distances would they become insupportable. The alacrity with which Lightfoot's (1979:27) figure of a 48-kilometer maximum distance for corn transport has been accepted is rather remarkable in view of the number of variables and unknowns that exist. In calculating foot transport costs for Mesoamerica, Drennan (1984b) concludes that a one-way distance of 275 kilometers is the probable upper limit for transporting food, a distance easily encompassing the Chaco region.

Given the relatively good climatic conditions reconstructed for the 900s (Rose, Robinson, and Dean 1982), crop shortages were probably infrequent and any inefficiency in redistributing foods probably could have been absorbed. With increasing climatic variability in the 1000s the necessity for goods movement probably increased, perhaps occasioning the dramatic increases evident in investment in the system (H. Toll 1985).

Given the relatively short duration of the peak operation of the Chaco system, inefficient transports may have been sufficiently frequent that the system became insupportable toward 1100, leading to the abandonment of large-scale transports as an adaptation. A period of favorable moisture in the early 1100s, concurrent with or following the cessation of intensive system investments, might have allowed continuation of some aspects of the system, though investment in construction and transport never again reached the level of the late 1000s. Historically, Pueblo ritual is heavily involved with food transfers, which serve to correct shortages on an intrapueblo level (Ford 1972b) and are extremely likely to have occurred prehistorically. The question of food movement for the Chaco system is one of scale and distance, both of which are shown by ceramic and dendrochronological studies to be regional and high volume for those items. Transport of thousands of beams and pots has a decided aura of inefficiency, and equal volumes or weights of foodstuffs would certainly provision a substantial population. Although this speculation does not demonstrate that food movement took place, it does have sufficient merit that such movements should not be ruled out on present evidence.

I am not in a position to argue with Sebastian about the purpose of the Chaco system, which she holds is to support the competitive drive of an emerging and consolidating elite. Nor can I debate adequately her views on the origins of political systems as they relate to Chaco. The concern here, rather, is with how the system functioned, which I persist in believing was to move large quantities of utilitarian goods or perhaps to facilitate movement of people to stored goods (E. Adams 1981:327). The longevity of the stable phase from around 900 through 1050 suggests that the majority of the population found it advantageous to support the system. The shortness of the major growth phase, perhaps from 1080 to 1110, indicates a change in perception. For such a system to persist at the level of organization likely, most of the population must believe that participation is to their advantage, and that perception is ultimately based on the maintenance of adequate subsistence.

SPECIALIZATION

The presence of specialists necessitates greater numbers of transactions and higher levels of integration. It can also provide elites with the means of controlling certain goods. Various specialties have been suggested for the Chaco system: among them are administrators and planners, builders, jewelers, and potters. Based on the quantity of production beyond local need and the quality of vessels produced, Shepard (1963) suggested that Chuskan potters may have been specialists. In an effort to identify the presence or absence of specialization more objectively, analyses of metric variability of gray wares in Chaco have been conducted (H. Toll 1985, 1986). These analyses show that there is less variability in Chuskan products than in others found in Chaco, but that the variability is not of an order that suggests quantum differences in production from other grayware makers. In fact, given the less specific nature of the groups to which the Chuskan vessels were compared, what is more striking is the consistency of all the vessels. It is likely that various settlements within the region did produce more of given items than did others, such as turquoise ornaments in Chaco and pottery in the Chuskas (see also S. Plog 1980a), and this level of specialization probably did contribute to reduced variability. Considerable question remains, however, whether or not any of these specializations was of a degree sufficient to require or imply a highly differentiated society. Group specialties occur at any level of organization, and they serve to facilitate broader areal ties and the adaptive advantages accruing thereto.

The presence of highly crafted items of wood, jet, and turquoise in a few sites raises the possibility that there were a few specialists in the production of "wealth," which could in turn indicate some attachment or support by an elite (Brumfiel and Earle 1987:5–7). Other than turquoise, however, too little is known about the sources and distribution of these products to postulate the existence of such specialists. Specialists in the production of nonwealth goods are more likely to be independent of elites and the establishment of political complexity (Brumfiel and Earle 1987). Determination of how the wealth and subsistence spheres interrelated in Chaco remains an important area of research.

EXCHANGE AND COMPLEXITY

Nonlocal items may be interpreted in a number of ways. If, for example, one feels that the Chaco system existed primarily to provide Mesoamerican states with turquoise or other commodities, then all the turquoise is readily explained as waiting in the staging area. Alternatively, if one is arguing for the presence of social differentiation, then ornaments, exotics, and unusual items become status markers. Review of the contexts and quantities of these materials, however, makes these interpretations seem tenuous. Although there are associations between burials and exotic goods at Bonito (see Akins 1986; Akins and Schelberg 1984), even there many of the large quantities of unusual items are not in clear association or even in the same room with burials. The well-known strings of beads from Chetro Ketl were sealed into niches, removing them from circulation. These "systemic removals" (following Rappaport 1968), much like intentionally destroyed items in trash mounds (H. Toll 1985) or plastered-over exquisite masonry, may represent means of binding people and areas to the system through contribution to it. Certainly there would have been individuals with greater say than others in how things were done, but it is important that the individuals themselves may have been de-emphasized.

There are, of course, a number of points that rest somewhat uneasy. From the perspective of what we know of the exchange system during the eleventh and early twelfth centuries, there seems to have been heavy east-west traffic between the Chuska Valley and Chaco. East to west, however, is contrary to what Gillespie's (1985) climatic model would predict; Gillespie shows that the San Juan Basin is located in such a way that shifts in the continental weather pattern have great impact on amounts of moisture received in the basin. The overall weather pattern is from west to east, so that the impact of shifts is seen north to south. Thus, a system that needs to account for moisture shortages seems more likely to show an emphasis on north-to-south movement than on east-to-west. Clearly, the system does bracket a wide latitudinal range, and some of the east-west emphasis that we see is an artifact of the analytical glass through which we are looking. If the premise concerning the function of the system is correct, then the Chuska traffic may be an indication that the central canyon was used as a place in which bonds with the rest of the region were maintained.

Flannery (1968) has argued that in order for exchange to occur between groups, those groups must be of similar complexity. The Chaco Anasazi and the Sedentary period Hohokam are both thought of as having developed more complex social forms than those of preceding periods and surrounding areas, yet evidence for exchange between the Phoenix Basin and the San Juan Basin in the eleventh and early twelfth centuries is remarkably slim. Except for shell and turquoise, the materials most readily associated with Hohokam and Chaco, there is little to suggest that there was any but the most indirect connection between the two groups through the western Anasazi. Does this indicate, then, that complexity in these two areas was not comparable? Or, was the complexity in these two "core areas" unremarkable given the surrounding areas? Was there more exchange than we are presently able to detect? Perhaps the Hohokam palettes, censers, and etched shells, and the Chaco inlaid jet, cylinder jars, and inlaid scrapers, which we consider special hallmarks of the respective areas, had meaning only in their original contexts and were not available for circulation. The abundance of shell at Hohokam sites and the analogous occurrence of turquoise in special contexts at Chaco, the similar level of occurrence of copper bells in both systems, and the presence of goods caching are clear indications that numerous parallel processes were operating in Anasazi and Hohokam society. The most important similarities are the likelihood that considerable labor investment was made in public structures such as ballcourts and great houses for large-scale gatherings of people, which would have provided opportunities to exchange products of subregional specializations, subsistence items, information, genes, and jokes. Certainly the timing of changes in these two systems as well as in the Mimbres is close enough that some overarching influence or connection must be contemplated.

Redman suggests that Chaco's apparently anomalous location and development were the result of social forces on a much larger scale. In North Africa, powerful centers characterized by their religious fervor developed in environmentally unlikely places because they were located in a position critical to trade between the Sub-Sahara and the Mediterranean (Boone and Redman 1982). Thus, there are intriguing parallels between these centers and Chaco, which also has an air of fervor about it, as seen in its densely packed, massive, over-engineered structures made of large beams from far away, its beautifully crafted masonry covered with coats of plaster, and its perfectly straight and much-too-wide roads. The pan-Southwestern trends and the African example redirect attention to Mesoamerica, but there are some serious deviations from Redman's parallel, such as the absence of any evidence that there is either a natural or a social resource to which Chaco could control access by virtue of its location. Although the impetus for the development of regional exchange systems can be found locally, interregional, macroregional, and supramacroregional forces were all clearly operating.

THE END OF THE SYSTEM CENTERED IN CHACO

The great reductions in goods movement, construction, and population that took place in much of the San Juan Basin in the A.D. 1100s very likely relate in some way to successive periods of drought between 1130 and 1160. Presumably, one impact of this period was considerable population relocation to more favorable areas, including the valleys of the San Juan and its northern tributaries and the Rio Grande valley. Loss of sufficient numbers of participants would of course cause exchanges to become inoperable, which could in turn cause further deterioration of the entire regional interaction system. As suggested above, the reductions in building scale, the stylistic changes apparent in ceramics and architecture, and the changes in great-house use may have resulted from years of over-investment in the system (an early form of deficit). A vestige of the system could continue in the early 1100s by virtue of a climatic reprieve, but the stage was set for rapid relocation and "truncation" of the system when moisture became scarce. Because the possibilities for exchange and the efforts made to facilitate it were important in the development of the Chaco system, the inability to sustain exchange was surely a strong catalyst for— if not a cause of—the system's curtailment. There can be little doubt that relationships and patterns that developed during the period when Chaco Canyon was a regional center persisted in the following century, but their form and content were significantly altered.

SUMMARY

The content of the Chaco exchange system observable archaeologically is dominated by very large volumes of transported subsistence and construction materials from within the Chaco region. Items that are likely to have represented wealth coming from outside the region are extremely rare relative to intraregional goods. Although the rare exotics are known mostly from Pueblo Bonito, large volumes of transported construction materials are present at all central canyon great houses, and intraregional ceramic imports are common at all site types.

Within the limitations of the fact that our knowledge of material distributions comes from a severely uneven and little-controlled sample, the concentrations and quantities of valuables suggest that some form of elite probably existed, though we have precious little evidence as to its nature or its size. The presence of valuables throughout the Anasazi sequence and in many contexts suggests that such an elite probably entailed an elaboration of existing symbols with the addition of some new privileges and duties. Mechanisms to reduce the visibility of an elite—to contemporaries and especially to archaeologists—are quite likely to have been in place. The volume and relative ubiquity of long-distance intraregional goods indicate that participation in the subsistence aspects of the system remained broad-based.

A number of interrelated factors came together at the end of the eleventh century and ended the system in its most complex form: climatic variability increased, population and goods movement may have passed thermodynamic limits, elite demands and levels increased. This short period of frenzied activity was followed by changes in the location of centers for and the organization of eastern Anasazi society, resulting in great reductions in activity in Chaco Canyon and much of the San Juan Basin in the first half of the twelfth century.

————— *Acknowledgments* —————

I am honored to have been invited to participate in this seminar, and I thank Jim Judge, Patty Crown, and the School of American Research for the opportunity to do so. In addition, Cathy Cameron has been helpful and generous with her data; Steve Lekson has been, as always, a source of good, provocative thinking; and Tom Windes, Peter McKenna, and John Stein have contributed to any good ideas that may be found herein.

Chapter 6

Sociopolitical Complexity and the Chaco System

LYNNE SEBASTIAN

FROM the time of the very earliest explorations in the Chaco drainage, the monumental quality of the ruins in Chaco Canyon has led to an assumption that the builders of these remarkable edifices must have been members of a socially and politically complex society. Subsequent discoveries, such as the excavation of a small number of rich and elaborate burials in Pueblo Bonito and a growing awareness of the far-flung and carefully engineered road network that converges on Chaco Canyon, served to reinforce that perception. Recently questions have been raised about whether or not Chaco was, in fact, a sociopolitically complex system, and I will discuss that issue below. But for the most part, the long-standing questions about the social organization of the Chaco system have been the following: How complex was it? What form did that complexity take? And what was the source or cause of that complexity?

As James Judge has pointed out in chapter 2 of this volume, explanations of the perceived complexity at Chaco have fallen into two categories: those that depend on contact with or heavy influence from the high civilizations in Mesoamerica, and those that consider Chaco to be a result of indigenous development. Although Charles Redman suggested at the seminar that we—or at least the Chaco team—had dismissed the importance of the Mesoamerican connection prematurely, it is my opinion that current evidence for Mesoamerican interaction or interference is insufficient to account in any substantial way for the developments in Chaco Canyon or the larger cultural system of which Chaco was a part. In this chapter, therefore, I will concentrate on previous indigenist explanations for the complexity of the Chaco system and offer an indigenist explanation of my own.

As explained in the Introduction to this volume, our discussions at the SAR advanced seminar were structured not only by our topics for comparisons between the two cultural systems (subsistence, settlement patterns, etc.), but by three general research issues: the origins of each cultural system, the causes of truncation of development in each system, and the means of defining and maintaining system boundaries. Here, I offer a model that attempts to account for the first two issues: the rise and eventual fall of a Chaco-centric cultural system. But before I can address rises or demises I must look at the third research issue, boundaries, and offer my particular version of what constituted the Chaco "system."

Crown and Judge (this volume) define a regional system as one marked by the exchange of goods and services. Although I think this is certainly true, I would add exchange of information as a very important third component in defining or identifying such a system. For my purposes here, I will define a cultural system very simply in terms of interconnectivity. A cultural system comprises "a set of individuals or groups that interact more frequently or intensely with one another than they do with individuals or groups that are not culturally defined as being part of the system" (Sebastian 1988:10).

· Clearly this definition is too vague to be fully operationalized archaeologically, making it impossible to draw boundaries around the cultural system. But I am not at all sure that this is a major drawback. I think that the very concept of "system boundary" may be inappropriate for prestate societies. In fact, I don't think that there is a *single* system in nonstate societies. Perhaps a better way of visualizing such societies would be as the intersection of overlapping interaction spheres. That is, the boundaries of the system would be very different depending on whether we were looking at trade and exchange, shared language, shared religious beliefs, or ties of marriage or alliance. In nonstate societies, in other words, definitions of "us" and "them" are even more situational than they are in states.

WAS CHACO A COMPLEX SYSTEM?

Much research into the degree of complexity at Chaco has been concerned with typological questions about which of a set of evolutionary categories the system most closely resembled, and I will discuss these arguments below. Other research, however, has questioned the proposition that the archaeological remains at Chaco represent a politically complex system at all. Two recent arguments against interpreting Chaco as a complex system have been presented by H. W. Toll (1985) and Gwinn Vivian (1989).

Although he has subsequently moderated his stand somewhat (see Toll, this volume), in his doctoral dissertation Toll (1985) responded to arguments that Chaco Canyon was the center of a redistributive economy controlled, administered, and manipulated by resident elites in the canyon great houses by offering a model of what might be called a nonadministered redistributive economy. In that work, Toll argued that the archaeological phenomena that we perceive as the Chaco system were the result of increasing levels of interaction—exchange, periodic aggregations, and cooperative building endeavors—intended to provide greater subsistence security for the participants in this interaction network. Noting that at least the early construction episodes at the great houses occurred during periods of low precipitation and thus of increased subsistence stress, Toll suggested that communal construction and other forms of periodic population aggregation were mechanisms for increasing cooperation and sharing during times of such stress. He argued that, in conjunction with these events, reapportionment of any available foods took place through exchange or other activities.

This model of cooperation, interaction, and sharing as a response to periods of serious subsistence stress is questionable on ethnographic grounds. Ethnographic evidence indicates that in times of environmental crisis and subsistence failure, sharing of food decreases or ceases altogether, even among fairly close kin (compare Firth 1936 with Firth 1959, for example, or see Colson 1979). Toll's reasons for offering this model have to do with his interpretation of the political structure of the modern Pueblos and with what he sees as a lack of evidence for "elites" in the Chaco archaeological record.

In discussing the modern Pueblo Indians, Toll asserts that "historic Pueblo organization places an added burden on arguments for elites [among prehistoric Pueblos]. That is, if powerful individuals are precluded in the analogue, then especially strong arguments are required for their demonstration" (Toll 1985:503). I would argue, however, that powerful individuals are by no means precluded in the analogue. Recent reassessments of political structure among the Hopi (Whiteley 1988) and the Zuni (Upham 1982) indicate that these supposedly classic egalitarian societies have, at least since European contact, exhibited marked social, economic, and political stratification based on control of land and access to ritual knowledge.

Toll is by no means the only archaeologist to argue for interpreting Chaco (or for that matter Hohokam, as Wilcox notes in this volume) as an egalitarian system based on analogy with ethnographically recorded Indian groups. Yet even if it were true that the modern Pueblos had a thoroughly egalitarian political structure rather than the class and power distinctions that they in fact exhibit, this would not be a compelling reason for denying the presence of powerful individuals in the prehistoric past. The Chacoan florescence took place more than 900 years ago. Hundreds, perhaps thousands of cultural institutions must have been lost, gained, and lost again through all those years and the many disruptive influences to which Pueblo culture has been subjected.

Vivian's recently published (1989) argument against considering Chaco to have been a complex society supports Clyde Kluckhohn's interpretation of Chaco Canyon's great-house/small-site settlement pattern as representing side-by-side occupation by two groups with different cultural traditions. This view was first espoused by Gordon Vivian more than 20 years ago (Vivian and Mathews 1965). Although Gwinn Vivian subsequently offered explanations of the great house/small site dichotomy based on differences in agricultural technology and social organization (Vivian 1970a, 1970b), he has returned to the concept of a canyon population comprising groups with two distinct cultural traditions.

I would be more comfortable with Kluckhohn's argument if the ethnographic cases that he used as examples of side-by-side residence of disparate cultural groups in the modern world—the Tewa on First Mesa at Hopi and the Laguna at Isleta—were not cases that would be virtually invisible archaeologically. And I would be more persuaded by Vivian's argument if it were supported by appropriate patterning of material culture items and technological variables. If it is true that two groups with distinct cultural traditions inhabited Chaco Canyon, one would expect that the items they made and used would exhibit stylistic, technological, and source differences (for traded items) reflecting those distinct cultural traditions and continuing ties to the regions of origin. Additionally, one would expect most of these differences to decrease with time as interaction and intermarriage led to acculturation. I have not examined the data with this question in mind, but it is my impression that material culture differences between great houses and small sites do not exhibit this patterning.

The other difficulty that I have with Vivian's model concerns the outliers. The widespread pattern, within the San Juan Basin and well beyond, of a great house surrounded by a community of small sites and the apparent evolution of this settlement pattern out of an existing community of sites seems to me to be best explained as resulting from an organic, systemic connection between the occupants of sites of these two types.

Both Toll's and Vivian's models of an egalitarian form of organization are unified, internally consistent, and provide explanations for much of what we perceive as the Chacoan cultural system. Although I think that a model based on differential political and economic power provides as good a fit with the archaeological data and a better fit with what we know about the behavior of ethnographically recorded societies, each of these models has interesting organizational implications and would be well worth additional study and testing.

HOW COMPLEX WAS IT?

One problem with arguments concerning sociopolitical complexity in prehistoric societies is that most of them tend to be based on very ethnocentric views about what "powerful individuals" ought to look like, ethnographically and archaeologically. In a cross-cultural study of political organization in prestate sedentary societies in the New World, Feinman and Neitzel (1984) examined the numbers and kinds of functions performed by leaders in the societies in their sample, the nature and extent of evidence for social differentiation, and the correlations among these variables. Among other things, they monitored the occurrence of those items generally considered by anthropologists to be markers of high status. They found only a moderate correlation between the number of leadership tasks that an individual performed and the number of status markers accorded to him (Feinman and Neitzel 1984:60), and equally important for the archaeological case, many of the status markers that they were examining would be invisible in the archaeological record.

Most of the personal power in the modern Pueblo world expresses itself not as possession of goods, but as possession of ritual knowledge. As Upham (1982:199) has pointed out,

> major errors in interpreting the Western Pueblo political structure have resulted (a) from underestimating the significance of ritual knowledge in the attainment of political leadership and (b) from failing to recognize the political significance of ceremonial position in these societies. The possession of ritual and ceremonial knowledge is the most powerful instrument in the acquisition of preeminent position in modern Western Pueblo society. These positions are maintained by restricting access to such knowledge.

The ritual-based nature of political power in these societies should not be interpreted as indicating that this power is not very much "real" in the material, this-worldly sense. As Dozier (1970:154) pointed out in his study of political activity among the Keresans, "despotic rule by the religious-political hierarchy did take place in virtually all the pueblos and across the years some Indians lost houses, property and land, and were evicted from their pueblos."

The other problem with many attempts to address the issue of sociopolitical complexity in prehistoric societies is the use of a typological approach. Was it a chiefdom? Was it a ranked or a stratified society? There are any number of good critiques of typological approaches to the study of human social and political organization. Flannery (1972), for example, objects to typological approaches because they tend to emphasize so-called prime movers as explanations for cultural change and because these prime movers virtually always relate to exchanges of matter and energy and ignore the third requisite of cultural systems: the transfer and processing of information.

Flannery views increasing cultural complexity as consisting of increases in two processes that permit progressively larger quantities of information to be collected, processed, and acted upon. These processes are *segmentation*, "the amount of internal differentiation and specialization of subsystems," and *centralization*, "the degree of linkage between the various subsystems and the highest-order controls in society" (Flannery 1972: 409). Flannery considers the commonly suggested prime movers of sociopolitical change to be simply triggers setting in motion mechanisms such as increasing segmentation and centralization. He argues that rather than trying to classify cultural systems into static types, we should attempt to identify the mechanisms regulating all cultural systems and the mechanisms through which the complexity of systems increases.

One recent critique of the use of typological approaches in general and of typological approaches to the explanation of cultural change in the American Southwest in particular has been offered by Lightfoot (1984). Lightfoot objects to typological approaches because the political types are defined as mutually exclusive so that there is no way to study processual regularities of sociopolitical change or to account for transitions from one type to another (Lightfoot 1984:2–3). He also objects to what he calls the undemonstrated and probably false assumption "that economic, demographic, social, and political traits change simultaneously with the shift from one evolutionary type to another" (Lightfoot 1984:3).

Another problem with typological approaches is that they require formulation of extremely high-level inferences because identification of a specific type demands the ability to recognize a whole constellation of cultural traits—some of them quite abstract. In practice, typological studies frequently become bogged down in questions of evidence, inference, and interpretation and lose track of the larger questions of system organization and cultural change that they originally set out to answer.

Given that the correlation between obvious status markers and politically powerful individuals is not particularly exact and that power bases can consist of something so nonmaterial as control of ritual knowledge, how are we to identify the presence of sociopolitical complexity in the archaeological record? Lightfoot's solution to this problem is to focus on the dynamics of the development of decision-making organizations and leader-follower relationships. He maintains that the critical questions in any study of sociopolitical organization are "What conditions stimulate the initial development of leadership positions and the subsequent expansion of the decision-making organization? [And] what processes underlie the individual achievement of such positions?" (Lightfoot 1984:22).

Although I disagree with Lightfoot about why complex systems arise and to some extent about how they arise, I feel that his rejection of a typological approach in favor of an emphasis on the process of leadership development is appropriate and that his focus on the roles of leaders and followers is a productive way to address questions of cultural complexity and sociopolitical evolution. We can examine sociopolitical change in prehistoric societies, I would argue, by looking not for evidence of leaders, but for evidence of *leadership*—evidence of a level of planning and organization and a potential for quick decision making that is beyond the capacity of acephalous societies.

EVIDENCE OF INSTITUTIONALIZED LEADERSHIP

A number of different classes of evidence could be offered to support an interpretation of sociopolitical complexity. I have selected five of the most commonly offered proxy measures for examination here: settlement pattern and site hierarchy, differential distribution of material culture items, architectural and construction data, burial data, and the presence of water control systems.

SETTLEMENT PATTERNS

Observations about settlement pattern and site hierarchy are among the most commonly offered evidence for sociopolitical complexity. Morphological differentiation and spatial patterning of archaeological remains, it is argued, reflect the social arrangements that were in place when those remains entered the archaeological record. In Chaco Canyon itself, the major site types are numerous small-house mounds (the Hosta Butte sites), the very large great-house or Bonito structures, and the smaller, more compact but formally laid out McElmo sites. Although there are some time-span differences among the three site types, we now know that the temporal sequence of Hosta Butte, Bonito, McElmo suggested by Vivian and Mathews (1965) is incorrect and that during the final years of the major occupation of Chaco Canyon all three site types were in use simultaneously. Thus, there were at least three morphologically distinct categories of major structures in use simultaneously at Chaco.

Beyond the canyon itself, throughout the San Juan Basin and beyond, there are "outlier communities" comprising at least two and often three morphologically distinct structure types: the great house, often a great kiva, and the small-house mounds. Some of these outliers developed in the midst of preexisting communities; others give evidence of having been established as full-blown outliers rather than having evolved in place. Thus the ancestral and scion outliers (Doyel, Breternitz, and Marshall 1984) appear to represent two different political processes or routes to architectural (and presumably organizational) specialization.

If we consider both Chaco Canyon and the outlier communities, we encounter what is probably the most persuasive settlement-pattern-based argument for organizational complexity in the Chaco system. The geographical extent of the Chaco system and the clear evidence for interconnectivity in the form of roads (Obenauf 1980; Kincaid 1983; Nials, Stein, and Roney 1987), potential line-of-sight signaling networks (Windes 1978), and architectural uniformities imply a level of integration beyond what can be achieved by simple individual-to-individual and family-to-family interaction.

MATERIAL CULTURE

A second class of archaeological evidence frequently used to infer the presence of social complexity is differential distribution of material culture items, especially exotic, imported, and high-energy-input items. As discussed above, the assumption that "those who have the power will have the goodies" is not always true in the modern cases that we can observe; the reverse argument is more often true, however. Where there is differential access to material goods, there is generally differential power as well.

There are some differences in ceramic assemblages between great houses and small sites in Chaco Canyon (H. Toll 1985:174) and in some of the outlier communities (Mills 1986:82–83; Sebastian and Altschul 1986: tables 7, 9). These differences occur both in proportions of imports and in vessel form distributions and relative frequency. None of the trends is overwhelming, however, and with the exception of the virtual absence of cylinder jars from all sites except great houses, these differences could conceivably be a result of fine-grained temporal differences. Lithic material type distributions are virtually the same in great houses and small sites, both in the canyon and beyond (Cameron 1984; Cameron and Young 1986).

In contrast to these utilitarian items, possible differentiation *has* been identified for subsistence items, for turquoise and other ornaments, and for long-distance imports. Vivian (1970b) and Akins (1985) found greater diversity of faunal species in great-house assemblages than in small-site assemblages, and M. Toll (1985) reports apparent differences in strains of maize between the two site classes. Mathien (1984) found a much higher incidence of turquoise, shell, and other ornaments in the great-house assemblages than in the small sites, and most of the macaws, copper bells, and other clearly long-distance imports were found in the great-house sites as well.

Clearly, problems of differential sample size, depositional context, and differential excavation and recording techniques make it difficult to offer any well-supported interpretations of these patterns. But the patterns have been tentatively identified, and further examination of these proposed differences in distribution certainly would be warranted.

LABOR INVESTMENT

Arguments about the degree and nature of cultural complexity within the Chaco system often cite the massive effort involved in constructing the great houses and great kivas. Recently the road network has been added to the list as further evidence of the ability to mobilize and direct massive quantities of labor. Now it appears that other kinds of constructions, such as water control systems and mounds and earthworks, should also be added to calculations of the public works capabilities of the Chaco system (Fowler, Stein, and Anyon 1987).

Steve Lekson (1986) has gone a long way toward demystifying the "labor investment" argument by providing rough but concrete figures for the person-months involved in particular construction episodes. He points out that "a 30-person crew could cut and transport beams for about 1–1.2 months a year over a 6-year period, and quarry and construct for 3.6 . . . months a year over a 4-year period, and build the single largest construction event in the Chacoan record" (1986:262).

When we consider, however, that some evidence indicates that individual construction episodes took place rapidly rather than over a period of years, that multiple construction episodes were likely to be going on at any one time, and that roads, mounds, water control features, small habitation sites, field houses, and a myriad of other facilities were being built and maintained at the same time, the apparent magnitude of effort comes into a different perspective. If we further consider that all of this was being done by people who were maintaining a widespread and highly active trade network, participating in a rich and potentially time-consuming ceremonial life, and, incidentally, making a living as agriculturalists and part-time hunter-gatherers in a very harsh and uncertain environment, it is difficult not to be impressed. And it is impossible to imagine that this level and diversity of effort could have been scheduled and carried out without benefit of some degree of institutionalized leadership.

BURIAL DATA

Perhaps the classic category of evidence cited by archaeologists to support arguments of sociopolitical differentiation is difference in mortuary treatment. Akins (1986) has compiled all available data on burials from canyon sites ($n = 135$; dates range from A.D. 500–900 through post–A.D. 1175). She found that from the very earliest period of great pueblo construction (A.D. 900) there are marked differences in mortuary practice between great houses and small sites. Small-site burials were variable in positioning and orientation but otherwise exhibit limited differentiation, most of which appears to be related to age differences. Great-house burials, on the other hand, exhibit differentiation in quantity of grave goods but are quite standardized in positioning. As a group, great-house burials contain markedly more accompanying artifacts (especially ceramics and ornaments) than small-site burials.

Akins also found (1986:135–36) observable stature differences between both males and females in large-site and small-site burials, with Pueblo Bonito males and females being an average of 4.6 centimeters taller than their small-site counterparts. Palkovich (1984:111), however, found similar incidences of nutrition-related pathologies in the great-house and small-site burial populations.

Again, sample size is small, but a pattern of differentiation in mortuary behavior and possibly even a population difference between large sites and small sites does seem to be indicated. And such a pattern, if it does indeed exist, would be yet another indicator of some degree of organizational complexity within the Chaco system.

WATER CONTROL

The last class of archaeological evidence for sociopolitical complexity to be considered here comprises the fairly impressive water control facilities that were built in Chaco Canyon (Vivian 1970a) and at some of the outlier communities (Sebastian and Altschul 1986). The implications of these features for the question of organizational complexity are far from clear, however. These are not irrigation facilities in the traditional sense, because they are designed to capture and distribute runoff rather than to extract water from some relatively permanent source and deliver it to agricultural fields. In one sense, this may indicate less organizational complexity, since disputes over water allocation are less likely and since scheduling of maintenance activities would be automatically set by the timing of runoff events.

On the other hand, operation of a system to capture and distribute runoff would seem to require greater speed and centralization of decision making than is possible with simple political organizations. When the flood is roaring toward the fields, there is no time to establish a consensus. Someone must already be empowered to mobilize and direct the labor needed to ensure that the water is used quickly and efficiently.

CONCLUSION

I would suggest that the evidence presented above indicates quite clearly that it is unlikely that the Chacoan archaeological record was produced by people with a decentralized, situational leadership structure. The level of planning and organization apparent in these remains indicates a degree of centralization and political specialization beyond the capacity of societies whose decision making is carried out within the framework of kinship and consensus. And the evidence for differentiation in site types, mortuary treatment, and distribution of material culture, though tentative, offers some hints to where we might look for leaders and followers in this system.

PREVIOUS EXPLANATIONS FOR THE COMPLEXITY OF THE CHACO SYSTEM

Explanations for the cultural complexity of the Chaco system developed in the 1960s and 1970s (e.g., Altschul 1978; Grebinger 1973; Vivian 1970a, 1970b) generally were grounded in cultural evolution and cultural ecology. Because these studies were published before the results of the Chaco Center investigations were widely known in the profession, most of them suffered from the lack of published modern data about Chaco. These works were valuable, however, because they represented the first serious, systematic, anthropologically based attempts to account for the remarkable archaeological remains of Chaco Canyon and the San Juan Basin.

Explanations of Chacoan complexity developed in the late 1970s and early 1980s were also grounded in cultural evolution and cultural ecology. Although highly variable in their particulars, they all share a single underlying premise based on two undeniable observations: (1) that the San Juan Basin is a harsh and uncertain environment, and (2) that the Chacoans appear to have developed some degree of sociopolitical complexity. The assumption based on these observations is that the Chacoans became complex in order to deal with the difficulties of the environment—that the cultural complexity was an adaptation to the problems of supporting an agricultural population in this arid region.

I find this premise unsatisfying for several reasons. For one thing, the most successful adaptation to a harsh and uncertain environment is one that depends on mobility, broad-spectrum resource use, depth of possible backup strategies, and flexibility in demographics and organization. Complexity decreases your options, dependence on agriculture narrows your resource base, population increase and increasing investment in structure and facilities decrease the potential for mobility.

This gives rise to the obvious question: What, exactly, does complexity do to increase the security of the cultural system that is sufficient compensation for the costs? It is, after all, difficult to imagine how such energetically expensive activities as carrying hundreds of thousands of trees from the Chuska Mountains to Chaco Canyon could have been an appropriate response to subsistence stress. The two basic answers offered to the question, What did complexity do for them?, come down either to increased cooperation and sharing in times of need (which I have argued against above) or to pooling and redistribution of subsistence resources to average out productive shortfalls.

The redistribution argument, especially as it was articulated in Judge (1979) and Judge and others (1981), was the first comprehensive attempt to account for the rise, operation, and fall of the Chaco system based on modern data. The main features of this model can be outlined as follows: The earliest great-house sites in Chaco Canyon are located at the mouths of the major side drainages, it was suggested, because they served as central places where foodstuffs grown in the drainages that these sites controlled were pooled and redistributed. Locations of the outlier sites were purposefully chosen so that these sites could control some desired resource: agricultural land, for example, or timber.

Under this model, the great houses with their multitudes of featureless rooms were explained as storehouses where resources were stockpiled for future redistribution. The road network was explained as a mechanism to facilitate movement of goods; the roads connect areas rich in different resources with Chaco Canyon and do not interconnect in the hinterlands, it was argued, because the canyon residents were administering an exchange network with themselves as the central node.

The formalization and elaboration of the ritual system, as expressed in the construction of the great kivas, was a means of sanctioning the redistribution system, and the great kivas themselves, with their frequently associated banks of small rooms, were loci at which redistributive events took place. And the collapse of the Chaco system, it was argued, was a result of a period of extended drought that depleted the stored resources throughout the system and left the central canyon unable to meet the demands of the system constituents.

Although I disagree strongly with redistribution-based models, I find the explanation outlined above to be an admirable example of how archaeological models serve to advance our understanding of the past. The redistribution model was internally consistent and relatively comprehensive, and it accounted for much of the then-known variability in the Chaco data. This model provided us with a unified argument about how the Chaco system might have operated, and it was falsifiable, so that further work could lead to model refinement or replacement and to an improved understanding of Chaco as a system.

As more information about the Chaco system became available, the fit between the evidence and the redistribution-based model became less satisfying. The lack of evidence for redistribution in ceramics (H. Toll 1984; Toll et al. 1980) and lithic materials (Cameron 1984) was troublesome. The evidence from Pueblo Alto indicated that periodic large "consumption events" (H. Toll 1984) seemed more likely than periodic redistributive events. Owing largely to these empirical findings, more recent interpretations of Chaco (e.g., Judge 1983; Judge and Schelberg 1984; H. Toll 1985) have tended to back away from strict dependence on the explanatory power of economic redistribution.

Even though redistribution is no longer discussed as a central mechanism in more recent models of Chaco, it is often an underlying assumption and occasionally is specifically invoked. Judge (1983), for example, eschews redistribution as an explanation for the functionings of the mature Chacoan system, but he falls back on the redistribution argument to account for the beginnings of the unique developments in Chaco Canyon. He suggests that the early town sites "functioned primarily as storage sites to accommodate resource pooling and redistribution within the drainage systems that they 'controlled'" (Judge 1983:36). Likewise, the early outliers are described as having developed in situ "from a BM-III/P-I base in a manner analogous to [communities] in the Canyon, for the same reasons, and to perform the same function (resource pooling and redistribution)" (Judge 1983:36).

In the same vein, Schelberg (1982:267) suggests that the function of increased complexity in the Chaco system was to "expand the productive base and increase the volume and variety of energy inputs such that the system [could] more effectively cope with stress." One means by which the productive base was increased, he argues, was through areal expansion of the system to encompass more environmental variability. The suggestion that security could be increased through expansion of the system to encompass a wider area implies moving material though the expanded system, and in fact, Schelberg indicates that short-term buffering strategies made available through increased complexity "are designed to move energy, materials, and manpower to critical sectors of the economy during times of need" (1982:266).

The problem with explanations for the complexity of the Chaco system based wholly or in part on the concept of a redistributive economy are numerous. Archaeologists who have considered the question of redistribution in chiefdoms (e.g., Peebles and Kus 1977; Earle 1977, 1978) have found (1) that redistribution is by no means the only (or even the major) form of exchange in these societies; (2) that where redistribution does occur it most often involves status goods and elite individuals and seldom is a major means of provisioning the population; (3) that redistribution normally arises *after* the complex political system is functioning, so that it is in no way causal to this increased complexity; and (4) that redistribution does not serve to integrate environmentally diverse areas, at least in the Polynesian cases studied.

In addition to these general problems with the notion of redistributive economies, there are specific problems with the proposed version of the Chaco system in particular as a redistributive network. The classic argument for the evolution of redistributive economies (Service 1962) suggests that sedentary populations in a diverse environment must specialize in the production of specific resources, and that the organizational requirements of getting the goods from an area where they are abundant to areas where they are needed give rise to an administrative hierarchy. In the Chaco case, the argument is that it is not environmental diversity that is being evened out through redistribution but variable rainfall and thus productivity. But the posited end result is the same: members of a group pool their resources, often placing them under the control of one individual, and then receive the redivided resources or some portion of them back again.

In the case of Chaco, the suggestion that redistribution functioned to reduce the risks of crop failure depends on the assumption that every farmer suffered from an equal probability of failure and so would be willing to pool his resources as insurance against the day when his turn to fail came. In fact, this assumption of equal probability of failure is true only if everyone is practicing dry farming and thus is dependent on the increment of rain that actually falls on his fields. As soon as floodwater farming and various forms of agriculture dependent on water control appear, we gain a new source of patterned variability overlaid on the random distribution of patchy rainfall. This new variability is patterned because under a random distribution of rainfall, those who are farming with runoff from a large catchment area will always have a higher probability of receiving at least some water than do those who are farming with runoff from a small catchment area, and those who are dry farming and thus are dependent on direct gain from rain falling on their fields will always have a lower probability of receiving the needed moisture than will farmers using un-earned water (i.e., water other than direct gain from rainfall) from drainages of whatever size (Vivian 1974). Thus, redistribution in the San Juan Basin would not have been insurance, a sharing of resources among equals, but rather a sort of prehistoric welfare state in which one segment of the population subsidized another segment—a possibility in small communities with close kinship ties, but not a possibility in a system even a fraction the size of Chaco.

An additional problem with the characterization of Chaco Canyon as the central node in a redistributive network is that the energy costs of transporting food on foot throughout the Chaco system would have been very high. Conflicting data exist on the subject of foot transport and energy costs (e.g., Lightfoot 1979 and Drennan 1984b). Low-bulk/high-calorie food items such as piñon nuts or dried meat can be economically transported over long distances, but I would argue that routine transport of high-bulk/low-calorie staples such as corn would reach a point of diminishing returns over distances much shorter than the apparent extent of the Chaco system. In an emergency, large loads of food could certainly have been transported long distances regardless of the cost, but such long-distance transport is unlikely to have been a routine practice.

Clearly, large quantities of material were routinely moved about within the area encompassed by the Chaco system. Some of the transported items were very large, and some of the distances were great. Certainly some of the transported material was food, and exchange or even redistribution of food within localized exchange networks very likely occurred. But even if redistribution of basic subsistence resources could in some way be made to account for local developments—for example, in the immediate vicinity of Chaco Canyon—an elite-administered redistributive economy simply cannot be invoked to account for the rise or functioning of the whole Chaco system.

Although he offers a redistribution-based explanation for the initial stage of great-house and outlier development, Judge (1983) quickly moves beyond redistribution to outline a functionalist explanation for the continued increase in sociopolitical complexity at Chaco. He suggests that because Chaco Canyon was resource poor compared with its neighbors, canyon residents used various sociocultural means, such as ritual elaboration and control over the trade in turquoise, to mitigate the precariousness of their agricultural adaptation.

Judge argues that originally processing and distribution of turquoise would have served as a buffer against resource deficiencies in hard times, and that eventually Chaco Canyon established itself as the dominant source of finished turquoise—an important ritual item and potentially a medium of exchange—in the San Juan Basin. Ultimately, he argues, the canyon leaders converted control over a critical ritual resource into domination of the ritual system itself. By scheduling and controlling large ritual events at the canyon great houses, he suggests, the canyon leaders were able to integrate "dispersed residences . . . into a single socioeconomic system" and to "control and regulate the distribution of both goods and services between dispersed residential communities such as the outlying components of the Chaco system" (Judge 1983:45).

I find many of Judge's suggestions about how sociopolitical complexity functioned within the Chaco system very compelling. These functional descriptions do not explain why or how this sociopolitical complexity arose, however. It is not that cultural complexity did not make life better for the people of the Chaco system. The presence of a leadership structure could have yielded many benefits: subsistence assistance in times of individual domestic failures of production, resolution of disputes, protection from aggression, opportunities to form a wide network of useful alliances, access to a wide range of imported goods. But none of these potential benefits from an in-place, functioning leadership structure can be offered as an explanation of the *origins* of that political phenomenon. Societies do not "get complex" in order to do any of these things.

AN ALTERNATIVE EXPLANATION FOR THE COMPLEXITY OF THE CHACO SYSTEM

In examining and ultimately rejecting the explanation that the complexity of the Chaco system was an adaptation to the harsh and uncertain environment of the San Juan Basin, I made an interesting observation that eventually led me to the radically different explanation of Chacoan complexity offered below. If the "social complexity as buffering mechanism" model were accurate, one would expect the greatest degree of elaboration, interaction, and centralization in the Chaco system to occur during long-term periods of low moisture/high risk, when the advantages of being part of a large, integrated network would be greatest. Conversely, during extended periods of above-average moisture, one would expect a weakening of the control or influence exerted by the central canyon, and an increase in local and regional autonomy.

In fact, although conditions in the San Juan Basin were never anything resembling Edenic, the most "phenomenal" aspects of the Chaco phenomenon occurred during a period of above-average rainfall (especially the critical summer rainfall); the apogee of cultural complexity and maximum extent of the system occurred during one of the wettest periods of the entire Anasazi era; and the collapse of the system was coincident with an abrupt shift to a period of below-average rainfall. If the complexity of the Chaco system was intended to serve as a buffering mechanism against the harsh environment of the San Juan Basin, it was a failure: it only worked when it was least needed, and it fell apart as soon as a real need arose.

In creating my own model of the sociopolitical dynamics of the Chaco system, I began with a hypothesis based on this observation that the exponential increase and abrupt decrease in energy investment in the Chaco system appeared generally to parallel a period of improvement and then rapid deterioration in the eleventh- and twelfth-century rainfall regime in the San Juan Basin. It was my expectation that the elaboration of the Chaco phenomenon would turn out to be a result of the availability of unusual amounts of "capital," in the form of surplus production, in the system. My first step was to consider how the availability of the hypothesized surplus could have led to the evolution of political differentiation and a leadership structure.

POWER AND LEADERSHIP

As noted earlier, in my attempt to understand how and why sociopolitical complexity arose in the Chaco system, I chose to avoid the methodological traps of typological approaches and to concentrate instead on the dyadic relationship of leader and follower. The complete arguments behind the nature of this relationship and the development and formalization of a leadership structure are long and complicated, and I have explored them in some detail elsewhere (Sebastian 1988:chap. 4). I will simply outline the major points here.

The leader-follower relationship is based on social power (Adams 1975; Mann 1986), which Haas (1982) has defined as the ability of one actor to get another actor to do something that he or she would not otherwise do through the promise, application, or threat of sanctions. Haas (1982:163–

64) defines the following elements of social power: the power base (some aspect of the environment that is important to the follower and controlled by the leader); the means of exerting power (the sanctions available to the leader); the scope of power (the magnitude of the response that the leader can extract from the follower); the amount of power (the probability that the follower will do as the leader asks); the extension of power (the number of followers per leader); and the costs of power (both the costs to the leader of exercising power—including applying sanctions—and the costs to the follower of doing or not doing what is asked).

Gregory Johnson (1978:100) has suggested that all would-be leaders must solve two problems: (1) ensuring that their followers acquiesce to and carry out their decisions, and (2) finding means to recruit and train successors so that organizational continuity will be maintained. I found this problem-oriented analysis to be a useful way of looking at the role of leaders, but I would qualify and add to Johnson's list.

First, I would argue that Johnson's initial suggested problem actually has two critical and very different components: The leader must both suppress segmentation (ensure that his followers do not physically pack up their goods and families and move beyond his sphere of influence) and legitimize his authority (find a means of ensuring that his followers do as they are told and do not ignore him, or worse). Second, I would emphasize that recruitment of successors is a problem that pertains to leaders in societies that have established institutionalized leadership. Third, I would argue that *the* critical problem for any would-be leader is the necessity to out-compete other would-be leaders. Competition is a central fact of leadership.

Having outlined the components of social power and established this framework of problems that would-be leaders must solve, I would like to combine these concepts with paleoclimatic information about rainfall patterns during the Chacoan period to develop an alternative model of the relationship between Chacoan sociopolitical complexity and the harsh and uncertain environment of the San Juan Basin. This alternative explanation, presented in the final section of this chapter, suggests that there is, indeed, a relationship between the difficulty of the environment and the complexity of the Chaco system, but that it is much less direct, less teleological, more systemic, and more satisfying from an anthropological perspective than the "complexity as buffering mechanism" explanations that have been offered before.

PRODUCTIVE POTENTIAL AND INVESTMENT IN STRUCTURE AT CHACO

The argument that agriculture would have been a risky business in the San Juan Basin is certainly well founded. For most of the history of human occupation in this area, low population density and high mobility were necessary to survival. Even the introduction of cultigens apparently did not decrease the importance of these backup strategies for a very long time. Ultimately, however, the Anasazi Southwest began to fill up. The option for farmers to return to the land as hunters and gatherers in times of crop failure was slowly being closed off. Survey and excavation data indicate that there was a major increase in storage space in Puebloan sites between the Basketmaker III and Pueblo I periods, and I infer from this that increased production and storage were replacing mobility as a backup strategy in times of agricultural failure. By planting and growing more food than they expected to need, farmers would have assured themselves of at least a minimal crop in most years and would have produced surplus for storage in many years.

Given a strategy of overproduction and multiyear storage, even a minor amelioration in the rainfall regime could produce a respectable surplus production. And as noted above, paleoclimatic data (Gillespie 1985; Hogan 1983; Rose 1979) indicate that just such an amelioration did occur between about A.D. 1020 and 1130. It was my initial hypothesis in carrying out the study summarized here that the Chacoans used some of this excess production to fund elaboration in the form of great houses, mounds, roads, imported ceramics, and other imported goods, and that when this climatic improvement crashed in a major drought, the elaboration became simply too expensive to support.

Before describing the means that I used to test this hypothesis, I might note that during the SAR seminar Redman commented with some surprise that Southwest archaeology appeared to have come full circle. After a period during which environmental causality was considered simplistic and passé, he observed, we seem to be returning to models in which climate and environment serve as prime movers. Although climate and environment do play a pivotal role in the model being developed here, I see that role as being one of providing an opportunity for sociopolitical development to take place. The *causes* of that sociopolitical development, however, were social roles and power dynamics that were widespread in Anasazi culture at the time.

To assess the hypothesized relationship between agricultural production potential and investment in structure and elaboration, I devised a computer simulation (Sebastian 1988:appendix) that used estimates of seasonal rainfall amounts based on tree-ring retrodiction and data on the effects of water stress during particular seasons on corn yield to model potential crop production for the years A.D. 900 to 1200. By factoring in multiyear storage and by using production beyond what was required for use and for storage as a measure of capital available to the system as a whole, I was able to model potential availability of surplus production within the Chaco system on a year-by-year basis.

When I compared these assessments of productive potential with investment in construction at great houses (which I used as a proxy measure of investment of energy in nonsubsistence pursuits in the system as a whole; Sebastian 1988:chap. 6), I found that the relationship between surplus production and investment in elaboration was more complex than I had expected and that it changed through time. In the early 900s, the first construction episodes at the three earliest great houses—Peñasco Blanco, Pueblo Bonito, and Una Vida—occurred in conjunction with three separate episodes of sharply *decreased* productive potential. Throughout much of the rest of the 900s productivity remained high, no new great houses were begun, and no identifiable additional construction was carried out at the existing houses. Then, in the late 900s and early 1000s, two more marked downturns in production were associated with initial construction at Hungo Pavi and at Chetro Ketl.

In the 1020s and 1030s this first pattern of association between productive potential and construction appears to have broken down. The only initial construction during this period occurred at Pueblo Alto, and it is not clear whether this construction was associated with the high potential of the 1020s or the productive downturn of the 1030s. Beginning by 1040, however, and continuing until 1100, a whole new pattern appears. In general this was a high-productivity era, but there were downturns, especially in the 1040s, 1080s, and 1090s. Throughout this entire period, however, there was a great crescendo of construction, across good times and bad times alike. The other very marked difference between this pattern and the first one is that all of the early construction episodes—those correlated with periods of low production—took the form of initial construction of a new great house. Eleventh-century construction consisted almost entirely of additions to these existing structures; in some cases, this was the first identifiable new construction at these sites in more than 100 years. The only new great house begun during this period was Pueblo del Arroyo.

Finally, between A.D. 1100 and the crash of the system in the 1130s or 1140s, yet a third pattern emerges. These were arguably some of the best years for agriculture in the whole time span of Anasazi occupation; production was consistently high, stores and surplus beyond stores would have been very abundant. Yet construction at great houses virtually ceased; the few additions that were made to the great houses consisted of arcs of rooms enclosing the plazas at these sites. The main construction in Chaco Canyon during this period involved a whole new building type—the McElmo structures, which were very different in scale, plan, and masonry technique from the massive great houses of the earlier period.

POLITICAL DIFFERENTIATION AND THE CHACO SYSTEM

Drawing together this information about the relationship between productive potential and investment in structure at Chaco and the notions of social power and problems of leadership presented earlier, I have developed the following possible explanation for the rise of sociopolitical complexity at Chaco. In the 700s and 800s, the shift to overproduction and storage as a backup in case of agricultural failure had created the potential for sociopolitical differentiation. There are two possible strategies for increasing production with low-level technology in an environment like the San Juan Basin: a labor-intensive strategy designed to capture and channel runoff to fields, and a land-extensive strategy that depends on multiple plantings, both temporally and spatially, to take advantage of optimum growing season and maximize the efficiency of use of the available water.

These two strategies create different population regulation problems, require different decision-making structures, and have differential effects on productive potential. Both strategies increase production, but the potential increase is higher for the labor-intensive strategy since only this strategy captures unearned water. Within a system of generalized reciprocity, this differential productivity can eventually lead to an asymmetry of power and obligation between neighboring, closely related corporate groups because one group can consistently afford to be more "generous" than the other. Such asymmetry of power and obligation would have occurred wherever groups pursuing these two separate strategies to increase production lived in close proximity to one another, but at Chaco Canyon a series of apparently unique developments arose from the context of this widespread pattern of incipient sociopolitical differentiation.

In the early 900s, a series of sharp downturns in agricultural production created opportunities for groups or individuals commanding the most productive lands to turn incipient power differences into actual positions of power, to become leaders by creating relations of obligation through generosity. One visible manifestation of these new relations was the ability to mobilize a sufficient labor force to build a large structure different in scale, formality, and construction techniques from all neighboring structures.

Suppression of segmentation may not have been a major problem for these would-be leaders because Chaco Canyon was a relatively high-productivity zone surrounded by many kilometers of low-productivity areas. Legitimation was probably achieved through generosity, possibly with an assist from the appearance that the group with consistently higher production was favored by the supernatural. The problem of succession does not appear to have been solved by these early leaders. Each great-house site experienced a burst of activity, and presumably of power, and then sank into 100 years or more of zero growth. As new periods of low productivity and thus of opportunity for developing relations of power came along, new leaders arose, apparently out-competing aging former leaders or their weaker heirs.

During the higher-productivity years of the 940s through 990, few opportunities to engender obligations through generosity arose. Traditional patron-client relations between the occupants of the great houses and some subset of the small-site residents in the canyon probably continued, but the scope of power involved in these relationships was probably low.

Between 990 and 1020 productivity became highly variable and was characterized by series of multiple low-yield years and of numerous low-yield years with only single higher-yield years in between. Two new great houses were built during these years, indicating a continuation of the pattern of would-be leaders taking advantage of productive downturns to develop a power base through generosity and mobilization of resources and labor. A new pattern of leader-follower relationships also seems to have been emerging at this time, however. The patron groups in the old great houses seem to have taken advantage of this period of variable productivity to somehow convert their continued greater productive success into permanent leadership roles relying on some power base other than generosity in times of low productivity. It may be that they promoted their continued agricultural success as evidence of special access to the supernatural realm and thus created permanent roles for themselves as mediators between the rest of the population and that realm. Whatever the source of their new, nongenerosity-based power, the residents of the great houses had become a permanent leader class.

The pattern between 1040 and 1100—nearly constant major construction, repeated additions to the old great houses rather than initiation of new great houses, constant construction through high-productivity and low-productivity periods—implies a very different leadership structure than that postulated for the tenth century. Segmentation appears to have been very effectively suppressed, given the impressive evidence of ability to mobilize labor to construct great houses, great kivas, mounds, and roads. Legitimation apparently no longer depended on generosity. The nature of construction at the great houses and the makeup of the trash mounds indicate that some types of specialized functions were being performed at the great houses, and the consistent association of great kivas with great houses implies that many of those functions were religious. The problem of succession also appears to have been solved. Most of the major construction took place as repeated additions to tenth-century and early eleventh-century great houses; all of the old houses underwent numerous building episodes.

It was the problem of competition, however, that seems to have been the preoccupation of political life in Chaco during the eleventh century. I have suggested (Sebastian 1988:chap. 6) that architecture served as a medium of competition at this time. Likewise, the evidence for periodic population aggregations at the canyon and the contemporaneous development of the roads and the outliers may indicate that the competition for followers among the canyon sites extended out into the rest of the San Juan Basin and beyond.

The archaeological record of the early 1100s in Chaco Canyon is dramatically different in many ways from that of the preceding period. Investment in construction declined drastically; activities at the great houses seem to have turned inward, with the plazas being enclosed, the trash mounds falling into disuse, and the space within the structures being more heavily used for domestic activities. Elsewhere within the Chacoan sphere of influence, the old pattern of heavy investment in construction of great houses, great kivas, and roads continued, but in the canyon emphasis shifted to the small, highly standardized McElmo structures.

Unfortunately, two virtually opposite explanations for this new pattern can be offered. Both are generally consistent with what is now known about the Chaco phenomenon, and it is impossible to choose between the two, given the currently available data. Both explanations hinge on hypotheses about potential effects on the system of marked production downturns in the 1080s and especially the 1090s. If we accept the proposition that legitimation of the eleventh-century leadership structure was based at least in part on mediation between the general population and the supernatural realm, the generally good rainfall regime of the period from 1050 to 1080 would have greatly strengthened the power base of these leaders. The question is, when the 1080s and 1090s brought repeated dry years, did the leaders lose face and lose power or were they strong enough to turn these stressful times to their advantage and consolidate their power over their followers?

If the effect of the production downturn was to weaken the religious power base of the canyon leaders, the early 1100s pattern can be seen as evidence of a retreat from systemwide involvement. The great houses turn inward and become more domestically oriented; the mounds and plazas fall into disuse because the crowds are no longer coming to the canyon for large periodic gatherings. Elsewhere in the old Chaco system, new would-be leaders are taking advantage of the power vacuum at the center to establish new, dynamic, highly competitive centers, drawing to themselves the crowds that once journeyed to Chaco Canyon.

Alternatively, when people who had experienced sufficiency and even abundance for two generations in the mid-1000s suddenly found themselves faced with critical subsistence shortages, the leaders in the canyon could, by careful management of this unfamiliar and frightening crisis, have turned followers into subjects, clients into retainers. Under this scenario, restricted access to great houses could imply increased status differences; increased domestic activity within these structures could indicate the presence of actual live-in retainers, craft specialists, and so forth. The cessation of competitive construction and sponsorship of periodic aggregations could indicate that the problem of competition had been resolved in the canyon and that the arena of competition had turned outward into the San Juan Basin and beyond. The burgeoning collection of great houses in the San Juan Valley could be viewed as a second-order center established to attract and incorporate into the larger Chaco system new follower or client populations from the Mesa Verde region. Additional excavation data from outliers, great houses, and McElmo sites will be necessary if we are to choose between these alternatives.

However we eventually come to interpret the pattern of early twelfth-century Chaco, there can be little question about what happened next. Beginning at 1130, a drought of catastrophic proportions hit the San Juan Basin. Construction at the canyon great houses ceased; hundreds of sites were abandoned or virtually abandoned, not only in the central basin but around the higher, better-watered margins as well. Eventually, after about 1180, the basin margins made a comeback, and in the 1200s there were new periods of dense population aggregation, large-scale construction, and probably intense political activity as well in these areas. But the old Chaco system as a social entity, as a particular form of political organization, was gone forever.

COMPARISONS AND CONCLUSIONS

One interesting point that was never raised, as far as I can remember, during the advanced seminar is the observation that in setting out to compare Hohokam with Chaco we definitely are in a realm of apples and oranges. Hohokam is a name applied to a very long-term, widespread, regionally variable cultural development. Chaco was an intensive, short-lived, regional variant within a much longer, more widespread cultural development commonly called Anasazi.

At least from the perspective of my topic, sociopolitical development, we would probably have been better advised to compare Chaco with Classic period Hohokam. As described by Wilcox in this volume, during the long period of Hohokam development through the Sedentary period, there is increasing evidence of supraresidential groups and intra- and inter-community integration, but little or no evidence, it seems to me, of socio-political differentiation, of leadership based not on kinship or particular circumstances but on social power.

In the early 1100s, however, there was a major reorganization in the Hohokam system—a contraction of the extent of the system, a decline in the presence of ballcourts, initial construction of platform mounds, a change in mortuary practices, and so forth, as described in the Hohokam chapters of this volume. Do these changes reflect a shift in the subsistence and/or belief systems that made sociopolitical differentiation possible? By the mid-1200s, according to Wilcox, there is fairly clear evidence of social (and presumably political) differentiation as a small proportion of the population took up residence on the platform mounds. Does this indicate a shift to institutionalized leadership?

I would like to see an analysis of the Hohokam data focusing on social power and leader-follower relations. How would events and conditions of the early 1100s and mid-1200s have contributed to the solution of the central problems of leadership—supression of segmentation, legitimation of authority, orderly succession, and competition? For example, does the apparent shift in community integrative structures from ballcourts to platform mounds reflect a shift in the ideological system that made it easier for an individual to acquire or legitimize social power over his neighbor? Wilcox and Gregory (this volume) note that activities on platform mounds were apparently hidden from public view behind palisades. Could this imply differential access to ritual and ceremonial knowledge, one source of social power?

As another example, Wilcox (this volume) notes that after A.D. 1200 the riverine villages were much more dependent on irrigation agriculture than ever before. Did this effective suppression of segmentation permit politically powerful corporate groups to increase and legitimize their authority? Does construction of habitations on platform mounds and of specialized tower structures at this time reflect the rise of institutionalized leadership and solution of the succession problem?

This School of American Research advanced seminar offered most of the participants a remarkable opportunity to learn a great deal about a cultural system other than the one he or she knew best (the single exception and cross-over scholar being Dave Doyel). Each of us saw things to envy and things to sympathize with in the control that the other team has over their data. I envy the Hohokam scholars their far greater understanding of intrasite patterning and demographics, for example, but sympathize with their lack of chronological control. No two of us who work with the Chaco data seem to be able to reach a consensus about what various patterns mean, but we are in relative agreement about when these uninterpretable things happened.

We heard things about the other system that startled us. Who could stand in the Phoenix Basin today, for example, and suspect that one possible explanation for the collapse of the Hohokam system is that they had too *much* water (that is, catastrophic floods damaged the irrigation system beyond repair)? And we encountered some interesting similarities between the two cultural systems: the early presence of specialized community integrative structures in both systems, for instance, or the strong evidence for major reorganization in both systems in the early 1100s.

From a sociopolitical perspective, perhaps the most interesting similarity between the two systems is this: The Chaco and Hohokam people were adapted to very different environments; their technologies, subsistence practices, and ideological systems were very different. Yet there is evidence to indicate that through time both systems shifted from a pattern of communitywide integrative mechanisms to one of integration based on institutionalized leadership. A comparative study of the two systems focusing on social power and solutions to the universal problems of political leaders could be very useful in indentifying factors that are endemic to the process of sociopolitical evolution and independent of the particulars of human adaptations to specific environments.

Chapter 7

The Hohokam:
Current Views of Prehistory
and the Regional System

PATRICIA L. CROWN

THE advanced seminar "Cultural Complexity in the Arid Southwest: The Hohokam and Chacoan Regional Systems" explored the origins, maintenance, and truncation of these regional systems. This chapter puts in perspective the papers written for the seminar by Hohokam specialists, providing an overview of Hohokam research over the last century and outlining the status of the Hohokam chronology debate. It also furnishes a brief review of Hohokam culture history and a working definition of the Hohokam regional system. The discussion is confined to the Salt-Gila, or Phoenix, Basin, since the research and prehistory of other portions of the "Hohokam" domain (for instance, the Tucson Basin) diverge in significant ways from that presented here. The Salt-Gila Basin core of Hohokam culture and the surrounding peripheral areas are illustrated in figure 7.1.

HISTORY OF HOHOKAM RESEARCH

The first professional archaeological excavation in the American Southwest was conducted in the Hohokam area. In 1887–88, Frank Hamilton Cushing and Frederick Webb Hodge directed excavations at Los Muertos, Los Hornos, Las Acequias, and Los Guanacos for the Hemenway Expedition. Described by Sylvester Baxter (1888) in a series of articles in the *Boston Globe*, Cushing's work brought the Hohokam area to the attention of the Eastern establishment. Unfortunately, Cushing (1890) failed to complete the publication of the results of these excavations.

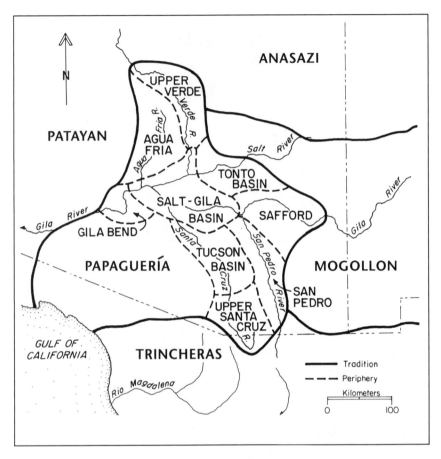

Figure 7.1. *The Hohokam area, including the Salt-Gila or Phoenix Basin core and surrounding peripheries.*

Work at the Casa Grande Site soon followed, conducted by Mindeleff (1896, 1897), Fewkes (1892, 1908, 1912), Pinkley (1935), Gladwin (1928), and Hastings (1934). A number of individuals, including Patrick (1903), Cummings (1926), Turney (1929), and Midvale (1965, 1968), surveyed prehistoric canal systems along the Salt and Gila rivers. Soon after the success of the Lindberg aerial photography of Chaco Canyon, Judd (1930, 1931) arranged for an aerial survey of Hohokam canals. The work of these researchers constitutes the basis for most recent reconstructions of the canal systems. Schmidt's (1928) excavations at Pueblo Grande and La Ciudad helped in formulating the first chronology for the Salt River valley.

The staff of a private research foundation known as Gila Pueblo contributed in large measure to the then-existing knowledge of the Hoho-kam. Their survey for red-on-buff pottery sites throughout the greater Southwest led to the definition of the Hohokam culture (Gladwin and Gladwin 1933), and their 1934–35 excavations at Snaketown, a large pre-Classic site located north of the Gila River on the Pima Reservation (Gladwin et al. 1937), laid the foundation for all subsequent work in the Hohokam area. The resulting publications outline a culture history and sequence that is largely in use today.

Exploration of Hohokam sites continued through the 1930s, funded in part by New Deal programs (Schroeder 1940; Halseth 1936; Hayden 1945, 1957). The Van Bergen–Los Angeles Museum Expedition worked at the Grewe Site near Casa Grande in 1930–31 (Hayden 1931; Woodward 1931). In 1945, Emil Haury's dissertation was published. A summary and interpretation of the work of the Hemenway Expedition at Los Muertos, it remains a major source for studies of the Classic period Hohokam (Haury 1945).

Over the next two decades, most publications documented projects in areas surrounding the Salt-Gila Basin, rather than in it, most notably the excavations of Ventana Cave (Haury 1950), University Indian Ruin (Hayden 1957), and Painted Rocks Reservoir sites (Wasley and Johnson 1965). These excavations, combined with surveys in areas surrounding the basin, increased our knowledge of variability in the area defined as the Hohokam periphery.

In the 1960s, researchers from Arizona State University undertook survey and excavation of Pioneer period sites in the Salt-Gila Basin, funded largely by the National Science Foundation (Ruppé 1966; Ives and Opfenring 1966; Morris 1969). Arizona State University also sponsored a series of field schools at Hohokam sites in the Salt-Gila Basin, including Mesa Grande (excavated in 1967), the Fitch Site (Pailes 1963), the Silo Site (Chenhall 1967), Pueblo del Monte (Weaver 1972a), Las Canopas (F. Plog 1980; Gasser 1980), the Broadway and McClintock Site, Los Hornos, and La Ciudad (Wilcox 1987a).

University of Arizona researchers tested two large prehistoric canals at the Park of the Four Waters in 1959–60, providing significant information on the engineering of Hohokam irrigation systems (Woodbury 1960, 1961a).

Haury instigated a second foray at Snaketown in 1964–65 to reassess aspects of the interpretations of the 1934–35 excavations, including the validity of the chronology, the origins of the Hohokam, their relationship with Mesoamerica, and the history of irrigation agriculture at the site

(Bohrer 1970, 1971; Haury 1967, 1976). The second excavation re-affirmed his faith in the original sequence but led to a revision of his interpretation concerning Hohokam origins (see below).

The 1960s also brought salvage work to the Hohokam area (Wasley and Johnson 1965). Highway projects led to excavations of several late sites (Johnson 1964; Hammack and Sullivan 1981) and to surveys of large tracts. The scale and scope of cultural resource management work increased throughout the 1970s and into the 1980s, primarily in connection with water control projects (Rice and others 1979; Brown and Stone 1982; Teague and Crown 1984), but also as a result of the CONOCO Florence project (Doyel 1974; Doelle 1976) and additional highway salvage work (Herskovitz 1974; Masse 1976). The National Park Service sponsored work at Casa Grande (Wilcox and Shenk 1977) and Snaketown (Wilcox, McGuire, and Sternberg 1981) that contributed significantly to our knowledge of these sites. Ultimately, cultural resource management work has led to more surveys and excavations in the Hohokam area than has "pure" research.

There have been advantages and disadvantages to this burgeoning of cultural resource management work. For many years, excavations at a few large habitation sites, most notably Snaketown, Casa Grande, Pueblo Grande, and Los Muertos, formed the basis for our interpretations of the Hohokam. Despite the obvious importance of these sites in prehistory, we had no real way to evaluate their representativeness. Cultural resource management work over the last two decades focused on smaller habitation and special-use sites, providing broader knowledge of Hohokam lifeways and culture history, as well as some perspective on the data from the larger sites.

The disadvantages of the cultural resource management work in the Hohokam area are the same as those for cultural resource management work elsewhere. Study areas selected on the basis of criteria such as the best place to engineer a highway or an aqueduct will not necessarily inform on questions of importance to Hohokam archaeologists. Placement of study areas limits potential research questions, and restricted funding limits the time and energy that can be expended in addressing them. Cultural resource management excavations have increased our knowledge of the Hohokam, but the sample of sites surveyed and excavated must still be viewed with considerable caution. It is impossible to say at this juncture whether or not we have access to data from a truly representative series of Hohokam sites; however, increased awareness of the magnitude of variability inherent in Hohokam material culture, subsistence economy, and settlement function suggests that we do not.

A number of recent projects have focused on archival data and museum collections, rather than collecting of new data, to address questions about the Hohokam. Studies utilizing archives or collections from Snaketown (Wilcox, McGuire, and Sternberg 1981; Seymour and Schiffer 1987), Los Muertos (Crown 1983a), and Casa Grande (Wilcox and Shenk 1977; Andresen 1985) are notable in this regard. Synthetic studies of Hohokam ballcourts (Wilcox and Sternberg 1983), platform mounds (Gregory and Nials 1985), intrusive pottery (Crown 1985a), and shell (McGuire and Howard 1987) have demonstrated the value of a regional approach. This trend will undoubtedly continue as costs of mounting surveys and excavations rise, and as the potential of the existing collections is realized.

The first Hohokam conference was held in 1973, reflecting the growing need for communication among researchers working at different institutions. A day-long symposium on Hohokam archaeology at the 1978 meetings of the Society for American Archaeology (SAA) emphasized the importance of disseminating unpublished cultural resource management data and demonstrated the burgeoning interest in the Hohokam area. Since that time, papers and symposia on the Hohokam have become staples of SAA meetings and Pecos conferences. Other Hohokam conferences were held in 1983 and 1987.

Two overviews funded by federal agencies (Berry and Marmaduke 1982; McGuire and Schiffer 1982) provide much more exhaustive discussions of the history of Hohokam research than can be given here (see also Doyel 1985a for an update of recent projects).

Research continues in the Hohokam area, but economic development and population expansion have permanently altered the sample of sites available for study in the Salt-Gila Basin. Although several recent projects have produced surprising amounts of information from largely developed areas (Cable and Doyel 1985; Wilcox 1987a), at least one projection estimates that 90 percent of the prehistoric sites in the Phoenix area have already been destroyed (Ayres 1965). Our interpretations are necessarily biased, and we are increasingly dependent on the records and assemblages of previous expeditions to provide a fuller picture of the past.

CHRONOLOGY

Fifty years of debate have not resolved the Hohokam chronology. Desert woods are not suitable for tree-ring dating, and datable species are seldom recovered in Hohokam sites. Whereas Anasazi and Mogollon sequences are built on hundreds of available tree-ring dates, the Hohokam chronology was structured using other absolute and relative techniques: radiocarbon, alpha-recoil, obsidian hydration, archaeomagnetism, thermolumines-cence, seriation, stratigraphy, and intrusive ceramic dating. The resulting data are open to multiple interpretations. The timing of events prior to A.D. 700 is particularly contested, with some consensus existing after that point. In this section, I will provide a brief overview of the major points of controversy concerning the Hohokam chronology (for a more detailed review of the debate, see Schiffer 1982; Berry and Marmaduke 1982; or Dean 1988).

Initial formulations of the Hohokam chronology involved relative dating using stratigraphy and pottery seriation (Kidder 1924; Schmidt 1928; Gladwin 1928; Haury 1932; Gladwin and Gladwin 1935). The 1934–35 expedition at Snaketown produced the first complete chronological se-quence, with definition of seven phases based primarily on stratigraphic data and seven recognized decorated pottery types. Assignment of calendar years to the phases entailed examining the occurrence of trade ceramics found at Snaketown but manufactured in portions of the Southwest where tree-ring dating was possible (Gladwin et al. 1937). An absence of well-dated intrusive ceramics for the earliest phases led Haury to make assump-tions about the length of these phases based on the better-documented length of the later phases (200 years). The justification for this approach was essentially that styles change at a constant rate through time, and, assuming no overlap in the manufacture of the defined types, each recog-nized ceramic type must have been manufactured over an interval equal to each other type. The resulting chronology was almost immediately chal-lenged, although the various revisions presented in the ensuing 30 years were based largely on the Snaketown data (Gladwin 1942, 1948; Wheat 1955; Di Peso 1956; Schroeder 1960; Bullard 1962).

The revisionists took issue primarily with the dating of the earliest Hohokam phases, or the Pioneer period. The excavators of Snaketown favored a "long count," with a sedentary, agricultural, pottery-producing lifestyle beginning in the Salt-Gila Basin at around 300 B.C.; the revisionists have consistently argued for a later beginning date for sedentism and pottery production, after A.D. 1. "Short count" arguments are based on essentially the same data as "long count" arguments, demonstrating that the existing data are open to multiple interpretations.

Two projects in particular attempted to gather data to refine aspects of the chronology: stratigraphic testing in nine sites in the Salt River valley (Schroeder 1940), and documentation and excavation of Pioneer period sites (Ruppé 1966; Ives and Opfenring 1966; Morris 1969). Unfortu-nately, neither project provided sufficient chronometric data to resolve the debate.

A major research focus for the second Snaketown excavations involved closer examination of the Hohokam chronology (Haury 1976), and samples were collected and analyzed by a variety of chronometric techniques. In some instances, the techniques brought to bear were in their infancy (for example, obsidian hydration, archaeomagnetism, and alpha-recoil), and the results obtained are subject to serious scrutiny today. Haury argued that the dates supported the original Snaketown chronology, although the data were conflicting in many instances and once again subject to multiple interpretations.

Soon after the publication of the Snaketown excavation results (Haury 1976), other researchers began critical reexamination of the data (Wilcox and Shenk 1977; F. Plog 1980; Schiffer 1982; LeBlanc 1982). Criticism centered on the purity of the deposits used in devising the pottery sequence, the interpretation of chronometric dates, problems with the use of intrusive ceramics in chronology building, the lag suggested by the chronology between events or styles in the Hohokam area and similar events or styles in the Anasazi and Mogollon areas, and possible problems created by the Hohokam use of "old wood." The reevaluations led to the development of four additional chronologies (fig. 7.2). As noted by Schiffer (1982:322), with all of the options we now have, one of the chronologies almost has to be correct.

Attempts were also made to tie the Hohokam chronology to better-dated areas of the Southwest by examining the occurrence of red-on-buff intrusive ceramics in tree-ring dated sites. Unfortunately, with few exceptions Hohokam ceramics in well-dated contexts are plain ware and decorated intrusives occur almost exclusively in undated contexts (Crown 1984a; Dean 1988).

Contract work produced increased opportunities for obtaining chronometric data and refining the chronology with material outside of Snaketown. Discovery of 81 Pioneer period pit houses in Phoenix resulted in seven new radiocarbon dates for seven of the structures and led investigators to conclude that the "short count" chronologies began too late (Cable and Doyel 1985:290). Recent work in Archaic sites in southeastern Arizona strengthens the argument for the existence of a sedentary agricultural lifestyle in the Sonoran desert by 500 B.C. (Huckell 1987). Dates from these and other early sites are discussed in greater detail in the next section, but additional data and objective interpretation of existing dates are needed to refine the existing Hohokam chronology. Two recent studies have attempted to synthesize the existing data (Dean 1988; Eighmy and McGuire 1988), and the tentative dating utilized here is based largely on the work of Dean (1988).

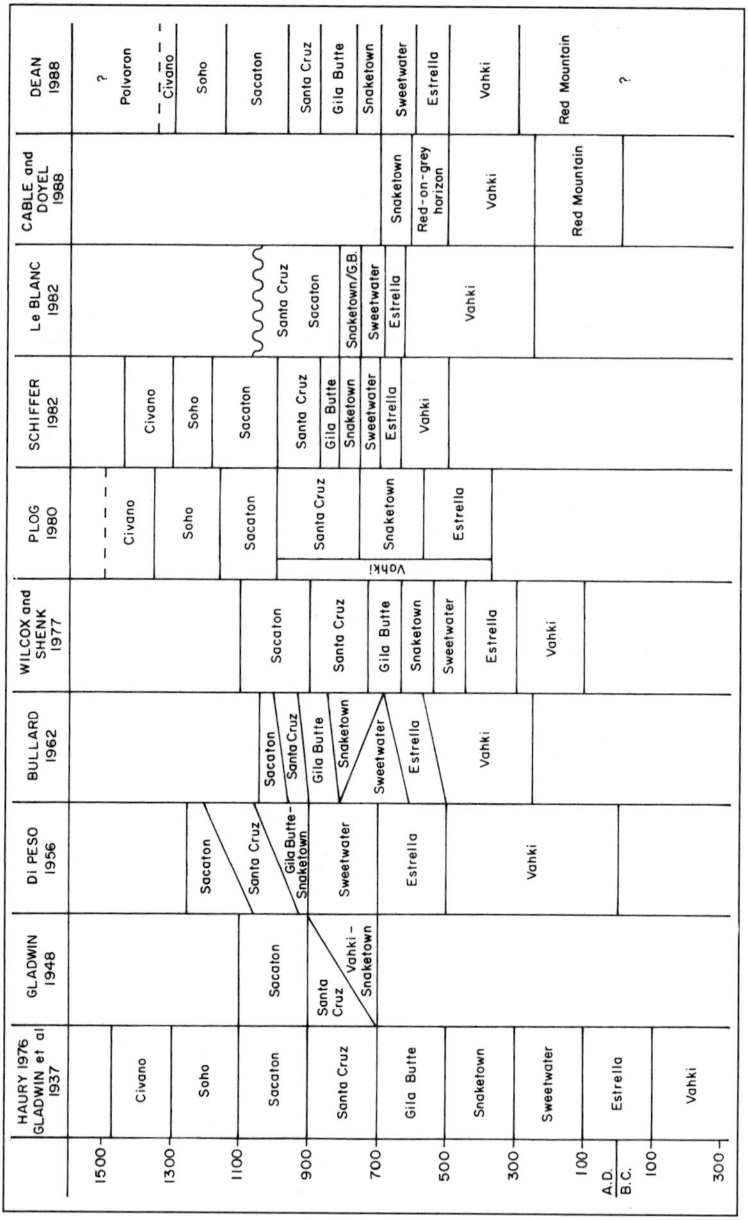

Figure 7.2. Various interpretations of the Hohokam chronological sequence.

THE HOHOKAM SEQUENCE

Disagreement over the timing of events in the Hohokam area makes discussion of its culture history difficult. Although no consensus exists, this brief background to the Hohokam may be helpful in reading the papers that follow. This section touches on Hohokam subsistence and economy, material culture, site structure, and interaction, leaving elaboration and greater detail to the chapters dealing specifically with these topics.

ORIGINS

An important source of debate over the last 50 years concerns whether an indigenous Archaic population developed into the sedentary, agricultural, pottery-producing Hohokam, or whether a migrant group from the south displaced the local population when it arrived with a full-blown, early version of Hohokam culture. The debate developed largely as a result of the considerable differences apparent between the latest known Cochise sites and the earliest known Hohokam sites in southern Arizona. On the basis of his work at Snaketown and Ventana Cave, Emil Haury first argued for indigenous development (Haury 1950). He later opted for the immigrant model because the second Snaketown excavations (Haury 1976) indicated that the Hohokam possessed a suite of advanced and nonlocal cultural traits, including irrigation, from the time of their first appearance in southern Arizona, implying immigrant status.

Other researchers argued for indigenous development of early sedentary horticulturalists in the Salt-Gila Basin, but suggested that the populations involved were not Hohokam. Gladwin (1948:217) considered the Pioneer period a local manifestation of Mogollon culture; Schroeder (1947) called the indigenous group the Hakataya; and Di Peso (1956) argued for a nonagricultural, pottery-producing indigenous group called the O'otam. All three researchers suggested that the Hohokam entered the Southwest from Mexico sometime between A.D. 750 and 900.

A basic problem with interpreting the origins of the Hohokam has been the dearth of data both from early Hohokam sites and from sites in northern Mexico. In the past five years, several projects have contributed new information on late Archaic and early sedentary adaptations in southern Arizona, and a clearer picture of the development of the Hohokam is now emerging.

Excavations in southeastern Arizona reveal evidence for horticulture (maize and probably beans), pit-house architecture, storage features, trash accumulations, cemeteries, an elaborate ground-stone industry, and imported shell ornaments dating to 1000–500 B.C. (Huckell 1987). The early sedentary horticulturalists occupying southeastern Arizona lacked ceramic manufacturing traditions. Plain ware and/or red ware pottery appears later, again in association with pit-house architecture. Sites with this early pottery include the Corona de Tucson Site, with dates of A.D. 200 to 500 (Huckell 1987), and a pit house at the Pueblo Patricio Site with dates of 968 to 390 B.C. and 336 B.C. to A.D. 212 (Cable and Doyel 1987; Dean 1988). Excavations in the 1960s in similar contexts produced dates of A.D. 420 to 660 at the Red Mountain Site (Morris 1969), and 43 B.C. to A.D. 197, A.D. 310 to 550, and A.D. 330 to 570 at AZ T:16:19 (Ives and Opfenring 1966:18). The earliest sites with Hohokam decorated sherds include the Dairy Site, dating between A.D. 400 and 500 (Fish et al. 1987), the Central Phoenix Redevelopment Agency Project dating of seven pit houses between 200 B.C. and A.D. 740 (Cable and Doyel 1985:291), and the Drag Strip Site dating between A.D. 580 and 800 (Ives and Opfenring 1966:26).

Currently, the question of Hohokam origins and the beginning of the Hohokam chronology seems to be largely a matter of semantics—that is, of how we define "Hohokam-ness." Sedentism and agriculture are unquestionably present in southern Arizona by 500 B.C. Pottery production is added to the repertoire prior to A.D. 300, but decorated pottery may not predate A.D. 400. The links between the technological changes and particular populations have not been made, so that it is not clear if a single indigenous population "progresses" to production of Hohokam decorated pottery, or if new populations enter the area with preexisting technologies (Bruce B. Huckell, personal communication, 1987). Until more is known about the prehistory of northern Mexico, it will be difficult to resolve this issue or to provide the kind of evidence necessary to demonstrate the presence of a migration in the archaeological record. However, current data seem to indicate that most, if not all, of the elements that we consider quintessentially Hohokam could well have developed among indigenous populations with input from the outside (Wasley 1960; Doyel 1976; Weaver 1972b). Many of these elements were present in southern Arizona at an early date, yet if we accept the Gladwinian definition (Gladwin and Gladwin 1933:4) of the Hohokam as "the people who were responsible for the red-on-buff pottery culture," the Hohokam chronology must now be viewed as beginning quite late. Such arbitrary divisions have little value for understanding processes of change in the past; however, to provide structure for the following discussion, the Hohokam are defined as sedentary, pottery-producing horticulturalists.

PIONEER PERIOD: RED MOUNTAIN AND VAHKI PHASES

Prior to A.D. 300, the earliest pottery appears in southern Arizona, marking the beginning of the Hohokam sequence. Red Mountain phase (pre–A.D. 300) components are characterized by small, square houses, shallow basin metates, corner-notched projectile points, flexed inhumations, clay figurines, and sand-tempered plain brown pottery (Doyel 1988). The succeeding Vahki phase dates from approximately A.D. 300 to 500, and ends when decorated pottery appears. Structures found during the Vahki phase at Snaketown had over 50 square meters of floor area, two side entries, and superstructures constructed of primary upright posts leaning against horizontal stringers supported by four interior posts. Reeds and brush covered the superstructure, with an outer coating of clay (Haury 1976:68). This wattle-and-daub, or jacal, architecture was present throughout the Hohokam sequence. The Vahki phase houses at Snaketown surrounded a central plaza area, with the three houses arrayed in cardinal directions (north, west, and south) around this open area (Wilcox, McGuire, and Sternberg 1981; but see Cable and Doyel 1985:297). These large structures may have had a ceremonial or special function (Gladwin et al. 1937:82; Gladwin 1948:118; Cable and Doyel 1985:294), although Haury (1976:68) argues that they were used for domestic purposes by extended families. Vahki phase structures at other sites are smaller in size (Ives and Opfenring 1966; Cable and Doyel 1985). Interior features include hearths located just inside the entries.

Vahki phase ceramics included a plain buff/brown ware and a polished red-slipped ware. Potters either employed scraping tools or used paddles and anvils for thinning vessels manufactured by coiling, and pots were fired in an oxidizing atmosphere. Human figurines, and chipped- and ground-stone artifacts (including stone palettes, perhaps used to prepare pigments) have been recovered in Vahki phase contexts. Carved and perforated shell ornaments and turquoise mosaics are the only known Vahki phase exotics, although this dating has been questioned (Wilcox and Shenk 1977:175). Cremations in pits or trenches (Haury 1976) and flexed and semiflexed inhumations occur (Morris 1969; Doyel 1988).

Haury (1976:149) argues that irrigation agriculture was present in the Vahki phase, although the dating of the earliest canal segment found at Snaketown is in dispute (Wilcox and Shenk 1977:180–81; F. Plog 1980: 13) and no canal segments dating to the Vahki phase have been discovered outside of Snaketown. Dry farming and floodwater farming were probably practiced at this time, with maize (Haury 1976:117), squash,

cotton (Fish et al. 1987), and perhaps beans (Huckell 1987) being cultivated. It is possible that early canals were constructed in the floodplains of
the major drainages, but subsequent flooding has long since obscured
their remains. Wild plants supplemented the diet, along with rabbit, deer,
rodent meat (Greene and Mathews 1976:368), and fish (Morris 1969).

PIONEER PERIOD: ESTRELLA, SWEETWATER, AND SNAKETOWN PHASES

During the remainder of the Pioneer period (A.D. 500–775), the large
structures of the Vahki phase continue to occur, together with smaller
structures (mean house size is 29.01 sq m). Square, rectangular, or ellipsoidal houses had single side entries, generally centered on one of the long
walls. Jacal superstructures were built inside shallow pits (houses in pits),
with the outer clay lining sloping to the surrounding desert floor (Wilcox,
McGuire, and Sternberg 1981). On the basis of floor area, Wilcox
(Wilcox, McGuire, and Sternberg 1981:166) argues that the economic
unit during this time period was an extended or expanded family, with
each family occupying a single house.

Habitation structures were still arrayed around a central plaza area, a
feature of all subsequent occupations at Snaketown (Wilcox, McGuire,
and Sternberg 1981:144). Trash mounds appear by the Snaketown phase
A.D. 700–775). One trash mound (Mound 40) at Snaketown was capped
with a layer of caliche, possibly a prototype of the later platform mounds
(Haury 1976:82).

Estrella Red-on-gray, the earliest known decorated ceramic manufactured by the Hohokam, appears in the Estrella phase (A.D. 500–600). The
pottery had thick red line work on a gray background, and artificially
enhanced grooves between coils occasionally decorated the exterior of
bowls. At least some of the vessels were manufactured with coils thinned
by scraping, although paddle-and-anvil thinning predominated. Subsequent Pioneer period decorated pottery exhibited gradually narrower
painted line work, shallower and sloppier exterior grooves, and lightening
of background paste through a more controlled firing atmosphere and
perhaps a different clay source. By the Snaketown phase, all vessels were
manufactured with paddle-and-anvil thinning, and hatched designs predominated on a buff background (Haury 1976). Gila Plain, a thicker
utility ware, appeared in the Pioneer period and continued as the utility
type throughout the remainder of the Hohokam sequence.

Shell and turquoise occur as exotics in Pioneer period sites, and bones of
macaws and a parrot, unquestionably intrusive from Mesoamerica, were
recovered in Sweetwater phase (A.D. 600–700) contexts at Snaketown
(Haury 1976:277). Cremation became the primary mode of disposing

of the dead, and urn burials appeared in the Snaketown phase (Haury 1976:164).

Evidence indicates the presence of canal irrigation by the late Pioneer period (Wilcox and Shenk 1977:180–81; Nicholas and Neitzel 1984:173). Late Pioneer period habitation sites may be patterned in distribution; they are located at intervals averaging 4.9 kilometers along the Gila River. The length of Pioneer period canal segments may determine this spacing (Wilcox 1979a:101).

Several of the river drainages outside of the Salt-Gila Basin produce evidence for late Pioneer period Hohokam occupation (Masse 1980a, 1980b), and Hohokam ceramics are found at sites in north-central and east-central Arizona (Crown 1985a).

COLONIAL PERIOD: GILA BUTTE AND SANTA CRUZ PHASES

The Colonial period is characterized by increases in the size of existing sites and the founding of new settlements in the Salt-Gila Basin. During this time period we also see the most visible expansion into the river drainages surrounding the basin.

During the Gila Butte (A.D. 775–850) and Santa Cruz (A.D. 850–975) phases, rectangular structures predominate at Snaketown (Haury 1976: 65), with a mean size of 22.2 square meters (Wilcox, McGuire, and Sternberg 1981:158); house size is generally smaller at sites outside of Snaketown. Wilcox (Wilcox, McGuire, and Sternberg 1981:166) suggests that an increase in the number of nuclear families constructing houses may account for the smaller house size during the Colonial period. At some sites, such as Snaketown, houses in pits predominate, while at other sites, house superstructures were positioned outside of the pit (true pit houses) (Sires 1984a). Spatial patterning in groups of structures in sites also becomes apparent in this period. Variously called house clusters (Wilcox, McGuire and Sternberg 1981:167), courtyard groups (J. Howard 1985), or structural aggregates (Sires 1984a:131), the patterning consists of two to four structures with entries focusing on a common extramural work area (courtyard) and typically associated with a cremation area (Gregory 1984; Sires 1984a:133). Sites consist of one or more house clusters, often separated by several hundred meters.

At Snaketown, six trash mounds were begun during the Gila Butte phase, in addition to the recapped Mound 40; five of these mounds ring the central plaza area. During the Santa Cruz phase, four additional mounds were formed and the existing Mound 39 was capped with caliche. A formalized crematory floor was also added late in the Santa Cruz phase at Snaketown (Haury 1976; Wilcox, McGuire, and Sternberg 1981:146). On the western side of the site, a ballcourt, measuring 62.6 by 31.7 meters and oriented east-west, was constructed during the Gila Butte phase (Haury 1976:78). At least one other ballcourt in the Salt-Gila Basin and four ballcourts outside the basin are assigned Gila Butte phase construction dates (Wilcox 1988a). Twenty-eight additional courts were constructed by the early Sedentary period (Wilcox 1988a).

There is still considerable debate over the specific activities associated with capped trash mounds (Gregory 1982) and with ballcourts (Wilcox and Sternberg 1983), but both certainly served an integrative function for the communities in which they occurred. Most Hohokam sites lack these features, and their appearance and proliferation signals increasing differentiation in the function of sites within the Hohokam area. Colonial period site sizes and types range from small, temporarily occupied fieldhouse sites (Crown 1985b; Cable and Doyel 1985), to farmsteads of from two to three houses, to hamlets with two to three house clusters or courtyard groups, to large villages, such as Snaketown, with two to five hamletlike subunits (Sires 1984a).

Decorated pottery during the Gila Butte phase exhibits attributes representing the culmination of technological trends begun in the Pioneer period. Scored exteriors, light buff backgrounds, and increased use of curvilinear scrolls, small design elements, and life forms characterize the pottery (Haury 1976:213–14). During the Santa Cruz phase, ceramic decoration reached its peak, featuring tightly packed and carefully executed motifs. Exterior grooves on bowls disappear, and the background on vessels is consistently light (Haury 1976:210).

Other forms of material culture changed little during the Colonial period, although decorative elements became more elaborated on materials such as stone palettes (Haury 1976:286). Amounts of exotic items, such as shell and turquoise, increased in frequency throughout this period, and the first mosaic plaques (mirrors) appeared in Gila Butte phase contexts. By contrast, the number of figurines found declined.

Disposal of the dead continued to involve placement of cremated remains in small pits (Haury 1976:164). Caches appeared at Snaketown initially during the Colonial period, consisting primarily of broken and/or burned ground-stone pieces buried in pits (Haury 1976:190).

We have evidence for increased farming along tributaries of the Salt and Gila rivers throughout the Colonial period (Crown 1984b), when the canal systems along the major rivers also expanded in size (Nicholas and Neitzel 1984:173; Wilcox 1979a:103, 105). In addition, there is clear evidence for dry farming along both major rivers and minor drainages. At the present time, it appears that the variety of plants grown and gathered increased during the Colonial period through "manipulation" of field weeds and wild plants, such as agave and little barley, and through the addition of new cultigens, including tobacco (Fish 1984; Miksicek 1984).

SEDENTARY PERIOD: SACATON PHASE

The Sedentary period, which encompasses just one phase, the Sacaton, is characterized by continued growth of existing habitation sites and expansion into more sites. Many large sites, such as Snaketown, reached their maximum size and complexity during the Sedentary. By the end of the period, significant numbers of sites were abandoned and population shifted into compact sites concentrated primarily along the major drainages.

Ellipsoidal houses were the dominant form in the Sacaton phase (A.D. 975–1150) at Snaketown (Haury 1976:73), with a mean size of 24.6 square meters (Wilcox, McGuire, and Sternberg 1981:158). The increase in house size over the Colonial period may indicate an increase in the number of extended or expanded families (Wilcox, McGuire, and Sternberg 1981:166). This pattern does not appear to hold in all portions of the Hohokam domain. At some smaller sites, rectangular structures predominated, and house sizes were consistently smaller (15.5 sq m) and roughly equivalent for both the Colonial and Sedentary periods (Sires 1984a).

Snaketown reached its greatest extent during the Sedentary period, with the addition of three new mounds around the central plaza area and the construction of a second ballcourt. One of the new mounds, Mound 16, was a completely artificial construction, built up of material excavated from the surrounding area with little trash admixture. The circular, flat-topped mound was capped with a caliche-clay mixture and surrounded by a pole palisade (Haury 1976:93–94). The second ballcourt was considerably smaller than the court constructed during the Colonial period, and was oriented north-south. The majority of the documented ballcourts in the Southwest were built and used during the Sedentary period (Wilcox and Sternberg 1983:131).

The trend toward increasingly finer control over decorated pottery technology and artistry reversed during the Sedentary period. Vessel forms were generally larger, and designs also were large and less carefully executed. There is some suggestion that pottery was mass produced by specialists during this period, accounting for the less careful workmanship (Abbott 1983; Crown 1983b). Red ware reappears after a several-century hiatus in its manufacture. There are few other innovations in material culture during the Sedentary, although etching of shell artifacts appears.

Caches buried during the Sedentary period consist primarily of broken/burned pottery rather than ground stone (Haury 1976:190). Burials of cremated bones in pottery vessels become more common, as do inhumations, although the latter remain a small portion of the total number of burials recovered. The inhumations found generally lie in an extended position, with the head oriented to the east (Haury 1976:172).

The known canal systems were expanded and new systems constructed during the Sedentary period (Nicholas and Neitzel 1984:174). There is evidence that domesticated amaranth (Fish 1984; Miksicek 1984) was added to the farming repertoire during the Sedentary period as well.

CLASSIC PERIOD: SOHO AND CIVANO PHASES

The Classic period, encompassing the Soho (A.D. 1150–1300) and Civano (A.D. 1300–1350?) phases, has traditionally been viewed as exhibiting the most radical departures from the gradual changes that characterize the preceding periods. On the basis of excavations conducted primarily at large sites, archaeologists have considered the Classic a time of change in architecture (from houses in pits to adobe or post-reinforced, caliche-walled surface structures); settlement patterns (from dispersed house clusters to aggregated villages within adobe walls); interaction spheres (with the decline of Hohokam traits in areas outside of the Salt-Gila Basin); community structures (with fewer ballcourts, more platform mounds, and the construction of the Great House at Casa Grande); material culture (with less red-on-buff pottery, a new polished red ware, and the disappearance of figurines, effigies, palettes, and elaborate projectile points); and burial practices (with the appearance of inhumations in addition to the traditional cremations) (Haury 1945; Doyel 1979). Explanations of these changes include environmental shifts (Doyel 1979; Masse 1981a; F. Plog 1980; Weaver 1972b), population growth accompanied by agricultural intensification (Grady 1976), a migration of peoples from the north (Gladwin et al. 1937; Haury 1945, 1976), and a breakdown of the economic hierarchy (Wilcox 1979a).

Recent research at smaller Classic period sites has shown that changes concomitant with the Classic period were less radical than previously perceived (Doyel 1977a; Crown 1984b; Sires 1984a; Teague 1984). Although shifts in architecture and settlement patterns are present in the Classic period, they do not preclude the continuation of earlier styles and forms.

The end of the Sedentary is accompanied by the abandonment of many sites, including Snaketown; founding of new sites; and a shift in the location of the ceremonial precincts of others. Much of the evidence for the Hohokam occupation (or influence) in outlying areas disappears, particularly in the Gila Bend, lower Verde, Flagstaff, Buttes (east of Florence, Arizona, on the Gila River), and San Pedro River areas (Doyel 1980; Wilcox and Sternberg 1983:137). The number of sites in the Salt-Gila Basin increases, and their populations tend to be confined to a more compact area. There is some debate over whether the Classic was accompanied by population decline (Doyel 1976:33–35) or by growth (Schroeder 1960; Grady 1976; Upham and Rice 1980:87; Teague 1984:152).

During the transition between the Sedentary and Classic periods, several new house forms occur alongside the "traditional" jacal structures (Sires 1984a:121), including houses with post-reinforced caliche walls, built in pits and lined with solid adobe, or with freestanding walls of cobbles set in adobe. These transitional structures average 22.1 square meters in size, larger than the Colonial and Sedentary period structures found at sites outside of Snaketown (Sires 1984a:121). During the Civano phase, rectangular, aboveground, coursed caliche structures appear alongside the jacal and post-reinforced structures, with walls averaging 28 centimeters in thickness. Flat roofs of primary beams, secondary crossbeams, thatch, and earth cover these solid adobe structures (Sires 1984a:123). Contiguous-walled "pueblos" of coursed adobe also appear in the Classic period, particularly at sites with ceremonial architecture. The rooms occur within compound walls, which not only enclose the habitation units but also provide a defined, enclosed work space. Noncontiguous structures in pits also occur within compound walls at some sites, although compound walls do not occur at all habitation sites. During the Civano phase, cremation areas are apparently associated with entire compounds or several house clusters, replacing the earlier pattern of a cremation area for each house cluster (Sires 1984a:138–39).

New types of ceremonial architecture appear alongside the earlier forms in the Classic period. At least during the Soho phase, new ballcourts were constructed and old ones continued in use; it is unclear if ballcourts were still in use during the Civano phase (Wilcox and Sternberg 1983:131). Platform mounds, all of which exhibit a consistent morphology, were constructed at 41 sites in the Soho phase. The mounds were constructed by building rectangular retaining walls of coursed adobe, filling these with trash or sterile soil, and capping them with caliche-adobe. In the Civano phase, no new platform mounds were constructed, but coursed or post-reinforced adobe structures were built on top of these mounds and used for habitation. The mounds are always enclosed within compound walls (Gregory and Nials 1985:373–74). The platform mounds often occur in sites with ballcourts, and typically lie to the southwest of the courts (Gregory et al. 1985). Sites with platform mounds occur along the Classic period canals at regular intervals of 5 kilometers (Gregory and Nials 1985:378), suggesting that the platform mounds operated within the irrigation system of the Classic period (Gregory and Nials 1985; Crown 1987a). Sites without platform mounds or ballcourts tend to cluster around these larger sites.

The Great House at Casa Grande was also constructed during the Civano phase (Wilcox and Shenk 1977:123). This massive coursed adobe structure was four stories in height and of unknown function.

The Classic period witnessed the decline of red-on-buff ceramics, the appearance of polychrome vessels, and a continued increase in the frequency of red ware ceramics. The Soho phase Casa Grande Red-on-buff exhibits different vessel forms (exclusively jars) and designs from Sacaton Red-on-buff, and is found in considerably lower frequencies than Sacaton Red-on-buff. Although Classic period red ware vessels have slipped and polished surfaces and sometimes smudged interiors, patterned polishing striations, and patterned fire clouds, these distinguishing characteristics appear occasionally on Sacaton Red vessels and thus represent a continuation of earlier technological characteristics (Abbott 1983). The Salado Polychrome ceramics that appear in the Civano phase, however, do represent a clear break with past ceramic manufacturing traditions. The vessels are thinned by scraping and fired in a reducing atmosphere; both techniques are innovations in Hohokam ceramics. Design styles are largely distinct from red-on-buff decorations. Although long believed intrusive to the Hohokam area, the Salado polychromes are now known to have been locally manufactured (Crown and Bishop 1987).

Figurine manufacture may have died out during the Classic period, although its reemergence during the Postclassic suggests that the tradition may have simply become less prevalent (Haury 1976:265; Crown and Sires 1984). Some artifact categories, including palettes and elaborate projectile points, did cease to appear in Classic period assemblages.

Burial patterns shifted toward more inhumations during the Classic, and an increased number of cremations were buried in vessels (Haury 1976). Inhumations tended to occur on the eastern side of Classic compounds, with heads oriented to the east (Sires 1983:585).

The basic subsistence pattern of dependence on a mix of wild, encouraged, and domesticated plants grown in a variety of locations remained largely unaltered during the Classic period. Irrigation systems expanded in the Salt River during this time (Nicholas and Neitzel 1984:175), and canal networks may have increased in length along the Gila as well (Midvale 1965; although see Crown 1984b).

Ultimately, then, the Classic period involved intensification of patterns introduced during the preceding period together with some innovations. When taken in combination, the Classic appears to be a time of more rapid change and departure from the existing pattern than earlier time periods, but the basic patterns remained Hohokam in nature.

POSTCLASSIC PERIOD: POLVORON PHASE

Sites in the Salt-Gila Basin were largely abandoned by the end of the Classic period. The succeeding Polvoron phase (A.D. 1350?–1450?) was only recently defined (Sires 1983; Crown and Sires 1984), based on scant data from several multicomponent sites with large Classic period occupations (Gregory et al. 1985; Andresen 1985) and from one single-component site (Sires 1983).

Polvoron phase architecture was characterized primarily by rectangular jacal pit houses arranged in house clusters focusing on courtyard work areas. Aboveground structures at a few large sites were reused (David H. Greenwald, personal communication, 1990). In some instances, Polvoron phase pit houses intrude earlier Classic period structures, particularly at sites with platform mounds. Polvoron phase structures sometimes occur on top of platform mounds, although no platform mounds or ballcourts were built during the Polvoron. The existing mounds were probably used opportunistically, since there is no indication that these features continued to function as they had during the Classic.

Salado Polychrome dominates the decorated pottery assemblage, with red-on-buff pottery occurring in such low frequency that the existing material may represent heirlooms. Red ware and plain ware were the most abundant types of the period. Red-on-brown pottery closely resembling Tucson Basin ceramics may have been manufactured locally during this period. Obsidian occurred at Polvoron phase sites in high frequencies, and figurines occurred as well, although these also may have been heirlooms.

Both cremations and inhumations continued as burial forms, and seated inhumations appeared at this time. A single cremation area served the entire population at each Polvoron phase site (Sires 1984a:136), while inhumations continued to be placed within habitation areas.

The largest irrigation systems may have been abandoned at this time

(Nials, Gregory, and Graybill 1989), although evidence suggests that smaller systems remained in use through the phase (Crown and Sires 1984:84–85).

It is not clear that the Salt-Gila Basin was continuously occupied up to the arrival of Europeans in the Southwest. Precise dating of the Polvoron phase and the relationship of Polvoron phase populations with the groups found in the area in the mid–1500s will have to await excavations of protohistoric sites.

DEFINING THE HOHOKAM REGIONAL SYSTEM

A regional system may be defined as "a number of interacting but geographically separate communities that were dependent on each other through the exchange of goods and services" (Judge 1984:8; see also Wilcox and Sternberg 1983:222, 231). The concept of a Hohokam regional system was first proposed by Wilcox (1979a, 1980). His discussions follow the inception, growth, and decline of Hohokam "systemic relations and interactions" from the emergence of sedentism to approximately A.D. 1450 (Wilcox 1979a:79). A major question arising from use of the concept becomes how to define a prehistoric regional system—that is, What material correlates can be used to interpret economic dependency through exchange of goods and services? For both the Chaco and Hohokam regional systems, characteristic forms of portable artifacts and architecture may be utilized in regional system boundary definition. However, it is important to distinguish between situations in which material items merely indicate movement of goods and those in which material items indicate formalized and continuing interactions through exchange of goods and services. In bounding the Hohokam regional system, the attempt was made to examine overlapping distributions of exchanged artifact types (ceramics and shell) and public architecture (ballcourts). The overlap in distributions should provide a reasonable approximation for sites interacting in a formalized and continuing manner.

The initial means of tracing Hohokam exchange relationships through time is by reference to the distribution of red-on-buff ceramics manufactured within the Salt-Gila Basin and occurring in other portions of the Southwest. Figure 7.3 reveals the known distribution of datable Salt-Gila Basin red-on-buff ceramics outside of the Salt-Gila and Tucson basins by phase (Crown 1984a:294). The distribution indicates that Pioneer period material occurs over a broad area. The boundaries outlined by the occurrence of Pioneer period material expand through the Sacaton phase, and then rapidly contract. Unfortunately, there are no distinct ceramics

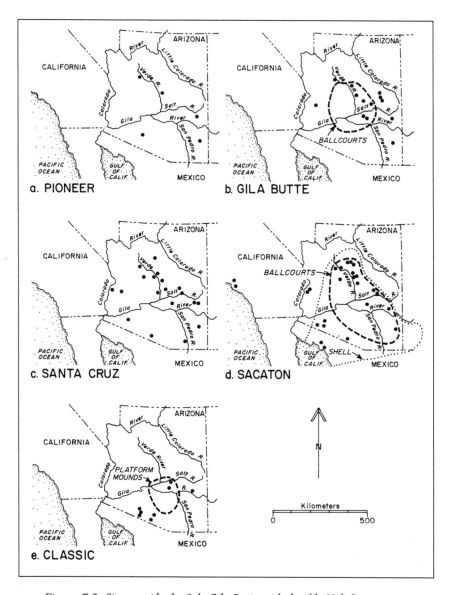

Figure 7.3. *Sites outside the Salt-Gila Basin with datable Hohokam intrusives by phase, compared with the location of ballcourts and shell artifacts (Gila Butte and Sacaton phases) and platform mounds (Classic period). Sites are indicated by single dots.*

characterizing the Polvoron phase, so that we are unable to distinguish Classic from Postclassic period materials in these plots.

The distribution of ballcourts provides a second means of bounding the regional system (Wilcox 1985:642), particularly when viewed in comparison to the distribution of red-on-buff ceramics (see Wilcox and Sternberg 1983:219–46 for a detailed discussion of the Hohokam regional system as viewed from the perspective of the distribution of ballcourts). No Pioneer period courts occur, but the distribution of Gila Butte phase courts and the later wider distribution of Sacaton phase courts are shown in figure 7.3. Not surprisingly, the distributions of red-on-buff ceramics and ballcourts overlap significantly.

For the Classic period, the distribution of platform mounds and datable Hohokam ceramics indicates the drastically altered patterns of Hohokam interaction and exchange (fig. 7.3).

A third means of defining the system boundaries entails the distribution of shell artifacts, highly recognizable and unquestionably exotic items exchanged through the formalized relations created by the regional system. Figure 7.3 outlines the distribution of "Hohokam" shell artifacts in the Sedentary period (McGuire and Howard 1987). A major problem with the use of these data is identifying the locus of production and mechanisms of exchange. As noted by McGuire and Howard (1987:120–21), finished items manufactured in the Trincheras area to the south of the Hohokam area are essentially impossible to distinguish from items manufactured in the Hohokam area itself, so that proof of formalized exchange relations between the Hohokam and groups in other areas with finished shell objects is impossible at this time. Nonetheless, the general distribution of shell artifacts is strikingly similar to that of Hohokam ceramics and ballcourts. By the Classic period, Hohokam exchange in finished shell artifacts is believed to have become bounded within the Salt-Gila Basin (McGuire and Howard 1987:134), although raw materials may have been exchanged over a broader area.

Taken together, these data suggest the establishment of formalized exchange networks between the Salt-Gila Basin inhabitants and populations outside this area during the Pioneer period. The construction of ballcourts probably strengthened these ties, and the system grew to maximum proportions in the Sedentary period. Reorganization or collapse of the system occurred by the early Classic, with distribution of ceramics, platform mounds, and shell all revealing drastically reduced boundaries for the system.

By these means, we can outline the boundaries of what we would designate the Hohokam regional system; however, we cannot indicate the processes responsible for the growth and decline of the system, or the mechanisms by which the boundaries were maintained. The conference papers explored these processes in detail. The chapters that follow thus provide greater insight into the nature of the Hohokam and their regional system.

Chapter 8

Form and Variation in Hohokam Settlement Patterns

DAVID A. GREGORY

A MONG the most significant trends accompanying the general inten-sification of Hohokam research that has occurred over the last two decades is an increased awareness of and attention to various aspects of Hohokam settlement patterns. Since its introduction into the conceptual rubric of archaeology in the early 1950s, settlement pattern and a number of closely related concepts that developed from it (settlement morphology, settlement system, subsistence-settlement systems, and so on) have been applied with salutary results in virtually every archaeologically known area in the New World. With respect to Hohokam studies, however, investigations guided by the great variety of productive research orientations associated with this concept were unfortunately slow to develop.

Several otherwise interesting historical reasons for this retarded progress are unimportant for present concerns; what is important is that this lamentable situation has now improved substantially. Research focused on Hohokam settlement patterns has proliferated with something of a vengeance, and we may now refer to studies dealing with topics that range from Pioneer period village structure (Cable and Doyel 1987) to the distribution of Classic period platform mound villages (Gregory and Nials 1985); from settlement distribution and land use along a single core area canal system (Crown 1987a; J. Howard 1987) to the composition and distribution of settlements in the near, intermediate, and far peripheries of the Hohokam region (Ciolek-Torrello and Wilcox 1988; Doyel and Elson 1985; Ferg et al. 1984; Wood 1985).

Recent advances notwithstanding, the challenge presented by this seminar—to deal with Hohokam settlement patterns on a regional scale; to relate those patterns to questions of the origin, development, and demise of the Hohokam regional system; and to address the question of how it is that these considerations, via comparisons with the Chaco system, improve the current understanding of cultural complexity in the prehistoric American southwest—is a daunting one. The task requires consideration of an interval spanning at least a millennium, coverage of an area that encompassed well over 100,000 square kilometers at its maximum extent, and examination of a general class of phenomena that has proven highly variable and quite complex in many respects.

To reduce the assignment to manageable proportions, the seminar mandates have been translated into a series of relatively simple questions. Extended answers offered for these questions lend a basic structure and orientation for the discussion that follows. First, the varieties and composition of Hohokam settlement types are treated: In what kinds of settlements did the Hohokam reside, and how were those settlements constituted? Second, patterns of settlement location and distribution and the nature of Hohokam settlement systems are considered: How were Hohokam settlements arrayed over the landscape, what spatial and functional relationships existed between and among individual settlements and groups of settlements, and how did perceived patterns vary through time and across space? Third, attention is turned to the explication of observed patterns: What factors influenced settlement location and distribution, how, and to what degree? Finally, conclusions and observations are offered concerning Hohokam settlement from a regional perspective, and comparisons and contrasts are drawn with the Chaco regional system.

HOHOKAM SETTLEMENT TYPES

The documented range of Hohokam sites may be ordered in a hierarchy of settlement types, based on variation in inferred population size and function. The upper tiers of the hierarchy are occupied by four general types, all representing a former locus of habitation and distinguished from one another by differences in relative population size, permanence of occupation, and the inferred range of functions formerly served by the settlement (see Doelle and Wallace 1986; Doyel and Elson 1985; Gregory 1984). These types are villages, hamlets, farmsteads, and field houses; examples of each are illustrated in figure 8.1.

Also recognized as components of Hohokam settlement patterns are a number of other functional site types, including agricultural fields, wild

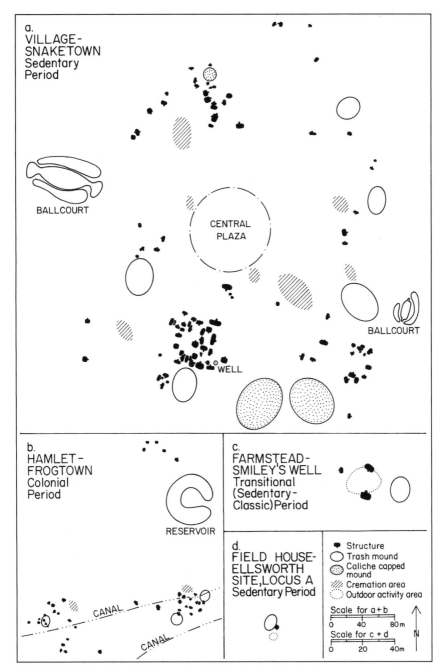

Figure 8.1. *Examples of Hohokam settlement types:* a, *village;* b, *hamlet;*
c, *farmstead;* d, *field house.*

resource procurement loci, quarries, shrines, and a number of other "limited activity" or "specialized activity" site types. Of primary interest here are those aspects of Hohokam settlement relevant to an understanding of the regional system and its component parts. Inferences concerning the nature and complexity of Hohokam society are founded in large part on data pertaining to permanent population aggregates, represented by villages and hamlets. The present focus will thus be on the characteristics and distributions of these two settlement types, with less attention given to farmsteads, field houses, and limited-activity or specialized-activity types; the nuances of the lower levels of the site hierarchy are beyond the scope of this paper.

Villages, the largest and most complex units in the Hohokam settlement hierarchy, are defined as settlements inferred to have been populated by more than approximately 100 individuals.[1] Occupation was year-round and continuous over a relatively long period of time, the duration of a phase or longer. Village sites routinely have facilities that are often absent from hamlets and always absent from other settlement types, including ballcourts and platform mounds. Although numerous village sites are known, relatively few have been subjected to intensive investigation; examples of the latter include Snaketown (Haury 1976), Los Muertos (Haury 1945), Las Colinas (Gregory, Abbott, et al. 1988; Gregory, Deaver, et al. 1988; Hammack and Sullivan 1981), La Ciudad (Wilcox 1987a; Rice ed. 1987a), Pueblo Grande (Hayden 1957), and Marana (Rice ed. 1987b).

It is uncertain when in the sequence villages first developed, but the evidence suggests that permanent settlements with populations exceeding 100 individuals were probably in existence by the late Pioneer period in several areas (Masse 1980a; Rice ed. 1987a). Village-level settlements eventually developed throughout the Hohokam region, with the largest examples and the greatest numbers of them found along the Salt and Gila rivers in the core area. In all areas, the largest villages emerged during the Sedentary and Classic periods. Maximum population size remains a matter for further investigation and debate; however, it is unlikely that any village ever exceeded 1,000 persons, and the actual maximum figure was probably considerably smaller.

Hamlets represent relatively smaller population aggregates, never having reached the theoretical 100-person threshold, yet they too were continuously occupied on a year-round basis and often witnessed occupations of similar duration to those of villages. A number of hamlets have been excavated (e.g., Gregory 1984; Elson 1986; Sires 1984b), and this common settlement type appears to have been present throughout the Hohokam sequence. The earliest occupation at Snaketown probably represents a small hamlet (Haury 1976; Wilcox, McGuire, and Sternberg 1981), and there is evidence to suggest that permanent settlements of this size were present during the late Archaic period in southern Arizona (Huckell 1988).

Farmsteads are settlements established primarily for the purpose of agricultural and related subsistence pursuits and are most often occupied by a single social group. This settlement type is conceived of as having been occupied seasonally, perhaps for only a few seasons, or as the repeated seasonal locus of residence for small social groups with continuing ties to one or more larger settlements. Farmsteads are essentially functional extensions of hamlets and villages. By virtue of repeated seasonal tenure, they may be represented by deceptively substantial archaeological remains. Examples of farmsteads have been documented through excavation (e.g., Doyel and Elson 1985; Sires 1984c), and, as with villages and hamlets, they were an aspect of Hohokam settlement patterns by at least the late Pioneer period (Greenwald 1988).

Field houses are individual structures and associated facilities established solely for the purpose of tending agricultural fields; they are inferred to have been occupied during periods of planting, growing, and/or harvesting of crops. Excavated examples show that field houses were a feature of the Hohokam landscape from the Pioneer period onward and over much of the Hohokam region (Abbott and Huntington 1983; Cable et al. 1983; Cable and Doyel 1987; Dart 1983; Deaver 1983; Doyel and Elson 1985; Greenwald and Ciolek-Torrello 1988). Crown (1983c) has provided an excellent discussion of field houses and farmsteads and their role in Hohokam settlement systems.

The definitions presented above contain a substantial heuristic element and are not meant to be precisely quantitative. They serve primarily as a means of ordering the available data in a reasonable manner, and they have been shown to have general empirical validity: All Hohokam settlement systems may be appropriately characterized as having these four settlement types or some subset of them as principal components. Furthermore, these types accurately represent the general scale of individual Hohokam settlements. Although variation in the composition and specific characteristics of settlements has been demonstrated, and although functionally integrated units consisting of multiple villages and other settlement types did exist (see below), *individual* settlements larger and more functionally complex than villages did not develop. True towns, cities, and urbanism were not features of the Hohokam landscape at any time during the prehistoric sequence.

SETTLEMENT COMPOSITION AND
INTERNAL ORGANIZATION

A number of studies have demonstrated patterned regularities in the makeup and internal structure of Hohokam settlements (e.g., Ciolek-Torrello and Greenwald 1988; Doyel ed. 1987; Gregory 1984, 1987; Wilcox, McGuire, and Sternberg 1981). Subsumed under the term site structure, investigation of such patterns promises to continue as an important and productive research emphasis in Hohokam studies. Site structure has been defined as "the basic patterns of organization imposed by a population on the form of their settlement," and refers to "the physical arrangement of facilities and space within the settlement, which may be defined in terms of the forms and distributions of architectural and other features, by the distributions of artifacts, or by both" (Gregory 1987:184). The architectural and other features that constitute basic elements of Hohokam site structure include structures that served as domiciles and as places for storage and other functions; public architecture and facilities such as ballcourts, platform mounds, and central plazas; areas for the disposal of domestic refuse; cemetery areas; and both generalized and specialized outdoor work areas and facilities, including large earth ovens.

RESIDENTIAL GROUPS

Patterned spatial relationships among and between sets of houses and associated features have been recognized as a consistent feature of Hohokam sites, in which the arrangement and orientations of houses define a spatial domain that contrasts with other spatially discrete units of similar makeup. Though variable in specific characteristics, these units seem to have been present throughout the prehistoric sequence. For purposes of analysis they may be argued to represent the basic building blocks of Hohokam habitation sites.

A consistent terminology with which to refer to these units has yet to be fully formulated and agreed upon, and a number of labels have been applied, including house groups or house clusters (Gregory 1984; Sires 1984b, 1984d; Wilcox, McGuire, and Sternberg 1981), courtyard groups (Henderson 1987a, 1987b; J. Howard 1985; Rice 1987a; Seymour and Schiffer 1987), and households (Doelle, Huntington, and Wallace 1987; Huntington 1986). Despite terminological variation, all of these labels refer to the same consistent and repeated associations of houses, sometimes accompanied by trash disposal areas, work areas, and cemetery areas (Gregory 1984; Henderson 1987a; Rice ed. 1987a). The inference that these constellations of features represent the spatial domains of the social groups that once occupied and used them would appear to be a secure one. It is also reasonable to infer that kin groups in some form are represented, and to refer to these entities as residential groups.

Systematic study of spatial and temporal variation in residential groups and the implications of that variation has begun only recently. Aggregation of residential groups into two or more larger contemporaneous units has been observed at some sites, with the larger entities being designated as village segments, precincts, or residential areas (Henderson 1987a; Huntington 1986; Rice 1987a, 1987b; Seymour and Schiffer 1987). These larger entities suggest the presence of social groups above the level of residential groups in the same settlement. A developmental cycle of domestic groups has been suggested as an important mechanism in the growth and development of residential groups (J. Howard 1987), and changes in residential group size and composition have been used to infer social change that transcended the level of individual settlements (Doelle 1988; Doelle, Huntington, and Wallace 1987; Huntington 1986). Continuity in the composition of groups through the Sedentary to Classic period transition has been observed, despite marked changes in architectural form and techniques (Sires 1987).

The principal dimensions of variation in residential groups appear to be the number and size of structures included; the manner in which the structures are associated with one another, including the degree of formality exhibited; the manner in which other features and deposits, particularly cemetery areas, are associated with the groups of houses; and the spatial relationships between residential groups within settlements, including spatial aggregation of groups into two or more larger units within a settlement.

BALLCOURTS, PLATFORM MOUNDS, AND CENTRAL PLAZAS

Ballcourts were the principal and most widespread form of public architecture in Hohokam sites during the Colonial and Sedentary periods. They are present in Hohokam villages by at least the early Colonial period and possibly during the Pioneer period, and they increase in number and distribution until the late Sedentary period. Few, if any, courts were built during the Classic period, and by the early Classic most had fallen into disuse. Most settlements have a single court, but as many as four have been documented in a single village (Wilcox and Sternberg 1983; Wilcox 1985). By the middle of the Sedentary period, ballcourts were present in nearly every core area village and hamlet, in many villages and some hamlets in the Hohokam periphery, and in some settlements lying outside the Hohokam domain (see figs. 7.3d and 11.2, this volume). The apparent absence

of ballcourts in the Papaguería is a notable and important exception to a
nearly universal Sedentary period distribution over the Hohokam domain
(Wilcox and Sternberg 1983).

Consistency of form wherever the ballcourts are found suggests a shared
conception of how to construct them and of the proper form and meaning
of the activities that were conducted in them. Wilcox (Wilcox and Sternberg 1983) has concluded that some form of the Mesoamerican ball game
was played in the Hohokam courts, and it is likely that basic elements of
Hohokam cosmology and world view were expressed and reiterated by
activities associated with the courts. Settlements with ballcourts may have
served as an integrative focus for local systems or for communities consisting of a number of small, dispersed settlements (e.g., Ferg et al. 1984).
Intersettlement relationships on a larger scale have been postulated on the
basis of variation in the number and size of courts in individual settlements, combined with the distribution of settlements with courts having
systematically variable orientations to the cardinal directions (Wilcox and
Sternberg 1983; Wilcox 1985).

A new architectural form, the platform mound, appeared in Hohokam
villages during the Sedentary period. Earliest documented examples are
simple accumulations of earth capped with a veneer of caliche-rich adobe.
They are quite small, measuring as few as 10 meters in diameter and less
than one meter in height (Gregory et al. 1985; Gregory, Abbott, et al. 1988;
Haury 1976; Wasley 1960). The unique form of construction, an encircling
palisade of posts or a surrounding post-reinforced wall, and the placement
of mounds within the villages where they are found all argue for their
special character. Later examples show growth in size, with post-reinforced
walls, and sometimes buttressing embankments, constructed to hold fill
that was emplaced to form the body of the mound; they also evidence a
shift in shape from circular to roughly square or rectangular with rounded
corners (Gregory 1987; Gregory, Abbott, et al. 1988; Hammack and Sullivan 1981; Wasley 1960; Wilcox 1987a).

In several documented examples there is evidence on top of the mounds
for a single structure of insubstantial construction, and sometimes for
smaller features such as hearths (Gregory 1987; Gregory, Abbott, et al.
1988; Hammack and Sullivan 1981; Wasley 1960; Wilcox 1987a). In the
case of Mound 8 at Las Colinas, a highly patterned arrangement of structures was closely associated with the mound—an arrangement that varied
systematically with seven sequential enlargements of the mound (Gregory,
Abbott, et al. 1988). Many of the structures were quite large (one exceeds
100 sq m in floor area), and they were arrayed in a uniquely formal

arrangement with the mound as a central focus. These characteristics created a marked contrast with contemporaneous structures and arrangements present elsewhere in the village (Gregory, Abbott, et al. 1988; Gregory, Deaver, et al. 1988). Excavation data from other sites having early platform mounds are not sufficient to demonstrate the association of similar arrangements, but a group of features immediately south of Mound 16 at Snaketown is suggestive (Haury 1976).

The unique character of platform mounds as components of individual settlements is apparent. In contrast to ballcourts, the mounds were restricted in terms of both spatial and visual access, and it is probable that highly specialized (ritual?) activities were associated with them. Whatever these activities may have been, available evidence shows that neither the mounds nor the structures associated with them served as conventional residential space during the Sedentary period.

During the first half of the thirteenth century, Hohokam platform mounds underwent a significant transformation in form and function. Existing mounds were modified into a sharply rectangular form, with the retaining wall being of coursed- rather than post-reinforced adobe construction and massive in character. A rectangular compound wall of similar construction was consistently built around this later form of mound, and almost without exception, Classic period mounds and compound walls are oriented with their long axes in a north-south alignment (Gregory et al. 1985; Gregory 1987). While palisades or walls around earlier forms separated nearby structures from the mounds themselves, Classic period compound walls enclose associated structures. Examples of mounds built after this transformation all have these characteristics (e.g., Doyel 1974).

Most importantly, a shift in function accompanied this marked change in form. Domestic architecture atop the mounds as well as in the space between them and the surrounding compound walls, inhumations on the mounds and within the compound walls, and associated cremation areas and trash mounds outside the compound walls are all characteristics indicating that the mounds served as the locus of residence for some social group or groups (Gregory 1987; Gregory, Abbott, et al. 1988; Hayden 1957; Wilcox 1987a). Many Classic period mounds are quite large. Even allowing for incorporation of earlier mounds in some cases, their construction would have required more labor than could have been supplied by the social groups that occupied them. Also of importance is the obvious physical contrast between the character of residential space on the mounds and within associated compound walls and that represented by other compounds within the same settlement that lacked platform mounds.

Thus, for the first time, there is clear architectural evidence for social differentiation involving status and power relationships among residential groups within Hohokam villages (Gregory 1987; Wilcox 1987a).

Sedentary period mounds have been documented only in the Phoenix (Salt-Gila) Basin and in the Gila Bend area, and the wider distribution of Classic period examples is largely restricted to canal-dependent communities of the Phoenix Basin (Gregory 1987; Gregory and Nials 1985) (see fig. 7.1, this volume, for a map of the greater Hohokam area). A number of Classic period examples have been found in the Tucson Basin (Dart and Gibson 1988; Fish, Fish, and Madsen 1988; Rice ed. 1987b) and in the area around the Picacho Mountains between the Phoenix and Tucson basins (Czaplicki 1984; Gregory and Nials 1985; Ciolek-Torrello and Wilcox 1988). These features are generally much smaller than most of their Phoenix Basin counterparts, do not show the extremely consistent morphology of the Phoenix Basin mounds, are associated with much smaller settlements, and may have been built relatively late in the Classic period (Gregory 1987; Gregory and Nials 1985; Gregory, Abbott, et al. 1988).

A consistent spatial relationship between platform mounds and ballcourts in Classic period settlements has been demonstrated, with courts most often located to the north, northeast, or east of the platform mound (Gregory et al. 1985; Gregory 1987). This pattern suggests contemporaneity of the features in many villages and that the conception of the proper placement of platform mounds was determined in part by the location of existing ballcourts. Interestingly, the appearance and period of development of platform mounds is roughly coincident with the contraction of the ballcourt (regional) system during the late Sedentary period (see Crown, this volume) and with the overall decline of ballcourts as the principal form of Hohokam public architecture (see Wilcox and Sternberg 1983; Crown, this volume; Wilcox, this volume).

The arrangement of residential groups, ballcourts, platform mounds, and other features into an encompassing concentric structure has been observed (Wilcox 1987a; Wilcox and Sternberg 1983; Wilcox, McGuire, and Sternberg 1981). Wilcox has shown that a central plaza was present in a number of pre-Classic villages (Wilcox and Sternberg 1983). A large open area may have defined the center of Snaketown from the beginning of its occupation, and central plazas may have been present at several Classic period platform mound sites (Wilcox, McGuire, and Sternberg 1981; Wilcox 1987a; Gregory 1987). Due to lack of excavation data from a sufficient number of larger settlements, and because the pattern is difficult to demonstrate on the basis of survey data alone, the pervasiveness of a concentric structure in Hohokam settlements is not yet known. Nonetheless, this aspect of Hohokam site structure seems to have considerable time depth and importance at least in the core area, enduring through changes in residential group size and composition and transcending the development of new forms of residential and public architecture.

At the most basic level, permanent Hohokam settlements were composed of a variable number of residential groups that have been identified archaeologically on the basis of patterned arrangements of houses and other features and facilities, the latter including work areas, areas for trash disposal, and cemetery areas. Two or more aggregates of residential groups have been observed at some sites, indicating the presence within settlements of social groups above the level of residential groups. In addition, two principal forms of public architecture were present: Ballcourts appeared early in the sequence and endured through the early Classic period, serving as highly public facilities; platform mounds appeared in the middle Sedentary period and underwent a developmental sequence in form and function, beginning as the loci of highly specialized (probably esoteric) activities with restricted public access and emerging in the early Classic period as places of residence for particular social groups. When both ballcourts and platform mounds are observed in the same settlement, their placement with respect to one another is relatively consistent.

SETTLEMENT LOCATION AND DISTRIBUTION

It has long been appreciated that water had a fundamental influence on the location and distribution of Hohokam settlements. Given the Sonoran desert environment in which the most characteristic expressions of Hohokam culture developed, this assertion is hardly revelatory. Nevertheless, this simple fact produced an important aspect of Hohokam settlement from a regional perspective: an overall linearity of settlement, with the principal aggregates of population consistently and more or less continuously distributed along major drainages and their larger tributaries. One has only to glance at the distribution of Colonial and Sedentary period settlements having ballcourts (see fig. 7.3b, d, this volume), or of Classic period core area platform mound villages (see fig. 7.3e) (Gregory and Nials 1985) to be convinced of the enduring validity of this general pattern; both are reasonable representations of the overall distribution of settlement and population in these areas and during these intervals (see also Doelle 1988; Wallace and Holmlund 1984). Recognition of this general pattern also calls attention to the importance of drainage basins as units for the analysis of settlement location and distribution (see Redman, this volume).

Though important, reiteration of the general linearity of Hohokam settlement is not sufficiently complete. As a more detailed and geographically representative body of data has accumulated, broad distinctions previously used to characterize Hohokam settlement patterns have proven inadequate (Haury 1950; Masse 1980a:215–16). A more productive emphasis of many recent studies has been on identification and subsequent investigation of Hohokam settlement systems: temporally and spatially bounded groups of functionally interrelated settlements that can be distinguished from, compared to, and contrasted with other similar groups. Studies dealing with settlement systems in the Salt and Gila drainages of the core area (Crown 1987a; Effland 1985; Gregory and Nials 1985; J. Howard 1987), in the Tucson Basin (Doelle 1985; Doelle and Wallace 1986), and in a number of intermediate and peripheral areas (Ciolek-Torrello and Wilcox 1988; Doyel and Elson 1985; Ferg et al. 1984) have now been accomplished.

Following the systemic perspective reflected in these studies, emphasis is placed here on the manner in which the general linearity of Hohokam settlement was variably expressed in systems that developed in particular drainage basins. Considerable attention has been paid to patterns in the core area, and it is appropriate and useful to begin with these better-known systems. Core area patterns reveal important facets of the complex and sometimes subtle interplay between environment and technology that was in large part responsible for the principal features of Hohokam settlement not only in the core area, but everywhere in the Hohokam domain.

CORE AREA PATTERNS

By the middle of the thirteenth century, a series of settlement systems having quite regular characteristics had developed along the Salt and Gila rivers in the Hohokam core area. These systems included from one to five platform mound villages and other smaller settlements, all associated with a single canal or canal system; hamlets, farmsteads, field houses, and sets of agricultural (dry-farming) features are also components of these systems. At least 16 such entities existed, and they have been most often referred to as irrigation communities (figs. 8.2 and 8.3) (Crown 1987a; Doyel 1981; Gregory and Nials 1985; J. Howard 1987). Irrigation communities are the only social and political units above the level of individual settlements that can be demonstrated to have been present during the prehistoric Hohokam sequence.

In those systems having multiple platform mound villages, spacing between the villages is remarkably uniform at approximately 5 kilometers; the first village is 5 kilometers downstream from the canal intakes, the second 10 kilometers away, and so on (Crown 1987a; Gregory and Nials

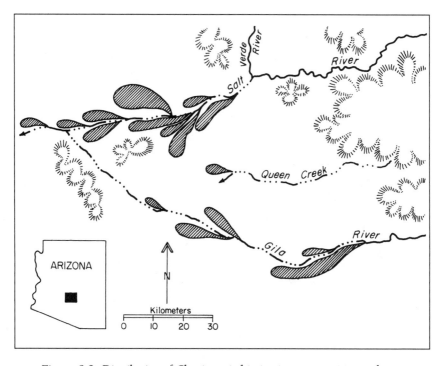

Figure 8.2. *Distribution of Classic period irrigation communities in the Phoenix Basin, indicated as hatched areas.*

1985). In single-village systems, the village is also approximately 5 kilometers downstream from the heads. As may be seen in figure 8.3, distance from a settlement to the river itself is quite variable, depending on the course of associated canals. The largest villages in multiple-village systems are often those located at the terminal end of the canal system that served the entire irrigation community. Villages comprising these irrigation communities are the only settlements where Classic period platform mounds are to be found in the Phoenix Basin; all but one of these mounds are associated with canal systems drawing water from the Salt or Gila rivers, the single exception being a platform mound village located along a canal system that drew water from Queen Creek (Crown 1984c). Finally, villages and other associated settlements are most often situated on the upside (or uphill side) of the canals.

The basic structure of these systems was clearly molded well before the Classic period. A number of Classic period communities had village-level settlements in the same locations during the Sedentary period, and some have a history that extends back to at least the Colonial and perhaps the

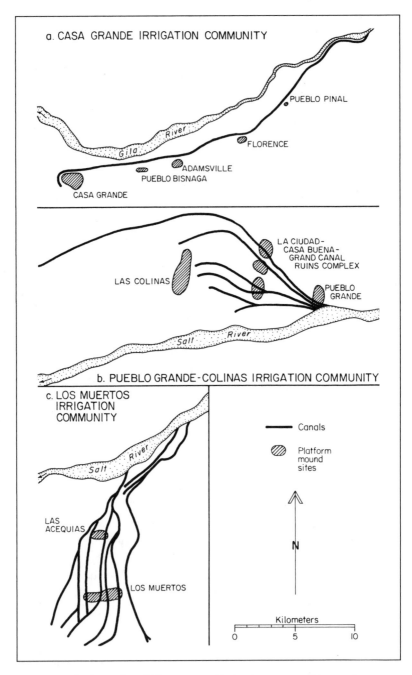

Figure 8.3. *Examples of Classic period irrigation communities:* a, *the Casa Grande community (after Crown 1987a);* b, *the Pueblo Grande– La Ciudad–Las Colinas community;* c, *the Los Muertos community.*

late Pioneer period. In the Salt River drainage, Pueblo Grande and La Ciudad are located on the same canal system, 5 and 10 kilometers downstream from the canal intakes, respectively; both were village-level settlements during the Colonial period and possibly during the late Pioneer period (Rice ed. 1987a; Wilcox 1987a). Extension of associated canals and incorporation of the village of Las Colinas (located 5 km downcanal from La Ciudad) into the Pueblo Grande–La Ciudad system has now been confidently dated to the early Sedentary period (Gregory, Deaver, et al. 1988). In addition, a number of single-village systems having similar characteristics did not endure into the Classic period. Snaketown and Oldberg in the Gila and the large Salt River villages of Van Liere and Cashion are examples of such systems. It was long thought that consolidation of Hohokam canals into large systems was principally a Classic period phenomenon (Doyel 1981). Accumulating evidence suggests that this consolidation and the accompanying development of multiple-village communities occurred at a much earlier date in many instances, and that the location and distribution of Classic period platform mound villages is simply a highly visible representation of a much older pattern.

The inference that irrigation communities functioned at some level as a single social and political unit is strongly supported by their association with the same canal system. All were dependent on the same intakes, and a minimal amount of coordination and cooperation would have been necessary for maintenance and repair not only of intakes but of the canals themselves (Crown 1987a; Gregory and Nials 1985; Nials, Gregory, and Graybill 1989). The degree to which this necessary cooperation fostered other organizational forms that transcended individual settlements is unknown and remains a topic for future research. It has been noted that the individual histories of irrigation communities may have varied considerably in terms of the length of occupation of constituent settlements and the relative complexity of relationships that developed between those villages and related smaller settlements (Gregory and Nials 1985).

It may be stated with certainty that settlement location and distribution in the core area were strongly influenced by a continuing commitment to canal irrigation agriculture, a commitment made in the plastic period during which core area settlement patterns took shape. As will be shown below, the original placement and subsequent expansion and consolidation of canals determined in a general way the location of individual settlements and many other aspects of the overall distribution of settlement in the Phoenix Basin. Similar factors appear to have operated along the Gila between the Salt-Gila confluence and Gila Bend (Midvale 1970, 1974; Wilcox and Sternberg 1983).

Not all core area populations lived in irrigation communities, and numerous nonriverine settlements have been documented. Wilcox has noted a series of Sedentary period (and earlier?) ballcourt settlements (villages?) at the base of the mountains at the northern and eastern margins of the basin (Wilcox and Sternberg 1983). The development of a series of Classic period villages and hamlets with platform mounds situated around the base of the Picacho Mountains and well away from the Gila River constitutes another variant case (Ciolek-Torrello and Wilcox 1988). Nonetheless, all known nonriverine settlements are comparatively small, and their occurrence and distribution are best understood and assessed against patterns documented for the canal-dependent communities along the Salt and Gila.

PATTERNS IN OTHER AREAS

The general linearity of Hohokam settlement was expressed quite differently in other areas. Unfortunately, other drainage basins have generally received less attention and study, and without the unifying thread of canals to aid in the identification of settlement systems, discovery and examination of patterns in other areas is somewhat more difficult.

Perhaps best understood is the Tucson Basin, where the general pattern is one of villages and smaller settlements distributed along the Santa Cruz River and its primary tributaries (Doelle and Wallace 1986). A few village-level settlements were present by the late Pioneer period, but Pioneer period population does not appear to have approached that of the Phoenix Basin during this interval. Some villages may have had ballcourts at this time, and it is certain that ballcourt villages were present during the Colonial period. A general increase in the number and size of villages and other settlements through time has been noted (Doelle and Wallace 1986). In contrast to those in the core area, Tucson Basin settlements are always located quite close to the watercourses along which they are found, rarely more than about 1.6 kilometers (1 mi.) from the channel.

More detailed studies suggest that specific sets of hamlets, farmsteads, and other settlement types were associated with particular villages. Though analogous to core area irrigation communities in that they represent functionally interrelated groups above the level of individual settlements, the composition of Tucson Basin communities, their locational characteristics, and the relative stability of patterns through time were quite different. Doelle and Wallace (1986) have defined a number of communities in the southern Tucson Basin, each composed of a primary village and associated smaller settlements. By the early Rincon phase, the spacing of villages (five of seven containing ballcourts) was quite regular, with an average distance between them of 2.8 kilometers. A major change is noted in the following middle Rincon phase, when a number of villages decline in population and a single primary village emerges along the same segment of the river where four or five were present in the preceding period. There is evidence of a similar concentration of population elsewhere in the basin during this period, and villages that endured appear to have undergone internal reorganization as well (Doelle and Wallace 1986; Doelle, Huntington, and Wallace 1987). Further changes in settlement location are seen during the Classic period, when there is a partial shift away from the Santa Cruz itself and into areas along major tributaries at the margins of the basin (Wallace and Holmlund 1984). Platform mound villages are present during the Classic period (Doelle and Wallace 1986; Fish, Fish, and Madsen 1988).

Prehistoric canals have been documented in the Tucson Basin (Bernard-Shaw 1988), but it is clear that the scale and importance of canal irrigation agriculture did not approach the level of the Phoenix Basin. It is also apparent that Tucson Basin canals had little if any effect on the location and distribution of settlements; observed patterns resulted from the interaction of other factors, which are discussed below.

Masse (1980a) has compared Hohokam occupation in the lower San Pedro drainage and the Papaguería, and he finds similarities in the general history of settlement. Although data are limited, village-level settlements appear to have been present in the lower San Pedro by the late Pioneer period (Masse 1980a). Thereafter, a sequence of settlement similar to that described for the Tucson Basin is suggested, with ballcourts built at some villages during the Colonial period and possibly during the Pioneer period (Masse 1980a). Interestingly, a middle Sedentary period contraction and reorganization of settlement similar to that described for the Tucson Basin has been noted in the lower San Pedro (Masse 1980a). General abandonment by Hohokam populations at the end of the Sedentary or perhaps during the early Classic period is suggested (Masse 1980a:220–22).

In the lower reaches of the New River drainage, a Colonial and Sedentary period occupation involving a single primary village and associated farmsteads and field houses has been documented (Doyel and Elson 1985). This occupation was apparently supported by a subsistence strategy involving small ditches that diverted water from New River; production of ground-stone artifacts using raw materials from a nearby source and exchange of those items to other communities also may have played a role in the occupation of this area (Doyel and Elson 1985). Small settlements of limited duration were present in a number of areas within the lower New River and Agua Fria drainages (Bruder 1983a; Rodgers 1978); these occupations all appear to have been related in part to agricultural pursuits using a variety of techniques appropriate to local settings and conditions, and many date to the Colonial and Sedentary periods.

Specific patterns of settlement location and distribution in other areas are still less well studied and understood. Along the Gila between the Buttes and Kearny, a pattern roughly similar to that described for the lower San Pedro may be perceived in the available data (Debowski et al. 1976). Occupation begins in the Snaketown phase, ballcourt villages are present by the Colonial period, and maximum population was probably reached during the Sedentary period. Somewhat similar patterns are present in the lower Verde, but canal irrigation agriculture may have played a greater role in this area (Fuller, Rogge, and Gregonis 1976). Hamlet- and perhaps village-level settlements were located along the middle reaches of New River and the Agua Fria during the Colonial period (Weed and Ward 1970; Weed 1972), but little is known of the overall history and distribution of settlement in these areas. The aforementioned areas as well as the Safford Valley, the San Simon Valley, the upper San Pedro, the upper Santa Cruz, the Agua Fria, and the Hassayampa remain in need of further study and analysis.

THE DETERMINANTS OF HOHOKAM SETTLEMENT PATTERNS

Those facets of Hohokam settlement discussed above reflect the continuing influence and interaction of a number of factors. Most important among these are (1) the abundance and characteristic forms of available water, in combination with local topography and the dominant technology for water management and control; (2) sociological factors, including status relationships and the differentiation of social groups; (3) cultural factors that may be best interpreted in terms of world view and cosmology; and (4) historical factors, which crosscut the first three and influenced the particular outcomes of their interaction. The results of that interaction as they relate to Hohokam settlement patterns and to the Hohokam regional system are now considered.

WATER, PHYSIOGRAPHY, AND TECHNOLOGY

It has been suggested that the overall linearity of Hohokam settlement distribution was a function of the distribution of available water. Acknowledgment of this general pattern does not imply that the availability of water alone can satisfactorily explain everything about Hohokam settlement. However, in combination with local topography and subsistence technology, the abundance and specific characteristics of available water produced basic patterns in Hohokam settlement location and distribution that are not yet fully appreciated.

It is a characteristic of perennial drainages in the Basin-and-Range province of southern Arizona that they may, during periods of low flow, "disappear" for some distance along their courses, with water present and moving only as underflow beneath the temporarily dry surface of the channel. The presence of surface water in such circumstances is determined by permeability of the underlying substrate. Flow may be entirely subsurface as the channel passes over relatively permeable basin fills, but it is forced to the surface when it encounters relatively impermeable bedrock masses. The variable presence of bedrock masses or "reefs" has a number of important implications, the most obvious being the more reliable supply of water available during periods of low flow (Nials and Gregory 1989; Nials, Gregory, and Graybill 1989). The creation of *ciénega* environments,[2] which have more abundant and more diverse resources, is another significant effect of these features in some cases (Effland and Rankin 1988; Hendrickson and Minckley 1984).

With respect to those drainages having their origins in the extensive mountainous zones of central Arizona (the Salt, the Gila, and the Verde), an analogous effect is produced at the places where the drainages debouch from the mountains. Here, a more reliable surface flow results from the long stretch upstream where the channel has incised the surrounding mountain ranges and flows for some distance over more or less continuously distributed and relatively impermeable bedrock. The net effect is the same, a zone where surface water is present for some distance before sinking into the porous valley fills as the river flows away from the bedrock masses of the upstream mountainous zone. A third situation in which the availability and abundance of water may be locally enhanced occurs in places where major tributaries have their confluence with the dominant stream.

For those Hohokam populations committed to canal irrigation agriculture, there were more specific reasons for the attractiveness of these locations. Annual periods of low flow probably coincided with the Hohokam irrigation season (Graybill and Nials 1989; Nials, Gregory, and Graybill 1989), and thus the necessary condition of water for irrigation would have been met at the appropriate times and on a more consistent basis at these places than at others. Bedrock reefs also create a natural hydraulic head in the stream, whereby the water's surface is actually higher at the point of the reef and for a short distance below it than it is either immediately up- or downstream. This circumstance facilitates diversion of water from the stream and onto adjacent land via canals. Particular physical characteristics of some locations may enhance these conditions, depending on the existence of surface bedrock masses on one or both sides of the drainage, the distance between these surface masses, their proximity to the channel, and so on (see Nials, Gregory, and Graybill 1989).

It was at and immediately below bedrock masses that the core area Hohokam consistently chose to situate the heads for their canals. Intakes for at least 10 of the 16 canal systems that served the Classic period irrigation communities discussed above were placed in these locations (Gregory and Nials 1985), as were those for the sequence of canals serving the long-lived village of Snaketown (Haury 1976). Put the other way around, Hohokam populations emplaced canal intakes at *all* those places along the Salt and Gila rivers in the Phoenix Basin where immediately adjacent bedrock masses are present. The heads for two other Salt River systems were located immediately downstream from the confluence of major tributaries.

In combination with downstream topography, the selection of canal intake locations had a number of fundamental effects on associated settlement patterns. Downstream topography dictated the ultimate course of canals and thus the general location and distribution of potentially irrigable land and associated settlements. Long-term use of these intake locations produced a remarkable stability in settlement location and distribution, and ultimately affected the size and shape of individual settlements and settlement systems. The longest-lived and largest individual villages, as well as the largest irrigation communities, were associated with canals having their intakes in the most favorable of these locations (Nials, Gregory, and Graybill 1989). Selective placement of canal heads also accounts for another as yet unmentioned aspect of patterning in core area settlement: the pairing of canal systems and irrigation communities on opposite sides of the respective rivers (see fig. 8.2).

A few selected examples serve to illustrate the degree to which local topography shaped the character of settlement within irrigation communities in the Phoenix Basin. Along the Gila, relatively well developed terraces are present. Potentially irrigable land is thus restricted to a rather narrow strip parallel to the river channel. The principal means for expansion of irrigable land in existing systems was downstream extension of main canals. The systems here, as well as those on the south side of the Salt below Tempe Butte (where the pediment rises quickly toward South Mountain, thus creating the same kind of narrow irrigable strip), were long and strongly linear in character. The Casa Grande system illustrates this effect, with villages occurring as rather compact units on the upside of a single long main canal (fig. 8.3a).

Along the north side of the Salt River below Tempe and Papago buttes, and on both sides of the river above these features, the less severe topography allows canals to be taken well away from the river, though in variable ways. In the case of the area occupied by the Pueblo Grande–La Ciudad–Las Colinas system, relatively flat terrain fostered development of a series of more or less regularly spaced main canals, stacked one upon another and reaching as far as nine kilometers away from the river channel. Three major clusters of settlements are situated along these canals at the expected five-kilometer intervals (fig. 8.3b). However, the stacked character of the canal system dictated that as canals were added to the system, associated settlements grew to the north and developed a stretched-out, north-south shape across the canals and perpendicular to the river. South of the river in the area of Los Muertos, where the topography is flatter still, the parallel mains are much closer together and run perpendicular to and directly away from the river channel. The village of Los Muertos is thus stretched out east-west across a series of closely spaced main canals, its elongate shape being parallel rather than perpendicular to the course of the river (fig. 8.3c).

It has been suggested that development and maintenance of the remarkably regular five-kilometer spacing of villages along canals is best explained with reference to universal spatial principles governing rural land use and resulting settlement distribution (Chisolm 1979; Crown 1987a). These principles involve optimum distance of daily travel to and from fields, and it may be argued that the continuity and stability of Hohokam occupation along canals produced a particularly unfettered example of these principles at work. Examples cited above illustrate the strength of the spatial pattern in a number of situations, from the strongly linear Casa Grande system in the Gila to the more complicated Pueblo Grande–La Ciudad–Las Colinas system in the Salt. The course of new canals was dictated by local topography, while the direction of growth in existing settlements and the location of newly founded ones was strongly influenced by the (conscious?) maintenance of the spacing between population aggregates along canals.

Outside the Phoenix Basin, where canal irrigation was not the dominant mode of water control and use, similar variables affected patterns of settlement, but in different ways and with different results. The attraction of favorable conditions created by bedrock masses manifests itself in the southern Tucson Basin, where Sedentary period communities discussed in the preceding section, as well as earlier and later settlements, were located immediately upstream from and adjacent to such a feature (Doelle and Wallace 1986; Effland and Rankin 1988); at least one other village in the northern portion of the basin appears to have been similarly located

(Wallace and Holmlund 1984). Whereas a commitment to canal irrigation dictated that water would be taken downstream and away from bedrock reefs, populations not employing canals situated themselves upstream. Here, the backup of subsurface water created favorable conditions for floodplain agriculture unaided by substantial canal systems, and it produced a relative abundance of wild plant and animal resources as well (Effland and Rankin 1988).

Those locations where major tributaries flowed into primary drainages also appear to have been favored by populations not dependent on canal irrigation technology. Village-level settlements are consistently found in such situations in the Tucson Basin (Doelle and Wallace 1986), along the Gila River above the Buttes (Debowski et al. 1976), in the Safford area, and along both the upper and lower San Pedro (Seymour 1989). Though the relationship is largely unanalyzed, it is probable that width of floodplain also played an important role in settlement location and distribution in areas where canal irrigation was not the dominant subsistence technology.

In the Papaguería, where perennial drainages are absent and the overall size of drainages is smaller, the location and distribution of population aggregates appears to have been determined primarily by the location and areal extent of areas suitable for dry-farming techniques, particularly ak-chin farming (see Masse, this volume). The confluences of principal drainages may have played a role in creating these situations. Construction of reservoirs served to mediate the scarcity of potable water and may have influenced the distribution, size, and longevity of settlements in particular locations. Reservoirs may have had similar effects on settlement in non-riverine portions of the Phoenix Basin (Crown 1984c).

In sum, much of Hohokam settlement in the core area and in other drainages may be explained with reference to the abundance and characteristic forms of available water, in combination with local physiography and the dominant local technology for water control and management. The effects of these variables are most clearly seen in the well-studied core area, where a successful commitment to canal irrigation technology produced regular and highly visible patterns. Although systematic analysis necessary to support the assertion has yet to be accomplished, it may be reasonably argued that much of the variation in Hohokam settlement will ultimately be explained with reference to bedrock reefs, confluences of major drainages, and width of floodplain.

SOCIOLOGICAL FACTORS

Many elements of Hohokam site structure are obviously tied to sociological variables; that is, they are attributable to variation in the size and composition of and relationships between and among social groups that occupied Hohokam settlements. Systematic study of spatial and temporal variation in residential groups and of the larger social units that may have existed in Hohokam settlements is in its preliminary stages. However, a number of observations may be made concerning the effects of sociological factors and their possible import.

The development during the Classic period of some degree of social differentiation within core area villages is demonstrated by the transformation of platform mounds into residential space. There is evidence to suggest that this development was accompanied by a general trend of increasing residential group size and increasing spatial and perhaps social distance between residential groups. Although there are not the systematic data to prove a thoroughgoing pattern, compounds in Classic period sites are widely separated from one another by distances of from 100 to 300 meters. Earlier residential groups appear to have been smaller and much closer together, with measured examples for the early Sedentary period being approximately 50 meters apart (Gregory 1984; Gregory, Deaver, et al. 1988).

If a greater degree of social differentiation and increased social distance between groups did indeed develop, different modes of integration may have been necessary within and between villages, one mode more vertical than horizontal in character. The decline of ballcourts and the ascendancy of platform mounds as the dominant form of public architecture in Hohokam settlements may also be related. Ballcourts appear to represent communal facilities, with all inhabitants of a given settlement or perhaps even multiple settlements having participated in activities associated with the courts. In both earlier and later forms, platform mounds are facilities involving restricted access, whether as the focus of esoteric activities or as the locus of residence for relatively high-status social groups. The contrast between the much wider distribution of ballcourts and the much more restricted one of platform mounds may be instructive in this regard as well. The ballcourt complex was encompassing and catholic in its appeal and ability to include a variety of groups over a wide geographic area, whereas platform mounds developed in a particular and geographically restricted social context: the canal-dependent villages and irrigation communities along the Salt and Gila rivers.

Development of social differentiation as expressed by the residential character of Classic period platform mounds did not occur uniformly across the Hohokam domain. It would appear that the trajectory of social change in the various drainage basins was variable, paralleling in some sense the overall variation seen in a number of aspects of settlement described above. As I have suggested, there is no evidence for the existence of any social or political entity above the level of the multiple-village irrigation communities of the core area.

WORLD VIEW AND COSMOLOGY

Several previously discussed patterns, as well as some significant alterations in Hohokam settlement not yet referred to, are appropriately discussed in terms of Hohokam world view and cosmology; that is, they were produced by a shared and consistent conception of the proper physical form of the features and facilities within settlements and of the proper spatial relationships among them—a conception wedded to a similarly shared understanding of the symbolic import of those forms and relationships. Such factors are elusive and difficult to quantify or examine using archaeological data. Some speculation is warranted, however, because of the potential importance of these factors in the explanation of social and cultural change among the Hohokam.

The influence of Hohokam world view and cosmology may be perceived in the following patterns: concentric arrangements of features and facilities around a central plaza, consistent spatial relationships between ballcourts and platform mounds, the physical form of ballcourts and platform mounds themselves, and a formal array of specialized structures around at least one early platform mound. All are patterns that may be argued to represent physical manifestations of a transcendent conception of the world and of the proper relationships between the individual, his or her fellows, and the cosmos. Such an interpretation becomes more interesting when a number of roughly contemporaneous changes in Hohokam settlement are considered.

The possibility that Snaketown was abandoned quickly, perhaps ritually, has been suggested, and the fact that a large percentage of burned houses date to the latest period of occupation at least raises interesting speculation (Wilcox, McGuire, and Sternberg 1981; but see Haury 1976; Seymour and Schiffer 1987). The hypothesis may be strengthened by the occurrence of other events at approximately the same time. It may be that not only the abandonment of Snaketown, but the abandonment or substantial reduction in size and importance of the large pre-Classic Salt River villages of Cashion, Van Liere, Las Cremaciones, and Villa Buena are all related; the minor but distinct shift in the location of the Grewe Site to become Casa Grande may also be part of the same phenomenon.

Snaketown is an interesting case in that its abandonment had lasting effects on settlement in the immediate area. Unlike the Grewe–Casa Grande transformation, where a relatively minor shift in the location of the village was effected, the area around Snaketown was never really occupied again by any significant population. Aside from two Classic period settlements that may be classified as farmsteads or hamlets (Haury 1976), and which are located at some distance from the former center of the older village, this location, favored for many centuries, was permanently abandoned. It is one of the few places where the Classic period pattern described above is violated: as previously noted, Gila Butte is one of those bedrock masses below which canal intakes were consistently placed, and Snaketown was located approximately five kilometers downstream from the heads of the canals that served the village. Why was this desirable location not occupied again?

Although existing data cannot completely resolve the issue, it appears that these changes occurred over a relatively short interval, sometime in the latter half of the eleventh century. It is also immediately preceding this interval that platform mounds began to be built and used at a number of sites, including Snaketown, and it is immediately following this period that a substantial contraction of the ballcourt distribution occurs. Though not strictly within the topic of settlement, it may be noted that substantial changes in the Hohokam cremation complex and in other aspects of Hohokam material culture occurred during this interval as well. Given the specialized characteristics of early Hohokam platform mounds, and a subsequent decline in the role of ballcourts as the principal form of Hohokam public architecture, it is suggested that these alterations had something to do with a shift in the cosmology and world view of the Hohokam, and that ballcourts and platform mounds provide concrete representations of opposing or alternative world views and cosmologies.

The latter part of the eleventh century appears to have been an important period of intellectual ferment and change among Hohokam populations, at least in the core area and perhaps in other drainage basins as well (Debowski et al. 1976; Doelle, Huntington, and Wallace 1987; Masse 1980a). The occurrence of these events in widely separated locations suggests large-scale factors at work. Environmental variables do not appear to provide a useful explanation, given the overall maintenance of environmentally based patterns across the area. An explanation involving the realm of ideas is plausible and deserves attention in future research.

HISTORICAL FACTORS

It is an accepted fact in the discipline of geography that historical factors often play a significant role in the development of settlement in an area or region. Because of a remarkable study in which tree rings were employed to reconstruct prehistoric annual discharge of the Salt River below its confluence with the Verde (Graybill 1989), there is the opportunity to assess Hohokam settlement patterns not only in terms of the general environmental and social processes discussed above, but against specific events or sets of events that may be inferred from the reconstruction. In this study, tree-ring series from the Salt and Verde drainages were used to retrodict the annual flow of the Salt River for the period from A.D. 740 to 1370.

To provide a basis for comparison of annual flows and an indication of trends on which correlations with archaeological data and geomorphic reconstructions could be based, the 640-year reconstruction has been characterized in terms of recurrence intervals of annual flows (Nials, Gregory, and Graybill 1989). This method treated annual flows in the same way that peak flow or flood events are dealt with in modern flood data. Figure 8.4 shows the results of this manipulation, while table 8.1 summarizes the inferred geomorphic effects during several periods isolated on the basis of annual flow characteristics and dominant geomorphic processes. These data provide a basis for discussion of both trends and possible events that occurred during the sequence. Because the data from the Salt River have shown it to be an excellent proxy for the Gila River (Graybill 1989), the conclusions reached may be tentatively extended to that drainage as well, thus including all of the Hohokam core area.

The implications of this study obviously extend far beyond a consideration of Hohokam settlement pattern, and a full treatment of those implications for Hohokam settlement is beyond the scope of this paper (see Nials, Gregory, and Graybill 1989). However, two periods of the reconstruction are of particular importance for present concerns with respect to the development and decline of the Hohokam regional system. The first of these is the period of frequent high-magnitude flows that occurred between 798 and 802, combined with the highest reconstructed flow of the entire 640-year reconstruction in 899. The second is the 33-year period of low discharge between 1322 and 1355, followed in 1356 by the highest annual discharge since 899.

It has been argued elsewhere that the flows of the early 800s would have had drastic effects on existing Hohokam canal systems in the Phoenix Basin, necessitating major repairs and probably resulting in the loss of several irrigation seasons (Nials, Gregory, and Graybill 1989). It has also been suggested that an event on the order of a maximum probable flood probably occurred in 899, with the floodwaters covering the entire geologic floodplain and once again necessitating major repairs and the loss of several irrigation seasons.

The Colonial and Sedentary period consolidation of canal systems and

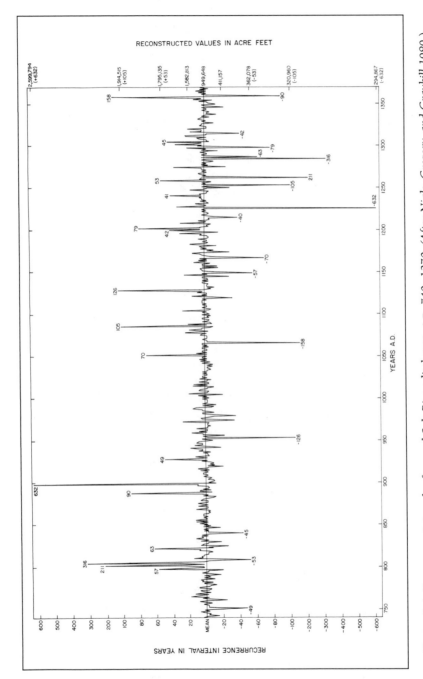

Figure 8.4. Recurrence intervals of annual Salt River discharge, A.D. 740–1370. (After Nials, Gregory, and Graybill 1989.)

TABLE 8.1.   *Periods of annual Salt River discharge and associated geomorphic processes*

Discharge Periods	Geomorphic Processes
A.D. 740–797	General stabilization of channel; strength of trend unknown
A.D. 798–899	Establishment of bar-braided channel, with channel widening and bank erosion, 797–822; possible weak trend toward stabilization from 838(?) to 889; bar-braided conditions by end of period
A.D. 900–1051	Trend away from bar-braided channel toward island-braided conditions; channel narrowing; all changes gradual
A.D. 1052–1196	Similar to preceding period, with some initial trend back toward bar-braided conditions possible as a result of infrequent high-magnitude flows; some channel avulsion possible, especially toward the beginning of the period; changes in conditions generally gradual
A.D. 1197–1355	Overall stable conditions with probable trend toward island-braided channel; some channel avulsion probable due to clusters of moderately high magnitude flows; progressive deepening of channel throughout period
A.D. 1356–1370	Marked lateral erosion and channel widening due to high-magnitude flow of 1356 following 30+ year period of low flow

Source: Nials, Gregory, and Graybill 1989.

the creation of multiple-village irrigation communities discussed above may be interpreted as directly related to these streamflow events. Seen in light of destructive high-magnitude flows, these alterations in Hohokam settlement would have had a number of important effects: the removal of most of the length of the canals from the geologic floodplain, a reduction in the number of intakes necessary for irrigation of a similar or greater area of land, and consolidation of the labor force necessary to deal with routine maintenance and repair as well as extraordinary conditions such as those inferred for A.D. 899. These changes appear to have followed close on the heels of the high-magnitude events of the ninth century.

The expansion of Hohokam settlement that fostered the name of the Colonial period may thus have been in part born of necessity. Hohokam settlement of the Tonto Basin (Haury 1932) and other previously unoccupied areas such as the Agua Fria, New River, and portions of the Verde may have resulted from the need to exploit new areas with similar characteristics. Establishment of small farming communities in previously marginal areas such as the lower New River drainage (Doyel and Elson 1985) may have been related as well. These streamflow events may also explain a minor and as yet unmentioned aspect of Hohokam settlement: the apparent presence of Hohokam populations outside the Hohokam area and in some cases as enclaves in non-Hohokam settlements (Halbirt and Dosh 1986; Morris 1970; Stafford 1978). Finally, it is of particular interest that the spread of Hohokam ballcourts to their widest distribution occurred in the period following the disruptive streamflow events discussed above.

The second period of interest is at the end of the reconstruction. The long period of low flow preceding the high flow of A.D. 1356 resulted in a general drying of sediments. This in turn produced increased bedload—and thus increased stream competence—during the high flows of 1356. Principal geomorphic effects during this period were channel widening and marked lateral erosion (table 8.1) (Nials, Gregory, and Graybill 1989). Thus, the apparently sound engineering decisions to place canal intakes in favorable locations immediately below bedrock masses may have proved in the long term to be disastrously poor ones. If sufficient lateral erosion took place, it would have been impossible to relocate canal heads far enough upstream to retrieve the canals without cutting through bedrock. It does not appear that the Hohokam were capable of this, and the flows of 1356 may have proven to be catastrophic as a result. In addition, single tree rings from the years 1380, 1381, and 1382 show indices greater than those for 899 (Nials, Gregory, and Graybill 1989). Even if the flows of 1356 were not ultimately destructive to Hohokam canals, flows of greater magnitude may have occurred less than 30 years later, thus delivering a final blow to the long-lived Hohokam canal systems of the Salt and Gila rivers. These remarkable systems were simply not adjusted to the unprecedented environmental variability faced in the fourteenth century. In the following period, population in the core area is much reduced, and there is no evidence for the existence of village-level settlements (Gregory et al. 1985; Sires 1984b).

Another important aspect of this consideration is that the communities in the Papaguería, the Tucson Basin, the San Pedro, and other areas would not have been affected in the same manner, given different factors that govern the flow regimes of their respective drainages and the absence of a commitment to canal irrigation technology. Thus the histories of these areas were either not influenced or influenced only indirectly by events that had direct and lasting impacts on the Phoenix Basin populations.

REGIONAL AND COMPARATIVE PERSPECTIVES ON HOHOKAM SETTLEMENT

Development of basic patterns and variation in Hohokam settlement size, location, and distribution may be best understood in terms of long-term interaction between environment and available technology. The strength and maintenance of observed patterns as well as some aspects of their disintegration are largely attributable to these factors. Overall continuity and longevity in Hohokam settlement location and distribution resulted from relatively successful technological and social adjustments to particular environmental characteristics and conditions. These adjustments were the basis for development and subsequent maintenance of subregional variation, and the principal geographic dimensions of variation in Hohokam settlement are thus local and areal rather than regional in scale.

Demonstrated patterns suggest that Hohokam settlement systems were characterized by a substantial degree of self-sufficiency, and they indicate strong inward tendencies in Hohokam interaction within particular drainage basins or naturally bounded portions of them. Variable adjustments by Hohokam populations to local and areal conditions were effective impediments to large-scale interaction, interdependency, and integration. The widespread distribution of Sedentary period ballcourts notwithstanding, there was never a regional Hohokam *settlement system* in the accepted sense of the term. There is nothing in Hohokam settlement patterns that may be readily argued to have developed as a result of economic interdependency or power relationships on a regional scale. Similarly, there is no evidence at the regional level for any centralization of settlement or for strategic positioning of settlements vis-à-vis access to or control of critical resources.

The strong local and areal focus in Hohokam settlement contrasts markedly with Chacoan patterns in a number of respects. One of the most impressive aspects of Chacoan settlement is the continuity in form that occurs on a regional scale. It is this regularity of form that was in part responsible for initial recognition of the geographic extent of the Chaco phenomenon (see Judge, this volume; Lekson, this volume), and refinement of the spatial parameters of the system has been based on the discovery of additional settlements having a particular set of morphological characteristics. Formal connectivity between these similarly constituted settlements is indicated by the remarkable road system that links many of them. Much as canals serve to demonstrate functional interrelationships between sets of Hohokam settlements, Chacoan roads provide strong evidence for analogous relationships between settlements on a much grander scale. The most characteristic expressions of settlement form and the connecting hub of the road system are to be found in Chaco Canyon itself. Whether or not centralized organization was a feature of the Chaco system, there was certainly a centralized locational referent for it.

The distribution of principal Chacoan settlements appears to defy any consistent explanation with reference to straightforward environmental variables such as the location of bedrock masses and resultant upwellings of available water that were so valued by the Hohokam. Whereas the basic dimensions of Hohokam settlement reflect the interplay of environment and technology in a relatively direct way, the location and distribution of Chacoan settlements seem in some sense to have ignored or defied the natural environment. At the very least, it may be argued that the manner in which the Chaco system articulated with the natural environment was much less direct than was the case for the Hohokam, and that environmental variables had significantly less influence on the overall location and distribution of settlements. There is some evidence that locations of certain Chaco outliers may have been determined by strategic access to or control over particular resources.

In sum, patterning in the form, size, location, and distribution of Chacoan settlements occurs on a geographic scale that is unlike anything that may be identified within the Hohokam area. The centrality of Chaco Canyon itself, the wide distribution of characteristic settlement form, the possible strategic location of some settlements, and a formal connectivity of settlements on a regional scale are all features entirely lacking in Hohokam settlement data. The lasting impression that results from a comparison of Hohokam and Chacoan settlement patterns is one of the evolution of local and areal systems on the one hand and an imposed locational geography on the other. As previously stated, a Hohokam settlement system that was regional in extent never existed; it appears that the Chaco phenomenon did in fact represent a settlement system of this scale.

Another characteristic that distinguishes Chacoan and Hohokam settlement is the relative difference in overall longevity and continuity of settlement location and distribution. Despite substantial changes in architectural form and function, significant environmental events, and shifts in cosmology and world view, the basic patterns of Hohokam settlement were

enduring ones. Whatever the Chaco system may have been, it was relatively short-lived by comparison. The rapid pace at which the system
developed reinforces the impression of an imposed locational geography
mentioned above. Reasons for continuity in Hohokam settlement have
been discussed previously, and the relatively short duration of the Chaco
phenomenon has been treated in several of the other papers prepared for
this seminar. In the case of Chaco, the organizational forms around which
the system developed may have been inadequate to the task of system
maintenance, an outcome perhaps also related in part to environmental
variation (see Vivian, this volume; Sebastian, this volume).

Finally, there is nothing in their respective settlement patterns to suggest
that either of the two systems influenced the origin and development,
maintenance, or demise of the other. The temporal coincidence of apparent
changes in Hohokam world view and cosmology and a florescence of the
Chaco system during the latter part of the eleventh century is of interest in
this regard, for it is really the only point at which the trajectories of the two
cultures coincide in any obvious way. However, this is a period of widespread change, and influences on a supraregional scale may be inferred.
There is no evidence for a direct linkage between the Hohokam area and
Chaco Canyon during this or any other period.

COMMENTS ON THE REGIONAL SYSTEM CONCEPT

Emphasis in the foregoing discussion has been placed on the strongly local
and areal focus of Hohokam settlement patterns. However, these tendencies did not halt the spread of ballcourts and the conceptions of reality that
governed their construction and use, the movement of (realistically) relatively small quantities of material goods over large distances, or the occurrence of other distributions or patterns having a regional referent. The
perspective derived from a review of Hohokam settlement does not deny
the importance of these large-scale distributions and patterns in the interpretation of Hohokam prehistory. Certainly the expansion and contraction
of Hohokam ballcourts represent significant changes in the prehistory of
the American Southwest.

The question is not whether or not these patterns are important, for they
certainly are. Difficulties arise when specific interpretations and meanings
are uncritically assigned to such patterns in the context of a too-narrow
usage of the regional system concept. Can these various distributions really
be taken as evidence for economic interdependency and enduring social
relationships, based on the exchange of goods and services on a regional
scale and (by extension) having important implications for the origins,

maintenance, and demise of the participating populations? Or, do they represent epiphenomena, resulting primarily from cumulative geographic proximity and small-scale but consistent down-the-line trade and interaction that had little or no effect on the essential character and ultimate survivability of local and areal systems? Are these two extremes the only plausible and approachable alternative interpretations in the attempt to define and explain patterns on a regional scale?

The answer to the last question is obviously no, and an important underlying theme of the seminar was the clarification and sharpening of these and other general issues surrounding appropriate use of the regional system concept itself. In Hohokam studies, there has been an implicit and unfortunate reification of the concept in recent years, whereby it has been to some degree turned from a useful analytic tool into an ill-defined prehistoric reality. Appropriate intermediate steps of critical evaluation and study are often skipped, and the "Hohokam regional system" has become in many instances an automatic source of facile explanations for observed patterns of almost any sort and at any scale, rather than an organizing concept around which continuing specification and investigation is carried out. It should not by this time have to be stated in such stark terms, but demonstrating the former parameters and significance of a prehistoric regional system is simply a great deal more difficult and complex than asserting and thereafter assuming its existence.

In the instance at hand, this fact is brought home rather forcefully when one versed primarily in Hohokam prehistory is confronted directly with comparative data from the Chaco case. A convincing argument may be made from these data that systematic and sustained interaction, economic interdependency, and integration on a regional scale were actually characteristic features of the Chaco system. Available evidence indicates that the Chaco phenomenon was probably a tangible entity that had direct, apparent, and in some cases highly formalized physical referents and social proportions for those populations that it encompassed. Put in a slightly different way, the analytic concept of a regional system appears in this case to match up particularly well with a real-world prehistoric counterpart. Conversely, existing evidence suggests that no such entity ever existed in the Hohokam area, and that regional relationships and connectivity of populations across the area were much less direct, less apparent, and less formalized. That is, the analytic concept of a regional system does not find a similarly close real-world counterpart in the Hohokam case.

The strength of the regional system concept lies in its ability to organize and guide the investigation of relationships between prehistoric populations on a regional scale, and not in its use as a classificatory device. If the concept is to retain its power and vitality, its analytic identity must be assiduously guarded; its application as a largely unexamined and amorphous characterization of what actually existed—an encompassing label—must be avoided entirely. With respect to careful application as an analytic concept, controlled comparison of the Chaco and Hohokam regional systems as documented in this volume has thrown up important new understandings. On the basis of that comparison, it is clear that the Chaco and Hohokam "regional systems" were very much not the same kind of beast, and that the simple labeling of them as "regional systems" reveals little or nothing about either.

If considered and attended to, critical perspectives on the regional system concept briefly discussed here and embedded in the other chapters in this volume will substantially enhance any future studies that attempt to deal with the relationships between prehistoric populations on a regional scale, regardless of specific geographic location. As the papers presented here attest in their various ways, judicious application of the concept has contributed to an expanded understanding of the Hohokam and Chaco phenomena and to the nature of social and cultural complexity in the prehistoric American Southwest.

———— *Acknowledgments* ————

I would like to extend my thanks to the School of American Research for providing both gracious hospitality and an unparalleled atmosphere for intellectual exchange and ferment. It is a rare treat indeed to be completely shielded from the everyday world and to be asked no more than to concentrate on those things in which one is most interested. I also thank the seminar participants for their attentiveness, enthusiasm, and thoughtful consideration and comment on the topics covered at the seminar and in this paper. In particular, I extend my appreciation to Patricia Crown and James Judge for giving me the opportunity to participate; for orchestrating a well-organized and highly productive interchange of ideas, perspectives, and good fellowship; and for their infinite patience.

———— *Notes* ————

1. Most estimates of population for Hohokam settlements have been derived from formulas that relate floor area to an inferred number of individuals that occupied living spaces. Such an approach requires relatively complete excavation data and demonstration of absolute contemporaneity for sets of living spaces—conditions that are particularly difficult to achieve and only rarely available for settlements at the upper end of the hierarchy. The problem is complicated further by shifts in architectural form that occurred between the Sedentary and Classic periods (see Crown, this volume). To provide a basic idea of the scale of settlements classified as villages, it is suggested that pre-Classic settlements having more than approximately 25 to 30 simultaneously occupied habitation structures and Classic period

settlements having more than approximately 5 to 7 simultaneously occupied compounds would qualify as villages.

2. Hendrickson and Minckley (1984:131) have defined and commented on cienegas as follows:

> The term cienega is . . . applied to mid-elevation (1000–2000 m) wetlands characterized by permanently saturated, highly organic, reducing soils. A depauperate flora dominated by low sedges highly adapted to such soils characterizes these habitats. Progression to cienega is dependent on a complex association of factors most likely found in headwater areas. Once achieved, the community appears stable and persistent since paleoecological data indicate long periods of cienega conditions, with infrequent cycles of incision.

Chapter 9

The Quest for Subsistence
Sufficiency and Civilization in the
Sonoran Desert

W. BRUCE MASSE

H OHOKAM culture provides an excellent vehicle for studying the relationships between socially complex societies and their local environments, especially the interplay between subsistence technology and environmental and social change. This is not to say that Hohokam archaeology is free of the vexing problems that beset archaeological study in general (see Crown's discussion of Hohokam chronology, this volume). However, several factors combine to enhance the meaningful study of Hohokam subsistence systems: excellent site visibility; often good preservation of floral and faunal remains; the preservation of sites such as plant-processing camps and dry-farming fields due to low modern population densities outside of urban centers; the surprising finding that extensive portions of Hohokam canal irrigation systems are still preserved; and, perhaps most significantly, recent detailed paleoenvironmental reconstructions of climate and streamflow.

In this chapter, I examine the role of subsistence in the growth and trajectory of the Hohokam regional system. The primary focus is on variability in agricultural technology within and between the various geographical components of the Hohokam regional system, along with an assessment of changes in agricultural subsistence through time. The Hohokam, adept at diversifying their agricultural strategies and coping with most environmental perturbations, deserve the appellation "First Masters of the American Desert" (Haury 1967). Even so, limitations inherent in their environment likely fostered constant tension between subsistence sufficiency, on the one hand, and population growth and social elaboration on the other.

THE SONORAN DESERT

Arizona is unusual in having within its boundaries portions of the four major subdivisions of the North American desert—the Mojave, Great Basin, Chihuahuan, and Sonoran deserts (Lowe 1964). The Sonoran desert is by far the richest subdivision in terms of species diversity and productivity. This desert, which occupies south-central and southwestern Arizona, western Sonora, and most of the Baja California peninsula, is characterized by an erratic and uneven biseasonal rainfall pattern that is unique among the Earth's subtropical and tropical deserts (Brown 1982:180). Winter and spring precipitation usually derives from exhausted Pacific frontal storms, whereas summer precipitation usually comes from convection storms of tropical origin along the Sonoran coastline. The late spring and fall are marked by low rainfall. Seasonal patterns generally are regular and somewhat predictable, but the duration and intensity of precipitation and drought episodes can vary dramatically from year to year.

The Sonoran desert has been divided into five biomes based on the combined effects of temperature, rainfall, elevation, and soil types (Turner and Brown 1982); two of these, the Lower Colorado River Valley and the Arizona Upland, were important for the Hohokam. The western and central areas of the Hohokam cultural range are dominated by the hotter (summer) and drier Lower Colorado River Valley biome, and the southern, eastern, and northern fringes of the Hohokam range are dominated by the wetter (summer) and somewhat warmer (winter) Arizona Upland biome.

The physiography of these two biomes is characterized by isolated, rugged, north-trending mountain masses that rise abruptly above the surrounding broad valleys (Wilson 1962:90–96). In general the relief is low, with peaks rarely rising more than 650 meters above the adjacent valley floors.

The Lower Colorado River Valley biome contains numerous large, gently sloping basins. Basin floors are dominated by the creosote–white bursage vegetation series. The saltbush series, common on the lower basin slopes, is notable in that much of its range is potentially cultivable.

The Arizona Upland biome is dominated by multidissected, sloping *bajadas*—broad aprons of soil formed by coalescing alluvial fans at the foot of mountain slopes, which often descend to the bottom of valley floors. Soils in the Arizona Upland are generally rockier and better drained than those of its neighboring biome. This combination of soil type and a precipitation regime averaging roughly 290 millimeters per year led to the development of some of the largest and most spectacular dry-farming systems in the prehistoric Southwest. Natural vegetation in this biome consists largely of the paloverde-cacti-mixed scrub series, which includes a number of economically important species such as leguminous paloverde and mesquite trees, and saguaro, prickly-pear, and cholla cacti.

The physiographic feature of greatest importance for the development of Hohokam society is the Gila River. The Gila and its principal tributary, the Salt River, together drain an area of approximately 186,000 square kilometers, with the Gila River originating in the mountains of western New Mexico and the Salt River in the mountains of east-central Arizona. Despite the fact that the Salt River watershed is only about one-fifth the size (33,760 sq km) of that of the Gila River, the Salt River (including the Verde River) has an annual streamflow of 965,000 acre-feet, nearly four times that of the combined Gila and San Pedro rivers (U.S. Department of the Interior 1962:24–25).

The Gila and Salt rivers probably were perennial during Hohokam times, although portions of the Gila River may have lacked surface flow during periods of extended drought or due to the intervention of canal irrigation (Hendrickson and Minckley 1984; Rea 1983). The larger tributaries, such as the Verde, San Pedro, Santa Cruz, and Agua Fria rivers, were likely also perennial, although certain stretches probably lacked surface flow due to local physiographic conditions and to periodic drought. The alluvial floodplains of all of these rivers supported broad areas of riverine marshland and mesquite *bosques* (thick stands of mesquite forest), along with occasional *ciénegas* (marshlands supported by perennial springs or by the upwelling of underflow due to the presence of impervious bedrock masses). These wetlands undoubtedly influenced the distribution of human population (e.g., Fish and Gillespie 1987; Waters 1987, 1988); however, the combined effects of periodic flooding and human intervention (particularly land clearing and irrigation) fostered habitat instability. Another important aspect of these river systems is the presence of one or more associated sets of natural terraces, formed during Pleistocene to early Holocene times (Péwé 1978). The height and breadth of these terraces played a prominent role in Hohokam agricultural strategies and practices.

MODELING SUBSISTENCE STRATEGIES IN THE HOHOKAM LANDSCAPE

The archaeological study of subsistence is a manifestly complex subject, one that goes far beyond the simple identification of food remains and the technologies used to acquire or produce the food. The past decade of accelerated research on the Hohokam has forced us to reconsider many traditional assumptions about the nature of Hohokam settlement and subsistence; however, data have accumulated so rapidly that no consensus has yet been reached on these subjects, and even basic terminology is inconsistent among the various researchers. I will provide brief definitions of the more important concepts as part of my modeling of the Hohokam landscape. These definitions differ substantially from those of other authors in this volume, reflecting my emphasis on the "community" (described below) as a conceptual unit for the empirical study of Hohokam subsistence.

SETTLEMENT AND LAND-USE FEATURES

The Hohokam archaeological landscape contains a wide assortment of features and site types that were once part of the functioning and evolving fabric of Hohokam society. This study focuses on four broad categories: habitation sites, environmental management features, agricultural lands, and wild plant extraction sites.

Wild plant extraction sites represent the residue from the seasonal gathering and processing of wild plant resources. Examples include camps, roasting pits, bedrock mortars and metates, and stone basket rings utilized variously for the gathering and processing of cactus buds and fruits, mesquite wood and beans, creosote products, and other such resources.

Agricultural lands consist of those areas utilized for crop production. They can exhibit a variety of field and water control features (e.g., rock piles, check dams, canals), along with roasting pits, field houses, and other features relating to field maintenance and the processing and storage of produce. Some agricultural lands, such as field areas utilized for floodwater farming, may be definable only through geomorphic setting or soil and pollen analysis.

Environmental management features relate to activities involved in the reduction of the potential effects of environmental hazards (as defined by Vink 1983:13). For example, it is possible that some check dams and stone terraces were purposefully constructed to limit soil erosion (Di Peso 1984) or, alternatively, to protect agricultural lands from unwanted inundation and sedimentation (Doolittle 1985). In a similar vein, it is possible that dikes and levees may have protected some Hohokam fields and villages from the effects of excessive flooding (Castetter and Bell 1951:134–35).

Habitation sites include all sites occupied on a seasonal or permanent basis that exhibit evidence of formal house structures. Formal houses are distinguished from other kinds of structures, such as ramadas and field houses, by the presence of features such as entryways, plastered floors and hearths, substantive wall and roof support posts, and an interior floor area of suitable size (greater than 7–8 sq m) for sleeping and for various domestic activities.

Habitation sites can be somewhat arbitrarily divided into three categories based on the number of contemporaneously occupied houses. Farmsteads consist of one or two houses situated near agricultural fields and presumably representing the residence of a single family or extended family. Hamlets are composed of approximately three to ten houses, usually close to agricultural fields and presumably representing the residence of two or more extended families. Villages consist of more than 10 houses situated near the choicest agricultural lands within the overall "community." These houses are commonly separated into two or more clusters, possibly representing discrete clans, moieties, or other social groupings beyond that of the extended family (Doyel ed. 1987). It is noted that because of the difficulty of accurately assessing the absolute contemporaneity of houses in Hohokam habitation sites, archaeologists possibly have tended to overestimate the size and character of most sites.

Villages can be subdivided further according to the presence or absence of public architecture, which includes ballcourts, plazas, and platform mounds. Villages with public architecture are referred to here as "focal villages," on the assumption that such villages served to integrate, both socially and economically, the residents of nearby farmsteads, hamlets, and small nonfocal villages; likewise, these villages were probably the focus of interaction on a broader regional scale.

THE HOHOKAM COMMUNITY, LAND-USE PATTERNS, AND THE COMMUNITY NETWORK

A community is a human population and its associated biotic and abiotic resources, which together constitute a self-sustaining and geographically restricted unit and whose members interact freely and possess a shared framework of social institutions and decision-making processes. Thus, I view a Hohokam community as consisting of a focal village and its associated "primary resource zones"; that is, those agricultural lands, water sources, and wild plant resources that were exploited on a regular basis and that met the demands of normal yearly sustenance for the members of that community. Although the Hohokam unquestionably were sedentary agriculturalists, animal products were also important, and the presence of optimal hunting grounds may have been an incidental factor in the establishment of most Hohokam communities. The community concept potentially can be extended to nonfocal villages as well, many of which may have contained public architecture subsequently destroyed or otherwise obscured.

Data gleaned from the recent spate of contract research projects are finally allowing archaeologists to look at Hohokam communities in their entirety (Crown 1987a; Fish, Fish, and Madsen 1989; Rice ed. 1987b; Teague and Crown 1984) rather than emphasizing isolated components, as was previously the case. These data suggest that Hohokam community settlement and land use can be broadly classified into two basic patterns: zonal and disjunctive.

Zonal Land Use. In zonal land use the exploitation of important subsistence resources occurs in distinct contiguous bands or zones that radiate from the residential areas of the community (Chisolm 1979; Roper 1979; Vita-Finzi and Higgs 1970), a pattern first recognized and defined by Von Thünen for early nineteenth-century rural northern Germany (Chisolm 1979). The most convincing illustration of a Hohokam zonal community is that of the early Classic period Marana Community, situated along the Santa Cruz River north of Tucson (Rice ed. 1987b). Suzanne Fish and her colleagues have defined several zones of settlement and land use beginning at the river and extending to the foot of the neighboring Tortolita Mountains (Fish, Fish, and Madsen 1989), with the observable limits of the community forming a pie-shaped wedge some 13 kilometers wide at the river's edge and narrowing to a point nearly 17 kilometers from the river.

Extending outward from the river axis, the land-use zones (in slightly modified form) include the Santa Cruz River floodplain (water supply, irrigation and floodplain-inundation farming, riparian plant and animal exploitation); an interfingering of the lowest river terrace with the upper margin of the floodplain (land use probably similar to that of the lower floodplain); the distal portions of several large, active, coalescing alluvial fans at the base of the lower bajada (ak-chin floodwater farming; primary residential areas, including a platform mound); the stable lower bajada surface immediately upslope from the residential area (dry farming); the middle portions of the bajada (wild plant gathering, hunting); the upper bajada slope and mountain pediment, an area with a high water table (water supply, dry farming, secondary residential area); and an unlabeled zone consisting of the mountain valleys and slopes (periodic large game hunting and wild plant gathering). Also included in this community are the somewhat isolated, steep-sided volcanic ridges bordering the Santa Cruz River, which likely were used for wild plant gathering and which also contain defensively situated residences with associated dry-farming agricultural terraces (Downum 1986).

Disjunctive Land Use. The second major Hohokam settlement and land-use pattern, and one much more subtle and difficult to identify archaeologically, is termed "disjunctive." Disjunctive land use refers to the regular and intensive exploitation of noncontiguous parcels of land, often many kilometers distant from one another. A classic ethnographic example of disjunctive land use is that of the biseasonal and bilocational residence pattern of the historic Tohono O'odham (Papago) of the Arizona Papaguería, who moved in a regular cycle between "summer field villages" and "winter well villages" (Castetter and Underhill 1935; Hackenberg 1964; Joseph, Spicer, and Chesky 1949).

The clearest Hohokam analog to the Tohono O'odham disjunctive land-use pattern is that of the pre-Classic period occupation of the Arizona Papaguería. The Hohokam presence in the Papaguería has long intrigued archaeologists because of perceived differences in settlement pattern, adaptation, and material culture between the Papaguería sites and those in the Gila and Salt river valleys (Masse 1980a, 1980b; McGuire and Schiffer 1982). These differences led Haury (1975:546–48) to divide the Hohokam into two discrete groups: the River Branch, who occupied the watered valleys of the Gila River and its major tributaries, and the Desert Branch, whose range largely coincided with that of the historic Tohono O'odham.

The most curious aspect of the Papaguerían Hohokam sites, and one with rather profound implications for our understanding of the Hohokam regional system, is the apparent complete lack of ballcourts. If the presence of ballcourts was indeed a key ingredient for "Hohokam-ness" and for participation in the Hohokam regional system (Wilcox 1985; Wilcox and Sternberg 1983; see also Crown, this volume, and Wilcox, this volume), then just who were the Papaguerían Hohokam?

There are three plausible scenarios to account for pre-Classic period Papaguerían settlement patterns. First, most Papaguerían sites may have been occupied by small, indigenous (non-Hohokam) populations (see Wilcox 1979b, 1980), who simply did not participate in the symbolic or ritual aspects of the Hohokam regional system.

The second scenario views the Papaguerían occupants as being largely or completely of Hohokam cultural affiliation, either by birth or by persuasion. These peoples exercised a primarily disjunctive land-use pattern within the Papaguería (Doelle 1980), with the lack of ballcourts resulting from small population sizes and the inferred biseasonal nature of settlement location. Economic (e.g., shell exchange; see McGuire and Howard 1987) and social ties should have allowed the Papaguerían Hohokam ready access to ballcourt activities at focal villages within the Gila Valley, thus obviating the need for ballcourts within the Papaguería itself.

The third scenario again views the Papaguería in terms of disjunctive land use, but with the Gila Valley playing a dominant role in this pattern. Although I do not discount the possibility that some occupants resided permanently at some sites in the northern Papaguería, I suggest that much or most of the pre-Classic period Hohokam manifestations in the Papaguería resulted from the seasonal movement of some Gila Valley villagers into what were essentially summer field villages. This pattern would help explain both the striking similarity in material culture between the two regions (Masse 1980b) and the lack of Papaguerían ballcourts. The "Desert" Hohokam and the "River" Hohokam were, according to this scenario, simply disjunctive land-use expressions of the same people.

Assuming that any one or a combination of these scenarios does indeed accurately reflect the nature of pre-Classic period Papaguerían settlement and land use, and further assuming that the disjunctive land-use pattern occurred in other portions of the Hohokam regional system as well, we are likely to have overestimated the population size for many Hohokam habitation sites and for the regional system in general. As pointed out by Redman (this volume) and other scholars, population size and distribution does indeed have a bearing on social complexity. If Gila and Salt river valley communities did contain even a small number of individuals who articulated in disjunctive fashion with settlements in other areas, such a situation must necessarily force us to reevaluate many aspects of Hohokam society, including the nature of trade and exchange (particularly as concerns marine shell; see Doyel, this volume) and the nature of residence patterns within individual communities. Just as Lekson (this volume) cautions us about the boundaries of the Chaco regional system, it appears that we should not define the limits of the Hohokam regional system solely on the distribution of public architecture.

Community Networks. Zonal and disjunctive land-use patterns are most easily observed and defined in the context of single communities (such as the Marana Community noted above). However, it is apparent that many Hohokam communities did not operate independently, but rather participated in larger political and economic units comprising two or more focal village communities. These larger entities are termed "community networks" to distinguish them from the individual communities themselves.

The most conspicuous type of community network is that of multiple communities linked together by a single irrigation system, a common occurrence along the Salt and Gila rivers. These irrigation community networks ranged in size and complexity from modest systems servicing just a couple of focal villages, to networks containing five or more sizable focal villages (Gregory and Nials 1985:table 1).

Linking multiple communities within a single irrigation system confounds the identification of boundaries for each individual community;

however, recent studies indicate that individual focal villages typically are spaced along each canal system quite regularly (Crown 1987a; Gregory and Nials 1985). Although there are a number of possible explanations for such spacing (Flannery 1976; Kus 1983; Paynter 1983), this pattern suggests that each focal village maintained its own primary resource zones in much the same manner as those villages not linked by canals. For example, regular spacing is evident in each of two irrigation community networks along the Gila River near Florence (Crown 1987a), with most of the associated communities exhibiting wedge-shaped zonal land-use patterns not unlike that of the Marana Community.

REGIONAL NETWORKS AND THE HOHOKAM REGIONAL SYSTEM

The foregoing discussion of Hohokam settlement and land use has dealt with features and components that for the most part are observable in the archaeological record and whose validity can be at least partially tested. It is when we proceed to levels of social organization and cultural articulation beyond single irrigation community networks that we run into our greatest problems of interpretive modeling and hypothesis testing. Did some "irrigation" community networks extend to communities outside the boundaries of their individual irrigation systems—or alternatively, were there community networks that were not linked at all to irrigation systems? Did two or more community networks (irrigation or otherwise) ever join together to create supracommunity or regional networks? And just what constitutes the Hohokam "regional system"?

To address the first two questions satisfactorily would far exceed my topical limits and perhaps the limits of our present data base itself, although aspects of these issues are touched on in this paper. It is necessary, on the other hand, to clarify my use of the "Hohokam regional system" concept.

I agree with the general tenor of Gregory's (this volume) well-reasoned assessment of the profound differences between the Hohokam and Chacoan regional systems, a theme echoed in all the papers in this volume. Likewise, I am sympathetic to his cautions regarding the often overzealous and uncritical use of the regional system concept by many students of Hohokam archaeology. Nevertheless, I am uneasy with a dichotomy that embraces the Chaco phenomenon as a regional system (as defined by Crown and Judge in the Introduction to the volume) but denies such status to the Hohokam.

The Hohokam regional system is more than just a heuristic organizing concept for use by Hohokam scholars. Chacoans certainly had their own peculiar and impressive brand of regional system, but the tenth- and eleventh-century Hohokam participated in something that should be considered a regional system as well. I firmly believe that the Hohokam had sustained economic (see Doyel, this volume) and social (see Wilcox, this volume) networks beyond those of simple irrigation community networks (see also Masse 1980a, 1982), and that several such regional networks variously existed and competed in Arizona's Sonoran desert. Our present inability to identify the exact configurations of specific networks, and to isolate the goods and services being moved and manipulated, reflects inadequacies in our current data base and research modeling. These regional networks most likely were dynamically fluid and unstable—a response to periodic large-scale environmental change, and in part a reflection on basic population structure.

SUBSISTENCE SYSTEMS

Throughout their more than 1,000-year span of culture history, the Hohokam—like the Chacoans and other Southwestern neighbors—utilized a subsistence economy comprising hunting, wild plant gathering, and agriculture. There have been several attempts over the years to ascertain the relative contribution and importance of each food source for the collective Hohokam diet (e.g., Haury 1975:543–45) and to quantitatively model Hohokam subsistence systems in general (e.g., Bohrer 1970; Gasser 1979; Masse 1980b:191–211). We are presently making rapid progress in the sophistication of our data recovery methodologies and interpretive frameworks (Gasser and Kwiatkowski 1988; Szuter and Bayham 1989), but it is still premature to treat Hohokam subsistence, at least in terms of the plant and animal remains themselves, in a quantitatively holistic fashion. The problems besetting the archaeological analysis of subsistence remains are many and varied, and they often go unrecognized (Masse 1989). The following discussion of Hohokam subsistence is therefore descriptive, rather than quantitative, in nature.

HUNTING

Hunting was always a significant component of Hohokam subsistence economy and undoubtedly provided the main source of protein during all time periods (Szuter and Bayham 1989). Earlier statements about the seeming lack of animal bones in some Hohokam habitation sites (e.g., Haury 1976:114–16) are most likely the result of inadequate data recovery methods. For example, use of a quarter-inch mesh screen for faunal recovery results in the loss of approximately 70 percent of the elements from an animal the size of a cottontail rabbit (Grayson 1984:table 6.2).

Despite the importance of hunting, however, Hohokam hunting technology appears to have been relatively simple, with larger animals taken primarily by bow and arrow and smaller game likely obtained with a variety of snares, traps, nets, and clubs.

Rabbits, especially jacks (*Lepus* spp.), dominate the faunal assemblages from all time periods and probably comprised the bulk of all animal protein consumed by the Hohokam. White-tailed and mule deer were also important food resources, as were (to a somewhat lesser degree) bighorn sheep, pronghorn, kit foxes, badgers, squirrels, and quail. Aquatic animals, such as mud turtles, ducks and other waterfowl, muskrats, and fish, constitute just a small percentage of the faunal remains from most Hohokam sites, but such specimens may be underrepresented due to screen-size bias. Snakes, lizards, and small rodents (pocket gophers, rats, and mice) are quite common in archaeological assemblages, but it is unclear whether or not they were actually eaten by the Hohokam (Szuter 1984). Domesticated dogs occur at Hohokam sites, but there is no evidence that dogs were eaten. Turkey remains are also present in small numbers, but these individuals probably were obtained (presumably by trade) from the mountainous areas of central and eastern Arizona.

Szuter and Bayham (1989) have identified what they feel to be meaningful patterns of regional and temporal variability in animal use by the Hohokam. I agree with their conclusion that subsistence and land-use patterns should have a profound effect on the distribution of animals and the manner in which they are procured. This situation is well illustrated by the distribution of jackrabbits and cottontail rabbits (*Syvilagus* spp.). Those areas most subject to human modification (e.g., large villages and agricultural field systems in valley floors) enhance the habitat of jacks, while degrading that for the more solitary cottontails (see also P. Johnson 1978). The expansion of Hohokam population and agricultural systems also would have impacted the larger game animals adversely while enhancing the habitats of mice, birds, and other animals—including jackrabbits—capable of utilizing cultivated and fallow fields (P. Johnson 1978; Rea 1979; Szuter and Bayham 1989).

I am concerned, however, by other interpretations of faunal assemblage variability presented by Szuter and Bayham (1989), including their suggestion that the Hohokam living in higher elevations and more mountainous regions relied to a much greater degree on large game (especially deer), and therefore considerably less on agricultural produce, than did their valley-floor cousins. In the first place, I agree with Vivian (this volume) that even areas seemingly marginal for agriculture have much greater farming potential than we have traditionally assumed. My skepticism also derives at least in part from the fact that several of the site assemblages forming the basis for these authors' sample are from poorly controlled or reported contexts (e.g., see Szuter and Bayham 1989:n. 7), including Gu Achi and Ventana Cave in the Papaguería. The analysis of the Ventana Cave material in particular fails to recognize that a sizable and presently unknown portion of Level 1 (and possibly Level 2) contains evidence of use during the protohistoric or early historic periods (ca. A.D. 1600–1800) rather than during the Hohokam occupation (Masse 1981b:39). This situation could have a profound effect on the interpretation of the artiodactyl index for these two levels (Szuter and Bayham 1989:fig. 8.5), as well as on other diachronic aspects of prehistoric animal use in southern Arizona.

Animals were utilized by the Hohokam for purposes other than food, of course, including skins and furs for clothing and containers; cut bone for tools and personal adornment; and a variety of bone tubes, skulls, horn cores, pierced jaws, and other such objects for ritual purposes. However, except for the presence of nonindigenous macaws, thick-billed parrots, and cardinals (Ferg and Rea 1983; Haury 1976:115–16)—apparently desirable for their brilliant plumage—substantive evidence for the long-distance trade of animal products (apart from marine shell) is lacking.

WILD PLANT GATHERING

Wild plant resources were critical for the Hohokam diet and for a variety of other purposes. Many edible plants were collected by the Hohokam, chief among them being mesquite pods, a major staple of the Hohokam diet. Other important gathered foods include saguaro fruits, hedgehog cactus fruits, prickly-pear cactus fruits and pads, cholla cactus buds, tansy mustard seeds, goosefoot seeds, screwbean pods, wild buckwheat, Indian wheat (*Plantago*), cattail, globemallow, and "Cheno-am" seeds (that is, seeds of various species of *Chenopodium* and *Amaranthus*). In addition to these edible plants, a number of species were important for construction (mesquite, cottonwood, paloverde, saguaro, common reed), firewood (mesquite, creosote), lac (creosote), smoking tubes (common reed), utensils (ironwood, cottonwood), and so forth.

Because of the importance of wild plants for many aspects of Hohokam livelihood, and due to the fact that most edible buds, fruits, pods, and seeds are seasonal and are thus available during just a short portion of each year, it is not surprising that wild plant gathering and processing camps and features are ubiquitous over much of the Hohokam cultural range (e.g., Doelle 1976; Goodyear 1975). In fact, since most edible plants need to be gathered during the same months in which agricultural activities are pursued (March through October), many of the small sherd-and-lithic scatters that dot the valley floors and gently sloping bajadas are probably seasonal camps supporting both farming and a wide range of wild plant gathering activities (Doyel 1984a; Gasser 1979; Masse 1980b). On the other hand, some of these sites may represent the remains of highly specialized activities involving but a single plant species (Goodyear 1975; Sullivan 1983).

As with hunting, there are as yet no clear trends observable in the use of wild plant resources through time, nor is there clear evidence for distinctive regional differences in the use of various plants. Nevertheless, there are some hints at potentially interesting patterns, such as the apparent great increase in the number of cactus gathering loci during the late Sedentary and Classic periods, in at least the Papaguería (Goodyear 1975; Masse 1980b). Similarly, the possibly abrupt appearance of what may be saguaro wine preparation pits during the Colonial and Classic periods in the Gila Valley (Doyel 1981:32; Haury 1976:156) is suggestive of local specialization, perhaps for ritual purposes.

In general, I agree with Bohrer (1970) that changes in the use of wild plants are intertwined with other aspects of the overall subsistence system. However, there are a number of factors other than simple crop failure that can alter the importance and use of wild plants. These include changes in collecting or preparation techniques, as well as the infusion of new forms of ritual and ceremonialism.

The Hohokam constantly tinkered with their environment, and both intentionally and unintentionally enhanced various wild plant resources. We still have much to learn about the Hohokam use of wild plants, but it is obvious from the archaeological landscape that wild plant resources were a critical component of most Hohokam communities. It is perhaps no accident that the presumed range of the Hohokam regional system (at least during the Sedentary period) closely matches the distribution of the saguaro cactus within the Sonoran desert. The range of the saguaro, in effect, represents the range of biotic and abiotic resources most likely viewed by the Hohokam as critical for their survival.

AGRICULTURAL SYSTEMS

Most late prehistoric Southwestern groups were proficient agriculturalists, utilizing a wide variety of farming techniques (Canouts 1975; Fish and Fish 1984; Glassow 1980; Haury 1976; Vivian 1974; Woodbury 1961b; Woosley 1980). However, no cultural group, including the Chaco Anasazi (Vivian, this volume), could match the Hohokam in terms of the diversity, magnitude, complexity, and sophistication of their aggregate technologies. The Hohokam were equally expert in three major agricultural technologies: floodwater farming, irrigation, and dry farming. Before discussing these technologies, I will first note the crops that were utilized by the Hohokam.

Crops. The past decade of intensive macrobotanical and palynological research has called into question the traditional notion that the maize-beans-squash triumvirate provided the basic sustenance for Southwestern populations. It is now apparent that there was considerable regional and temporal variation in the kinds and amounts of agricultural produce used by the Hohokam, perhaps in response to local water availability (and other environmental factors), as well as to various social and economic factors (Gasser and Kwiatkowski 1988).

Ford (1985:343–44) has defined three broad "agricultural complexes" that impacted prehistoric Southwestern populations: the Upper Sonoran Agricultural Complex, including the common bean, the bottle gourd, and summer squash introduced from western Mexico during the first millennium B.C.; the Lower Sonoran Agricultural Complex, including cotton, crop plants somewhat resistant to high temperatures, and four beans, two squashes, and a grain amaranth, all introduced into the Sonoran desert from Mexico between approximately A.D. 500 and 1200; and the Southwestern Agricultural Complex, representing the domestication of plants indigenous to the Southwest. Ford (1985) notes only six such plants in the latter complex (Sonoran panic grass, little barley grass, devil's claw, agave [*Agave parryi*], and two tobaccos [*Nicotania* spp.]), and suggests that all six were developed late in prehistoric times or perhaps even in early historic times. Recent studies, however, indicate that this list can be broadened substantially both in time depth and in number of species. For example, it seems likely that both agave and little barley grass were cultivated during the Pioneer period (Gasser and Kwiatkowski 1988). Other possible cultivars include chia, sunflower, dropseed grass, pigweed, yucca, cholla cactus, additional species of agave (e.g., *A. murpheyi*), and chiltepine.

The Hohokam benefited not only from the crops, but also from the field environments that they created. A number of edible weeds flourished in cultivated and fallow garden plots, including groundcherry, tansy mustard, spurge, plantain, Indian wheat, globemallow, purslane, and horse purslane. As previously noted, a number of food animals proliferated in field areas as well, including rabbits, cotton rats, wood rats, packrats, and sphinx moth larvae (Rea 1979).

Floodwater Farming. Two different agricultural practices are subsumed under the term "floodwater farming": floodplain inundation (overbank

flooding) and ak-chin farming. Floodplain-inundation farming, the cultivation of river floodplains after spring or summer freshets (Castetter and
Bell 1951), requires the presence of a perennial stream, or at least a
semiperennial one that flows and floods with enough regularity for floodplain wetting and enrichment to be a normal expectation. This type of
agriculture does not usually require a major labor investment, although it
is sometimes necessary to clear trees and other riparian plants. Dikes and
short canals may also be constructed in particularly favorable floodplain
locations. Given the locations of late Archaic and Hohokam sites with
respect to documented riverine marsh locations (likely choice areas for
floodplain-inundation agriculture), it is probable that this technology was
practiced by the Hohokam throughout their cultural sequence (Waters
1988).

Ak-chin farming consists of capturing rainfall runoff for use in field
areas. Recent geomorphological studies (e.g., Waters and Field 1986),
ethnographic study (Nabhan 1983), and archaeological surveys (Fish,
Fish, and Madsen 1985; Fish et al. 1988) indicate that ak-chin farming was
a vitally important agricultural method for the Hohokam (Gasser and
Kwiatkowski 1988; Nabhan and Masse 1986) and apparently permitted
sizable villages to be constructed on middle and upper bajada slopes far
away from the channels of perennial and semiperennial streams (e.g., Craig
and Wallace 1987). Ak-chin farming appears to have been burgeoning by
A.D. 900 and was seemingly utilized during the Pioneer period as well.

"Ak-chin" is derived from the Papago ak ciñ, which means "mouth of a
wash," referring to the location where historic Papago fields were often
located (Nabhan 1986). Nabhan's (1982, 1983, 1986) study of Papago ak-
chin farming has shown that such fields can be located at all points along
the distal and proximal portions of alluvial fans and can even occur along
the discontinuous channel (Waters and Field 1986) that connects the two
ends of a fan. Ak-chin fields are also common on the braided portions of
major ephemeral wash systems such as the Vekol and Santa Rosa washes in
the northern Papaguería (Nabhan and Masse 1986).

Generally more labor intensive than floodplain inundation, ak-chin
farming may even approach the intensity of labor input required by dry-
farming methods. It often employs features such as brush weirs and small
ditches to capture and channel sheetflow to individual agricultural plots,
and these features require frequent repair or cleaning. In addition, flooding
often changes the character of the runoff patterns, so that field and associated feature locations will frequently have to be moved considerable distances. This instability of field location is in marked contrast to irrigation
and dry farming. However, floodwater farming (both ak-chin and flood-

plain inundation) does have the decided advantage of continuous nutrient enrichment due to the decomposition of floodwater-introduced detritus (Nabhan 1983).

Dry Farming. Dry farming consists of a suite of agricultural techniques constructed to use direct rainfall or to divert rainfall runoff short distances to field locations. Dry farming is distinguished from ak-chin farming in that field locations for dry farming are usually located on flat river terraces and gently sloping bajada tops rather than on active alluvial fans.

Dry-farming features are found across much of the Hohokam regional system area, but are most prevalent in the Arizona Upland biome and the wetter portions of the northeastern corner of the Lower Colorado River Valley biome. Dry-farming features are seemingly absent from the western Papaguería and Gila Bend areas, presumably because low local precipitation levels would have inhibited such technology. It has been suggested (Crown 1987a) that some dry-farming systems date to as early as the Gila Butte phase (circa A.D. 750–800), but most appear to date after A.D. 900.

Dry-farming systems can range from very simple to quite complex, and from a few hundred square meters to scores of hectares in area. The major types of dry-farming features are schematically depicted in figure 9.1 (see also Masse 1979; Vivian 1974). Channeling borders presumably served to channel runoff and prevent it from debouching prematurely from the bajada or terrace slope; check dams, contour terraces, bordered terraces, and perhaps revetment terraces apparently served as soil and moisture traps for individual garden plots (see, however, Doolittle 1985). Bordered gardens (also referred to in the literature as "waffle gardens") aided in moisture conservation from direct precipitation; protective borders helped prevent erosive sheetflow from damaging crops planted on fields with slopes greater than about 5 degrees; and catchment basins (termed "retention basins" by Crown 1987b), which were filled by runoff and direct precipitation, may have provided water for drinking, pot irrigation, or for irrigating downslope fields. Gravel-mulched bordered gardens have been identified archaeologically in the Safford Valley, but it is unclear if they were constructed and used by the Hohokam occupants of this region.

Rock piles are by far the most ubiquitous dry-farming feature. These are groups of unmodified cobbles that have been gathered into clusters, mounds, or quasilinear arrangements. Rock piles are often found together with other features (especially check dams, and contour and bordered terraces), but are also commonly found alone.

I suggest that Hohokam rock piles are the residue from two distinct types of activity, which also may be largely temporally discrete. The first

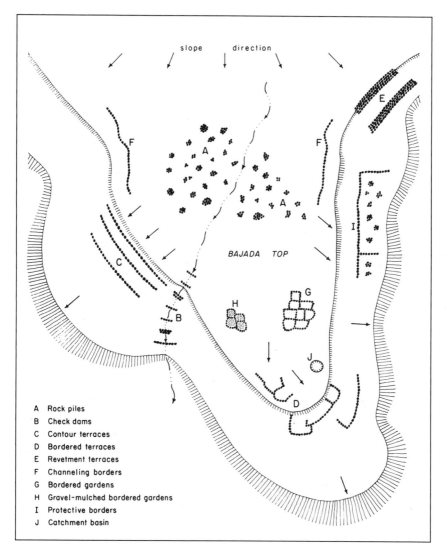

slope   direction

BAJADA   TOP

A   Rock piles
B   Check dams
C   Contour terraces
D   Bordered terraces
E   Revetment terraces
F   Channeling borders
G   Bordered gardens
H   Gravel-mulched bordered gardens
I   Protective borders
J   Catchment basin

Figure 9.1. *Schematic representation of various types of Hohokam dry-farming features.*

activity is simply that of the removal of stone from potential field areas, dating primarily between A.D. 900 and 1050 (Masse 1979). There is little evidence that the Hohokam cleared stone solely to augment runoff for downslope fields, as has been documented for dry-farming systems in Israel's Negev desert (Evenari, Shanan, and Tadmor 1971). The second activity is the purposeful gathering of stones to provide a suitable substrate for cultivating agave (and possibly cholla); other crops, such as corn, were at least sometimes planted in adjacent cleared areas (Fish, Fish, and Madsen 1989; Fish et al. 1985). This intensive use of agricultural mounds for agave production may be restricted largely to the late Sedentary and early Classic periods (ca. A.D. 1100–1250), although some systems may date to as early as the late Colonial period (Craig and Wallace 1987).

Irrigation. Hohokam irrigation systems (at least those extending onto the terraces away from the river floodplains) appear to have first developed during the Snaketown period, around A.D. 600–700 (Wilcox and Shenk 1977:180–81; Wilcox, McGuire, and Sternberg 1981:204). Perhaps the simplest Hohokam irrigation system is that reported from Montezuma's Well in the Verde Valley (Schroeder 1948), where a Sedentary period irrigation system diverted water from the outlet of a permanently flowing artesian spring (Montezuma's Well) to nearby agricultural plots. Somewhat more complex systems are those that divert water from small perennial or semiperennial streams into field areas several hundred meters away (Doyel 1984a; Doyel and Elson 1985). In a very real sense this is simply an elaboration of ak-chin farming, with the brush weirs and small ditches of the ak-chin system replaced by more substantial weirs and longer canals. Even more complex systems were probably associated with irrigation in the floodplains of the major perennial and semiperennial streams. A late Colonial or Sedentary period irrigation system has been documented recently in the floodplain of the Santa Cruz River near Tucson (Bernard-Shaw 1987); it is possible that such irrigation was similar to that known for the historical Pima Indians (Haury 1976:fig. 8.4; Wilcox, McGuire, and Sternberg 1981:fig. 6).

The most complex irrigation systems known for the Hohokam are those along the Salt River in and around the modern city of Phoenix (Ackerly 1988; Ackerly, Howard, and McGuire 1987; Herskovitz 1981; Masse 1976, 1981, 1987; Nials and Gregory 1989; Nicholas 1981; Nicholas and Feinman 1989; Nicholas and Neitzel 1984).

Figure 9.2 schematically depicts the major components of Phoenix Basin irrigation systems. The components depicted in this figure are derived from both excavation and the interpretation of aerial photographs (e.g., Masse 1981; Nicholas and Feinman 1989), and they are named with reference to modern irrigation terminology (see Nials and Gregory 1989). Three basic types of canals are suggested for Hohokam irrigation systems: main canals, distribution canals, and field laterals. Main canals extend from the canal intake to the first major junction at which the channel size is significantly reduced. Distribution canals represent those canal segments

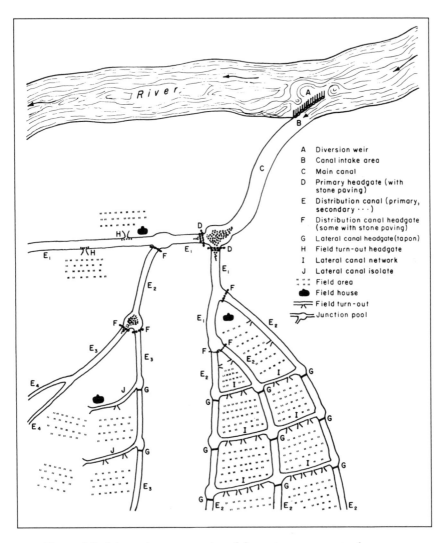

Figure 9.2. *Schematic representation of the major components of a Phoenix Basin Hohokam irrigation system.*

branching off the main canal or from other distribution canals that serve to conduct water to villages and to field laterals.

The terminal segment of a Hohokam irrigation system is the field lateral, which conveys water directly onto field areas. There are two distinct types of laterals. The term "lateral network" refers to laterals that are arranged in parallel sets, usually coupled with multiple distribution canals to create a weblike effect (fig. 9.2); the resulting grid parcels represent individual field areas (Israelsen and Hansen 1967; Nials and Gregory 1989). Lateral networks were the hallmark of the early Classic period.

By contrast, the "lateral canal isolate" did not necessarily operate in tandem with other laterals, and may have conveyed most of its water to fields situated near the lateral's mouth. Lateral isolates usually extend at an acute angle from the distribution canals and appear to be associated primarily with pre-Classic period irrigation.

There are a variety of other water conveyance features associated with Hohokam irrigation systems, including canal junctions (some with elaborate post-and-mat headgate structures, junction pool areas to slow and control water flow, and extensive stone pavings to retard erosion; see Ackerly, Howard, and McGuire 1987; Ackerly 1988); tapon post-and-mat structures to raise canal water level to facilitate debouchment into field laterals and turnouts; and field houses. However, despite the large size and seeming complexity of the Phoenix Basin irrigation systems, the Hohokam lacked certain critical engineering features, including permanent dam structures, drop structures, the general use of artificial linings to retard water seepage, and apparently a conception of the use of drainage canals (Masse 1987; Nials and Gregory 1989). These omissions prevented the Hohokam from achieving the level of sophistication necessary to deal successfully with various environmental hazards such as field waterlogging and salinization and the destructive effects of catastrophic river flooding.

Nicholas and Feinman (1989) have recently introduced the interesting proposition that at some point during the Classic period the Hohokam began to link different networks together by means of various crosscut canals. They suggest that such linkage, which was deduced from Nicholas's (1981) detailed and valuable study of several sets of aerial photographs, represents a response to decreased water availability for individual networks and to an increase in overall social differentiation.

While not wishing to dismiss their model outright, I nevertheless expect that Nicholas and Feinman's crosscut canals are, in fact, remodelings within irrigation community networks. The envisioned supra-irrigation community networks probably never existed, at least not in the form suggested by Nicholas and Feinman. Irrigation networks did not grow by simple accretion but achieved various temporal configurations through a combination of both gradual expansion and episodic large-scale change (see also Ackerly, Howard, and McGuire 1987). The nature and magnitude of these episodic changes are coming into clearer focus as we refine our analytical models and data recovery methodologies (Masse 1988; Nials, Gregory, and Graybill 1989).

THE ENVIRONMENTAL FACTOR

Recent detailed paleoenvironmental reconstructions have greatly enhanced our potential for understanding Hohokam culture history. Specifically, these include (1) the detailed reconstruction of climate and hydrological conditions in the lower Colorado Plateau (Dean et al. 1985; Euler et al. 1979), the broad parameters of which can be applied to southern Arizona (Jeffrey S. Dean, personal communication, 1987); and (2) Donald Graybill's (1989) reconstruction of Salt River annual streamflow for A.D. 740 to 1370. Both studies represent an important attempt to correlate aspects of environmental change or stasis with human behavior.

The period from A.D. 600 to 750 in the Colorado Plateau generally was a time of aggradation and high effective moisture, and at the same time there was little in the way of rapid oscillation in dendroclimatic variability. This situation would be likely to favor the development of irrigation systems, as well as other agricultural technologies.

The years 750 to 950 are characterized by degradation, low effective moisture, and the high likelihood of rapid oscillations in dendroclimatic variability. Such a situation would have had an adverse effect on all three major forms of Hohokam agriculture. However, beginning around 900 to 950 and continuing until about 1100, effective moisture is quite high and aggradation is prominent; dendroclimatic variability is characterized by infrequent oscillations after A.D. 1000. These are ideal conditions, especially between 1000 and 1150, for the growth and expansion of all three major Hohokam agricultural technologies.

Beginning around 1100 to 1150, there is a gradual decrease in effective moisture, which culminates around 1350 and continues low for the remainder of the Hohokam sequence. There is a short but prominent period of degradation between 1100 and 1150, but aggradation is again the rule between 1150 and 1300. Dendroclimatic oscillations are not pronounced (at least in terms of rapid shifts) during the period from 1000 to 1350. These various conditions would have fostered a decline in the suitability of dry farming beginning around 1150 to 1200, and perhaps would have had deleterious effects on irrigation and ak-chin farming in the period from 1100 to 1150. These technologies (excluding dry farming) would have been satisfactory, however, during the period from 1200 to 1350.

The years A.D. 1350 to 1550 were marked by rapid and dramatic oscillations in dendroclimate and included greatly depressed effective moisture values and a major cycle of degradation. This situation would have had a profound and lasting unfavorable impact on Hohokam agriculture.

Our understanding of the relationship between environment and Hohokam irrigation has been brought into sharper focus by Graybill's (1989)
recent statistical coupling of historic tree-ring widths and Salt River
streamflow in order to retrodict prehistoric streamflow patterns from the
analysis of prehistoric tree-ring widths. He has thus estimated Salt River
discharge for each year between 740 and 1370, assuming that years of
exceptionally large streamflow also may have witnessed catastrophic flood
episodes (Ackerly 1988; Nials, Gregory, and Graybill 1989). Gregory has
detailed aspects of this reconstruction in the previous chapter, and the
reader is referred to his discussion and to the graph depicting the reconstructed streamflow (see fig. 8.4).

HOHOKAM SUBSISTENCE AND SOCIETY

It should be readily apparent that the Hohokam regional system was
closely intertwined with the variable fabric of climate and environment. I
shall conclude this paper with a synopsis of what I feel are the salient
characteristics of the Hohokam regional system. This task will be accomplished by briefly sketching certain temporal segments of Hohokam
culture history, highlighting the perceived effect of environment and subsistence change on the growth and trajectory of the regional system.

THE BEGINNINGS OF THE REGIONAL SYSTEM

I place the origins of the Hohokam regional system in the latter portion of
the Snaketown phase (ca. A.D. 700). It was at this point that the Hohokam
first began to settle in, or at least interact with, areas away from the Gila and
Salt rivers (e.g., the Tucson Basin, lower San Pedro Valley, northern Papaguería, and lower Verde Valley).

The catalysts for initial regional system growth presumably included the
development of irrigation agriculture (the idea for which may have been
introduced from Mexico along with cotton and other crops of the Lower
Sonoran Agricultural Complex), the regularization of long-distance trade
and exchange, and population growth that would have been facilitated by
the other two factors. Settlement locations and the incipient boundaries of
the regional system seem to coincide with those areas most favorable for
floodwater and irrigation farming and for the gathering of mesquite and
cactus products. These boundaries also coincide with the margins of other
cultural groups (e.g., the Mogollon of southeastern Arizona), who, like the
Hohokam, were going through a period of initial societal expansion and
integration.

I suggest that the initial construction of ballcourts did not take place

until after these regional populations had been in place for a few generations, and that the formalization of economic and social ties was the
primary impetus for their construction.

THE COLONIAL TO SEDENTARY PERIOD TRANSITION

Despite the notable artistic achievements of the Santa Cruz phase Hohokam at Snaketown (Haury 1976) and elsewhere, I do not view these
populations as being either very large or very socially complex. The devastating floods in the Salt River (and probably the Gila River) between 798
and 805 in all likelihood led to experimentation with dry-farming techniques and perhaps ak-chin farming as well. As noted by Nials and his
colleagues (1989), these floods seemingly led to the commingling of small
Hohokam groups with non-Hohokam populations outside the boundaries
of the regional system (Haas 1971; Halbirt and Ciolek-Torrello 1985;
Morris 1970). The return to more stable environmental conditions after
A.D. 805 may have muted the full development of these alternative subsistence and settlement strategies.

During the period from 823 to 887, the Hohokam probably became
increasingly reliant on their irrigation systems, with community irrigation
networks "incrementally expanded" (as defined by Doolittle 1984) by the
construction of new distribution canals and their associated farmlands and
small villages or hamlets. However, it is likely that the large streamflow
discharge in A.D. 888, and especially the presumed disastrous flooding
accompanying the huge discharge of 899, completely interrupted Hohokam irrigation practices for one or two years (Nials, Gregory, and Graybill
1989). It may have been several years into the first decade of the tenth
century before the irrigation systems were fully repaired.

This situation, although similar to that of the 798 to 805 flooding, was
apparently even more disruptive, given the larger size of irrigation community networks and the populations that they serviced. Due to limitations
inherent in these strategies, the demands of basic sustenance could not be
met simply by the intensification of hunting and wild plant gathering;
therefore, the Hohokam had to rely, once again, on ak-chin and especially
dry-farming practices. I suggest that those villages and hamlets on the
terminus of irrigation community networks may have been completely
abandoned for a substantial period of time due to the absence of potable
and agricultural water, with the displaced populations establishing new
settlements in areas favorable to ak-chin and dry-farming techniques. Even
villages at the proximal ends of irrigation community networks—or those
that previously had relied on floodplain irrigation and floodplain inundation agriculture—may have participated in this partial Hohokam diaspora

by implementing or intensifying disjunctive patterns of land use. This overall pattern illustrates Boserup's (1981:6) observation that important technological changes usually accompany large-scale population movements.

The Hohokam regional system reached its maximum size as a result of the population movements at the beginning of the tenth century and the subsequent "niche-packing" that occurred during the next 150 years as the Hohokam strove toward full utilization of their environment. Settlements founded as a consequence of the A.D. 899 flooding not only helped to assuage the immediate effects of that flooding, but continued to grow and thrive with the aid of increasingly advantageous environmental conditions of ak-chin and dry-farming practices.

In fact, the very success of those settlements situated in areas somewhat marginal for irrigation agriculture had a profound effect on the nature (and perhaps even the eventual demise) of the Hohokam regional system. The new settlement and subsistence patterns required substantial restructuring of the mechanisms for regional economic and social integration. I suggest that the proliferation of "late Colonial" and Sedentary period ballcourts, and even changes in ritual orientation (as defined in Wilcox and Sternberg 1983), represent the attempt by Phoenix Basin communities to maintain some control over regional economic exchange and alliance systems in the face of the sudden decentralizing settlement shift. These efforts resulted in some community craft specialization, such as large-scale pottery manufacturing at Snaketown (Haury 1976), and in the still somewhat poorly understood networks controlling the collection, manufacture, and distribution of marine shell items (McGuire and Howard 1987) and the distribution of other exotic artifacts (Doyel, this volume).

Despite these trappings of social complexity, I do not believe that any pre-Classic period community network achieved a chiefdom-level organization. Such complexity was thwarted by the relatively low population density existing across most of the Sedentary period Hohokam landscape, coupled with a settlement and subsistence pattern which in times of environmental stress fostered population movement and the development of alternative systems of agricultural production less intensive than that of irrigation (see also Powell 1983).

COLLAPSE AND REORGANIZATION OF THE REGIONAL SYSTEM

It is somewhat ironic that the most striking transformation of Hohokam culture, the collapse of the regional system at around A.D. 1100, has no clear-cut environmental correlate as do the changes at A.D. 798 to 805 and 899. On the other hand, the large streamflow in 1052, and especially four sizable discharges that occurred between 1080 and 1090 (including a 105-year recurrence event at 1087), may have played a role in the collapse. There is strong corroborative evidence from Pueblo Grande (Masse 1976, 1981, 1986) and La Cuenca del Sedimento (Ackerly 1988; Masse 1987) of severe flood damage to irrigation systems in the Phoenix Basin at about this time period, and once again major portions of Hohokam irrigation systems seem to have been incapacitated.

The destruction of irrigation systems is not sufficient by itself to explain the abandonment (or general settlement relocation) of broad areas of the Hohokam regional system, including communities utilizing non-irrigating methods of agriculture; thus, it would seem that other factors were also at play. For example, there is a slight period of hydrologic degradation between 1100 and 1150, which may have affected the subsistence base of some regional communities, but even this should not have the effect of complete settlement reorganization or abandonment.

Another hypothesis deserving serious consideration is that the more powerful irrigation community networks (especially those near Phoenix) may have attempted to forcefully recruit labor to assist in the repair of their canal systems, or perhaps levied a tribute (apart from labor itself) to help defray the costs of system repair and to provide sustenance during the repair period (see also Wilcox 1979b; Wilcox and Sternberg 1983). Such a scenario is consonant with the reorganization of the regional system, the rise of Classic period sociopolitical complexity, and the presence of numerous fortified or defensive hilltop sites that ring the Phoenix Basin. This may also help to explain why the reorganization of the regional system is not a uniform process, as might be the expected response to a single catastrophic environmental event, but rather seems to occur in various episodes between about 1080 and 1130.

THE HOHOKAM CLASSIC PERIOD

In referring to the demographic and social changes that occurred in southern Arizona around A.D. 1100 as a "reorganization," I suggest that the Hohokam regional system did not end, per se, but instead simply changed character, albeit rather drastically. Part of this configurational difference may reflect a change in emphasis from disjunctive land use to zonal patterns of control over important subsistence resources, especially in relation to irrigation agriculture. Such circumscription, regardless of cause and even in the absence of overall population increase, would have created a patchwork of densely populated areas (such as the Salt River valley around Phoenix and the Tonto Basin), each comprising one or more regional networks. This settlement pattern would have facilitated the development of vertical hierarchies of social complexity and control (i.e., the "minimal chiefdom" defined by Carneiro 1981), as well as the spread and acceptance of various cosmological and religious belief systems emanating from Mexico, as noted by some of the other contributors to this volume.

The Hohokam Classic period exhibits several striking examples of the relationships between environment, subsistence, and social structure. For example, the apparent shift in emphasis to the growing of agave in dry-farming fields between about 1150 and 1250 appears to be a response to decreases in effective moisture, which would favor the cultivation of agave over less drought-resistant crops. At the same time, it should be noted that agave played an extremely important part in social rituals throughout central and northern Mexico (such as the drinking of the fermented beverage *pulque* in rituals of sacrifice), and it may be that the Hohokam began to utilize agave for similar ritualistic purposes.

It seems likely that the Phoenix Basin Hohokam, especially those populations on the Salt River, relied increasingly on their irrigation systems during the period from 1100 to 1358. The systems were expanded to their greatest extent by at least 1200 to 1250, and the often striking regularity in the placement of distribution canals and lateral networks along the medial and terminal portions of some networks reflects a good working knowledge of structural design and system management. I do not believe that such systems were derived solely by means of simple incremental expansion; rather, large segments of each irrigation community network may have been constructed as a unit.

The streamflow data from the period between 1197 and 1276 exhibit a number of unusually pronounced highs and lows, with the high discharges most often separated by a decade or more of moderate to low flow. This situation would have necessitated the frequent remodeling of canals near the proximal portion of each system (as is evidenced at La Cuenca del Sedimento), made expansion of the canal systems difficult, and hindered the production of crop surpluses. The power of the Phoenix Basin regional networks may have been weakened as a result, which may have fostered the development and political strengthening of competitors such as the Tucson Basin Hohokam and the somewhat heterogeneous populations along the eastern portions of the Hohokam regional system (i.e., the lower San Pedro Valley, Safford Valley, and Globe-Miami area). These groups eventually crystallized into the Salado culture (Doyel and Haury 1976).

The period from 1277 to 1298 witnessed either moderate or extremely low streamflow, followed by a 17-year period (1298–1314) with five large flows and two smaller, but still sizable flows. It is my belief that many or most of the irrigation systems around Phoenix were largely inoperable

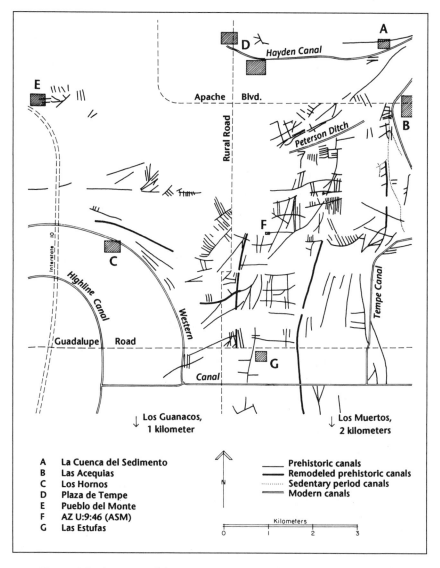

Figure 9.3. *A portion of the Las Acequias–Los Muertos irrigation community network as seen on an aerial photograph taken in 1967. (Courtesy Landis Aerial Photography, 3 January 1967, #B-26.)*

throughout much of the latter period. I suspect that many remodeled canals were constructed shortly after 1314, presumably as a major concerted effort over a period of just one or two years to reestablish the main distribution canals and some of the associated farmlands. Figure 9.3 depicts the locations of remodeled canals that appear to date to this period.

This irrigation system repair effort resulted in the last, brief flowering of Hohokam culture. The period 1315 to 1357 had moderate or low streamflow, which seems to coincide with the cultural manifestations that scholars have traditionally considered as the Civano phase of the Hohokam Classic period (Doyel 1981; Gumerman and Haury 1979; Haury 1945, 1976). Although low water flows may have occasionally hampered crop productivity, it was generally an environmentally favorable time for the Hohokam, especially compared with the previous century.

The final environmental nail in the Hohokam coffin took the form of a major discharge year in A.D. 1358 (a streamflow recurrence interval of 158 years), coupled with the beginnings of the exceptionally severe period of low effective moisture and hydrologic degradation, which persisted until the middle of the sixteenth century. Most irrigation systems (especially on the Salt River) probably were destroyed by the presumed catastrophic flooding in that year, or perhaps by the hypothesized flooding in A.D. 1380–82 noted by Gregory in the previous chapter; the systems seemingly were never reestablished. With the agricultural base largely destroyed, the Hohokam Postclassic period (the Polvoron phase of the Classic period) witnessed the final dissolution of Hohokam society.

Despite the general tenor of this chapter, I am not a strict environmental determinist and I admit that my treatment has glossed over many critical aspects of the Hohokam regional system—including the impact of Mexican products and cosmology, information and product exchange with other Southwestern cultural groups, and structural changes in various specific regional Hohokam communities. Nevertheless, it seems likely that the Hohokam regional system germinated and was nurtured by the beneficence of the Sonoran desert and the Gila River; that it changed character when confronted by major environmental perturbations; and that it collapsed when the oscillations of the cultural system were unable to buffer the oscillations of the environmental system. The Hohokam mastery of the American desert was, in fact, simply a prolonged illusion. The desert was master, and the Hohokam were never quite able to throw off the shackles of their environmental bondage.

————— *Acknowledgments* —————

I thank my fellow volume contributors for five days of intensive interchange, and I particularly thank the Hohokam cohort, with whom I have enjoyed a long and rewarding professional relationship. Emil W. Haury, William H. Doelle, Jerry B. Howard, Suzanne R. Fish, Paul R. Fish, Donald A. Graybill, Arthur W. Vokes, Robert E. Gasser, Gary Huckleberry, Gary P. Nabhan, Charles H. Miksicek, and

Neal W. Ackerly have also stimulated much of my recent thinking about Hohokam subsistence. Howard, Gasser, Doelle, Paul Fish, Cory D. Breternitz, John C. Ravesloot, Glen E. Rice, and Bettina Rosenberg kindly provided me with unpublished data and manuscripts. Charles Sternberg did his usual skillful magic on the illustrations. To each of these individuals, *aloha* and *mahalo*.

Chapter 10

Hohokam Exchange and Interaction

DAVID E. DOYEL

THE greatest time depth and subsequent elaboration of Hohokam cultural expression is found in a physiographic province referred to as the Phoenix, or the Salt-Gila, Basin. This region contains just under 6,400 square kilometers (4,000 sq. mi.) of Sonoran desert vegetation surrounding the drainage and confluence areas of the Gila, Salt, San Pedro, and Santa Cruz rivers. Some researchers (Di Peso 1956; Hayden 1970) have suggested that the appellation "Hohokam" be restricted to this area. Others have applied the term to an area in excess of 80,000 square kilometers (50,000 sq. mi.) encompassing most of south-central and southern Arizona (Haury 1976; Doyel 1979). This region defines the area within which Hohokam pottery and other characteristics are most commonly found.

If the Hohokam region is restricted to the major desert river valleys listed above and extended somewhat to the south into the Papaguería, an area of 43,000 square kilometers (27,000 sq. mi.) is defined, which is roughly equivalent to the area encompassed by the Chaco regional system (Judge, this volume). Although Hohokam procurement and exchange activities (in shell, salt, obsidian, turquoise, etc.) clearly went beyond these limits, the great majority of exchange of goods and services undoubtedly occurred within the 43,000-square-kilometer area. As Haury (1976), Doyel (1984b), and Masse (this volume) have pointed out, this area roughly defines the distribution of the Sonoran desert in southern Arizona, where intensive agriculture could be practiced along with the harvesting of mesquite, cactus, and animal products.

Long-distance trade in shell and stone is documented for the preceramic horizon and for the Pioneer period of the Hohokam sequence (A. Howard 1987; Bostwick and Shackley 1987), but it is between A.D. 700 and 1400 that the operation of Hohokam commercial systems is most apparent. It will be suggested herein that the Hohokam initiated, maintained, and regulated numerous corridors of commerce both within and beyond the boundaries of their own distinctive regional system. Commerce included the movement of prestige items, utilitarian and ornamental products, foodstuffs, and information. Both material products and site structural properties reveal the operation of these ancient economic systems.

Trade, commerce, exchange, and interaction all have rather vague connotations. My thinking closely follows that of Colton (1941:308), whose definition of commerce includes both trade (the exchange of items among or between parties) and other activities that do not involve actual exchange but still would be considered activities of a commercial nature (long-distance expeditions, resource acquistion, production for exchange, etc.). This definition does not require a standard medium of exchange (money), but it does imply that institutional mechanisms existed to effect the flow of a wide variety of products and materials.

Trade was of great importance to the historic Pima and Papago Indians (Russell 1908; Underhill 1939). The redistribution of food, the exchange of food products for labor, and other social and economic conventions have been documented. A limiting factor in the study of prehistoric exchange is that not all items exchanged will remain identifiable in the archaeological record. For example, to acquire corn and wheat from the neighboring Pima, the Papago traded numerous perishable goods: cactus seeds, syrup, and fruit; agave cakes and fiber; wild gourds; peppers; acorns; sleeping mats; baskets; dried meat of deer and mountain sheep; buckskin; various pigments; salt; and so forth (Underhill 1939:103). Given that the Pima and Papago inhabited the same environment as the Hohokam and that prehistoric trade between the Papaguería and the Phoenix Basin has been demonstrated, the above caveat should be kept in mind in any attempt to reconstruct prehistoric Hohokam exchange.

Because the Pima did not express significant complexity in social organization, it is felt by some authorities that the prehistoric Hohokam also lacked any strong tendencies toward social complexity (Haury 1976; Woodbury 1961a). The Pima and Papago, however, did not build hundreds of miles of canals, 225 ballcourts, or over 60 platform mounds; neither did they maintain an economic system encompassing some 80,000 square kilometers in area. They possessed neither the population levels nor the complex settlement hierarchies documented for the prehistoric period. The Hohokam cultural sequence reveals a dynamic record of growth and change, which cannot be fully understood by the use of static, historically based analog models (Doyel 1979:550).

MESOAMERICAN MATERIALS

The relationship between the Hohokam of southern Arizona and other cultural groups located farther to the south has been a continuing subject of debate for several generations. Close affinity to Mesoamerica seemed to be indicated when several well-known Mayanist archaeologists verified the presence of a ballcourt at the site of Snaketown (Gladwin et al. 1937:38). For the next 40 years, the ruling hypothesis held that the Hohokam were immigrants into southern Arizona from Mesoamerica (see Doyel 1981 for a summary). The presence of capped mounds, clay figurines, polished red ware and red-on-buff pottery, and other attributes were used to support this position. Although the history of research in the Chaco region contains battle lines drawn between the "Mexicanist" and the "indigenist" models (see Judge, this volume; Toll, this volume), no one has seriously suggested the wholesale movement of Mesoamerican immigrants into Chaco Canyon. The history of research in the Hohokam region contains a similar range of Mexicanist to indigenist models, but also includes immigration theories to account for the archaeological record. This discrepancy is explained by the presence of a well-documented Basketmaker sequence in the Chaco Basin and, until recently, a corresponding lack of documentation on the elusive Pioneer period in the Phoenix Basin.

The nature of Hohokam-Mesoamerican relationships will continue to be debated for several generations to come. Meanwhile, tangible physical evidence does exist to document trade and interaction with a number of Mesoamerican populations. Although a few pottery sherds of suspected southern origin have been found (Haury 1976), most objects of Mesoamerican manufacture recovered from Hohokam sites are ceremonial in nature and are found in restricted contexts, usually in cemetery areas.

Of the 500 copper bells found in Southwestern sites, fewer than 200 are from the Hohokam region (Sprague 1964; Haury 1976:278; Nelson 1981: 398–420). Most of the copper bells in Hohokam sites date to the Sedentary period and were found at Snaketown (28) and Gatlin (60). Copper bells dating to the Classic period (26) came from a large number of sites, most containing platform mounds, but provenience data for many of these are lacking (Nelson 1981:403). The discovery of copper bells in the late fill of the Gatlin platform mound (Wasley 1960:259–60) and in a masonry wall of a Chacoan kiva in the Bis sa'ani Ruin located near Chaco Canyon (Breternitz, Doyel, and Marshall 1982:443), both dating to the early 1100s, suggests a similarity in offeratory behavior that is indeed intriguing.

Approximately 100 pyrites-encrusted, sandstone-backed mirrors (or plaques) have been recovered from Hohokam sites dating to the Colonial and Sedentary periods. They are thought to reveal clear evidence of direct contacts with Mesoamerica (Gladwin et al. 1937; Woodward 1941), and some are said to contain Mesoamerican designs, such as flying parrots and images of Tezcatlipoca (a major Toltec-Aztec deity). Most were recovered from rich cremation burials at Snaketown (80) and Grewe (14). The distribution of mosaic mirrors is restricted to the Hohokam region, except for the two recovered from Pueblo Bonito (Nelson 1981:423, 446–47). Di Peso (1974) has suggested that these artifacts point to the presence of Mesoamerican religious cults among the Hohokam.

Of the 200 scarlet macaws, military macaws, and thick-billed parrots recovered from archaeological sites in the Southwest, fewer than 3 percent (5 individuals) are from Hohokam sites; these date to between A.D. 700 and 1100. In contrast, 35 are from Chaco, 48 are from the Wupatki area, and over 50 have been recovered in Late Mogollon or Western Pueblo sites (Hargrave 1970:53; Nelson 1981:390–97). The infrequent occurrence of these birds in the Hohokam region and their common occurrence in other areas after 1100 is enigmatic, but suggests that the Hohokam were not strong participants in the ceremonialism emanating from the Casas Grandes region of northern Mexico, the presumed source of the exotic birds (Di Peso 1974).

SHELL

Because of its durability, its ubiquity, its restricted source areas, and its adaptability to a wide range of form and style, marine shell has traditionally been of interest to Southwestern scholars (Gladwin et al. 1937; Haury 1945; Di Peso 1956; Nelson 1981; Vokes 1983; McGuire and Howard 1987). The Hohokam probably served as middlemen and as producers and traders of shell products (Colton 1941; Tower 1945). The discovery of specialized tool kits, shell-manufacturing debris, and whole shell caches from various sites supports the inference that people in the Papagueria and Phoenix Basin areas were involved in the production of shell items for exchange (Haury 1976:305; A. Howard 1983, 1985). Hohokam pottery has been recovered from coastal sites in southern California and along petroglyph-marked trails leading to the source areas for Gulf of California shell (Hayden 1972; Nelson 1981). Several authors have suggested that shell may have been used as a medium of exchange (Doelle 1980; Marmaduke and Martynec 1986). Among the Pima, a shell necklace was equal to a metate in exchange value (Colton 1941:319).

Quantitative data on shell, such as weight, assemblage variation, and counts, are not systematically reported by all authors. Exceptions include Ann Howard's recent study (1985:460), based on a sample of 20,000 items from 63 sites, and Richard Nelson's (1981:174–97) inventory of 100 site collections, which contained 4,400 bracelets, 350 pendants, 200 *Conus* tinklers, 2,850 beads identifiable to genus, and 65,000 disc beads.

Additional comparative data on the distribution of shell and other artifacts from selected Hohokam sites is reported here. As a potentially useful measure of comparison, sherd-to-shell recovery ratios have also been provided (table 10.1). It should be pointed out, however, that such ratios should not be used for direct interpretive purposes without considerable qualification. For example, the Escalante Ruin group has one of the highest sherd-to-shell ratios listed (56:1). As stated elsewhere (Doyel 1981:13, 19), the sherd samples from these sites could have been increased significantly if time had permitted more excavation in the associated trash mounds. Snaketown has one of the lowest ratios (275:1), yet this site is thought to be one of the few pre–A.D. 1100 shell production centers located in the Phoenix Basin (McGuire and Howard 1987:122; Seymour 1988). The low ratio is a result of the extensive stratigraphic excavations conducted at Snaketown in the 1960s, which generated a staggering 1,500,000 sherds (Haury 1976).

Sites with platform mounds (Snaketown, Gatlin, Escalante, Brady Wash, and Las Colinas) all reflect high shell species diversity but widely different sherd-to-shell ratios. Lago Seco is a specialized shell jewelry manufacturing site located in southwestern Arizona; compare the high ratio from this site (21:1) with Snaketown, where one of the lowest ratios occurs. These data underscore the problem of using such ratios to address issues of exchange and the organization of production, as has recently been attempted (Teague 1985). Future studies should be sensitive to variable excavation strategies, sample quality, site formation processes, and refined temporal control.

Although exceptions do occur (Wasley and Benham 1968:279; Hayden 1957:171), shell artifacts are common on most Hohokam habitation sites. We can compare the figures in table 10.1 with the results of the Chaco Project excavations, which yielded a total of 203 pieces of shell from all sites (Toll, this volume). Nearby, two seasons of excavations in the Late Bonito phase Bis sa'ani Community yielded a total of 22 shell artifacts (Debowski 1982:1093).

STONE AND MINERALS

That portion of the Phoenix Basin located between Casa Grande Ruins, Los Muertos, and Las Colinas lacked good-quality resources for the production

TABLE 10.1. Shell items, potsherds, and other artifacts recovered from selected Hohokam sites

Site	Shell Items	Species	Minerals	Sherds	Sherd-to-Shell Ratio
Snaketown (Source: Haury 1976)	5,440	33	21	1,500,000	275:1
Cashion Site (Source: Antieu 1981)	795	5	5	37,228	47:1
New River (8)[a] (Source: Doyel and Elson 1985)	248	10	4	93,328	375:1
Gatlin Site (Source: Wasley and Johnson 1965)	284	17	2	32,442	115:1
Escalante Ruin group (4) (Source: Doyel 1974)	506	15	17	28,700	56:1
Salt-Gila (18) (Source: Teague and Crown 1982–83)	2,534	22	?[b]	478,485	189:1
Pueblo Grande (Source: A. Howard 1985)	2,120	?	?	?	?
Las Colinas (Source: Hammack and Sullivan 1981)	972	20	5	134,382	138:1
Santa Rita (8) (Source: Ferg et al. 1984)	486	13	8	29,329	60:1
Tucson Aqueduct Project (6) (Source: Callahan 1988)	1,392	23	10	159,000	114:1
Lago Seco (Source: Huckell 1979)	711	13	0	15,500	21:1
Totals	15,488			2,508,394	162:1

[a] The number of sites containing shell is indicated in parentheses.
[b] ? = unknown.

of ground- and chipped-stone tools. Although local river and terrace gravels supplied the basalts and quartzites that dominate most lithic assemblages, the Hohokam were willing to trade or travel to acquire specialized formal tools, minerals, raw materials, and ornaments. Products traded include a variety of minerals utilized for ornamentation and ceremonial activities, as well as finished stone tools utilized for subsistence functions such as resource processing and food preparation.

GROUND-STONE TOOLS

Field research to the north of Phoenix has revealed numerous specialized sites for the production of manos and metates dating between A.D. 850 and 1050 (Hoffman, Doyel, and Elson 1985; Bruder 1983b). These activities focused on an unusual phase of brown- to gray-colored quartz-basalt stone, also known as New River andesite (Schaller 1985, 1987). One recent estimate suggests that over 4,000 metates could have been produced at one of the larger New River production sites (Hoffman, Doyel, and Elson 1985:683). Thin-section analysis has suggested the presence of New River quartz-basalt 30 kilometers to the south at the large village of Las Colinas, where it represents 30 percent of the ground-stone assemblage during the Sedentary and Classic periods (Doyel and Elson 1985). Similar material has been identified at other sites in the Salt River valley (Mitchell 1988).

The high incidence of severe dental infection among the Hohokam (Merbs 1985:138; Barnes 1987) may have encouraged selection of good-quality stone for grinding corn. The self-sharpening properties and the availability of New River quartz-basalt apparently supported an active exchange system with the villages to the south along the Salt River, where the local gravels are dominated by orthoquartzites (Kokalis 1971). Red-on-buff pottery, shell jewelry, and other items appear to have been traded into the New River area from the south (Doyel 1985b). The absence of suitable stone for grinding implements has also been noted along the Gila (although the Santan Mountains may represent a local source), where similar exchange networks may have developed (Haury 1976:273; Schaller 1987).

PROJECTILE POINTS

Thousands of projectile points have been recovered from cremation deposits at Hohokam sites dating prior to A.D. 1100 (Wasley and Johnson 1965; Haury 1976; Nelson 1981). Many of these are made from nonlocal stone, such as quartz, chert, chalcedony, and obsidian. Haury (1976:277) notes the paucity of obsidian raw material and debris at Snaketown, although obsidian points were common; he also suggests that chert may have been traded in from southeastern Arizona. This evidence, combined with technological analysis, suggests the production of projectile points by specialists (Crabtree 1973:31; Haury 1976:297).

Shackley (1988:754) has identified at least 18 sources of obsidian within the southwestern region. Studies indicate that late Archaic and Hohokam populations were utilizing a number of sources located primarily within Arizona (Bostwick and Shackley 1987). It appears that changes in the use of source areas occurred over time, with northern sources more dominant during the pre-Classic period and southern sources becoming dominant during the Classic. It is also possible that particular projectile point styles are correlated with the type of obsidian used (Landis 1988:435). Obsidian raw materials become more widespread during the Classic period, and caches of obsidian nodules have been found at various sites, including Escalante, Casa Grande, and Pueblo Grande (Doyel 1974; Hayden 1957; Nelson 1981:233–40).

OTHER STONE

Bernard-Shaw (1983:433–34) has suggested that tabular knives, used for agave processing, were being traded. Tabular schist and slate utilized for the production of palettes (over 325 were recovered from Snaketown) were probably obtained for production by specialists (Haury 1976:286). Other stone items circulated through the system include schist slabs and axes (Colton 1941:314). A large number of axes, including numerous unfinished specimens, were found at Pueblo Grande, possibly suggesting a manufacturing function for this site.

MINERALS AND ORNAMENTAL STONE

Haury (1976:376) lists over 20 different minerals from Snaketown. A similar number was recovered from the Escalante Ruin group; in total, these weighed 2,800 grams (6.2 lbs.) and included red ochre, copper ores, chrysolite, limonite, gallena, and other materials (Debowski 1974). Haury (1976:276–79), Wood (1985:248–50), and Nelson (1981:238) identify source areas for some of these minerals, but more research is badly needed. The source areas for most of these items lie outside of the Phoenix Basin.

Argillite was used to produce rings, pendants, beads, nose and lip plugs, overlay, and carved effigy vessels. Source areas include the Del Rio mines in the upper Agua Fria–middle Verde area and the northern Tonto Basin (Bartlett 1939; Fish and Fish 1977:42). Stone bowls made of argillite were found along with raw material at the Cashion Site, and 14 carved stone objects made of argillite were recovered from cremations at Snaketown (Antieu 1981:195, 227; Gladwin et al. 1937:126).

Lange (1982) has reported sites northeast of the Tonto Basin dating between 900 and 1100 which contain red-on-buff pottery, shell, and extensive evidence of steatite reduction and manufacturing. Harris (1974: 26, 86) concluded that the Hohokam occupation of the nearby Vosberg area was directed primarily toward the exploitation of steatite and serpentine.

Turquoise is rare in Hohokam sites prior to the Sedentary period. Approximately 4,000 beads and 300 pendants have been inventoried, with the majority of the beads coming from caches (Nelson 1981:357, 363). Little waste material from manufacturing has been found. Compare these figures to the 56,000 pieces found in a single room in Pueblo Bonito, or to the estimated one-half million pieces from the entire site (Mathien 1984:180; Toll, this volume). Turquoise beads from Snaketown submitted for neutron activation analysis suggested a source near Baker, California (Haury 1976:277), whereas additional analysis of other beads from Snaketown suggested a source area near Cerrillos, New Mexico (Nelson 1981: 383–84; Weigand and Harbottle 1987). Ravesloot (1987:151) has reported turquoise excavated from a site in Tucson, some of which is apparently from Cerrillos. A Colonial period site also located near Tucson is said to contain more than 2,000 pieces of turquoise derived from a source in southeastern Arizona (American Antiquity 1987).

CERAMICS

Hohokam ceramics represent the longest prehistoric ceramic tradition in the Southwest, lasting over 1,500 years and representing a unified tradition through time and space (Haury 1976; Zazlow and Dittert 1977; Masse 1982). Formal analysis of stylistic and technological attributes has detected variations suggestive of differences in the place of production and the presence of local styles of decoration among the plain, red, and red-on-buff wares (Neitzel 1984; Crown 1983b; Cable 1985). Studies of temper reveal that production and distribution systems for plain ware were different than for red ware and decorated pottery (Abbott 1983:105). Production centers for red-on-buff and the later red wares have been proposed by numerous researchers (Doyel 1977a, 1981; Abbott 1983:106), but the possibility of multiple manufacturing loci has not been excluded. Petrographic analysis has supported the nonlocal origins of buff ware in some areas (Doyel and Elson 1985). It is suggested here that specialized production of pottery among the Hohokam began during the Pioneer period and is reflected in different ways throughout the remainder of the sequence.

NONLOCAL CERAMICS: OVERVIEW

Although non-Hohokam pottery entered the Phoenix Basin from all directions, it does not appear to have entered in great quantity. Crown (1985a) reports a total of 28 nonlocal pottery vessels from the entire desert region; most occur as burial goods at sites containing public architecture. From a total of 2,513,965 sherds recovered from numerous sites spanning the entire sequence, intrusive pottery sherds number slightly more than 2,100, or 0.0009 percent (Doyel 1987, 1989). My recent analysis of intrusive pottery recovered during the 1925–40 excavations at Pueblo Grande suggests that a nonlocal vessel entered the site once every seven years between A.D. 700 and 1400, although the rates of exchange varied through time.

Crown (1984a, 1985a) has recently published an important study of ceramic interaction in the Hohokam region. Differential distributions of certain pottery types led her to propose that the major rivers served as barriers to ceramic exchange. I have since inspected three additional intrusive sherd collections, including the recent excavations at Las Colinas (Beckwith 1988), the material from Pueblo Grande, and from La Ciudad (Wilcox 1987a); this sample more than doubles that available to Crown. These sites contain ballcourts and platform mounds and are located in Phoenix on the north side of the Salt River along the same irrigation network. Table 10.2 shows the results of this analysis, and also includes data from both excavations at Snaketown and Las Colinas. It should be noted that no claims can be made for sample comparability across these cases.

NONLOCAL CERAMICS IN THE SALT RIVER VALLEY

Tusayan/Kayenta pottery types are common at most sites. Interestingly, the second highest category for each site is different; for Las Colinas, southern Arizona pottery is strong; at La Ciudad, Little Colorado White Ware is second; at Pueblo Grande, corrugated brown ware is the second commonest intrusive. Significant differences are also present in other categories (i.e., Hopi, Little Colorado, Cibola, corrugated brown ware, etc.).

A glaring difference in results relative to Crown's study is apparent when the Cibola White Ware category is inspected. Crown's data (from Las Colinas, 1968 excavations only) revealed that no Cibola White Ware was being obtained at sites on the north side of the Salt River. This conclusion can now be attributed to sampling error, as both La Ciudad and Pueblo Grande contain significant amounts of Cibola wares (19 of 130 vessels at

TABLE 10.2. *Percentages of intrusive ceramics recovered from selected Hohokam sites for all time periods*

Pottery Type	Snaketown[a] (824)	La Ciudad[b] (171)	Pueblo Grande[c] (368)[e]	Las Colinas[d] (1968/1982) (443/1,536)	(Total: 1,979)
Mogollon/Mimbres	58	–	–	–/1	1
Kayenta/Tusayan	26	47	30	28/59	52
Hopi	–	10	9	5/1	2
Little Colorado	–	12	4	7/4	4
White Mountain Red Ware	–	1	5	–/*	*
Cibola White Ware	1	11	7	*/1	1
Corrugated Brown Ware	1	4	18	–/1	1
Southern Arizona[f]	2	9	17	53/15	24
Western Arizona	–	–	†	–/‡	–
Prescott	–	–	2	4/1	2
Other	13	6	7	3/17	14

Note: Total sherd sample is 3,342. Total number of sherds from each site is given in parentheses.
[a]Source: Haury 1976:328. Includes both 1935 and 1964–65 excavations.
[b]Source: Wilcox 1987a.
[c]Source: Doyel 1987.
[d]Source: Crown 1984:258 for 1968 excavations; David Gregory, personal communication, 1987 for 1982–83 excavations.
[e]Total includes sherds identified to ware categories but not to type.
[f]Includes what is probably locally made sand-tempered pottery.
*Trace amounts.
†David Gregory has identified (but not counted) Lower Colorado Buff Ware in the Pueblo Grande collection.
‡A total of 4,066 sherds of Lower Colorado Buff Ware was excluded from these calculations.

Pueblo Grande dating between 800 and 1350). Other types, such as San Carlos Red-on-brown, were also reaching the north side of the Salt River in some quantity. These new data seriously undermine the "rivers-as-boundaries" hypothesis suggested by Crown (1985a:449–52).

A point of clarification is necessary for the "southern Arizona" pottery, most of which is Tanque Verde Red-on-brown. Tucson Basin wares have long been noted for their extensive use of sand temper (Doyel 1977b, 1984b), just as the Phoenix Basin Buff Ware is well known for its ground mica-schist temper. It is now suspected that plain and decorated sand-tempered pottery was being produced in the Phoenix Basin between the Colonial and Classic periods (Weed 1972; Antieu 1981; Crown 1981;

Doyel and Elson 1985), suggesting that some of the so-called southern Arizona wares could have been produced in the Phoenix Basin, thus overly inflating this category.

NONLOCAL CERAMICS IN THE PHOENIX BASIN

Little is known about Pioneer period ceramic trade, other than the fact that Mogollon pottery is present throughout the sequence at Snaketown. Since the 300 sherds of San Francisco Red found at Snaketown represent 30 percent of the intrusives, the Mogollon/Mimbres figure for the "Between Salt and Gila River" column on table 10.3 stands out when compared to neighboring areas. Currently, this is viewed as a problem of sampling, not of boundary definition.

The Colonial and Sedentary periods are remarkably consistent across the Phoenix Basin when the frequencies of nonlocal types are plotted. Haury (1976:328) notes the common presence of Kana'a Black-on-white and Deadman's Black-on-red at Snaketown. The combined totals for Kana'a Black-on-white and Floyd Black-on-white comprise 4 and 5 percent, respectively, for Snaketown and Las Colinas, while the combined figures for Deadman's Black-on-red and Black Mesa Black-on-white are identical at 15 percent apiece at each site. These data suggest that the Snaketown and Las Colinas populations had similar access to Kayenta decorated pottery during the Colonial and Sedentary periods. Local differences include Mogollon Brown Ware at Snaketown, while Lower Colorado Buff Ware is present at Las Colinas. For comparative purposes, it can be pointed out that Black Mesa Black-on-white was the most common non-Hohokam trade ware found in the Phoenix Basin. This type is also commonly found on Chacoan sites in the San Juan Basin, which could lead to speculation about the role of Kayenta pottery-producing people in interregional exchange networks.

Striking differences between the Gila and the Salt river valleys began to occur in the late Sedentary period, during what may be referred to as the Santan phase (A.D. 1100–1200). Tusayan Black-on-red and Sosi Black-on-white were not recovered from Snaketown (Haury 1976:328), but they are common in the Salt River valley, representing combined totals of 6 and 3 percent, respectively, at Las Colinas and Pueblo Grande. These types are also found in association with Sacaton Red-on-buff in the Gila Bend area (Wasley and Johnson 1965:28). Their absence at Snaketown suggests that either the population had been cut off from the supply source or the site was abandoned before these types became trade wares. The absence at Snaketown of Holbrook Black-on-white, which represents 2 percent of the

TABLE 10.3. *Source areas of intrusive ceramics found in Hohokam sites for all time periods (by percentage)*

Pottery Type	North of Salt River[a]		Between Salt and Gila Rivers[b]		South of Gila River[c]
	2,716	(611)	1,441	(1,039)	351
Mogollon/Mimbres	*	–	30	(30)	12
Kayenta/Tusayan	46	(22)	16	(9)	1
Hopi	3	(3)	3	(4)	2
Little Colorado	4	(5)	*	(–)	–
White Mountain Red Ware	1	–	1	(1)	*
Cibola White Ware	3	–	5	(8)	3
Corrugated Brown Ware	3	–	*	(–)	–
Southern Arizona[d]	24	(53)	29	(42)	78
Western Arizona[e]	2	(10)	–	(–)	*
Prescott	2	(3)	–	(–)	–
Other[f]	13	(3)	15	(5)	5

Note: Total sample size, indicated by source area in the column heads, is 4,508 sherds. This number is updated from Crown's total of 2,001 (Crown 1985a:441). Crown's numbers, where they differ from the author's, are given in parentheses.

[a]Approximately 93 percent of this sample is from the multicomponent sites of Las Colinas, La Ciudad, and Pueblo Grande; 73 percent is from Las Colinas.

[b]Approximately 57 percent of this sample is from the two excavations at the pre–A.D. 1100 site of Snaketown. (Source: Haury 1976:328.)

[c]Approximately 78 percent of this sample is from the post–1100 sites of Los Fosas and Casa Grande Compound F.

[d]Includes Tucson Basin (dominant), San Carlos, and Dragoon series.

[e]The Lower Colorado Buff Ware from Las Colinas is not represented in these figures.

[f]This category includes unidentified Anasazi, Mogollon, Trincheras, and other types.

*Trace amounts.

Las Colinas assemblage and 4 percent of the Pueblo Grande assemblage, further suggests that the latter alternative may be the case. Support for this inference comes from a reanalysis of the archaeomagnetic dates from Snaketown, which concluded that no samples can be shown to postdate A.D. 1050 (Eighmy and Doyel 1987). Furthermore, the ceramic assemblage contains little red ware and few late Sedentary period design styles, both of which increase at other sites in the region after 1050.

Crown (1985a:442) has attempted to partition the Classic period into more meaningful time units, but the sample with good dates is too small to be reliable. The pottery types found in this period overlap any one phase; Casa Grande Red-on-buff and Tanque Verde Red-on-brown both date between 1150 and 1450. Of the 65 projected intrusive vessels dating to the Classic period at Pueblo Grande, only 19 are datable to the early Classic, and all except one of them overlap phases (Doyel 1987).

Kayenta and Tusayan types dating to between 1050 and 1200 are common in the Salt River valley; they are not well reported from the Gila, but few sites dating to this period have been excavated there.

The later part of the Classic period (Civano phase) can be recognized by the presence of types postdating A.D. 1300, including White Mountain Red Ware, Jeddito Yellow Ware, and Salado Polychrome (Gila-Tonto). At Pueblo Grande, there are more types (14) present between 1300 and 1400 than during any other time period, suggesting a resurgence in long-range trade for nonlocal pottery types (47 projected vessels). Although they were long considered to be an intrusive type (Doyel and Haury 1976), recent research has suggested that the Gila-Tonto polychromes were produced in the Phoenix Basin, where local copies of Tanque Verde Red-on-brown also were manufactured (Crown 1983b:310; Crown and Bishop 1987; David Gregory, personal communication, 1986).

Some mention should be made of the related Tucson Basin sequence. Little Tucson Basin pottery entered the Phoenix Basin prior to the Classic period, and thousands of Phoenix Basin Buff Ware vessels occur in the Tucson Basin region during the Colonial and Sedentary periods. By the late Sedentary to early Classic transition, this situation became reversed, with a cessation of Buff Ware traffic to the south around the time that Snaketown was abandoned. Tanque Verde Red-on-brown appears in the Phoenix Basin in large quantity after 1200, but its point of departure need not have been the Tucson Basin, and, as suggested, some of it could have been manufactured within the Phoenix Basin.

HOHOKAM CERAMICS OUTSIDE THE HOHOKAM REGION

Little new data have been reported since Crown (1985a) completed her study of the approximately 9,000 Hohokam sherds found outside of the Hohokam region. Both Colton (1941:317) and Haury (1976:327) have commented on the small amount of buff-ware pottery found in other culture areas. Crown (1985a:446) has reported that the ratio of Hohokam decorated to plain vessels leaving the region is the reverse of the ratio of nonlocal vessels entering the region. This suggests that the vessels entering the Hohokam region probably had intrinsic value (most were used as burial goods), whereas the Hohokam wares leaving the region probably contained something of value, presently unknown (perhaps salt or lac).

TIME AND SPACE TRENDS

Figure 10.1 graphically summarizes our present understanding of Hoho-kam long-distance commerce between about 800 and 1100. Intensity of commerce during this period was particularly strong to the north, includ-ing the Agua Fria–Verde Valley region. Production areas were established in the north, perhaps in part to meet the demand for Tusayan pottery in the south (Geib and Callahan 1987). McGuire and Downum (1982) have proposed that the Hohokam exchanged shell for Tusayan pottery, probably up the Verde Valley.

The Hohokam maintained mining interests in the sub–Mogollon Rim country between the Verde Valley and Point-of-Pines. Trade routes passed through this region heading toward Cibola. The Kiatuthlanna Ruin yielded an average of four shell bracelets per burial, whereas some burials had as many as 20 (Roberts 1931:162, pl. 46). Haury (1976:321) also notes the presence of Hohokam-type shell bracelets at Pueblo Bonito. The Hohokam and Chaco regional systems shared a border along the Little Colorado River, which may have facilitated the exchange of Hohokam shell and cotton products for Cerrillos turquoise. Mention should also be made of the stone palettes, shell artifacts, and ceramic design styles found in Mogollon/Mimbres sites dating from the Three Circle to the Classic Mim-bres phases (Gladwin et al. 1937:125; Haury 1945:152; Brody 1977:89–95).

Phoenix Basin–western Papaguería contacts are discernible through a shell-based exchange network (Masse 1980b; Doelle 1980; McGuire and Howard 1987). Quantities of ceramic, shell, and other Phoenix Basin products can be identified in the lower and middle San Pedro and Santa Cruz drainages, but these districts are only weakly represented in the Phoenix Basin (Doyel 1984b:157). A critical question thus remains regard-ing the asymmetrical structure of interaction between these areas.

During the early Classic period, interregional exchange networks were reorganized. The Gila Bend sites ceased to be suppliers of marine shell, and new trade routes opened across east-central Papaguería to the Tucson Basin (Teague and Crown 1984; Vokes 1983). Some sites in the Phoenix Basin, such as Pueblo Grande and Las Colinas, became production centers for shell bracelets and other products (A. Howard 1985). By about 1100, most of the objects for which the Hohokam are best known (except shell) ceased to be manufactured; these included stone palettes, stone bowls and effigies, and most decorated pottery forms (censors, thick-walled vessels, figurines, bowls). By the same date, offeratory projectile points were greatly reduced in style and quality.

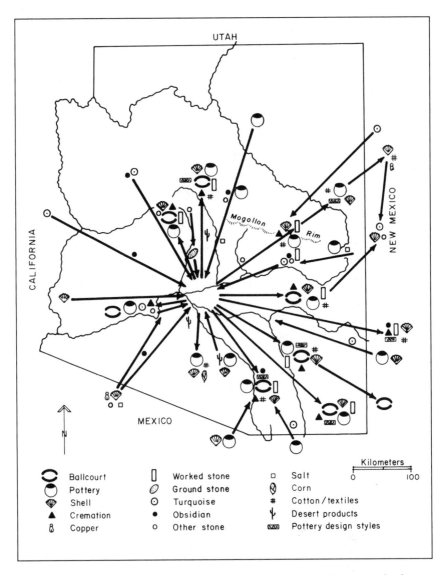

Figure 10.1. *Hohokam exchange systems. Operated through a network of ballcourt communities located between the Little Colorado River on the north and the international border on the south, these systems reached their maximum extent between A.D. 800 and 1100. (Modified from Doyel 1979:551.)*

Also by A.D. 1100, the thin veneer of Anasazi ceramics across the Phoenix Basin was interrupted and local variation became apparent. By 1250, access to Tusayan types was cut off to the Salt River Hohokam. Other widely traded types dating to the thirteenth century, such as St. John's Polychrome, McDonald Corrugated, and Tularosa Black-on-white, are absent or minimally represented, suggesting a recession in long-distance ceramic exchange during the Soho phase (Doyel 1981).

Around A.D. 1300, Gila and Tonto polychrome became common, while Jeddito Black-on-yellow and Tanque Verde Red-on-brown pottery also appeared at sites throughout the Phoenix Basin. Other products continued to circulate through the system, including obsidian, stone axes, tabular knives, minerals, and ground-stone tools. Shell jewelry maintained its popularity, and some forms, such as shell bracelets and *Conus* tinklers, were further elaborated (Haury 1945). It is possible that the large pueblos forming at this time between Flagstaff and Zuni obtained considerable amounts of worked shell from the Hohokam.

PROCUREMENT STRATEGIES

No prehistoric road systems like those surrounding Chaco Canyon have been found to connect Hohokam villages. River systems and canal corridors provided preferred routes of travel for both people and their products. Local trail systems have been reported (Wilcox, McGuire, and Sternberg 1981; Doyel and Elson 1985), but systematic work is needed to record remaining trails before they are lost forever.

Six different procurement strategies were developed by the Hohokam to conduct long-range commerce: (1) expedition to source, (2) acquisition through middlemen, (3) down-the-line acquisition, (4) interaction at or near source, (5) colonization, and (6) ritual integration or regulation.

Strategy 1 (expedition to source) includes the shell trade and spans distances of over 600 kilometers. Similar expeditions could have been organized to acquire turquoise, obsidian, and other products. Multiple-product trips may have occurred; for instance, shell expeditions could have involved acquisition of Sauceda obsidian and salt, which would have enhanced the payoff for the trip.

Strategy 2 (use of agents or middlemen) has also been suggested for the shell trade. Participants from the Trincheras cultural tradition of northern Sonora may have served in this capacity, but opinions are divided on this issue (Woodward 1936; Haury 1976; McGuire and Howard 1987). Other groups could have served as middlemen for the Phoenix Basin Hohokam in a variety of areas from the Agua Fria to the San Pedro River valley. Jernigan

(1978:213) suggests that the Mogollon acted as middlemen in Hohokam-Anasazi commercial endeavors.

Some authors (Fish 1983; Teague 1985) have stated that Hohokam commerce was often of the down-the-line variety (strategy 3), in which products are expected to exhibit predictable falloff rates from distance to source. Research has suggested that some artifact classes (carved-stone bowls, pipes, etc.) were independently incorporated into receptor site assemblages (Fish, Pilles, and Fish 1980). McGuire and Downum (1982) have suggested that products moving in either direction respond to local forces and will not necessarily reflect similar falloff rates, implying the existence of some level of control and differential product values. Some materials coming in from the Colorado Plateau may have been received as down-the-line goods.

Strategy 4 (interaction near source) refers to a presence in a geographically removed location, presumably due to commercial interests in a local material or product. An example is the Hohokam pit house located within a local village in the upper Verde Valley near Perkinsville, where evidence reveals procurement and production of local argillitic stone (Fish and Fish 1977). This strategy may also involve the use of trading partners.

Colonization of frontier areas (strategy 5) for commercial motives has been a popular concept for decades. Roosevelt 9:6 in the Tonto Basin and Palo Parado in the middle Santa Cruz have been described as Hohokam "site-unit intrusions" (Di Peso 1956). These developments have also been attributed to the operation of *pochteca*-like organizations (highly organized, itinerant Aztec merchants or traders; Schroeder 1966) or to directed colonialism by the Hohokam sociopolitical hierarchy (Wood 1985).

Strategy 6 (ritual integration) is represented by non-Hohokam sites that contain evidence of Hohokam ritual patterns, such as ballcourts and cremation burials. Examples include Wupatki, Winona, and Ridge ruins (McGregor 1941) and the Stove Canyon Site near Point-of-Pines (Neely 1974). Complex levels of interaction between Hohokam and non-Hohokam populations occurred at these sites, and local and nonlocal products are present (Doyel 1981; Wilcox and Sternberg 1983).

TRADE ROUTES

One approach to reconstructing prehistoric trade is to investigate those routes known to have been used by ethnohistorical populations. The four maps I consulted that show aboriginal trade routes are very different (Colton 1941; Tower 1945; Jernigan 1978; Crown 1985a). Jernigan (1978:

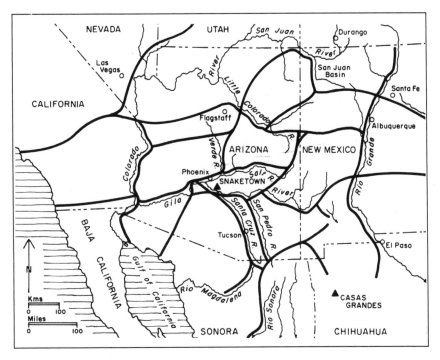

Figure 10.2. *Trade routes connecting the California coast and the plains of eastern New Mexico at* A.D. *1100 (after Colton 1941). The Hohokam were well situated to play an active role in Southwestern exchange networks.*

212) assumes that most routes followed major drainages (the Gila, Salt, Verde, etc.). Three maps show strong east-west routes, including a Phoenix Basin-to-Mimbres route following the Gila River. Crown (1985a: 448) emphasizes north-to-south travel and shows no routes crossing from Arizona into New Mexico from the Mexican border north to Zuni, while both Colton and Tower show four east-west trails in the same area (fig. 10.2). Riley (1987:119–22) has suggested that the entire Pimería Alta was "deeply" involved in trade and that the historic period Pima served as important middlemen along four major trade routes.

Several general observations can be made from the available evidence. Hohokam territory was strategically located for the acquisition of certain products of interest to other Southwestern populations, most notably salt and shell. All rivers between the Little Colorado River and the Mexican border drain through the Phoenix Basin, creating natural transportation corridors between the California coast on the west, the Plains on the east,

Cibola in the north, and Mesoamerica to the south. Geography also facilitated the movement of products adapted to the desert climate, such as cotton, agave, and lac.

Certain Hohokam sites were well positioned relative to the trade routes, including the Gila Bend sites; Cashion, near the confluence of three major rivers; Azatlan (Wilcox 1985), near the confluence of the Verde and the Salt; and Snaketown, near the confluence of the Gila, the Santa Cruz, and the Queen Creek delta. These areas and others, such as the Hodges and Palo Parado sites to the south, were also well suited for agriculture due to broad floodplains and access to water for irrigation, giving the settlements several natural advantages in terms of differential access to strategic resources.

TOWARD QUANTIFICATION

It has been demonstrated that Hohokam exchange systems were geographically extensive and broadly based on a variety of raw materials and products. Similarity in morphology and constituent materials has prompted the suggestion that production was organized and in some cases specialized. Specialized production is often associated with emerging cultural complexity, but for the Hohokam, and for the Southwest in general, quantification of key variables remains elusive. To address this question, several material products are evaluated in terms of production costs.

Hohokam ceremonial projectile points were abundant at leading villages and are thought to have been made by specialists. What production costs were associated with this element? Let us assume that 30 villages contained 5,000 points each, that it took 1.5 hours to make each point, and that such points were manufactured for a 200-year period. These estimates would suggest that 750 points were made each year, consuming an average of 1,125 person-hours. In other words, it would take 0.55 person-years per year to account for the 150,000 points. This would suggest that a few part-time specialists could handle the work—mobilization needs and travel time to source notwithstanding.

Shell products are also thought to have been made by specialists. Acquisition would have involved a long-distance travel component, which would figure prominently in production-cost estimates. For example, if whole shells were brought into the area, rather than being partially manufactured at the source, transportation costs would increase significantly. The average *Glycymeris* shell used for bracelet production weighed between 80 and 100 grams, while a finished bracelet weighs about 10 grams.

Both strategies were apparently employed, as shell blanks have been found at source areas and shell caches have been found in Hohokam sites.

For purposes of estimating production costs, let us set the number of *Glycymeris* bracelets at 100,000. Pueblo Grande and Snaketown have yielded 1,200 and 1,800 specimens, respectively, and only portions of these sites have been excavated. Also, *Glycymeris* bracelets were a common trade item. Let us assume, furthermore, that the shells were carried back as whole specimens. The bulk weight of the raw material would be 9,000 kilograms (19,800 lbs.). Assuming a person could carry 9 kilograms (20 lbs.) per trip (plus food and water) and that a round trip to Rocky Point required 20 days, it would require 1,000 trips (9.6 person-years) to acquire the raw materials. Given that most (but not all) shell bracelet manufacturing took place over a 700-year period, it would have required a trip every 8.5 months to keep the Hohokam supplied with *Glycymeris* shells.

Experimentation has suggested an average time of three hours to produce a shell bracelet. Our 100,000 bracelets would require 300,000 person-hours or 144 person-years to complete. Adding the 9.6 person-years for travel to the 144 person-years for production, a total production cost estimate of 153.6 person-years is achieved. Again using the 700-year production span, an average of 0.22 person-years per year would account for the 100,000 bracelets. Stated differently, if one person worked 60 days a year making two bracelets a day, the result would be 120 bracelets per year and 2,400 bracelets over a 20-year production life. If one person made 120 bracelets a year for 700 years, the total would be 84,000, thus accounting for most of our estimated number. It is entirely possible, of course, that our estimate represents only a fraction of the actual number of bracelets manufactured. Furthermore, this estimate applies only to bracelet manufacture, and does not include the tremendous amount of time invested in manufacturing beads, cut-shell pendants, *Conus* tinklers, rings, and other forms of jewelry, using over 20 different species of shell. From this exercise, it would appear to be a reasonable inference that each village would have needed perhaps three or four part-time specialists to produce the necessary volume of shell materials for both local consumption and exchange.

Appropriate production-cost estimates could also be developed for metates, axes, tabular knives, pottery production, and so on. (See Rafferty 1982 for an interesting discussion of mica-schist mining for pottery temper near the site of Snaketown.) Greater research efforts are necessary in this direction. Future studies must focus more on quantification, source area identification, and the context of discovery.

THE ORGANIZATION OF EXCHANGE

Not all materials were moving within the same spheres of exchange inside the Hohokam region. The distributions of Mesoamerican goods, obsidian, carved stone, some shell items, minerals, and other materials suggest that a prestige sphere of exchange focusing on leading villages began operating during the Colonial period (Nelson 1981; Doyel 1977a, 1979; McGuire and Howard 1987). A "utilitarian sphere" of exchange, involving stone tools and other products, and a "social sphere," including common shell, pottery, textiles, and basketry, also appear to have been operating; objects circulating through these spheres may have served as bridewealth or as payment for services or obligations. Trade fairs and markets held at sites with ballcourts and plazas facilitated the operation of these levels of exchange. To identify the dynamics of exchange, more behaviorally specific models are needed, such as those developed by Flannery (ed. 1976) for the early Mesoamerican village and recently applied to the New River Hohokam by Doyel (1985b).

Specialization in different products by different villages is apparent, influenced by their proximity to natural resources (volcanic stone, ceramic temper, clay, etc.) or access to trade routes, or both. The Papaguerían shell industry, for example, took advantage of proximity to coastal shell beds as well as convenient access to trade routes between the coast and the Hohohokam core. Choice also played a significant role in specialization, whether product manufacturing or food production. Vokes (1983) discusses specialization in the production of shell jewelry in the Phoenix Basin. Other communities specialized in the production of cotton, agave, or other plant products (Gasser 1981, 1988).

Significant variation in Hohokam adaptation to differing local conditions has been documented. In the Santa Cruz drainage, for example, floodwater farming was emphasized over irrigation, and specialization in agave and fiber production was a focus of one community (Fish and Fish 1988). Along the Gila River, irrigation and other agricultural techniques were incorporated into a diversified subsistence strategy (Crown 1987a). Population reached its highest density along the Salt River, where multiple villages associated with single irrigation systems was a common pattern (Gregory, this volume). Specialized economies and competition for resources characterized the latter phases of occupation in the Salt River valley (Doyel 1988; Gregory and Nials 1985). Given the adaptive diversity cited above, it is likely that the structure of exchange systems varied by area. This perspective suggests that the traditional concepts of core and periphery as applied to Hohokam exchange should be envisioned less as a wheel with spokes than as a series of overlapping adaptive areas, interaction spheres, and cultural traditions that expressed variation through time and space (Doyel 1976:35).

By the Sedentary period more than 225 ballcourts had been constructed in a region encompassing 80,000 square kilometers and a wide range of natural resource diversity. Numerous individuals have suggested that one of the functions of ballcourts was to facilitate the exchange of people and goods (Grebinger 1971; Haury 1976; Doyel 1981; Wilcox and Sternberg 1983). Recently, evidence has come to light that may strengthen this inferred relationship between the Hohokam ballcourts and exchange. The Terrace Garden Site in the New River drainage contained a large ground-stone tool-manufacturing area in association with a small, stone-lined ballcourt; numerous petroglyphs and a series of trails also were associated (Doyel and Elson 1985). The court was located in a cleared area and was surrounded by large sherd and lithic scatters that revealed evidence of limited occupation, perhaps camping. Associated materials date the activities at this site to between 850 and 1050. Available evidence supports the interpretation that the court was associated with a specialized economic activity, in this case ground-stone tool manufacturing. This discovery may strengthen the general association of ballcourts with commercial and exchange activities.

The Hohokam ballcourt network continued to expand until 1050 or 1100, at which time subsystem collapse and reorganization occurred (Doyel 1981). Recognizably Hohokam elements disappear from the far and intermediate peripheries, a situation that appears to signal a reorganization of the regional economic system. Massive platform mounds were then constructed primarily within the Phoenix Basin. Competition for resources is suggested by the presence of hillside forts during this period of organizational and ideological transition (Doyel 1981; Gregory 1987).

The presence of Salado Polychrome pottery, adobe "great houses," and changes in the function of the platform mounds from ceremonial to occupational use identify the post-1300 phase in the Phoenix Basin. Increasingly vertical organization is suggested, based on the presence of more private walled space in sites, a reduction in public activities such as ball games, a wider range of functions associated with the mounds, the control of larger territories by some mound communities, and the disappearance of individually oriented artifacts in burial contexts (Fish and Fish 1988). Wilcox (1987a) has suggested that the mound dwellers were participants in a widespread Salado interaction sphere involving elite-to-elite alliances through marriage, whereas Teague (1985) associates control of craft specialization and trade with the mound sites. Others have suggested a growing secularization of Hohokam society (Doyel 1980; Dean 1987). Interpretation is made less certain by the lack of a representative sample of Classic period communities, with a bias toward mound sites. Based on current evidence, it would appear that the presence of platform mounds at villages facilitated the flow of products and people, as had the ballcourt network of earlier generations.

SYSTEM GROWTH, MAINTENANCE, AND DENOUEMENT

Existing research data provide the basis for a simplified scenario for the long-term growth and evolution of the Hohokam regional system. By A.D. 1, people of the southern Archaic tradition had added domesticated plants to their native inventory, and basic technological advances such as improved food processing and storage had been added to a more substantial architectural technology. Settlements consisted of small hamlets containing both small and large houses, the latter serving the dual purpose of residences for leaders and communal meeting places (Cable and Doyel 1987). A clay figurine complex consisting primarily of anthropomorphic forms reflected socioreligious concepts borrowed—along with agriculture and other material cultural attributes—from peoples living to the south. Small amounts of turquoise, shell, and exotic pottery have been found, documenting the existence of long-distance exchange or procurement during this early period.

By the beginning of the Snaketown phase, increased technological sophistication led to the development of irrigation agriculture. Complex feedback processes involving technology, social organization, improved crop varieties, ritual elaboration, and immigration from outlying areas resulted in system expansion throughout the Phoenix Basin. By the Sedentary period, villages had become larger and had expanded into a variety of ecological niches. Irrigation systems and trade networks continued to expand. Increasing social complexity is suggested by mound architecture and mortuary variability. Competition over resources perhaps exacerbated by environmental variation during the Classic period led to further intensification of subsistence strategies and local variation among subpopulations. Increasing social complexity is indicated by the development of new settlement plans and specialized facilities.

System growth was stimulated by agricultural intensification and population growth within areas that became increasingly circumscribed through time. Exchange networks served a variety of purposes in system maintenance, including reducing local resource imbalances, circulating personnel, acquiring rare resources for the elite to underwrite their authority and for other social purposes, and enhancing sociocultural integration within local communities and throughout the region.

After 1300, the socioeconomic mechanisms that had promoted harmony and resource sharing throughout the region were no longer operative, and the system collapsed by the year 1400. Explanations for the truncation of the Hohokam regional system include a variety of models ranging from environmental catastrophe (flooding, soil salinization) to sociocultural processes (population growth, organizational collapse, overspecialization). Some researchers attribute the demise of this once-active system to extralocal causes such as the truncation of the Mixteca-Pueblo trade route by 1250, trade competition with the growing center of Casas Grandes in Chihuahua, and the departure of the Mesoamerican *tracadores* (pre-Aztec itinerant traders) who had dominated the late pre-Classic Hohokam trade network (Kelley 1980:62–65). Others maintain that the Hohokam-Mesoamerican connection was always casual, with few "organized mercantile overtones" (Haury 1980:114). Perhaps future research will produce a middle-ground position between these competing explanatory frameworks.

New evidence suggests that unpredictable flood episodes interspersed by long dry periods may have severely impacted Hohokam irrigation systems (Gregory, this volume; Masse, this volume). It is possible that their limited technology was insufficient to mount a satisfactory response to these challenges. Overspecialization and competition, perhaps coupled with environmental deterioration due to long-term use, contributed to the demise of the fourteenth-century cultural pattern; still, the collapse of this once-dynamic system remains a mystery. Similar forces appear to have been at work on a pan-Southwestern scale. Interruption of regional trading patterns may have been a contributory cause as well as a result of these unsettled conditions. By the time of the Spanish *entrada*, population levels were less than one-tenth the estimated prehistoric level. Reduced storage, increased residential mobility, impermanent architecture, and reduced social complexity during the early historic period all point to a more diversified and less elaborate lifeway than that of the inhabitants' probable ancestors, the Hohokam.

HOHOKAM AND CHACO CULTURAL GROWTH AND EXCHANGE

Comparison of growth patterns between the Chaco Basin Anasazi and the Phoenix Basin Hohokam suggests many more similarities than differences.

Both regions reveal long, in situ growth sequences beginning in preceramic times. Both areas witnessed the development of agriculturally based economies, and each contained site hierarchies, public architecture, high-status burials, and well-developed ceremonial and astronomical systems. Both systems had rituals involving caches and ritual breakage of finely made items such as carved-stone and ceramic vessels. Platform mounds and plazas are present in both areas. Plazas and elevated public structures were ancient concepts among the Hohokam, but only became prominent among the Chaco Basin population after A.D. 900 or so. Another architectural pattern found in both areas is an increased concern for specialized storage space late in the cultural sequence. Both areas also contain sites interpreted as defensive that appeared during periods of reorganization: the Trincheras sites in southern Arizona and, in the Chaco Basin, Mesa Tierra, Crumbled House, and sites on Chacra Mesa, among others. Both regions reveal an abundance of exotic materials. Turquoise and shell are found in sites in both regions, in nearly reverse frequencies.

Some participants in this symposium (Gregory, this volume; Wilcox, this volume) see little contact between the Hohokam and the Chaco regional systems. If only to provide an alternative perspective, I propose that it is possible that cotton, shell, lac, and many of the "Mesoamerican" items found in the Chaco region could have been passed along through the Hohokam interaction network operating between A.D. 850 and 1050 (see Schroeder 1981 for further discussion). More subtle clues should also be investigated. For instance, Red Mesa Black-on-white pottery from Chaco is identified by the use of a balanced and opposed interlocking scroll motif that incorporates hatched design elements—a design style that appears first on Snaketown Red-on-buff Ware in the Hohokam region.

The two regional systems reveal some basic differences in economies and cosmology, although variation exists within each region. The Anasazi were primarily floodwater farmers in an arid environment characterized by highly localized resources, and their great kiva organizational system had ancient roots in the Colorado Plateau area. Although a diversity of agricultural techniques has been documented for their region, the Hohokam did develop the most extensive and elaborate irrigation systems in aboriginal North America in an environment characterized by considerable resource redundancy. Their culture reveals clear connections with cultures to the south in Mesoamerica. It remains to be seen how these cultural and environmental differences influenced the role and structure of exchange systems, although there are reasons to suggest that differences did exist (Doyel 1983). Chaco Canyon appears to have operated for a time as a central place, but an analogous situation did not exist in the Phoenix

Basin—although the Salt River valley between Mesa and Phoenix did contain more villages than Chaco Canyon and probably a much higher population density. There is no evidence in the Hohokam region to suggest the sort of ritual pilgrimages or communal feasting now advanced for Chaco Canyon (Toll, this volume). There are no roads in the Hohokam region that connect primary villages and pass by rows of small rooms with exterior doorways, as there are at Pueblo Alto, Chetro Ketl, or Pueblo del Arroyo. Because of resource scarcity and unpredictability, the growing populations in the San Juan Basin probably relied to a greater degree on alliance formation, ceremonialism, and redistribution than did the Hohokam of the Phoenix Basin. As Charles Redman pointed out during the seminar, the marginal nature of the environment could well have limited the growth of sociocultural complexity in both areas. The Hohokam, however, always had access to greater resource diversity, which may be why the desert river valleys remained occupied long after Chaco Canyon was abandoned.

DISCUSSION

If a regional system is to be defined as geographically separate communities dependent on each other through the exchange of goods and services (Crown, this volume), then it would appear that such systems existed within both the Hohokam and the Chaco regions. Active exchange systems are documented for both regions, and there may also have been materials and ideas exchanged between these two systems. Toll (this volume) has forcefully demonstrated the exchange of considerable quantities of ceramics within the Chaco system. Although the same quality of evidence regarding ceramic exchange does not yet exist for the Hohokam region, clear evidence for exchange in marine shell and a variety of other goods does exist for the Hohokam.

Gregory's (this volume) interesting point that greater regional integration may have been achieved among the Chaco subpopulations should not be accepted without qualification. It is entirely likely that the elements of Chaco currently receiving the most attention—roads and road-associated features—lasted only a brief time, perhaps less than a generation, and therefore are not characteristic of the entire Bonito phase sequence, which lasted over 200 years. It should also be pointed out that the roads identified to date relate mainly to the central canyon (like spokes on a hub) and do not appear to integrate the various communities lying outside the Chaco core area. Conversely, it can be shown that Hohokam irrigation systems were in place for at least 700 years. Very specific patterning in the structure of Hohokam settlements has been identified throughout the Phoenix Basin; such patterning spans at least several centuries of the Hohokam sequence.

It is entirely possible that the differential distributions of critical resources (agricultural land, water, and food sources) between the two areas was an important factor in the seemingly divergent trajectories taken by the two systems. Gregory may be correct in suggesting that interdependency among Hohokam settlements beyond the level of the local community may have been more indirect than it was within the Chaco system. In order to learn more about how exchange integrated Hohokam and Chacoan culture, it will be necessary to identify more precisely the ways in which local communities exploited the resources available to them. These data can then be utilized to place community exchange and interaction within a better-documented regional system framework.

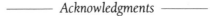

Acknowledgments

Charles Adams, David Breternitz, David Gregory, Emil Haury, and Alexander Lindsay provided valuable assistance in the analysis of the trade pottery found at Pueblo Grande. Harold Colton and Lyndon Hargrave had inspected the collection some 50 years ago, and their findings were also helpful. Patty Crown, Sharon Debowski, Ann Howard, Doug Mitchell, Paul Fish, John Ravesloot, David Schaller, David Wilcox, Richard Nelson, and Deni Seymour were generous with their information and assistance. Debbie Bowman typed several versions of the paper, and the City of Phoenix provided administrative support. Thanks to Patty Crown and Jim Judge for organizing the symposium.

Chapter 11

Hohokam Social Complexity

DAVID R. WILCOX

THE study of what we today call Hohokam archaeology began in November 1694 when Father Eusebio Kino and Juan Manje described several ruins in the Gila Valley (Burrus 1971:219–22). Father Kino held mass in the Casa Grande, thus consecrating it as a part of Western culture (Burrus 1971:207). A century and a half later, William Emory (1848) led a reconnaissance expedition along the Gila, describing the ruins and claiming the area for the United States. Interest in the history and prehistory of the American Indian accelerated in the late nineteenth century, as ways were sought to assimilate Native Americans into the American republic. Furthering the cause of assimilation was Mary Hemenway's motive in sponsoring Frank Hamilton Cushing's work in the Salt River valley, the earliest professional excavation program in the American Southwest (Cushing 1890, 1892, 1893).

Basing his insights on his knowledge of Zuni society, Cushing interpreted Classic period Hohokam social structure as nonegalitarian (Cushing 1890)—an opinion that ran contrary to the evolutionary perspective of Lewis Henry Morgan (1877) and Adolf Bandelier (1892). Interestingly, although Morgan's evolutionism was generally rejected, his belief in the egalitarian character of American Indians was widely adopted by the new discipline of anthropology. In the American Southwest it continues to be the dominant interpretation (Eggan 1950; Spicer 1962; Dozier 1970; Ford 1972b; Riley 1982), although, among archaeologists, this issue has become rather heated (Martin and Plog 1973; Cordell and Plog 1979; Wilcox 1981, 1988b; Upham 1982; Hunter-Anderson 1981; Whittlesey 1982; Graves 1987).

The model of Hohokam culture change formulated by Harold Gladwin and Emil Haury in the 1930s held that the Hohokam were an egalitarian, tribal society whose settlements were randomly organized like Pima *ranch-erías*—dispersed communities spread out over stretches of a kilometer or more along the Gila River (Gladwin 1930; Gladwin and Gladwin 1935; Gladwin et al. 1937). In his 1934 Harvard dissertation, Haury (1945) argued that the data that had persuaded Cushing (1890) are better explained by postulating a migration of Salado populations who lived peacefully side by side with the Hohokam (see also Schmidt 1928; Gladwin 1930). Although A. V. Kidder (in Kidder, Cosgrove, and Cosgrove 1949: 147) expressed skepticism about this "lion-and-lamb" hypothesis, it was widely accepted (Wormington 1947; McGregor 1965), and Haury (1976) has continued to defend it.

Even before the incredible acceleration of Hohokam studies that began in the middle 1970s, confidence in Haury's Salado migration hypothesis had waned. Richard Ambler (1961), Charlie Steen (1965), William Wasley (1966), Donald Weaver (1972b), and, most definitively, David Doyel (1974, 1981) showed that continuities of cultural development existed from the Sedentary through the Classic periods that eliminated the basis for the migration hypothesis. Subsequent work further documents the in situ development of Classic Hohokam culture (Hammack and Sullivan 1981; Gregory and McGuire 1982; Gregory 1987; Teague and Crown 1984). This means that the possibility that there was some kind of Hohokam social complexity is viable (Martin and Plog 1973:312–17; Wilcox and Shenk 1977:171–99) and that the patterns that Cushing (1890) was the first to see need to be reexamined.

ADVANCES IN HOHOKAM ARCHAEOLOGY

Rapid advances have been made in Hohokam archaeology during the last 15 years. We now know far more than did Cushing, Gladwin, and Haury, and substantially more than we ourselves knew a mere decade ago. The questions it is now possible to ask and the data currently available have transformed the debate about the nature of Hohokam social complexity. Yet these changes are very little known beyond the relatively small circle of active Hohokam archaeologists, and the problem of communication is compounded by our continuing failure to achieve a working consensus about the Hohokam chronology (Schiffer 1986; Dean 1988; Eighmy and McGuire 1988).

In spite of the progress that has been made, we still have a long way to go before important basic issues are resolved. Consider, for example, the fact that Cushing (1890) was the first person to sample almost completely a Hohokam village (Haury 1945; see also Brunson 1989). He also is the *only* person to have accomplished this task in a large site. We have learned how to ask good questions about households, suprahouseholds, village segments, settlements, and settlement networks, but many of the answers still elude us because appropriate samples have not yet been collected or analyzed (Wilcox and Shenk 1977:190; Wilcox 1979a; Wilcox, McGuire, and Sternberg 1981; Wilcox and Sternberg 1983; Doyel and Elson 1985; Seymour and Schiffer 1987; J. Howard 1985; Huntington 1986; Elson 1986; Elson and Doelle 1987; Doelle and Elson 1986; Henderson 1987c; Rice ed. 1987b; Wilcox 1984, 1987a; Doyel 1988).

The value of the SAR advanced seminar was that it challenged us to find ways to communicate our ideas to a larger audience in spite of the problems mentioned above. It also challenged us to begin thinking about how to compare apparently similar regional systems, thus stimulating anthropological generalizations. In what follows, I discuss recent advances in the understanding of Hohokam social organization on scales ranging from the household to macroregional fields of interaction, identifying critical questions that remain unanswered. At the same time, I hope to show that new opportunities exist for pursuing the issue of Hohokam social complexity. In conclusion, I will sum up the current state of the debate about Hohokam social complexity.

SOCIAL GROUP DOMAINS AND THEIR ACTIVITY STRUCTURE

The first modern settlement analysis of a Hohokam site was Doyel's (1974, 1981) study of the Escalante Ruin group, a Classic period site in the Gila River valley. Doyel's methodology was similar to that used by James Hill (1970) in the Broken K Pueblo analysis. Functional room types based on size categories were defined, and their distribution showed that only a few household-size groups had lived in the Classic period compounds or on the mound.

Quite a different approach was applied in a study of the architecture of the Casa Grande, the four-story structure that gives its name to the Casa Grande Ruins (Wilcox and Shenk 1977; see also Wilcox 1975, 1982). A depositional concept of a "living surface" provided a framework within which the behavioral boundaries of absolutely contemporaneous social groups could be identified using relational logic. The archival data from two previous expeditions to Snaketown (Gladwin et al. 1937; Haury 1976) also proved amenable to this kind of analysis (Wilcox, McGuire, and Sternberg 1981).

The concept of a "house cluster" was empirically defined as "adjacent houses of the same phase whose doorways share a common focus" (Wilcox, McGuire, and Sternberg 1981:155). It was inferred that these house clusters were the domains of "primary groups" (Goody 1972). Many archaeologists find it more convenient to call these groups "households" (Wilk and Rathje 1982; J. Howard 1985; Huntington 1986; Henderson ed. 1987). Although recognizing that serious pitfalls may be hidden by a too-facile assumption that the archaeological construct is identical to what ethnographers choose to call households (see Netting, Wilk, and Arnould 1984), I shall nevertheless adopt that terminology here for the social groups that inhabited the house clusters.

House clusters have now been identified at numerous Hohokam sites (Gregory 1984; J. Howard 1985; Huntington 1986; Elson 1986; Doyel ed. 1987; Henderson 1987c; Henderson ed. 1987; Rice ed. 1987b). The methodology used has not always been identical, but comparable results seem to have been achieved. At Snaketown, few of the areas on which doorways focus were excavated. Data from other sites now show, however, that these areas are indeed outdoor courtyards.

Suprahousehold groups have also been identified as occupying "village segments" or "precincts" (Sires 1983; J. Howard 1985; Huntington 1986) and the so-called loci at Los Solares (see Wilcox 1987a:42, 45–46; Rice ed. 1987b). They often are associated with a discrete cemetery, which documents the distinct social identity of these groups (Anderson 1985). Earth ovens also are often associated with these domains, indicating a production function on this suprahousehold level. The earliest appearance of such groups so far documented is at Los Solares in the early Santa Cruz phase, a few generations after large-scale irrigation was adopted. Centuries later, the Classic period compounds were clearly demarcated suprahousehold groups (Haury 1945; Sires 1983; Anderson 1985; Wilcox 1987a). Each had its own trash mounds and cremation cemetery that served the needs of three to five nuclear households within the compound. In contrast to the earlier suprahouseholds, the Classic period ones had a more formally marked boundary (the compound wall), which served to restrict access to information about matters internal to these groups (such as surplus holdings). Interestingly, some burials were placed inside the wall (inhumations) and others outside of it (cremations and some inhumations). It seems very likely that these suprahousehold residence units were also corporate groups, probably with their own property rights.

Identification of two kinds of residence units in Hohokam sites has opened up many new opportunities to study the structure of their distribution in settlements of different sizes and different locations in the cultural landscape. A similar dichotomy has also been documented in the ninth-century Pueblo I Dolores villages in southwestern Colorado (Orcutt, Blinman, and Kohler 1988; Kane 1989). The appearance of these suprahousehold residence units is coincident with the nucleation of the earliest Anasazi villages in the northern San Juan Basin, and that process parallels a similar social evolution in the Hohokam area at the same time. Great kivas and the distribution of red-on-orange pottery in the northern area, like ballcourts and red-on-buff pottery in the south, imply further that these processes are organizationally comparable. Detailed comparisons of these phenomena are needed. Regrettably, similar behavioral analyses of Chacoan sites have yet to be attempted.

A third kind of residence unit is the settlement. Horizontal complexity in Hohokam settlement size has now been well documented. Field houses and other temporary activity loci, farmsteads (both seasonal and permanent), hamlets, and villages have been distinguished (Ward 1978; Crown 1985b; Doyel and Elson 1985; Doelle and Elson 1986).

Following Sanders, Parsons, and Santley (1979:56), I define a "small nucleated village" as a settlement with 100 to 500 people. How households and suprahousehold groups are distributed in these different kinds of settlement, how they are structured in each, how that distribution is related to the developmental cycles of the two kinds of domestic group, and how those relationships may have changed through the phases of Hohokam culture history are wide-open research questions of considerable importance.

As such research is pursued it should be possible to investigate a series of collateral questions: When did suprahousehold groups first attain a distinct identity? Were there differences in internal organization or changes in organization of domestic groups in time or space? Were there wealth differences, or differences in production or consumption functions? Were hamlets in nonriverine settings structurally equivalent to suprahousehold groups in riverine sites (Sires 1984b), or were they composed of *segments* of several different suprahousehold groups?

Unfortunately, few such studies have been conducted and only ad hoc observations can as yet be reported. I am fascinated, for example, by the fact that each house cluster at Siphon Draw, a nonriverine site in the Phoenix (Salt-Gila) Basin (Gregory 1984), had its own cemetery, whereas cemeteries in riverine villages are apparently associated with suprahousehold groups (Henderson ed. 1987). Does this indicate that the social identities of households in nonriverine hamlets like Siphon Draw were unique (and thus were not part of suprahousehold groups there), but that they were linked to larger groups in the riverine villages? If so, what does this pattern imply about the integration of social networks, exchange flows between the riverine and nonriverine sectors, subsistence buffering, and so forth?

CRAFT SPECIALIZATION

Craft specialization implies a specific kind of horizontal social complexity that is often apparent during and after the emergence of more vertically complex societies (Redman 1978a; Blanton et al. 1981). So far, most Hohokam evidence in this regard is equivocal or weak. At Snaketown in the Sedentary period, for example, the evidence for pottery making seems to be concentrated in the unusually dense aggregate of house clusters north of Mound 40, while shell working occurred in several different areas that did not include the pottery-making one (Seymour 1988). Mica-schist that was used for pottery temper was mined from Gila Butte, and the Gila Butte site may have had a monopoly on this resource (Rafferty 1982). Sacaton Red pottery may have been produced by specialists (Abbott 1983). Differential distributions of other artifact classes are also suggestive of craft specialization (Kisselburg 1987; Henderson 1987c).

One of the best cases for a form of craft specialization and division of labor has been documented in the Tucson Basin. At the West Branch site on the southwest side of the basin, pottery-making artifacts were ubiquitous in nearly all of the Sedentary period Middle Rincon phase households (Huntington 1986). Petrographic analyses show that the pottery at this site was made from local materials. On the east side of the basin, at the Tanque Verde Wash site (Wallace and Heidke 1986), also a Middle Rincon phase component, few pottery-making artifacts were found and much of the pottery was made from materials from the *west* side of the basin. These data suggest that distinct production and consumption zones for utility pottery may have existed in the Tucson Basin in the Sedentary period.

For the middle Classic period, another case of differential production and consumption zones has been documented that is even larger in scale. Spindle whorls—both bead and centrally perforated sherd whorls—are common in platform mound sites. Their distribution is correlated with the distribution of weft-wrapped cotton textiles, and the Basin-and-Range zone of southern Arizona was certainly a good place to grow cotton (Di Peso 1956; Wilcox 1987a). The combination of bead and sherd whorls may have been a technological means of producing the different weight threads needed to make weft-wrap openwork textiles (Wilcox 1987a:158). If so, it is highly significant that bead whorls are virtually absent from the upper Salt drainage, but weft-wrap openwork does occur there (Kent 1957; Di Peso 1956; Wilcox 1987a). I infer that the Basin-and-Range zone was a production zone for cotton textiles that were in part consumed in the upper Salt transition zone (Wilcox 1987a). Bridewealth in connection with elite intermarriage may have been the social mechanism that produced this distribution (Wilcox 1987a:161–62).

SITE STRUCTURE

Site structure is a dynamic concept that refers to the way space is organized for human activity. Because it changes as people reconfigure the space they occupy to suit new needs, site structure must be understood as a series of physical reorderings that an archaeological site has gone through during the course of its occupation. Stimulated by K. C. Chang's (1958) study of Neolithic social groups, Southwestern studies that defined the methodology for this concept include Rohn (1965), Dean (1969), and Wilcox (1975, 1982). In the last decade or so, these ideas have been used to interpret Hohokam sites and the changes they underwent throughout the Hohokam chronology.

PRECLASSIC PERIOD

The restudy of Snaketown (Wilcox, McGuire, and Sternberg 1981) demonstrated that Hohokam villages are structured much more formally than was recognized by earlier students (see Haury 1976:353). What I discovered was that the area in the center of the site that is outlined by a peculiar rectangular contour line had been extensively excavated, and in its central portion *nothing at all* (no features and no artifacts) was found. It was noted that the caliche was unusually close to the surface. I feel certain that this area was a large plaza and was present at Snaketown throughout its 900-year history (Wilcox, McGuire, and Sternberg 1981:136; Wilcox 1987b).

Once this fact is recognized, the formal relationships of other features to the central plaza become obvious (fig. 11.1). In the Sedentary period, for example, the plaza was ringed by eight mounds, all of which were artificially built (Haury 1976), quite possibly with dirt scraped from the plaza area. At least two of these mounds were capped with caliche, and the lowest one, Mound 16, was surrounded by a palisade (Haury 1976:84–94). Mound 16 is an early version of what later became platform mounds (Gregory et al. 1985). Inside the ring of eight artificial mounds are the largest houses; the largest cemeteries; the richest caches, burial lots, and floor assemblages (see Nelson 1986); and the largest aggregates of house clusters (Wilcox, McGuire, and Sternberg 1981:163–75). This is not a random distribution!

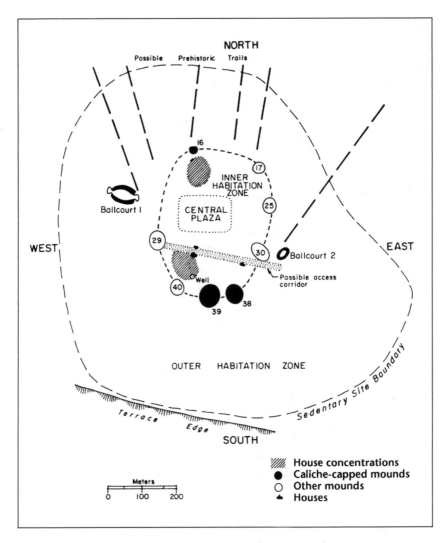

Figure 11.1. *Parameters of Snaketown's Sedentary period site structure.*
(After Wilcox et al. 1981:142; Wilcox and Sternberg 1983:91.)

House 66:8, with its 60 vessels and 28 copper bells, is located in this
central precinct (Nelson 1986; Seymour and Schiffer 1987); it may have
been a sodality (or moiety) storeroom (Wilcox 1987b). Figure 11.1 shows
that a linear space without Sedentary houses partitions the central precinct
into northern and southern halves. It is flanked by two extra-large houses
that may have been council chambers (Wilcox, McGuire, and Sternberg
1981:182), and it links Mound 29, the highest artificial mound, with the

southern end of the small ballcourt. This partitioning also divides the ring of eight artificial mounds into two groups of four, a sacred number among many New World societies. Because these data remain unique, one might dismiss them as chance relationships; on the contrary, I hypothesize that they indicate a moiety organization and other sodalities that crosscut it (Wilcox 1987b). Such a system is very like that reported for the historic Pueblo peoples (Kroeber 1917; Ortiz 1969). The generality of such relationships should be tested with comparable data from other Sedentary sites.

In *Hohokam Ballcourts and Their Interpretation* (Wilcox and Sternberg 1983), one chapter was devoted to assembling site structure information on a series of other settlements so that the generality of the pattern seen at Snaketown could be evaluated. At Snaketown, a large east-west ballcourt was located on the west side of the plaza and a small north-south court was on the east side (see fig. 11.1). At Villa Buena, near the junction of the Salt and Gila rivers, I found that these relations were reversed: that is, a large east-west court was on the east side of a large flat area (plaza?), and a small north-south court was on the west side. At Martinez Hill in the Tucson Basin, an entirely different configuration was found: a large north-south court lay on the west side of a large flat area (plaza?), and a small east-west court was on the east side (Wilcox and Sternberg 1983:133–74; see also Wilcox 1985).

The data on ballcourt distributions and orientations (Wilcox and Sternberg 1983; Wilcox 1985, 1988a) make it clear that Hohokam village sites are not identical to one another in every respect. Rather, a system involving both horizontal and vertical complexity of functions may be indicated (but see below). The vertical levels are as follows: (1) sites with a large ballcourt (in most cases, these sites also have at least one and often several small courts); (2) sites with only one or more small courts; and (3) sites without ballcourts. The differences of ballcourt orientation within vertical levels 1 and 2 may indicate horizontal complementarity of ceremonial activity (Wilcox 1987b, 1988c).

How large were the largest villages? Emil Haury (1976:356) thought it plausible to infer that Snaketown at its apogee had 2,000 residents, with 7,000 houses being built throughout the occupation. In the course of my restudy, I argued that no more than 1,000 houses were ever built there, a finding supported by David Abbott's excellent simulation study (Abbott 1985). Dismayed that my calculation for number of houses was one-seventh of Haury's (1976:356) guesstimate, I went with an assumption of an average house-life of 50 years for the Sedentary period to derive a maximum population of about 1,000 people, half of Haury's estimate

(Wilcox, McGuire, and Sternberg 1981:185–97). An average house-life of 15 years is more conservative and sensible, however, and I would now argue that Snaketown at its height had no more than about 300 people (Wilcox 1987b). This is also the scale of the Galaz Village in the Mimbres area (Anyon and LeBlanc 1984:187–92). These were not large villages (see Sanders et al. 1979:56).

CLASSIC PERIOD

The internal complexity of Hohokam villages increased during the Classic period. The compounds surrounding the central platform mound (Ruin 1) at Los Muertos are larger than the ones farther out, and the same pattern is apparent at Casa Grande Ruins, where a central precinct of large compounds surrounds a large north-south ballcourt and a possible plaza area southeast of the court. A concentric zone of small compounds surrounds the central precinct. One of these, Compound F, has been excavated (Woodward 1931; Hayden 1957); it was successively rebuilt during the late Soho and Civano phases (Andresen 1985) and thus was contemporaneous with the large compounds (Fewkes 1912; Hayden 1957). In addition to the ballcourt and a possible plaza, the central precinct was the location of two platform mounds (in Compound B) and a four-story structure, the Casa Grande (in Compound A), that probably was an astronomical observatory (Molloy 1969; Evans and Hillman 1981; Wilcox 1987b). A nonrandom distribution of social functions is thus indicated, as is differential access to these important facilities by the suprahousehold residence groups occupying the large compounds.

Over 40 platform mound sites are known in the Phoenix Basin (Gregory and Nials 1985; Wilcox 1987a). The mounds vary in overall size, the complexity of their construction history, the size of their compounds, the number of other associated features, the size of the settlement in which they occur, and so forth. Four levels of vertical complexity that probably are correlated with different social functions are as follows: (1) sites with a platform mound, a Casa Grande tower, a ballcourt, and numerous compounds (Casa Grande, Pueblo Grande, La Ciudad, Las Colinas?, and Mesa Grande?); (2) sites with a medium-sized platform mound and several other compounds (Escalante, Los Hornos, Villa Buena II, Las Acequias, Los Muertos); (3) sites with a single platform mound/compound and no other compounds (Casa Buena, Pueblo Ultimo, Brady Wash); and (4) sites without a platform mound (Grand Canal?).

Three of the five sites in level 1 are on the same macrocanal system (Pueblo Grande, La Ciudad, and Las Colinas). Pueblo Grande has the largest platform mound (Turney 1929), and Las Colinas the largest number of platform mounds (four); both sites are larger than La Ciudad. Pueblo Grande controlled the canal head, while Las Colinas occupied the end of the system where the most irrigable land may have been. The existence of a political hierarchy among these settlements is an intriguing possibility (see Wilcox 1988c).

The population of Classic period villages is most difficult to estimate. Complete site plans are available for only one site, Los Muertos, where 35 compounds were documented by Cushing (Brunson 1989). If we first multiply this figure by 75 percent to factor out the possible late Soho component, and then by 20 to 30, an estimated size of a suprahousehold group in any one compound, then a total population of 520 to 780 is reached. Assuming that not all of the Los Muertos compounds were absolutely contemporaneous, a guesstimate of 600 seems most reasonable. It should also be noted that Cushing chose Los Muertos for excavation because he felt that it was representative, not because it was the largest village; the largest probably was Mesa Grande (Cushing 1893; J. Howard 1987). Multiplying 600 times 40 villages suggests a middle Classic period population in the Phoenix Basin of approximately 24,000.

REGIONAL NETWORKS OF PUBLIC ARCHITECTURE AND CEREMONIES

The people living in individual settlements were not wholly autonomous. They depended on people in other settlements for spouses, exchange goods, and information—all of which were critical to their survival. Thus, above the level of the site we must consider larger social systems or fields of intersection. The larger level most studied by Hohokam archaeologists is the region.

A decade ago, when I first proposed that the concept of Hohokam culture should be reinterpreted as a "regional system" (Wilcox 1979a, 1980), the idea was put forward as a methodological or metatheoretical concept. I was skeptical of the Gladwinian model of migrations (Wilcox and Shenk 1977) and proposed that a less biased way to investigate alternative hypotheses (including migration) about the behavioral interactions of local populations with one another (which the distribution of red-on-buff pottery and similar death ritual or ritual paraphernalia indicated) was to approach the problem from the standpoint of a regional system. Artifact distribution, principally of red-on-buff pottery, was the primary criteria for defining the region.

Gregory (this volume; see also McGuire 1988) finds that the idea has become reified, a danger I recall Fred Plog warning me about in 1979. In the interim, it has nevertheless had a salutary effect on Hohokam studies. In my ballcourt monograph I attempted to make the idea theoretically specific by postulating a particular model of an evolving regional system based on parameters of the ballcourt network. The focus of "regional" definition thus shifted from artifacts to public architecture. In subsequent work, I have not hesitated to modify this model as new data seemed to warrant, and this process should continue. While reification ("ruling theories" in Chamberlin's [1965] sense) certainly must be guarded against (see Dean 1987), I believe the regional system idea still has considerable utility as a way to think about the interactions among local groups.

Two kinds of Hohokam public architecture provide points of departure for thinking about social interaction among the people in a large set of settlements—or regional system—having such architecture. These are ballcourts (Wilcox and Sternberg 1983) and platform mounds (Gregory and Nials 1985; Gregory, this volume; Wilcox 1987a). Both have been systematically studied, although new examples continue to be discovered, necessitating a rethinking of earlier theories. They also serve to define "regions" of very different size, and the nature of intersection that they imply is not the same. Furthermore, the "regional system" definable using ballcourt data changed far more through time than I had originally postulated (Wilcox and Sternberg 1983; see Wilcox 1988a), and it seems likely that the platform mound "system" was equally dynamic.

BALLCOURTS

The best-known forms of Hohokam public architecture are ballcourts (fig. 11.2); over 200 courts at 163 sites are known. These features are large, oval depressions, normally surrounded by earthen embankments, where a version of the Mesoamerican ball game probably was played. Emil Haury (in Gladwin et al. 1937) first formulated this hypothesis, which eventually was eloquently challenged by Edwin Ferdon (1967). The central argument of my ballcourt monograph (Wilcox and Sternberg 1983; see also Wilcox 1986a) is a reply to Ferdon's challenge. The formal differences between Mesoamerican and Hohokam courts can be explained as due to independent invention if (1) the ball game, not the ballcourt, diffused northward, and (2) the courts are functionally comparable. A case can be made for both propositions (Wilcox and Sternberg 1983). The first Hohokam courts were built during the Gila Butte phase (Gladwin et al. 1937:41; Wilcox and Sternberg 1983). Pioneer period figurines, however, which Haury (1976: 265) recognized as probably ballplayer representations, support the hypothesis that the game was played in southern Arizona even before the first courts were built.

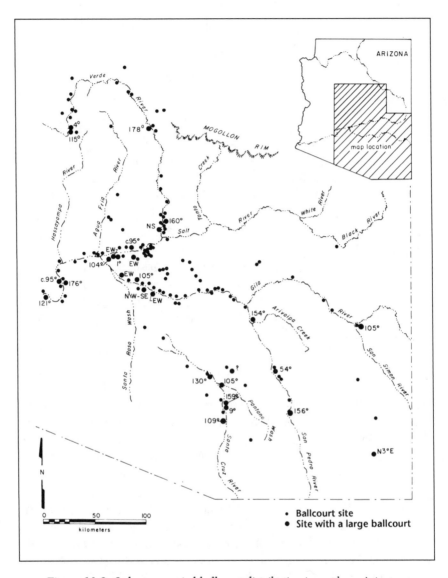

Figure 11.2. *Sedentary period ballcourt distribution in southern Arizona. The long-axis orientation of large ballcourts is given in degrees east of true north (e.g., 105°) or directionally (e.g., NS).*

The largest Hohokam court ever built was at Snaketown (Wilcox and Sternberg 1983). It was also one of the earliest, and it was refurbished and maintained at least into the very late Colonial period. It is still evident on the landscape today and might easily have been used throughout the Sedentary period. It thus could have been contemporaneous with the small court at Snaketown that was built during the Sedentary period; the two courts then would have been functionally complementary, with different ceremonies conducted in each. At the Citrus Site, similar complementarity has been reported (Wasley and Johnson 1965:40–41), and it may have existed at many other sites (see Wilcox and Sternberg 1983; Wilcox 1986a, 1988a); unfortunately, we cannot be certain of this. William Doelle and Henry Wallace (1986) present valuable arguments favoring the view that the large courts in the Tucson Basin are Colonial facilities, most of which were abandoned before the end of the Sedentary period. It is presently impossible to choose between these hypotheses. It should be noted, however, that there are both large and small Colonial period courts (Wilcox 1985, 1988a), so some kind of functional differentiation is assured.

What are the implications of ballcourts as public architecture and ceremonial facilities? I argue that ballcourts indicate the operation and evolution of a ceremonial exchange system that more or less continuously linked Hohokam settlements into a polythetic regional system (Wilcox and Sternberg 1983; Wilcox 1985, 1986a, 1987b, 1988a) (see fig. 11.2). By "polythetic," I mean that the nature of interaction and its archaeological expression were visible across the set of interacting settlements (see Mayo 1949; Needham 1975). Rectangular great kivas indicate an analogous network centered on the Mimbres Valley (Anyon 1984), whereas circular great kivas form a monothetic network centered on Chaco Canyon (cf. Lekson, this volume).

The principal evidence for a Hohokam regional system is seen in the ballcourt orientation data (Wilcox and Sternberg 1983:210–17; Wilcox 1988a). Three periods are apparent: (1) early Colonial through early Sedentary, when the widest range of orientations and greatest size variability is present; (2) the late Sedentary, when sharply differentiated large and small courts are present; and (3) the early Classic, when the large courts are abandoned (by about A.D. 1200) and the system is sharply curtailed. In the last period the range of orientations of the large east-west courts is seen in the newly emergent platform mounds and compounds. During all three periods, each local area exhibits a wide range of variability in court orientations, and the large courts tend to alternate back and forth from east-west to north-south as one moves up- or downriver. If the ballcourt ceremonialism of each site complements that of its neighbors, these patterns may be explained as the manifestation of a system of intervillage ceremonial exchanges among corporate groups or sodalities. Participation in this system changed radically from the beginning to the end of the three periods. The Tucson Basin south of Los Morteros, for example, may have dropped out as early as A.D. 1000 to 1100 (Wallace 1988; Doelle and Wallace 1988a), whereas the Flagstaff area did not join the system until the middle 1000s (Wilcox 1986c).

PLATFORM MOUNDS AND TOWERS

The nature of the Hohokam regional system changed fundamentally in the early Classic period when two other forms of Hohokam public architecture—platform mounds and Casa Grande towers—became important. David Gregory's studies of Mound 8 at Los Colinas (Gregory, Abbott, et al. 1988) contribute substantially to our knowledge of platform mounds. His findings (this volume) show that platform mounds were the center of special precincts within Classic period villages where activities were conducted that were hidden from general view behind palisades. On the east, north, west, and south sides of Mound 8, a succession of houses were built whose locations, sizes, floor assemblages, and other associations show that they were not ordinary habitations but ritual facilities that were differentiated by function. Suddenly, in the mid-1200s, a new pattern was imposed: the mound was built up with a massive rectangular retaining wall, habitation structures were built on top for the first time, and the mound was surrounded by a massive rectangular compound wall (Gregory, this volume). What does all of this mean?

One conclusion should be clear: the people who began living on top of the mounds were not ordinary residents. Data from Mound A at La Ciudad (Wilcox 1987a) show that only one to three households were living on these medium-sized mounds. A similar situation is evident at Escalante (Doyel 1981), but only fragmentary data are available from all other platform mounds (but see Haury 1945; Brunson 1989). While recognizing that the nature of occupation on the largest platform mounds (Mesa Grande, Pueblo Grande) may have been quite different, and that occupation of any kind on the smallest mounds is questionable, I believe that the La Ciudad and Escalante data are reasonably taken as representative of the second vertical level of Classic period sites defined above.

Two striking conclusions that emerge from an analysis of the floor assemblages on these mounds are that they had a very large number of storage rooms compared to the pattern apparent in small compounds (Wilcox 1987a; Sires 1983; Andresen 1985), and that their architectural history is consistent with the developmental cycle of a single large house-

hold group (Wilcox 1987a:115–17). Thus, the people living on the platform mounds in the second level of Classic period sites probably were
members of high-ranking corporate groups with considerably greater
wealth than those in other compounds (corporate groups). They were an
elite that probably was invested with sacred authority to mediate for the
larger community with the gods, having taken over ritual functions previously handled by religious sodalities. The rank order in size of compounds—the largest at or near the platform mound and the smaller ones
farther away—is probably correlated with social rank among the corporate
groups (Wilcox 1987a, 1988c).

The Casa Grande, also known as the Big House of the Casa Grande
Ruins, is like a platform mound in that it is a habitation structure erected
on an artificially filled first story. Platform mounds, however, also had
courtyards on top, which the Casa Grande lacks; the Casa Grande really is a
four-story tower, while the structures on platform mounds were at most
two stories high (Wilcox and Shenk 1977; Wilcox 1987a). As a tower, the
Casa Grande served as an astronomical observatory (Molloy 1969; Evans
and Hillman 1981; Wilcox 1987b), and its occupants would have had
control of the information necessary to regulate the calendrical ceremonial
system. The value of the tower for managing the irrigation system on canals
that linked multiple settlements has also been suggested (Valcarce and
Kayser 1969).

Two other Casa Grande-like towers have recently been identified. One is
a three-story structure partially excavated by Frank Cushing (1893) in
1887. It lies about 670 meters (2,230 ft.) north-northeast of the Pueblo
Grande platform mound (Fewkes 1910:425). The base of this structure,
the first professionally excavated prehistoric building in the American
Southwest, is still partially extant, although it is in imminent danger of
destruction by freeway construction (Cory Breternitz, personal communication, 1988). The second tower was Mound B at La Ciudad, which has
already been destroyed. Frank Midvale, who excavated it in 1929, described it as a "tower," an identification which his map confirms (Pilles
1967; Wilcox 1987a).

If there were three towers, I believe there probably also were others.
Given their other characteristics, Mesa Grande and Las Colinas might have
had them; at least, current data do not preclude this possibility.

In the published version of my dissertation (Wilcox and Shenk 1977), I
showed that the Casa Grande was built during a single construction
episode that involved assembling nearly 600 roof beams (each about 4 m
long) from over 100 kilometers (60 mi.) away, and digging up, puddling,
and transporting to the building site some 1,100 cubic meters (1,500 cu.

yds.) of caliche. That effort required many times the labor necessary to build most houses or even entire compounds. The ability to mobilize this kind of labor in a short time is impressive, and it is evidence that some degree of vertical complexity is plausible.

DEATH RITES

Burial assemblages have long been a focus for testing hypotheses about social differentiation (Brown 1971a; Peebles and Kus 1977). Unfortunately, Hohokam burial data have not yet been assembled in a way that permits systematic comparisons. Nevertheless, several conclusions are possible. First, if there were significant differences in status, its costumes were perishable textiles or feathers that have yet to be documented. Second, nothing comparable to the wealth of Mississippian burial assemblages (see Brown 1971b; Peebles and Kus 1977) is present in the Hohokam area. The adult burials on Ruin I at Los Muertos (Haury 1945; Brunson 1989) or Mound A at La Ciudad (Wilcox 1987a) had relatively few artifacts with them. Nevertheless, Cushing's analysis (Cushing 1890:176) is worth considering:

> Since the art-remains of the Ultra-mural houses [pit houses] and mounds were invariably . . . those obviously of an Industrial class of people, while within both the communal buildings and the Temples more luxurious articles, as well as abundant sacred paraphernalia occurred, the inference became irresistible that of the three or four Classes or Castes constituting the populations of these cities, the highest was that which occupied the Temples [platform mounds], presumably a Hereditary Chief-Priesthood; the second, that which occupied the better portion of the communal dwellings presumably an initiated and gentile Priesthood; the third, that which, in common with the latter, occupied the same communal houses and were buried in the pyral mounds pertaining thereto, – the ordinary or "younger" gentile class; and, finally, that which, as an Outcast element ·. . . namely the dwellers in the Ultra-mural structures, whose remains were also buried in what . . . we may call the Ultra-mural pyral mounds . . . common or working people.

A third conclusion that we can make about Hohokam death rites is that differences in burial location and treatment of the body are the chief indicators of social differentiation in the Classic period burial assemblages. The most unique burials are inhumations in "sarcophagi" (Fewkes 1912;

Cushing 1890; Wilcox and Sternberg 1981), which have been found on Ruin I at Los Muertos and in Fewkes's Clan House A in the central precinct at Casa Grande Ruins; the latter case had painted symbols associated with it (Andresen 1983). Inhumations also occur in other contexts on platform mounds (with infants or children in storage room floors and with adults in courtyards), in compounds off of the mounds, or in cemeteries or isolated contexts outside of compounds (Wilcox 1987a). Cremations normally occur in cemeteries east or north of the compounds (Haury 1945; Sires 1983).

Significant changes occurred over time in the ritual of death and probably in beliefs about death. Beginning apparently in the middle Colonial period, numerous cremation cemeteries appeared in riverine settlements; they have yielded a distinctive set of ritual paraphernalia (palettes, censors, carved shell) that are the hallmarks of Hohokam cultural identity. Abruptly, at about A.D. 1100, and concurrent with the disintegration of the regional network of ballcourts, that distinctive assemblage of ritual paraphernalia ceased to be used (Doyel 1980, 1988; Wilcox and Sternberg 1983; Wilcox 1987b; Gregory, this volume). Cremation burial continued, but Classic assemblages have a higher "dependency ratio" of nonproducers to all age classes than do Preclassic ones, suggesting a change in the definition of adulthood and beliefs about who had the right to be cremated (see Morris and Brooks 1987).

A final conclusion that can be reached is that beliefs about death were probably closely tied to beliefs about life and the role of different people in both the upperworld and the underworld (Binford 1971). The greatest complexity in Hohokam burial practices is apparent during the middle Classic period (Brunson 1989).

I believe that a much wider comparison than has yet been attempted among New World societies and their beliefs about death, burial ritual, and burial locations and assemblages is necessary if we are to have more than ad hoc arguments about the interpretation of these data. Connections between Mesoamerica and the American Southwest have been well documented, although the mechanisms of interaction are still uncertain (Gladwin et al. 1937; Di Peso, Rinaldo, and Fenner 1974a; Weigand 1978, 1979; McGuire 1980; Mathien and McGuire 1986). The rise of Paquimé (Casas Grandes in northwestern Chihuahua) appears to have brought with it new ideologies about death (see below). The spread of the kachina cult from the Little Colorado River valley into the Rio Grande also transformed conceptions of the relationship between life and death, although in a very different way. A better understanding of these processes should bring with it an improved comprehension of how social status was conceived in the later prehistory of the Southwest.

CULTURAL LANDSCAPES

One of the most exciting developments in current Hohokam studies is the growing corpus of data from the intensive surveys being conducted by Paul Fish, William Doelle, and others who are systematically filling in the huge blank areas between the Phoenix and Tucson basins and the area west of the Tucson Basin (Fish and Fish 1988; Craig and Wallace 1987; Dart 1987; Ciolek-Torrello and Wilcox 1988). Ten years ago, Hohokam archaeology was site-centric; everything was compared to Snaketown. The ballcourt study (Wilcox and Sternberg 1983) created a different image, that of a regional network (see fig. 11.2), although the methodology involved little more than connecting the dots. Network analysis has a lot of potential (Hage and Harary 1983), but it has yet to be attempted seriously in Hohokam studies (but see Wilcox 1988c).

At first glance, the traditionally recognized core-periphery structure of Hohokam site distributions (Gladwin and Gladwin 1935; Gladwin et al. 1937) appeared to be confirmed by the ballcourt data, although in a somewhat more complex way (Wilcox and Sternberg 1983:219–22; see also Wilcox and Shenk 1977:171–99). In addition to the string of riverine villages or hamlets practicing irrigation—the core zone—three peripheral zones were identified: (1) an inner periphery of nonriverine sites within the Phoenix Basin located less than a day's travel from the river, some of which had small ballcourts, irrigation, or reservoirs; (2) an intermediate periphery of river basins contiguous to the Phoenix Basin where irrigation agriculture was possible; and (3) a far periphery that included the Flagstaff area, the upper Salt River drainages, the Safford Valley, and southeastern Arizona.

This model presents a basin-centric view of Hohokam prehistory that is currently being challenged (Fish et al. 1987; Doelle and Wallace 1988a; McGuire 1988; Gregory, this volume). The Tucson Basin may not have been a passive recipient of influence from the Phoenix Basin, as some versions of the core-periphery model suggest (Wilcox and Shenk 1977).

Just as the Mimbres regional system jettisoned all Hohokam traits after A.D. 1000 (Anyon 1984; Minnis 1985), so too did the Tucson Basin— possibly becoming the center of a red-on-brown O'odham region in the 1000s (Doelle and Wallace 1988a; McGuire 1988). In each case, independent access to the wealth represented by seashells may have been involved. Fish designs on Mimbres Classic Black-on-white indicate that culture's direct access to the Gulf of California in the Guaymas area (Jett and Moyle 1986), and the route is remarkably like Paquimé's later shell route (Di Peso, Fenner, and Rinaldo 1974b:385). Similarly, increasing influence by Tucson Basin populations in eastern Papaguería (McGuire 1988) could have established connections with O'odham populations in the Altar Valley, and hence to the Gulf of California. Redefining the structural relationships within the Hohokam networks and how they changed as the nature of regional and macroregional interactions changed remains one of the central challenges of Hohokam archaeology.

Between the basins there certainly was a "rural" population of unknown relative proportion to the various basin populations (Ciolek-Torrello, Callahan, and Greenwald 1988; Fish and Fish 1988; Dart 1987). A series of ballcourts and small platform mounds are now being discovered in this interbasin zone (although some were reported long ago; see Huntington 1914).

The zone between the Tucson and Phoenix basins may have been an important reservoir of population whose integration with the basin populations defined a significant regulatory mechanism. Southern Arizona is a wide-open environment, little constrained by the bonds of natural circumscription. Even within the irrigated zone, three to four times more land was available than was irrigated at any one time (Nicholas 1981; Gregory, this volume). The ballcourt network, too, was an open system marked more by continuities of interaction than by boundaries (see fig. 11.2). How then, if an increase in vertical complexity is associated with social control (Carneiro 1970, 1981; Cowgill 1975), could social control have come about in the Phoenix Basin or elsewhere when avoiding it was apparently so easily accomplished by moving away?

The answer to this question seems to be relatively straightforward. Greater social circumscription came about after A.D. 1100 when the regional ballcourt network disintegrated, severing connections between the Phoenix Basin and its intermediate peripheries (Wilcox and Sternberg 1983; Wilcox 1987a; Doelle and Wallace 1988a). Concurrently, most of the inner periphery, or nonriverine area, of the Phoenix Basin was abandoned (Teague and Crown 1984; Doyel and Elson 1985), as were nonriverine areas west of Tucson (Dart 1987; Doelle and Wallace 1988a). A profound result of these processes was that the structure of the networks integrating the Phoenix and Tucson basins with outside areas changed fundamentally. Several primary sites such as Snaketown and Las Cremaciones were abandoned, and the locations of others such as Villa Buena and Casa Grande shifted a quarter of a mile or so and were reorganized (Wilcox and Sternberg 1983). The rank of some sites in the site hierarchy fell (for example, Villa Buena and Hodges), while that of others rose (Casa Grande, Mesa Grande, Martinez Hill). Changes in the crop mixes produced in different areas and the patterns of consumption also changed substantially. In some areas, agave began to be grown in large quantities (Fish, Fish, and Madsen 1985; Doelle, Dart, and Wallace 1985). Cotton was also grown and manufactured into textiles in much greater quantity than ever before (Gasser and Miksicek 1985; Wilcox 1987a).

The result of these settlement abandonments and shifts in the Phoenix Basin was the emergence of three site clusters, one on the Salt River, where Pueblo Grande became the most centrally located site, and two smaller ones on the Gila (Wilcox 1988c). The emergence of such site clusters, which probably were politically integrated in some way vis-à-vis their neighbors, was a general process in the Southwest during the Pueblo III or early Classic periods (see Upham 1982; Jewett 1989). Warfare among these polities eventually resulted in widespread regional abandonment (Upham and Reed 1989; Wilcox 1989), but new forms of macroeconomic relationships also resulted that produced some of the most complex (and interesting) sociopolitical systems to evolve in the aboriginal Southwest (Wilcox 1988b).

After A.D. 1200, and in conjunction with the processes described above, the flow of water in the Salt and Gila rivers was much less predictable (Gregory, this volume). It thus appears that Hohokam populations were much more at risk than ever before. Along with boundaries defining local settlement systems, fortified sites were built, suggesting that conflict increased (Wilcox 1979b, 1988c, 1988d, 1989; Doelle and Wallace 1988a). Fleeing to the countryside to escape famine or oppression was clearly possible in the Colonial and Sedentary periods, but not during the Classic. To survive, the riverine villagers apparently had to buckle down and make the irrigation systems work for them as never before. For these systems to succeed, social control and the coordination of different interest groups was essential to ensure that labor was mobilized whenever necessary and in whatever numbers were needed to keep the canals operational. This is the ecological context that characterizes the moment when 40 or so families moved onto the tops of the platform mounds and began administrating the lives of their people.

MACROREGIONAL FIELDS OR SYSTEMS

From the time of the first Snaketown work (Gladwin et al. 1937), it has been certain that Hohokam culture change was related in some way to external forces originating in Mesoamerica. Iron-pyrites mirrors, macaws, *Strombus* (conch) shells, copper bells—all rare valuables—entered southern Arizona from the south. That they played significant, if poorly understood, roles in the ritual life of the Hohokam is widely accepted. Yet how these items reached the Hohokam and what the social mechanisms were remain matters of vigorous debate and empirical obscurity (Di Peso 1974; Kelley and Kelley 1975; Plog, Upham, and Weigand 1982; Mathien and McGuire 1986). The fact that Piman is a dialect of the Tepiman language, which links southern Arizona with the Chalchihuites area in Zacatecas and Durango, Mexico, where close stylistic relationships with the Hohokam are found (Kelley 1971), strikes me as a potentially significant clue to how Hohokam-Mesoamerican connections were effected (Wilcox 1986a, 1986b).

Of greater current interest is the possible role played by the rise of Paquimé in northwestern Chihuahua in producing greater social complexity in southern Arizona and New Mexico. Recent reexamination of the wood from Paquimé has shown that the sapwood rings are mostly missing (Ravesloot, Dean, and Foster 1986). This means that the chronology of the Medio period pertains to the thirteenth and fourteenth centuries, coeval with the Hohokam Classic period.

Paquimé was at its height during the Paquimé phase, which correlates with the Hohokam Civano phase. This is when the Hohokam platform mounds were occupied. Paquimé had a monopoly on the production and distribution of valuables such as copper bells, macaws, and *Conus* tinklers (Di Peso 1974), which were important in the Hohokam Classic period political economy. I have postulated elsewhere (Wilcox 1988b, 1988d) that Paquimé was the center of a macroeconomy that included the Phoenix Basin Hohokam in a tertiary sphere of interaction. When Paquimé declined and was abandoned during the early fifteenth century, the entire macroeconomy centered on that site disintegrated, and regionwide abandonment followed. Massive floods in the Phoenix Basin (Gregory, this volume) may have influenced abandonment there, but this process was also linked to processes in a macroregional field of interaction about which archaeologists are only beginning to ask questions (see Haury 1976). This, too, is an area requiring further research before the issue of Hohokam social complexity can be fully addressed.

SUMMARY

Hohokam archaeology has come a long way in the last 10 to 15 years. The facile conception of the Hohokam as an egalitarian, tribal people like the Pima who lived in randomly structured villages has given way to a more complex picture. A multiplicity of scales of interaction became more horizontally and vertically complex during the millennium and a half during which Hohokam culture evolved. What began as a polythetic web of interconnections became increasingly differentiated as social and cultural boundaries formed. Following the adoption of large-scale irrigation, corporate kin groups emerged and became crosscut by sodalities that were integrated regionally by a ceremonial exchange system. When this system disintegrated circa A.D. 1100, sharply circumscribed local systems emerged that began to interact with one another in new ways. Both internal and external ecological and social factors then conjoined to produce a short-lived expression of vertical social complexity in the Phoenix Basin when more than 40 families moved onto the platform mounds. By the middle of the fourteenth century the civic authority of these elite groups was lost, and within another century Hohokam culture as a historical tradition disappeared.

Much remains to be learned about Hohokam archaeology. Its changing articulation with macroregional fields is perhaps the greatest unknown, but is by no means the least important area requiring new research. As I have sought to show in this paper, however, questions at every level remain unanswered, and it is far from certain that we have even learned what questions to ask. The advanced seminar, by compelling us to compare our ideas with those generated about adjacent regions, where different regional systems emerged and disintegrated, helps us all to think more clearly about our work and to report it in a way that others can understand.

——— *Acknowledgments* ———

Louella Holter's flawless typing, Emilee Mead's excellent draftsmanship, and Evelyn Wong's gracious assistance at the Bilby Research Center, Northern Arizona University, made the task of manuscript preparation a pleasure. Exceptional thanks are also due to the seminar participants for a stimulating and productive time. For her enduring support, I would like to thank my wife, Susan. Any and all problems, errors, or unwarranted speculation remain my responsibility alone.

Chapter 12

The Comparative Context of
Social Complexity

CHARLES L. REDMAN

IN this volume, various authors appraise to what extent either the Hohokam or the people of Chaco Canyon attained a level of social development that could be appropriately called "complex society." Before evaluating the merits of each case, it is useful to consider briefly the concept of social complexity, its essential elements, and its relevance to the prehistoric American Southwest. To provide a comparative perspective for the preceding chapters, I will also present an overview of the development of complex society in two examples from the Old World. Although distinct, each case highlights general processes that may have relevance to the Southwestern cases. Moreover, both of the Old World societies left written records that provide a political and social context for the archaeologically observed developments.

In assessing the meaning of complex society, scholars have relied on various measures and the existence of selected traits. Probably the first systematic analysis, and in some ways the most insightful, was V. Gordon Childe's definition of civilization (Childe 1951). The ten traits he associated with civilization were large populations, specialization of labor, concentration of surplus, class-structured society, state organization, monumental public works, long-distance trade, standardized artwork, arithmetic, and writing. It is clear that the two Southwestern societies we are concerned with exhibited some of these traits but lacked others. This eliminates them from being identified as civilizations in Childe's scheme, but it leaves open the question of degree of social complexity.

Anthropologists have responded to Childe's all-or-nothing trait-list approach with a series of models of alternative social and community forms that allow for a progression of social types. The two best-known systems are the alternate social relational forms of Morton Fried (1967) and the series of community organizational forms of Elman Service (1962, 1975). Fried posits that the criteria used to differentiate status in a society are a useful means of classifying societies into either egalitarian, ranked, stratified, or state societies. At least for the moment, the case for a true state society in the Southwest seems weak, so we will limit our discussion to the three alternative forms.

In an egalitarian society, as defined by Fried, there are as many positions of prestige in any given age-sex classification as there are persons capable of filling them. In a ranked society, limitations are placed on access to valued status positions, resulting in fewer positions of valued status than the number of people capable of achieving them. Various techniques are employed for limiting status positions to certain persons or families, the simplest being birth order. Fried (1967) suggests that the notion of rank is not inherent in human beings but is the result of economic and other external factors. In a stratified society, there are institutionalized differential relationships among its members with respect to means of subsistence. The means of allocating positions of preferred status are more formalized, and with these high-status positions comes privileged access to economic and political power.

Service's system parallels Fried's, but focuses on alternative community forms as identified in the ethnographic record. Service (1962, 1975) proposes four ideal societal types: bands, tribes, chiefdoms, and states. This typological scheme has been utilized by many archaeologists as a guide to interpreting archaeological remains (Sanders and Price 1968; Renfrew 1974). Bands are small, territorial hunting-and-gathering groups that lack social techniques for integrating local groups into larger aggregations. The major development that distinguishes tribes from bands is the creation of techniques to integrate local groups into a larger society (see Braun and Plog 1982). A chiefdom is comprised of several groups more or less permanently organized into a hierarchical social system. A well-developed form of Fried's ranked society, a chiefdom does not have social classes in the modern sense, but some of its members attain social positions that carry enhanced power and privilege (see Feinman and Neitzel 1984).

Some scholars will argue either of two extreme cases: that prehistoric Southwestern groups never attained more than egalitarian social relations (Whittlesey 1978), or that fully developed states existed in the Southwest (Di Peso 1974; Upham 1982). The scholars represented in this volume, however, seem to be taking the more middle-of-the-road position that they are dealing with a ranked situation, in Fried's terminology, or a tribe or chiefdom, in Service's. Although this position provides some interpretive models to work with, like other scholars I find the distinction between these social types to be too rigid and difficult to identify in the archaeological record.

Recently, some scholars have suggested that alternative forms of social complexity can be best understood as a continuum and best identified by measurement of key variables rather than by assignment to a particular category. One such approach focuses on the degree of internal differentiation found, and the means and levels of decision-making apparatus that existed (G. Johnson 1978; Flannery 1972). This approach derives from an interest in Old World civilizations whose written records have provided insights into the workings of early administrative hierarchies. Although written records are lacking for the Southwest, the concern with levels in a decision-making hierarchy is useful. Other scholars have attempted to represent alternative forms of society in terms of their measurable "heterogeneity" (McGuire 1983) or the nature and frequency of their bounded groups (Kowalewski et al. 1983).

Given the various approaches other authors have taken to measuring and understanding complex societies, what do I consider the key aspects of social complexity? Having done fieldwork in both the Old and New World and with societies at civilizational and precivilizational levels, I have pondered the question frequently. One immediate observation I can make is that the material remains themselves are not the answer to the puzzle of social complexity. There are no striking differences between a Neolithic and an early state community in terms of the buildings people lived in and the material inventory they utilized. This judgment reflects the ethnographically observable fact that for many people in a preindustrial state society, material lifeways are not qualitatively different from those of their predecessors in a prestate situation. I believe that the essential characteristics that distinguish complex societies from their predecessors are newly emergent forms of social relations. The two domains of relations that interest me are those reflecting group "interdependence" and those enhancing the "legitimization" of the new social order.

Some form of interdependence among individuals exists in all societies, but in complex society it attains a higher order. Specialization of production, exchange of goods, and control of new forms of knowledge all reach scales and intensities previously unknown. Moreover, interdependence in simpler societies often acted to equalize the distribution of goods among people. In a complex society this redistribution has been altered to provide unequal distribution of goods and access to productive resources. Although in most prestate societies some generalized form of balanced reciprocity underlies the movement of goods and services, this seems no longer to be the case in complex societies, in which these movements appear to be asymmetrical. It is the "value added" through collection of surpluses, unequal exchanges in redistribution of goods, and direct accumulations through taxes, conscription, and corvée labor that provides the economic basis for elite groups and nonproductive specialists. Hence, interdependence establishes a set of social relationships that allow certain groups to exert control over others, while at the same time providing an economic basis sufficient to support these groups, often in a sumptuous manner.

But if balanced reciprocity has dominated human society for the majority of its existence, how does a seemingly unbalanced situation such as the complex society I portray come into being? I believe the answer lies in the fact that the people on the "short" end of the exchanges feel that they are getting their true value in return, or at least feel that they are contributing the excess value to something they consider important. For a social order to exist that unequally distributes wealth, access, and control, a convincing ideology that "legitimizes" this seemingly unfair situation must have been developed. An effective ideology portrays the nature of society in such a way that it makes sense for the extant, yet asymmetrical, social relations to exist. Issues of birthright, religion, special knowledge, the afterlife, and the value of the elite all may play a role in justifying the relationships as ultimately balanced, despite the fact that they may seem unequal to an outsider.

Ideologies may be communicated through creation myths, religion, national ethics, school education, canonical art, ritual performance, state-sponsored architecture, or many other media. The message itself may be very direct, but more often is communicated implicitly. It frequently takes the form of a physical symbol represented in art or ritual, or of a symbolic individual or action communicated through myth, religion, or education. Archaeologists may find evidence of it in the way individuals were constrained to move through architectural complexes (Fritz 1986) or in the control of craft specialists in the production of standardized art (Davis 1984).

John Fritz's theories of how architecture was sometimes designed to communicate ideas about social order were first applied to the archaeological remains at Chaco Canyon (1978). Fritz focuses on how the magnificent architecture in Chaco Canyon appears to have been built according to a master plan, employing symmetrical positioning and repeating detailed themes. Fritz posits that a basic symmetry can be seen at several scales in the construction of both ceremonial and domestic buildings. This carefully planned and controlled architectural construction had two effects: first, only those with access to this special knowledge could design the construction of important buildings; and second, while living or performing rituals in these buildings the inhabitants would be forced to follow certain pathways and see certain vistas, all of which contributed to a prearranged effect. Fritz hypothesizes that the impact of these orientations is to provide a parallel on the ground to the cosmological divisions in the universe, and thereby to reinforce the class distinction between the two major divisions in the population (John Fritz, personal communication, 1986). Although Fritz does not address Hohokam material, similar arguments might be constructed for the use of platform mounds, compound walls, and ballcourts in central Arizona.

Several scholars have begun to examine how ideologies, in particular those dealing with legitimizing the social order, are developed and maintained (Cohen 1978). In trying to understand the invariance of Egyptian art, Whitney Davis examines the impact the tight control of early pharaonic canonical art had on the craftsman and on the viewer (1984). Davis (1984:1–2) suggests that both processes serve to reinforce the power and elevation of the ruling group:

> The canon was a systematic "rule-book" for making correctly formed images and for transmitting standards of production from one generation to the next . . . The goal, seemingly, was to obtain a high level of *invariance* between different images, produced at different times and places by different artisans . . . Invariance in discursive or representational practice is in part an expression of the despotic power of an authoritarian state, capable of enforcing uniformity in the public expression of intellectual effort among all members of its population.

The origin and initial acceptance of this uniformity of behavior is not clear. Davis has identified several competing art styles that flourished at the beginning of the Old Kingdom period in Egypt, but by the end of that period, when pharaonic power had coalesced, the canonical style had triumphed.

One approach to the maintenance and transmission of special knowledge that may form an important element of the ideology of a complex society is through secrecy. This secrecy may be embedded in limited-membership groups, such as the secret societies associated with kiva rituals in the American Southwest (Brandt 1980), or it may be controlled by those who hold a particular role in society, such as the blacksmiths of the West African Mande (McIntosh 1984). Brandt has found that among some contemporary Pueblo groups a variety of important information about the ritual cycle and economic affairs is shared only by members or directors of certain secret societies. This information is sought after by other groups and is highly valued within the general society, to the point that individuals or groups can elevate themselves into positions of power on the basis of it.

Susan McIntosh (1984) has suggested, on the basis of ethnohistoric information, that among the Mande and other African peoples, the black-smiths as a group were the only members of many societies to possess crucial sets of information. Of special interest to McIntosh was the detailed knowledge of iron technology, which, it seems, was tightly controlled for some period of time by a few blacksmiths and their associates. The power this would give those individuals is obvious, and we find that in many villages, the shamans were also blacksmiths. In order to prevent the dissemination of this privileged knowledge, the belief was introduced into the culture that working with iron was somehow ritually impure and could damn those practitioners who were not of the appropriate blacksmith class. This combination of a crucial technology, a set of beliefs to restrict its dissemination, and the elevation of a group of individuals to exalted posts is particularly suggestive as a potential element in the origin of complex societies.

There is another aspect of complex societies that I believe is important in their characterization, but that is really only susceptible to humanistic analysis. This is the "sophistication" of the society, expressed in both its products and its on-going lifeways. Creativity, art, science, statecraft, and eventually literature all seemed to have flourished within the context of complex societies. To what extent these expressions are simply the products of the economically more advanced society or are at the core of what makes the society more complex is a subjective assessment. My own concern with legitimization and ideology has led me to believe that they are more central elements than many archaeologists are willing to acknowledge. However, I do not offer any particular methodology to handle the measurement of "sophistication," but only offer it up as an issue to be considered.

In sum then, how do these general theoretical approaches help us illuminate for these two possibly complex Southwestern societies the three major domains of inquiry addressed in this volume: growth, maintenance, and truncation? Simply put, I believe the answer lies in a thorough evaluation of *interrelationships*. In order to conduct such an evaluation, one must be able to recognize what the component units of economic and social self-sufficiency are and how they interrelate. In the development toward complex society these units and their relationships change with emerging asymmetries and dependencies. As asymmetries come to characterize a complex society, there must also be emplaced some means of legitimizing the social hierarchy to the populace. This legitimization is often promulgated by an elite group and may find some manifestation in material remains. Otherwise, the evidence for the changing nature of interrelationships is difficult to assess. The various chapters in this volume touch on this issue in a number of ways, but none addresses it in the theoretical perspective I have presented. I will describe two cases from the Old World in which very different forms of interrelations characterized the complex societies that developed. These two cases contain significant similarities with and differences from the social sytems treated in this volume.

Interpersonal and group dynamics are key elements in understanding complex society, but as many authors in this volume make clear, relations to the environment are also crucial. Characteristics of the environment, both the ability to support a population and the variability of annual climate, are detailed at some length in the chapters by Masse, Vivian, and Judge. Among my objectives in presenting cases studies from the Old World is to examine what might be some key aspects of the environmental conditions leading to complex society. Without pretending to control the Southwestern data as well as the authors of the previous chapters, I will put forward some speculations of my own toward the end of this chapter.

COMPARATIVE OLD WORLD CASE STUDIES: MESOPOTAMIA AND NORTH AFRICA

The origin of civilization in the lowlands of Mesopotamia probably represents the earliest human experiment with social complexity and is among the best studied. Without going into great detail or exploring all the alternative theories, I will present a few ideas and insights that might prove useful in examining the American Southwest. Geographically, Mesopotamia has certain parallels with the core area of the Hohokam, being a hot, dry, alluvial plain traversed by two rivers and bounded by mountainous zones. Although the size of Mesopotamia and the flow of its rivers are far greater than the Salt-Gila rivers and their basin, both areas were difficult to settle without irrigation agriculture. In both cases the mountainous areas and upland valleys were inhabited far earlier than the lowlands, and they supported rainfall agriculturalists.

It is my contention (1978b) that it was the movement of groups into the relatively unoccupied ecological niche of lowland Mesopotamia that stimulated the processes of increasing social complexity. Once plants suitable to the arid saline environment could be developed and irrigation technology was perfected, the alluvial plains of Mesopotamia and the Salt-Gila river valleys could be the setting for highly productive agricultural regimes capable of supporting higher population densities than the surrounding upland regions. Early textual sources tell us that Mesopotamia was a great producer of plant and animal products. Primary among its exports were grain, cloth, and manufactured ceramics. In return, raw materials for both everyday life and elite activities flowed into Mesopotamia. The textual sources go on to indicate that at the core of this system of production and exchange was a redistributive economy directed by a religion-based elite. As yet, we have no archaeological evidence of the large storage facilities alluded to in the texts, but we do have large temple platforms, or ziggurats, thought to be associated with this religious-economic elite. In sum, the early growth of Mesopotamian urban centers is seen as a product of agricultural intensification and local production prompted by the environmental opportunities and necessities. We believe that this society was multi-ethnic and class stratified from very early times.

Concomitant with the growth of urban-size settlement in a core zone located in the Mesopotamian lowlands was a growth of impressive, but not urban-size, settlements in the secondary highland areas. These were usually centered in river valleys in better-watered localities, but still in environments that would benefit from water control apparatuses. A subject of active field research and debate, these secondary florescences appear to have utilized languages and cultural trappings distinct from the more uniform culture of Mesopotamia itself. Hence, we are looking not at colonial expansion, but at development that probably was a response to the increasing needs and opportunities created by the growth in Mesopotamia.

Is the picture of Mesopotamia's situation I have presented in broad brushstrokes relevant to the Hohokam? Some would argue that the Salt-Gila Basin should not be compared to the Mesopotamian core—that it appears to be more similar to one of Mesopotamia's peripheral states, with Mesoamerica acting as the core. This latter parallel is attractive, in that the scale of the secondary river valleys of Mesopotamia is closer to that of the Salt-Gila river valleys, with mountain resources lying in close proximity. However, I find that the evidence points to the Hohokam heartland as being a more independent than peripheral development in terms of subsistence and the majority of trade activities. In addition, the Hohokam seem to lack natural resources that could be shipped to Mexico, a type of exchange that was part of the trade relationship between the secondary centers and the Mesopotamian core. I would argue that many aspects of the geographic situation and the cultural polarities that existed in lowland Mesopotamia can be seen in the southern deserts of Arizona, with the Hohokam occupying what would appear to be the lowland core.

This does not mean that I intend to minimize the importance of Meso-america in the growth of social complexity among the Hohokam. To the contrary, I believe that the external forms of many of the civilizational trappings utilized by the Hohokam demonstrate a strong Mesoamerican influence. My interpretation is that the forces that gave rise to the complex-ity in Hohokam society were internal to the region and primarily involved intensification of agricultural production and local subsistence exchange. However, the structure of some of the integrative institutions, elite goods, and probably the belief systems and ideologies that accompanied them, derived ultimately from Mesoamerica.

Accepting the parallel with Mesopotamia as useful, what archaeological indicators characterize the Mesopotamian situation that might have paral-lels in the Southwest? Although I have spoken of Mesopotamia as if it were a single entity, which culturally it appears to have been, it was comprised of distinct subareas, often containing politically autonomous groups. In fact, when we trace demographic developments in different parts of Meso-potamia as the society approached urbanism, we find that several different trajectories were followed (R. Adams 1981), of which there are two ex-tremes. In the first path of development, all settlement categories seem to grow in tandem; in the second, the larger settlements increase in size at the cost of the surrounding smaller sites. As for architectural manifestations, traditional scholarship in the region has associated the platform mounds with the religious elite and has identified buildings on top of these mounds as temples, based on their consistency in design. Mesopotamian scholars also identify a more limited set of buildings as "palaces" and associate their occurrence with the rise of a later secular elite. In the realm of material inventory, it is interesting to note that pre-urban decorated ceramics came to be characterized by highly stylized geometric painting, both mono-chrome and polychrome (Halafian and Samarran wares). Early urban pottery continued the geometric design tradition, but became more sim-plified and often less well executed as skilled craftspeople devoted their talents to other media (stone bowls, metalwork, etc.). Examples of repre-sentational, and sometimes monumental, art, as well as early examples of writing, also came with the beginnings of urban life. On a very simplistic level, then, Southwestern decorative arts paralleled the precivilizational arts of greater Mesopotamia in the fifth millennium, already a period of substantial movement of goods around the region and some hypothesized cooperative political alliances. Interestingly, the effigies and depictions of human and animal forms in Hohokam crafts may reflect the advanced position of Hohokam society on the road to complexity.

The second Old World case that I would like to present is quite different in its structure and results. It emanates from fieldwork done in northern Morocco by myself and former graduate students (Redman 1986; Boone, Myers, and Redman 1990). We have attempted to explain the rapid rise and large geographic extent of the medieval Islamic states of North Africa, whose distinctive form was first recognized in the literature by Ibn Khaldun (1967) in the fourteenth century. These issues have been much debated, largely among French historians. In looking at this situation as anthropologists, I believe we have discerned some general processes that may apply in many secondary state situations.

We propose that social processes can be best understood as they impact individuals and groups of individuals within societies, each group acting to maximize its own situation, rather than as they impact the total society. Fredrik Barth (1962) first focused anthropological attention on the importance of these groups in his discussion of entrepreneurship. Barth argued that entrepreneurial activity clusters along barriers or discontinuities between discrete spheres of economic activity that involve the circulation of goods and services, and that it takes advantage of the relatively scarce means by which these barriers can be breached (Barth 1962, 1967). We proposed that entrepreneurship conceived of in this way was a major generative factor in the growth of complexity and urban centers in medieval North Africa and possibly in other parts of the world, such as the American Southwest.

From the eleventh through the fourteenth century, a political-economic situation existed in the western Mediterranean that gave rise to a series of successive dynastic states that were focused in North Africa but whose power and influence extended much farther (Ibn Khaldun 1967). We suggest that at two principal loci there emerged discontinuities in the flow of goods and services sufficient to foster the growth of aggregations of entrepreneurial activity amounting to urban proportions. The first locus is the geographically intermediate position of the Maghreb, situated between the gold-producing regions of sub-Saharan Africa (Ghana and the Sudan) and the centers of mercantile activity in the Mediterranean Basin. This discontinuity fostered the rise of the dynastic administrative capitals of interior Morocco that were concerned with facilitating this long-distance trade. The second locus of discontinuity in North Africa is at the geographic periphery of the dynastic empires: the Mediterranean and Atlantic coasts to the north and the edge of the Sahara to the south. We refer to urban centers that developed in these regions as coastal entrepôts; involved in a variety of transshipment activities, they rarely wielded political authority.

The founders of the interior dynasties and their followers may be considered religious-political entrepreneurs who were able to transform local tribal circumstances into a more broadly based and strongly integrated administrative unit. They were primarily concerned with maintaining (and taxing) the long-distance trade and with extending their influence to include as much of the trade network as possible. This goal was accomplished, in part, by redirecting the pattern of blood feuds and tribal warfare to the periphery of the empire through the institution of the *jihad* (holy war) and by laying an overarching and integrative currency of belief (Islam) over the diverse tribal mosaic. Thus, the conduct and spread of Islam played a major role in bringing a number of scattered, autonomous, and often mutually hostile tribes into the framework of a broadly based theocratic state (Boone, Myers, and Redman 1990:54–55).

In its basic form, the foregoing theory suggests the existence of urban centers of two very different types within a single state network. The first type, the dynastic capital, would be politically powerful but might not have vigorous economic activities of its own. The second type of urban center, the coastal entrepôt, would have a wide range of economic activities but often little political or military power. In neither case would the growth of these cities rely primarily on agricultural intensification or well-organized mechanisms of producing and locally redistributing basic goods. In fact, it seems entirely possible that the North African state political apparatus was created and solidified without regard to the preexistence of either cities or an established local urban network.

The North African case thus appears to be distinct from the more frequently described situations in Mesopotamia and Mesoamerica, where there is general agreement that complexity arose at least in part out of a need to control a growing population and to oversee the redistribution of locally produced goods. To the extent that a local production sector emerged in North African cities, it was after the establishment of the dynastic capitals and was a response to the demand created by the substantial numbers of people involved in the administrative, religious, and military activities of the newly formed state. Hence, the centers of state power, or dynastic capitals, were located in areas that were geographically central with respect to the movement of goods and the control of long-distance trade routes; efficient centralization of local production was not their purpose. These areas would have to have reasonable agricultural potential, but not the tremendous potential required of states relying on surplus agricultural production as the basis of their wealth.

Although the dynastic capitals of the North African states were the undisputed centers of political power and were the settlements most completely recorded in historical documents, they, in turn, relied for their very existence on the growth of economically active communities on the periphery of their territory. These coastal entrepôts, as we have called them, were involved with extraction and transshipment of goods, required the full range of economic activities, and often contained larger populations than the capital. Moreover, these entrepôts were often weakly controlled by the dynastic capitals and sometimes independent of them.

Although Mesopotamia and medieval North Africa are very different from anything in the Southwest, I have presented these cases because I believe they are examples of very dissimilar trajectories toward complexity and that in each situation we might find some insight into the Southwestern efforts at complexity. As has already been pointed out, I find intriguing parallels between the environmental situation in Mesopotamia and the conditions of the lower Salt-Gila drainage. Although the comparison is somewhat less obvious, the characteristics of the Chaco phenomenon led me to look for conditions that parallel the North African example I have presented. Among the parallels I have identified are the low population density, far-flung road system, and the location of Chaco in the geographic center of the San Juan Basin, even though this was not the most productive locality. In the Chaco system, agricultural intensification and control of a densely populated region do not seem as prominent as do the spread of cultural markers and the spatial organization of the system. Unlike the Hohokam system, the Chaco network would have controlled access to natural resources that could be of value to other groups, both in the Southwest and perhaps in Mexico. As in the North African situation, the valuable resources may not have been located on land directly controlled by the people of Chaco Canyon, but the Chacoans did control territory that the goods would have to pass through. I would argue that the Chaco phenomenon, like the Hohokam system, is the result of local forces, but in the case of Chaco I would maintain that economic opportunities created by external societies may have been essential in promoting the rise to complexity.

APPLICATION TO THE AMERICAN SOUTHWEST

By reviewing some basic definitions of complexity and these two examples of very different courses toward complex society, I believe a number of potentially important issues have been raised. Central to any evaluation of social complexity is a thorough examination of the nature of the system. In both Southwestern cases we are confronted with systems of great geographic extent, at least according to the distribution of some traits. The essential question is, What is the nature of relations within these systems?

Are the various groups and subregions economically and politically interdependent? That some goods are traded over long distances and that select stylistic motifs are found at these same dispersed settlements does not necessarily imply a strongly linked system. In the seventh-millennium Near East, we know that some goods (obsidian, in particular) moved over great distances and that some art motifs and even ceremonial behaviors were replicated over much of the same area, but no careful scholar would believe that there was any substantial economic interdependence or political control beyond the level of individual settlements.

At some point in the development of intercommunity relations, however, the distribution of shared art styles and other normative behavioral patterns does indicate the possible presence of economic interdependence, political control, or both. Reliably attributing meaning to widely distributed art styles is among the great challenges facing archaeologists today, and efforts are being made to determine local production versus importation of certain ceramic styles (cf. Crown and Bishop 1987; Toll, this volume). Tracing the role of these imported or imitated goods will also be necessary before definitive statements can be made on intercommunity relations.

Another category of evidence used in the Southwest and elsewhere to indicate the presence of economic control and possible political domination is the existence of a regional settlement pattern of large sites interspersed with smaller sites. The implication is that the larger sites serve as primary economic, political, or religious centers, providing higher-order services to the surrounding communities in return for their agricultural produce or conscripted labor. My own experience with that type of regional settlement pattern in the El Morro Valley of west-central New Mexico has led me to doubt that large and small sites in close proximity are necessarily interdependent (Watson, LeBlanc, and Redman 1980). The actual size-distribution of sites in the valley could be characterized as a three-tiered hierarchy, with the largest settlements having perhaps a thousand rooms. However, our excavations and characterization of these sites did not indicate any clear evidence of reliance of the smaller sites on the larger sites, or vice versa. At least in this case, the size of a settlement does not seem to equate with its place in an economic or political hierarchy.

What I would look for, instead, to indicate interdependence among sites would be differentiation in the activities taking place at these sites, as well as evidence for the presence of institutions representing the upper levels of the hierarchy. The impression received from most Chaco and other Anasazi sites is one of repetitiveness: similar room plans and similar site layouts recur, in both relatively small and large sites. Large sites, in fact, appear to be simply multiples of small sites. To the extent that this is true, these sites do not reflect a complex hierarchical system. The Chaco phenomenon does reveal some tendencies toward differentiation, however. The great kivas and massive architecture used in both central and peripheral sites are suggestive of a central institution. Moreover, there are examples of even larger, perhaps interregional, great kivas. At least one of these, Casa Rinconada, holds a very prominent location in Chaco Canyon (cf. Fritz 1978).

Hohokam communities reveal the possible presence of central institutions even more clearly than do those at Chaco. The existence of ballcourts, the focus of settlements around platform mounds, and the ultimate construction of compound walls to enclose these mounds all indicate to me that an early form of hierarchical control was establishing itself. Until we know more about what went on in the buildings on top of the platform mounds and in the compounds that surrounded them, any inference that these housed central institutions will remain largely hypothetical.

Archaeological evidence appears to indicate that one important attribute of complex society is missing from both Chaco and Hohokam. There is general agreement among the authors of this volume that the population density in both areas of the Southwest was relatively low. Given the size and complexity of architectural constructions in both regions, I was surprised at this assertion, which undermines the possibility of a truly complex society. One of the major reasons that politically and economically complex societies have emerged around the world is in order to manage both people and resources. Pressure from increasing population does not seem to have played a role in Chaco or Hohokam. In fact, I am continually surprised at the small numbers of people who appear to have lived in the prehistoric Southwest given its impressive archaeological remains. I expect that these low population estimates will be confirmed by new evidence and will also be seen in other regions of the Southwest.

Again, looking closely at the archaeological record, I am surprised that many large sites have relatively little accumulation of trash, indicating either a small population or a brief span of occupation. Sites with long continuous occupations are rare, and most local regions are occupied densely for only short periods of time. This pattern contrasts sharply with that of the Near East, where many communities are inhabited more or less continuously for several thousand years. It is a further indication of the overall low population in the Southwest and should force us as researchers to reevaluate our models for mobility in settlements. The Hohokam are something of an exception to this pattern of inhabiting settlements for only relatively short periods of time, and clearly remained in the Salt-Gila area for close to a thousand years. This is one more piece of evidence that might

point toward the existence of greater social complexity among the Hohokam than at Chaco, but I wonder how permanent the populations in these
sites were and if they were very large at any one time.

The low-population-density settlement pattern posited for both our
Southwestern regions leads one to ponder parallels with the North African
situation, where control of the productive abilities of local populations was
not the prime motive for the development of increasing social complexity.
What was necessary for the North African scenario was the existence of a
more advanced neighboring society that provided the demand for materials. A similar influence from Mesoamerica would be the parallel situation
in the Southwest, but most authors in this volume have backed away from
positing any direct reliance of Chaco or Hohokam on the unquestionably
complex society to the south. I think that this position has been overstated.
But rather than look for Mesoamerican "influences," I would recommend
that researchers examine the impact on the Southwest of the presence and
needs of Mesoamerican population centers, which could have been an
important generative factor in the growth of Southwestern complexity.
Admittedly, there is an absence of hard data on this exchange or contact,
but that is true in the case of Mesopotamia and the Indus Valley as well.
Although there is almost no material evidence of contact between these two
areas in the archaeological record, contemporary written records are very
clear about its frequency and importance, and archaeologists are quick to
cite it as a prime mover in stimulating developments in the Indus Valley.

The factor that is cited often in this volume as causing major changes in
the Southwest is the environment (cf. Masse, this volume). Although I
accept the ever-present role of climate and environmental resources in
shaping Southwestern society, I was surprised to see them considered such
active elements in fostering societal change. Admittedly, many societies in
the American Southwest were built on the environmental edge of subsistence and were susceptible to minor perturbations in the climate. However,
the societies we are discussing are two of the major achievements of
prehistoric North America. At least in the Hohokam case, the achievement
is long lived and is based largely on being able to control climatic forces to
the benefit of its citizens. Despite the powerful evidence reviewed in this
volume, I resist accepting these climatic events as the prime movers in
societal development, especially when it comes to the major transforma-
tions and ultimate demise of the Hohokam.

One reason these climatic factors have come to the fore, once again, as
prime movers, is that new evidence has been discovered that can be
correlated with identifiable changes in the archaeological record. It is the
unambiguously clear nature of this data that makes it appealing to us, and

it is the lack of competing sets of unambiguous evidence that makes it difficult to look elsewhere for causal mechanisms. Nevertheless, I would urge researchers to look further into other domains of explanation, even though the nature of the data they must deal with is far less precise and less easily understood.

The recommendation I am making is that the growth, extent, and truncation of Chacoan or Hohokam society can be best understood by focusing on the changing nature of group relationships. This requires us to redirect our investigations toward the nature of the actual systems we are investigating. One key to this effort can be found in understanding the ideological basis of those systems, especially the elements that define their boundedness. Archaeologists have traditionally sought answers to this question by delineating the distribution of distinctive ceramic types. We now recognize that these distribution studies must be redone, and that greater care must be taken to distinguish ceramic markers that have been traded from distant centers from imitations made by local producers. In addition, the role that various ceramic wares played in the economic and social life of the community must be explored. What were the identity-conscious social units of the prehistoric Southwest? Were they parallel to, and did they overlap with, economically self-sufficient units? How did these units differentiate themselves, and how did they articulate, especially within the Chacoan and Hohokam systems?

The answers to these questions may not be easily found, but they are at the core of assessing the complexity of these societies. We are no longer satisfied with determining only the distribution of a particular style of decorated ceramic; instead, we must begin to look at patterns of doing things as the "style" of a local community or broader society. The answers we now seek concerning style should extend not only to characteristic building techniques and decoration of artifacts, but also to technologies for solving problems of subsistence and mobility and traditional ways of relating to neighboring groups. I expect that we must seek these answers, among other places, in the great houses of Chaco and the platform mounds and ballcourts of the Hohokam. If these two societies were composed of constituent interdependent units, bounded in their own right but closely intertwined in other ways, then we must find the integrating mechanisms that bridged the divisions and created the greater whole. Identifying these networks and understanding the processes of integration are great chal-lenges, but they are at the core of complexity if it truly exists.

Chapter 13

Synthesis and Conclusions

PATRICIA L. CROWN AND W. JAMES JUDGE

THE papers in this volume address various aspects of the Chaco and Hohokam regional systems and provide interpretations for the growth, maintenance, and dissolution of these systems. In this chapter, we summarize the conference discussions and compare the two regional systems.

SUMMARIES

Within any group that undertakes intense scrutiny of a complex system there can never be full accord, but the following summaries of the Chaco and Hohokam regional systems represent areas of general agreement among the seminar participants.

CHACO

The San Juan Basin hosts an extremely variable and diverse environment and is subject to a largely unpredictable climate. In such an area, the organization and maintenance of a complex interactive social system cannot take place unless some basic subsistence functions are satisfied. Regardless of how overtly political or ritual the manifest function of the system may have been, its latent purpose was to solve the problem of getting its available food and its consumers in the same place at the same time.

Most of the seminar participants agreed that the Chaco system originated to solve an economic need, possibly an environmentally triggered shortage of food. Judge suggests that the tenth-century response to this need was primarily extensive in nature—that is, involving the cultivation of more land—while Vivian feels it was intensive, consisting of the development of water control mechanisms. The latter suggestion might offer an appropriate answer to the question why the system originated in resource-deficient Chaco Canyon, which was not the center of the populated areas of the basin at that time. Perhaps Chaco was the only place in the San Juan Basin that would facilitate water control of the sort that was implemented in the A.D. 900s. However effected, increased agricultural yield seemed to result in a localization of power in a few sites in the canyon. Thus the system began.

As the system matured, its structural aspects became increasingly formalized, with great houses, great kivas, and roads as its hallmarks. Impressive as the kiva and great-house architecture was, at least relative to surrounding sites, it was the road system that distinguished the Chaco phenomenon. The roads were wide, carefully engineered features, frequently maintained and remodeled. More than 320 kilometers of road have been mapped; admittedly, only a portion of the original system. In terms of their overt characteristics, the roads seem to represent an unnecessary expenditure of labor in a resource-deficient environment, a luxury not required for simple human mobility. Serving as avenues of transport for goods and people, their true function must have been that of integrating the Chaco regional system.

In Chaco Canyon itself, nine large and formal sites were built by the year 1100. During the latter part of this building period, construction reached almost frenzied proportions: roof beams were imported great distances, and existing room space evidently exceeded local habitation and storage needs. Though the canyon undoubtedly emerged as the architectural and ritual center of the regional system, it may not have been the demographic center. Debate continues about the population of the core area, but it is possible that the number of full-time residents was relatively low, augmented periodically by larger groups visiting the canyon for ritual purposes.

Though not all the seminar participants concur with Lekson that the geographical extent of the system covered most of the Colorado Plateau, all would agree that an area of more similarities than differences can be delineated as Chacoan, that the system can be bounded architecturally, that it served an economic function, and that it was large. Vivian would agree on the ultimate economic basis of the system, though he feels the outlying components were developed by emigration from Chaco rather than incorporation of existing communities into the Chacoan sphere, the position held by Judge. Toll also favors an economic base, terming it redistributive, though he does not see the need for the system to have been administered by elites. Sebastian does not see the system as basically redistributive, but does see ritual leadership as a strong component.

The role of turquoise in the development of the system remains poorly understood. Very large quantities occur archaeologically in Chaco Canyon, though the nearest source is over 160 kilometers to the east. Considerable evidence of turquoise processing has been found at sites in the canyon. Though the Chaco turquoise may have been exported to other regions, such as the Hohokam and Mexico, most authors would agree that it served a ritual purpose.

The exact character of the ritual aspect of the system is not fully understood. If there were periodic visits to the canyon by processions via the formalized road system, as Judge (1989) has suggested, then such visits could have functioned overtly to reaffirm participation in the system, and that reaffirmation could well have been votive (i.e., involving the ritual destruction of material items), as apparently was the case at Pueblo Alto. During such ceremonial events, a great deal of information would be exchanged, and that information could well have been vital in supporting the system's latent function, that of moving food to people or people to food within the San Juan Basin. Overtly, however, the system would have been identified by a shared ideology.

If there is agreement that the regional system had a ritual base, one might then ask how Chaco Canyon maintained ritual control. Judge suggests that an answer might lie in Chaco's serving as a central archive of esoteric knowledge, such as maintenance of the region's ceremonial calendar. The concept of calendrical control would explain the apparent visual communication system operative in the San Juan Basin during the Classic Chacoan period. We are hard put to determine what activities, other than the simultaneous commencement of ceremonies, would require communication through visible signals over such a vast area.

A significant change took place in the system in the early 1100s. Whether this involved reorganization, intensification, or a shift in the system's center from Chaco to the San Juan River is not understood at this time. In any event, by the mid-twelfth century the Chaco system was truncated, or "decapitated" in Lekson's terms. There is little argument that this truncation was climatically induced, given the extent of the drought that took place in the late 1100s.

Most of the Chaco scholars represented in this volume would agree that regardless of the overt characteristics of the Chaco system, as manifested in its material correlates, it ultimately served its members by functioning to even out scarce resources—effectively to make them predictable to the individual. In that sense, the system could be considered "redistributive" regardless of how this may or may not conform to a formal or classic anthropological definition of redistribution.

As long as the basic economic needs were satisfied by the system, its overt character could have changed through time, expressed in social, political, ceremonial, ideological, or other manifestations. Increasing population also could have triggered changes in the manifest system. Correspondingly, as the material correlates changed, our interpretations and explanations of the Chaco system change. But we must keep in mind that during all these changes, the economic needs of the system continued to be satisfied. It was when these needs were no longer met that the system failed its members.

HOHOKAM

The origins of the Hohokam system lie in ties between populations in southern Arizona that extend back into the Archaic period. Exotic items recovered in sites from even that early stage indicate movement of goods within an area extending from northern Sonora into southeastern Arizona. Although this interaction and exchange does not indicate economic dependency, it does provide a foundation for the increasing interaction and dependency that develops later.

The distribution of ballcourts provides an initial basis for delimiting boundaries for the Hohokam regional system. Red-on-buff pottery manufactured in the Salt-Gila (Phoenix) Basin "core" area was widely traded over an area that roughly corresponds to the distribution of ballcourts. This area encompasses most major tributaries feeding the Salt and central Gila rivers, areas often referred to as the "peripheries" of the Salt-Gila Basin core. Hohokam shell ornaments were most abundantly distributed within this broad area as well. This correlation of architectural forms with exchanged artifact types suggests that the ideological unity indicated by the ballcourt system was accompanied by exchange and economic interaction. As suggested by Crown, red-on-buff pottery distributions also indicate that, although the amounts of goods moved probably increased through time, the rough boundaries of the area in which pottery moved did not change substantially from the Pioneer through Sedentary periods. Ties that extended back perhaps as far as the Archaic became most visible archaeologically with the appearance of the ballcourts.

Ballcourts appeared after A.D. 775 in the Colonial period, and the number of ballcourts increased through the Sedentary period. No additional courts were constructed after 1150. We do not know what specific activities occurred in association with the ballcourts, or how populations at sites without ballcourts were tied to those having these features. Participants in the seminar generally agreed that the ballcourts provided a mechanism for face-to-face interaction between populations that resulted in greater dissemination of goods, services, and presumably marriage partners. Despite their shared stylistic concepts, material culture, and the widespread construction of ballcourts, the populations occupying the area defined by the courts were not united as a sociopolitical body, nor did they act in concert in economic transactions. Instead, coordination of effort seems to have occurred only at the level of each irrigation community (defined as the sites located on a single canal) or each ballcourt community (defined as the sites participating in the activities associated with a single ballcourt or set of ballcourts).

The Hohokam regional system, then, was an area encompassing multiple smaller communities integrated by ceremonial ideology and economic exchange, with the whole unified by a common subsistence base, technology, and style. The boundaries defined for the system were not environmentally defined, although Masse notes an association between these boundaries and the limits of irrigable land, floodwater farming, and the cultivation of mesquite and cactus products. Rather, the boundaries were defined culturally by a shared ideology.

The manifest function for the interactions associated with the ballcourts probably entailed movement of material goods, with a latent function lying in creating alliances for access to food, marriage partners, and land. The Salt-Gila Basin had fertile, irrigable soil, and the resources it lacked, such as shell, were primarily those that enhanced the quality of life rather than those important for survival. The uncertainties of the capricious southwestern environment probably made alliance with groups in surrounding areas attractive as well. Several of the seminar participants argued that unpredictable environmental events, particularly flooding of the canal system, stimulated the Hohokam to diversify both their subsistence base and their contacts with groups outside the Salt-Gila Basin.

The Hohokam regional system had declined by A.D. 1150, a process manifest in the disappearance of Hohokam traits from many peripheral areas that retained population and complete abandonment of other areas. The ballcourt system gradually died out and was abandoned by 1200 to 1250 (Wilcox 1988a). The limits of exchanged core-area Hohokam ceramics reveal this contraction as well. The population in the Salt-Gila Basin core reorganized, occupying new settlements, forming new types of settlements, and building more platform mounds. All of these changes culminated in the construction of habitations on platform mounds, signaling a more complex social hierarchy than had existed previously.

The collapse of the Hohokam regional system thus involved reorganization rather than abandonment of the core. We could not reach a consensus on the causes for this collapse. Factors suggested as contributing to the collapse include greater environmental uncertainty or fluctuation, changes in the availability of or access to specific resources (shell?), and collapse of other regional systems in the Southwest (Mimbres/Chaco) with consequent effect on the Hohokam. Ultimately, the population occupying the Salt-Gila Basin may have become part of a larger regional system involving the Salado or Tucson basin populations (Doelle and Wallace 1988b; McGuire 1988).

COMPARISONS

The participants in this conference provided a variety of possible explanations for the growth, maintenance, and dissolution of the Chaco and Hohokam regional systems, and we spent the last day of the seminar assessing the parallels that exist in these two contemporaneous Southwestern systems. Although the geographic areas represent two of the best-known and most thoroughly documented portions of the southwestern United States, our discussions were constantly hampered by lack of adequate data. Large pieces of the cultural puzzle are missing. In both areas, excavations have focused on the large, complex sites to the detriment of other portions of the settlement system. Modern urban and agricultural development impedes complete understanding of the Salt-Gila Basin Hohokam, but as Wilcox notes, recent intensive surveys are fleshing out the remaining portions of the Hohokam domain. Despite these problems with the existing sample of sites, we were able to compare and contrast the Chaco and Hohokam regional systems.

ORIGINS AND GROWTH

As Redman argued, complexity develops as a means of managing people and resources. The Hohokam and Chaco regional systems achieved a complexity greater than that of neighboring, contemporaneous portions of the Southwest. The course the "management" of people and resources took in these regional systems was tied to the local environment and the availability of resources. Both the Chaco and Hohokam systems occupied large geographic areas in arid environments, and both systems developed out of dispersed, low-density sedentary populations. Differences existed in the core areas of each system, however, particularly in the availability of arable land and in the potential to intensify production on this land. Major differences also existed in the availability of nonsubsistence necessities and luxury items. We will turn first to the impact of productivity and the management of subsistence resources on the development of the two regional systems.

As the center of the Chaco regional system, Chaco Canyon is a resource-deficient core, and most conference participants felt that the reasons behind the origin and development of the system lay in the need to access resources from richer areas outside this core. The potential for agricultural intensification within the canyon itself was relatively low. Thus, the primary response to stress (induced by population increase or climatic deterioration) was to adopt an agriculturally extensive strategy; that is, to put more land under cultivation. A secondary response was to intensify through the development of water control mechanisms that captured summer runoff. These two strategies (extensive and intensive) combined to effect the system origins.

Chaco's extensive strategy was intended to compensate for the unpredictable nature of precipitation patterns in an already marginal environment. Toward that end, it became necessary to subsidize that portion of the labor force whose investment did not result in effective crop yield due to the vagaries of the unpredictable climate. This subsidizing augmented the need for a centralized alliance network capable of managing resource distribution over a wide area. As a result, control of that network became firmly grounded in ritual, since ritual would be the only perceptible means of controlling the climate and accessing rainfall.

In the Chaco area, initial expansion took place to the southwest of the canyon, incorporating existing communities that had access to greater resource diversity. Preexisting exchange networks intensified as a function of this expansion, with an increase in the amount, and perhaps the kinds, of exotic goods. Public architecture appears at some sites at this time, signaling disparity in site function and formality, and perhaps some common ritual base, made manifest architecturally.

By contrast, the Hohokam Salt-Gila Basin core is a fertile area with high potential for agricultural intensification. Once the engineering of the irrigation systems was mastered, the potential of the land for agricultural production was as great as any in the Southwest. Dry-farming and floodwater-farming technologies provided additional avenues for exploiting nonirrigable land and diversifying land holdings and crops across a broader environmental landscape. Construction and maintenance of the irrigation systems required management of people and scheduling of activities on a year-round basis.

Although no evidence exists for coordination of activities above the level of the individual main canal network (at least until late in the sequence), populations living along each canal had to participate in canal construction, maintenance, water allocation, and dispute resolution. Management of people thus was a major impetus for the development of complexity within the Salt-Gila Basin core area. But how does this relate to the origins of the broader regional system?

Wilcox (1988a) argues that the regional system developed to ameliorate the discrepancies in access to food and exotics brought about by the development of irrigation agriculture in the core area and lack of irrigable land in most outlying areas. The rapid core-area population growth following the development of irrigation altered existing exchange networks between populations living in the core and those in peripheral areas. The ballcourt system provided a ceremonial basis for continuing interaction among these populations. In contrast, Masse (this volume) argues that the core-area Hohokam were stimulated to intensify contacts with surrounding groups to diversify their subsistence base, perhaps in response to devastating flooding of the canal system. Regardless of the impetus for interaction, the Hohokam probably never reached the full farming potential of the Salt-Gila Basin. Groups living in surrounding, less fertile areas may have needed the core-area produce to supplement their more meager harvests.

Control over agricultural resources thus provided an initial basis for the development of sociocultural complexity in each area, although the basis for subsistence system inequality was very different. Chaco Canyon had land that was only slightly better for agriculture than that of most surrounding areas, and the whole Chaco area was marginal for agriculture. The Salt-Gila Basin, on the other hand, had tremendous agricultural potential, much greater than most surrounding areas. Although flooding might destroy the canal system periodically, in good years the basin lands had potential to produce a surplus. In return, the Hohokam of the core area may have wanted access to nonsubsistence material goods, including "luxury" items, and perhaps also to labor. This leads us to the differences between the two areas in the availability of nonsubsistence resources.

Evidence indicates that populations in both Chaco Canyon and the Salt-Gila Basin exchanged nonsubsistence items with surrounding populations in all time periods. In Chaco, ceramic and lithic evidence points to a strong interaction between the canyon and the Chuska area to the west. Procurement of timber for roof beams may have been focused in that direction also, though the actual sources of construction beams are not known at present. Turquoise procurement points to interaction between populations in the canyon and the Cerrillos area near Santa Fe to the east. It is not clear, however, that these resource areas were controlled from the canyon. Chacoan outliers are known in the Chuska area, but not as far east as Santa Fe. Exotic items such as macaws and copper bells show definite interaction with Mexico, and these and other trade items led to early speculation of a purely Mesoamerican origin of the Chaco system, a position no longer widely held. In marked contrast to the Hohokam, however, the Chaco core was not the source of subsistence surplus for sites outside the canyon. Instead, it probably functioned most importantly as a center of ritual exchange.

The Hohokam may have acted as middlemen in exchanging some nonsubsistence goods. They also produced items for exchange, and there is clear evidence for manufacture of specific items by specialists. They imported nonsubsistence objects in return, many of them nonutilitarian in nature. Such exchange probably served to formalize relationships between populations, and particular artifact categories probably served as markers of status or role within Hohokam society. The recovery of Hohokam ceramics in association with specific resources outside of the area, such as salt mines, shell-collecting areas on the Pacific and Gulf of California coasts, and rock and mineral mines, indicates travel to or interaction with populations at these locations. There is no evidence for direct control over these resources, as might be indicated by the location of sedentary sites in the vicinity. Although continued access to such resources was apparently important to the Hohokam, their physical survival did not directly depend on these resources. Survival in a broader sense may have necessitated the formation of ties through exchange, and thus formed the basis for the origins of the regional system. The ballcourt system provided a ritual context for continuing interaction and exchange.

For both regions, inequality in agricultural potential and available resources promoted interaction with surrounding populations and, eventually, the formalization of this interaction through ritual. In both cases as well, maximum expansion of the regional systems took place largely during a period of relatively favorable climate.

SYSTEM MAINTENANCE

The shape of the systems at their maximal state mirrors their critical resources. For the Chaco regional system, this entailed expansion to the west and northwest, and intensified exchange with the Chuska area via the road network. Although Chaco Canyon was itself not rich in resources, its importance lay in its location in the center of an area from which it could control resource distribution through the management of people in a ritual context. The Chacoan road system constructed by A.D. 1100 provided a formal and visible confirmation of the exchange networks in the regional system and of the ritual basis of the networks.

As complexity grew in the Chacoan case, system control was assumed by its leaders through the management of ritual information and its maintenance as esoteric knowledge. Growing complexity in the eleventh century is evident in developed site hierarchies, differences in treatment of the dead, and differences in access to exotics. There was no consensus at the conference on the existence of elites, social stratification, or formal leadership categories. At some point in time, Chaco's subsistence strategy shifted to an intensive focus, and quite sophisticated irrigation systems designed to capture runoff were developed in the core area. This probably took place fairly late in the eleventh century (ca. 1075) after regional population increases made reliance on further extensive strategies inefficient.

By contrast, Hohokam expansion outside of the core area occurred primarily along major drainage systems, emphasizing both the greater subsistence potential of these systems and their role as networks of transport and communication between populations. The location of the Hohokam core area was conditioned by the presence of fertile, irrigable land, and it probably gave the core Hohokam a surplus in most years—a surplus that allowed them to exchange food with surrounding populations in return for nonsubsistence goods and labor. Within the core, management of the critical, but highly productive, land and water resources required the control of labor. This control appears to have been accomplished at the level of the irrigation community.

The ballcourt system, developed after A.D. 775 but reaching its maximal extent by 1150, provided a formal, and ritual, context for exchange between groups in the Hohokam regional system. Ballcourts served as places for ritual games, exchange of trade items, and social interaction. Within the basin core, they may also have provided a mechanism for population integration that crosscut the ties formed by the irrigation communities. By integrating populations belonging to diverse irrigation communities, such a mechanism would help prevent conflict over access to water and land among the different irrigation communities on a single drainage. In the absence of any political centralization in the core area, the ballcourt system would thus encourage peaceful relations. Outside the core area, ballcourt games or rituals provided mechanisms for social interaction and exchange in subsistence and nonsubsistence products. Unlike Chaco Canyon, the Hohokam core area did not control esoteric ritual knowledge or redistribution of resources. Rather, ritual and resource exchange occurred throughout the system (with the possible exception of the Papaguería) at apparently a roughly equivalent level. The absence of ballcourts in the Papaguería remains a mystery, although Masse (this volume) suggests that seasonal population movement into the area from sites elsewhere with ballcourts might account for the patterning found.

In the Hohokam area, ritual leaders certainly existed, but more important (and perhaps overlapping) social roles may have resided in management of the individual canal networks and decision making over allocation of land and water resources. As in the Chaco area, the existing complexity between A.D. 950 and 1150 is reflected in site hierarchies, differential treatment of the dead, and differential access to exotics. However, the existence of elites, social stratification, and formal leadership categories remains a subject of debate.

Though both areas developed extensive forms of public architecture, the character of that architecture differed in each region. In Chaco, public architecture took the form of great houses, great kivas, and roads; among the Hohokam, public architecture included ballcourts, plazas, and capped trash mounds or platform mounds. A significant difference between the two systems in the eleventh and twelfth centuries may have resided in the visibility of, or access to, ritual: Chacoan ritual in great kivas was restrictive, occurring behind walls, whereas Hohokam ritual in ballcourts was available for viewing. The restrictive nature of Chaco's ritual would have been in keeping with the need to maintain its esoteric aspect.

Although conference participants were reluctant to make population estimates, when prodded they agreed that population for the Salt-Gila Basin core area could be estimated at 15,000 to 30,000 for the period from approximately A.D. 900 to 1150, and population for the Chaco core area at about 2,500 to 5,000 during the same period. On a regional scale (i.e., throughout the San Juan Basin), the Chacoan population might well have been comparable to that of the Hohokam.

DECLINE OF THE REGIONAL SYSTEMS

The environment was seen as an important factor in the decline of both regional systems, although the nature of the stimulus may have been different. The periodicity of subsistence failure in each system differed, with greater frequency and probably greater severity in the Chaco area. This difference resulted in greater mobility of people in the Chaco regional system and greater stability among the Hohokam. The severity of the drought from 1130 to 1175 simply exceeded the Chaco system's capacity to compensate for such contingencies, through either technological or social means. System decline in the Chaco core area is manifest by abandonment, at least in the relative (if not absolute) sense, by the late 1100s. This course of action would be expected, given the Chacoans' primary focus on managing people: since there was little they could do to manage the drought-stricken resources, the people simply moved instead. Whether those in control of Chacoan ritual played an active role in orchestrating the abandonment, or whether the system simply dissolved through the people's dissatisfaction and subsequent fission, is not clear. The possibility of translocated reorganization in southwestern Colorado would support the former scenario, however.

In Chaco, some systemic reorganization may have preceded the rapid twelfth-century decline, but the relationship between this decline and the Classic period just before it is not at all clear. The reorganization appears archaeologically in extensive remodeling of existing structures: making the rooms smaller, and abandoning kivas and filling them with trash, among other things. Judge (1989) interprets such changes as reflecting a shift in the canyon core from a primarily ritual status to a more residential status, suggesting that control of the Chaco system may have moved north to the Aztec-Salmon area on the San Juan River. Lekson (this volume), however, feels that the Chaco system reached its peak during this period of reorganization, and that the remodeling reflected an increased need for storage facilities.

System decline in the Hohokam area is viewed mostly in terms of reorganization. Occupation of the Salt-Gila Basin area continued, with an organization generally viewed as more complex. Widespread abandonment of many outlying areas and the dominance of non-Hohokam material culture in others signal the demise of the Hohokam regional system outside of the core area. Within the core, a larger network of irrigation canals and regular placement of platform mounds suggest the continued importance of land and water management, with perhaps increased central control over these resources on a canal-specific basis. The occurrence of habitation rooms on top of the platform mounds indicates the development of greater social stratification, again probably tied to the management of land and water resources. Hohokam reorganization may have resulted from increased environmental variability, from changes in access to and availability of exchanged goods, or even from the collapse of neighboring systems such as Chaco. The latter possibility is difficult to imagine, though, since there was evidently little interaction between the two systems during most of their existence.

There is some indication that the level of social complexity manifest in Chaco prior to the collapse was maintained later in an altered form (perhaps in a less formally ritual regional system) in southwestern Colorado during the thirteenth century. Thus, substantive reorganization actually may have taken place in a different location and environment. In contrast, Hohokam reorganization seems to have taken the form of declining Hohokam influence outside the Salt-Gila Basin and of gradually increasing social complexity within it. In any case, basic variability in the physical environment (climate, topography, arable land, potential for water control, etc.) may ultimately explain most of the differences in the processes associated with the decline of these two systems.

Ultimately, the fates of the two regional systems differed. The Chaco system developed to distribute unequal resources more evenly, and it failed when resource scarcity reached a critical point in all portions of the system. Success in the Chaco system was tied to the ability of the core to utilize the all-encompassing ritual metaphor to orchestrate movement of people and resources. No level of complexity or control could manage insufficient resources resulting from consistent failure to meet necessary crop yields. Neither would there have been any mechanism to move people who were unwilling to participate in the ritual system any longer.

The Hohokam system was more loosely bound together, presumably as networks of relations between populations both inside and outside the core, formalized through ritual interaction over a broad area. Management of resources and labor continued in the core area at what was probably an even greater level of complexity after the regional system collapsed. The basic network of relations between populations inside and outside altered, but the core-area populations continued to thrive in their fertile valleys for another two centuries. The difference between the Hohokam and Chaco regional systems may lie in the availability of subsistence resources in each region and the fact that the core-area Hohokam were probably rarely dependent on other areas for their subsistence needs.

It is interesting that in both areas, quite complex sociocultural systems with a great number of parallels developed contemporaneously in relatively marginal climatic regimes. Equally interesting, however, are the questions how and why both flourished and declined as regional neighbors with apparently little formal interaction. Perhaps this phenomenon attests to their success as systems, each adapted to its particular regional environment. As long as each was successful, there would be little immediate need for formal interaction—and no need to create mutual interdependency as a survival mechanism. And as long as the two could thrive without competing for the same resource base, there would be no need for aggressive interaction.

It would be interesting (though perhaps futile) to speculate that had the drought of 1175 not occurred, and had Chaco, given another hundred years, expanded into the resource area already controlled by the Hohokam (i.e., the eastern Salt-Gila catchment area), perhaps interaction of some nature would have been forced on the two systems, altering substantially the course of Southwestern prehistory.

REGIONAL SYSTEMS

As used as a conceptual framework in this seminar, regional systems are characterized by economic interaction and stylistic unity of a magnitude greater within a population than outside of it. The efficacy of the regional system concept for understanding the prehistory of the Chaco and Hohokam areas must be considered as a final point of inquiry. Does this concept enhance our understanding, or merely add another level of complexity to the way archaeologists view the past? By focusing on economic interaction within the two areas, have we overlooked other significant types of interaction, such as conflict, ritual, symbolic exchange, or supraregional contacts?

The regional systems in the two areas appear to have some important similarities that may be of significance to defining more precisely the nature of the regional system concept:

1. Both systems developed to ameliorate inequalities in the availability of resources across the landscape. We can thus argue that regional systems tend to develop in areas with (broadly defined) patchy resource availability.
2. Both systems increased the available environmental diversity through expansion of interaction networks. Development of regional systems appears to involve expansion into areas of diverse environments and variable resources.
3. Both systems are believed to have involved exchange of material and nonmaterial goods in the context of ritual interaction in public settings. Public architecture thus appears to function in regional systems to draw populations from diverse areas for the purpose of exchange and interaction.
4. Both systems developed in a period of relatively favorable climate, and environmental conditions are believed to have influenced the character of subsequent developments in each case. In arid environments the development and demise of regional systems is thus closely tied to environmental conditions.
5. When the two systems collapsed, it was the most fertile areas agriculturally that continued to be occupied, regardless of their former position in the system. At a given level of technology, then, there are limits to the amount of resource stress a regional system can ameliorate.

Major differences exist in these two systems as well, and these divergences can be equally informative. The first major difference is grounded in the environmental disparities between the two regions. The Chaco system had a resource-deficient core, and surplus production elsewhere may have permitted continued occupation of that core and other marginal portions of the system. The Hohokam, on the other hand, had a fertile core, and outlying populations in environmentally deficient locales may have depended more on the core for surplus production than vice versa (although see Masse's chapter, this volume, for a differing viewpoint). Regional systems can thus develop for the same reasons in quite different environmental situations, and the forms they take will differ accordingly.

The second significant difference between the two systems lies in the ritual realm. Ritual knowledge was hoarded at Chaco, and people and resources were managed through control of this ritual information. Ritual knowledge does not seem to have been controlled by any areal segment of the population in the Hohokam area; rather, ritual provided mechanisms to integrate population and exchange material goods, labor, and marriage partners. This is an important distinction. By controlling ritual, Chaco Canyon became a true core, or focus, for interaction via the road system. In this sense, it achieved a greater level of complexity through orchestrating movements of people and resources on a yearly basis.

There is no evidence for anything comparable in the Hohokam area. The "core" is considered a core primarily because of its greater longevity of occupation, surplus potential, early large sites, and production of material items found in other parts of the Southwest. However, there is no evidence for centralized control from this core, or orchestration of population movements into or out of the core. Increasing evidence suggests that the "peripheries" diverged from the Hohokam core through time, and that these areas developed with little interference or perhaps even influence from the core. Recovery of core-area Hohokam ceramics over the same area covered by the ballcourts does imply interaction and exchange between these areas, but few would argue that this interaction was of a magnitude or formality comparable with the Chaco situation. Clearly then, centralized control is not a necessary characteristic of ongoing economic interaction or regional system development in Southwestern societies.

Although the regional system concept has utility as an analytic tool for comparing these two geographic and cultural areas, it cannot be considered equally useful in defining a stage in regional population dynamics that has the same form, content, or history in a broader context. The generalizations we can draw from comparing the Chaco and Hohokam regional systems are perhaps less grandiose than we would like, but may point the way for future comparisons and research in other portions of the American Southwest.

The School of American Research advanced seminar was successful in addressing many of the complex issues raised prior to the conference, and many more questions were proposed in the ensuing discussions and resulting papers. Much of our work in the future will focus on these questions. Clearly, the seminar has provided a solid foundation for further research on the development of social complexity in the prehistoric arid Southwest.

References

Abbott, David R.
1983 A technological assessment of ceramic variation in the Salt-Gila aqueduct area: Toward a comprehensive documentation of Hohokam ceramics. *In* Hohokam archaeology along the Salt-Gila aqueduct, Central Arizona Project: Material culture. Ed. L. S. Teague and P. L. Crown. Arizona State Museum Archaeological Series, no. 150, vol. 8, pp. 3–118. Tucson: University of Arizona.
1985 Unbiased estimates of feature frequencies with computer simulation. American Antiquity 50:4–11.

Abbott, David R., and Frederick W. Huntington
1983 Excavations at Casas Pequeñas (AZ U:15:97), Hohokam field houses in the Queen Creek area. *In* Hohokam archaeology along the Salt-Gila aqueduct, Central Arizona Project: Small habitation sites along Queen Creek. Ed. L. S. Teague and P. L. Crown. Arizona State Museum Archaeological Series, no. 150, vol. 5, pp. 101–204. Tucson: University of Arizona.

Ackerly, Neil W.
1988 Prehistoric agricultural activities: Hohokam irrigation cycles, A.D. 700–1100. Manuscript, Arizona Department of Transportation, Phoenix.

Ackerly, Neil W., Jerry B. Howard, and Randall H. McGuire
1987 La Ciudad canals: A study of Hohokam irrigation systems at the community level. Anthropological Field Studies, vol. 17. Tempe: Office of Cultural Resource Management, Arizona State University.

Adams, E. Charles
1981 The view from the Hopi mesas. *In* The protohistoric period in the American Southwest, A.D. 1450–1700. Ed. D. R. Wilcox and W. B. Masse. Arizona State University Anthropological Research Papers, no. 24, pp. 321–35. Tempe.

Adams, Richard N.
1975 Energy and structure: A theory of social power. Austin: University of Texas Press.

Adams, Robert McC.
1981 Heartland of cities: Surveys of ancient settlement and land use on the central floodplain of the Euphrates. Chicago: University of Chicago Press.

Akins, Nancy J.
1982 Perspectives on faunal resource utilization, Chaco Canyon. New Mexico Archeological Council Newsletter 4:23–29.
1984 Temporal variation in faunal assemblages from Chaco Canyon. *In* Recent research on Chaco prehistory. Ed. W. J. Judge and J. D. Schelberg. Reports of the Chaco Center, no. 8, pp. 225–40. Albuquerque: Division of Cultural Research, National Park Service.
1985 Prehistoric faunal utilization in Chaco Canyon: Basketmaker III through Pueblo III. *In* Environment and subsistence of Chaco Canyon, New

Mexico. Ed. F. J. Mathien. Publications in Archeology, no. 18E, Chaco Canyon Studies, pp. 305–446. Albuquerque: National Park Service.

1986   A biocultural approach to human burials from Chaco Canyon, New Mexico. Reports of the Chaco Center, no. 9. Santa Fe: Branch of Cultural Research, National Park Service.

Akins, Nancy J., and John D. Schelberg
1984   Evidence for organizational complexity as seen from the mortuary practices at Chaco Canyon. In Recent research on Chaco prehistory. Ed. W. J. Judge and J. D. Schelberg. Reports of the Chaco Center, no. 8, pp. 89–102. Albuquerque: Division of Cultural Research, National Park Service.

Altschul, Jeffrey H.
1978   The development of the Chacoan interaction sphere. Journal of Anthropological Research 34:109–46.

Ambler, J. Richard
1961   Archaeological survey and excavations at Casa Grande National Monument, Arizona. M.A. thesis, Department of Anthropology, University of Arizona, Tucson.

American Antiquity
1987   Current Research. American Antiquity 52:859.

Anderson, Keith
1985   Hohokam cemeteries as elements of settlement structure and change. In Anthropology of the Desert West, essays in honor of Jesse D. Jennings. Ed. C. J. Condie and D. D. Fowler. University of Utah Anthropological Papers, vol. 110, pp. 179–202. Salt Lake City.

Andresen, John
1983   Hohokam murals at the Clan House, Casa Grande Ruins National Monument. The Kiva 48(4):267–78.

1985   Pottery and architecture at Compound F, Casa Grande Ruins National Monument, Arizona. In Proceedings of the 1983 Hohokam Symposium, part 2. Ed. A. E. Dittert Jr. and D. E. Dove. Occasional Paper, no. 2, pp. 595–640. Arizona Archaeological Society, Phoenix Chapter.

Antieu, John M.
1981   The Palo Verde archaeological investigations. Museum of Northern Arizona Research Paper, no. 20. Flagstaff.

Anyon, Roger
1984   Mogollon settlement patterns and communal architecture. M.A. thesis, Department of Anthropology, University of New Mexico, Albuquerque.

Anyon, Roger, and Steven A. LeBlanc
1984   The Galaz Ruin, a prehistoric Mimbres village in southwestern New Mexico. Albuquerque: Maxwell Museum of Anthropology and University of New Mexico Press.

Arnold, Dean E.
1980   Localized exchange: An ethnoarchaeological perspective. In Models and methods in regional exchange. Ed. R. E. Fry. Society for American Archaeology Papers, no. 1, pp. 147–50.

1985   Ceramic theory and cultural process. Cambridge: Cambridge University Press.

Ayres, James E.
1965   A summary of archaeological sites in Maricopa County. Manuscript, Arizona State Museum Library, University of Arizona, Tucson.

Bandelier, Adolf F.
1892   Final report of investigations among the Indians of the southwestern United States, part 2. Papers of the Archaeological Institute of America, American Series, no. 4. Cambridge, Massachusetts.

Bannister, Bryant
1965   Tree-ring dating of archaeological sites in the Chaco Canyon region, New Mexico. Southwestern Monuments Association Technical Series, no. 6(2). Globe, Arizona.

Barnes, Ethne
1987   Analysis of human burials from the site of Casa Buena. In Excavations at Casa Buena along the Squaw Peak Parkway. Ed. J. B. Howard. Soil Systems Publications in Archaeology, no. 11. Phoenix, in press.
1988   Inhumations recoved from Casa Buena: Skeletal analysis. In Excavations at Casa Buena: Changing Hohokam land use along the Squaw Peak Parkway, vol. 2. Ed. J. Howard, pp. 619–91. Soil Systems Publications in Archaeology, no. 12. Phoenix.

Barth, Fredrik
1967   Economic spheres in Darfur. In Themes in economic anthropology. Ed. R. Firth, pp. 149–74. London: Tavistock.

Barth, Fredrik, ed.
1962   The role of the entrepreneur in social change in northwest Norway. Bergen: Universitetsforlanget.

Bartlett, Katherine
1939   A prehistoric "mine" of red argillite, resembling pipestone, near Del Rio, Arizona. Museum Notes 11(12):75–78. Flagstaff: Museum of Northern Arizona.

Baxter, Sylvester
1888   The old New World. The Boston Herald, 15 April 1888. Salem, Massachusetts.

Beckwith, Kim E.
1988   Intrusive ceramic wares and types. In The 1982–1984 excavations at Las Colinas: Material culture. By D. Abbott, K. Beckwith, P. Crown, R. T. Euler, D. Gregory, J. R. London, M. Saul, L. Schwalbe, M. Bernard-Shaw, C. Szuter, and A. Vokes. Arizona State Museum Archaeological Series, no. 162, vol. 4, pp. 199–256. Tucson.

Bernard-Shaw, Mary
1983   The stone tool assemblage of the Salt-Gila aqueduct project sites. In Hohokam archaeology along the Salt-Gila aqueduct, Central Arizona Project: Material culture. Ed. L. S. Teague and P. L. Crown. Arizona State Museum Archaeological Series, no. 150, vol. 8, pp. 371–444. Tucson: University of Arizona.
1987   Prehistoric canals and charcos at the Los Morteros site in the northern Tucson Basin. Technical Report, no. 87–9. Tucson: Institute for American Research.
1988   Hohokam canal systems and late Archaic wells: The evidence from the

Los Morteros site. *In* Recent research on Tucson Basin prehistory: Proceedings of the Second Tucson Basin Conference. Ed. W. H. Doelle and P. R. Fish. Institute for American Research Anthropological Papers, no. 10, pp. 153–74. Tucson.

Berry, Claudia F., and William S. Marmaduke
1982 The middle Gila Basin: An archaeological and historical overview. Flagstaff: Northland Research.

Bice, Richard A.
1983 The Sterling Site: An initial report. *In* Collected papers in honor of Charlie R. Steen. Ed. N. L. Fox. Papers of the Archaeological Society of New Mexico, no. 8. Albuquerque.

Binford, Lewis R.
1971 Mortuary practices: Their study and their potential. *In* Approaches to the social dimensions of mortuary practices. Ed. J. A. Brown. Memoirs of the Society for American Archaeology, no. 25, pp. 6–29.

Blake, Michael, Steven A. LeBlanc, and Paul E. Minnis
1986 Changing settlement and population in the Mimbres Valley, southwestern New Mexico. Journal of Field Archaeology 13:439–64.

Blanton, Richard E., Stephen A. Kowalewski, Gary Feinman, and Jill Appel
1981 Ancient Mesoamerica: A comparison of change in three regions. Cambridge: Cambridge University Press.

Bohrer, Vorsila L.
1970 Ethnobotanical aspects of Snaketown, a Hohokam village in southern Arizona. American Antiquity 35:413–30.
1971 Paleoecology of Snaketown. The Kiva 36(3):11–19.

Boone, James L., J. Emlen Myers, and Charles L. Redman
1990 Archaeological and historical approaches to complex societies: The Islamic states of medieval Morocco. American Anthropologist 92(3):630–46.

Boone, James L., and Charles L. Redman
1982 Alternate pathways to urbanism in the medieval Maghreb. Comparative Urban Research 9:28–38.

Boserup, Ester
1965 The conditions of agricultural growth: The economics of agrarian change under population pressure. Chicago: Aldine.
1981 Population and technological change: A study of long-term trends. Chicago: University of Chicago Press.

Bostwick, Todd, and Steven Shackley
1987 Settlement strategies and lithic technology: An examination of variability in hunter-gatherer and agriculturalist chipped stone assemblages in the Sonoran desert. Paper presented at 1987 Hohokam Symposium, The Archaic-Hohokam transition. January 30–31, Tempe, Arizona.

Bradfield, Maitland
1971 The changing pattern of Hopi agriculture. Royal Anthropological Institute, Occasional Paper, no. 30.

Bradley, Bruce A.
1974 Preliminary report of excavations at Wallace Ruin, 1969–1974. Southwestern Lore 40(3–4):63–71.

1988   The Wallace Ruin: Interim report. Southwestern Lore 54:2.

Brand, Donald D., Florence M. Hawley, Frank C. Hibben, and Donovan Senter
1937   Tseh So, a small house ruin, Chaco Canyon, New Mexico: Preliminary report. University of New Mexico Bulletin, Anthropological Series 2(2). Albuquerque.

Brandt, Elizabeth A.
1980   On secrecy and control of knowledge: Taos Pueblo. In Secrecy: A cross-cultural perspective. Ed. S. K. Tefft, pp. 123–46. New York: Human Sciences Press.

Braun, David P., and Stephen Plog
1982   Evolution of "tribal" social networks: Theory and prehistoric North American evidence. American Antiquity 47:504–25.

Breternitz, Cory D.
1982   An overview of principal research themes and explanatory models for the Chaco Canyon region. In Bis sa'ani: A late Bonito phase community on Escavada Wash, northwest New Mexico. Ed. C. D. Breternitz, D. E. Doyel, and M. P. Marshall. Navajo Nation Papers in Anthropology, no. 14, pp. 19–44. Window Rock, Arizona.

Breternitz, Cory D., and Michael P. Marshall
1982   Summary of analytical results and review of miscellaneous artifacts from Bis sa'ani Pueblo. In Bis sa'ani: A late Bonito phase community on Escavada Wash, northwest New Mexico. Ed. C. D. Breternitz, D. E. Doyel, and M. P. Marshall. Navajo Nation Papers in Anthropology, no. 14, pp. 433–48. Window Rock, Arizona.

Breternitz, Cory D., David E. Doyel, and Michael P. Marshall, eds.
1982   Bis sa'ani: A late Bonito phase community on Escavada Wash, northwest New Mexico. Navajo Nation Papers in Anthropology, no. 14. Window Rock, Arizona.

Brisbin, Joel M., and Charlotte J. Brisbin
1973   North McElmo no. 8: Kiva 8 (Ida Jean Site). Manuscript, Crow Canyon Archaeological Center, Cortez, Colorado.

Brody, J. J.
1977   Mimbres painted pottery. Albuquerque: School of American Research and University of New Mexico Press.

Brown, David. E., ed.
1982   Biotic communities of the American Southwest: United States and Mexico. Desert Plants 4(1–4).

Brown, James A.
1971a   Introduction. In Approaches to the social dimensions of mortuary practices. Ed. J. A. Brown. Memoirs of the Society for American Archaeology, no. 25, pp. 1–5.
1971b   The dimension of status in burials at Spiro. In Approaches to the social dimensions of mortuary practices. Ed. J. A. Brown. Memoirs of the Society for American Archaeology, no. 25, pp. 92–112.

Brown, Patricia E., and Connie L. Stone, eds.
1982   Granite Reef: A study in desert archaeology. Arizona State University Anthropological Research Papers, no. 28. Tempe.

Bruder, J. Simon

1983a Archaeological investigations at the Adobe Dam alternative site no. 4, Phoenix, Arizona. Museum of Northern Arizona Research Paper, no. 27. Flagstaff.

1983b Archaeological investigations at the Hedgpeth Hills Petroglyph Site, Phoenix, Arizona. Museum of Northern Arizona Research Paper, no. 29. Flagstaff.

Brugge, David M.

1980 A history of the Chaco Navajos. Reports of the Chaco Center, no. 4. Albuquerque: Division of Cultural Research, National Park Service.

1986 Tsegai: An archeological ethnohistory of the Chaco region. Santa Fe: National Park Service.

Brumfiel, Elizabeth M., and Timothy K. Earle

1987 Specialization, exchange, and complex societies: An introduction. *In* Specialization, exchange, and complex societies. Ed. E. M. Brumfiel and T. K. Earle, pp. 1–9. Cambridge: Cambridge University Press.

Brunson, Judy L.

1989 The social organization of the Los Muertos Hohokam: A reanalysis of Cushing's Hemenway Southwestern Expedition data, 100 years later. Ph.D. dissertation, Department of Anthropology, Arizona State University, Tempe.

Bullard, William R., Jr.

1962 The Cerro Colorado site and pithouse architecture in the southwestern United States prior to A.D. 900. Papers of the Peabody Museum of American Archaeology and Ethnology, vol. 44, no. 2. Cambridge: Harvard University.

Burrus, Ernest J.

1971 Kino and Manje. Sources and studies for the history of the Americas, vol. 10. Rome: Jesuit Historical Institute.

Cable, John S.

1985 The prehistoric ceramic assemblage from block 24-east. *In* City of Phoenix, archaeology of the original townsite: Block 24-east. Ed. J. S. Cable, K. S. Hoffman, D. E. Doyel, and F. Ritz. Soil Systems Publications in Archaeology, no. 8, pp. 183–210. Phoenix.

Cable, John S., and David E. Doyel

1985 Hohokam land-use patterns along the terraces of the lower Salt River valley: The Central Phoenix Project. *In* Proceedings of the 1983 Hohokam Symposium, part 1. Ed. A. E. Dittert Jr. and D. E. Dove. Occasional Paper, no. 2, pp. 263–310. Arizona Archaeological Society, Phoenix Chapter.

1987 Pioneer period village structure and settlement pattern in the Phoenix Basin. *In* The Hohokam village: Site structure and organization. Ed. D. E. Doyel, pp. 21–71. Glenwood Springs, Colorado: American Association for the Advancement of Science.

Cable, John S., Wilma Allen, Laurie Blank-Roper, and David E. Doyel

1983 The archaeology of a Hohokam field house site—block 28-north. *In* City of Phoenix, archaeology of the original townsite, block 28-north. Ed. J. S. Cable, S. L. Henry, and D. E. Doyel. Soil Systems Publications in Archaeology, no. 2, pp. 9–204. Phoenix: Professional Service Industries.

Callahan, Martha M., ed.
  1988   Hohokam settlement along the slopes of the Picacho Mountains: Material culture. Museum of Northern Arizona Research Paper, vol. 35, no. 4. Flagstaff.
Cameron, Catherine M.
  1982   Chaco Project lithic overview. Manuscript, Division of Cultural Research, National Park Service, Santa Fe.
  1984   A regional view of chipped stone raw material use in Chaco Canyon. *In* Recent research on Chaco prehistory. Ed. W. J. Judge and J. D. Schelberg. Reports of the Chaco Center, no. 8, pp. 137–52. Albuquerque: Division of Cultural Research, National Park Service.
  1985   The chipped stone at Pueblo Alto, Chaco Canyon, New Mexico. Manuscript, Division of Cultural Research, National Park Service, Santa Fe.
Cameron, Catherine M., and R. Lee Sappington
  1984   Obsidian procurement at Chaco Canyon, A.D. 500–1200. *In* Recent research on Chaco prehistory. Ed. W. J. Judge and J. D. Schelberg. Reports of the Chaco Center, no. 8, pp. 153–73. Albuquerque: Division of Cultural Research, National Park Service.
Cameron, Catherine M., and Lisa C. Young
  1986   Lithic procurement and technology in the Chaco Canyon area. *In* Archaeological survey at Chaco Culture National Historic Park. Ed. R. B. Powers. Reports of the Chaco Center. Santa Fe: Division of Cultural Research, National Park Service. In preparation.
Canouts, Veletta, assembler
  1975   An archaeological survey of the Orme Reservoir. Arizona State Museum Archaeological Series, no. 92. Tucson: University of Arizona.
Carlson, John, and W. James Judge, eds.
  1987   Astronomy and ceremony in the prehistoric Southwest. Papers of the Maxwell Museum of Anthropology, no. 2. Albuquerque.
Carneiro, Robert L.
  1970   A theory of the origin of the state. Science 169:733–38.
  1981   The chiefdom: Precursor of the state. *In* The transition to statehood in the New World. Ed. G. D. Jones and R. R. Kautz, pp. 37–79. Cambridge: Cambridge University Press.
Castetter, Edward F., and Willis H. Bell
  1951   Yuman Indian agriculture. Albuquerque: University of New Mexico Press.
Castetter, Edward F., and Ruth M. Underhill
  1935   The ethnobiology of the Papago Indians. University of New Mexico Bulletin 275, Biological Series, vol. 4, no. 3. Albuquerque.
Chamberlin, T. C.
  1965   The method of multiple working hypotheses. Science 148:754–59.
Chang, Kwang Chi
  1958   Study of the Neolithic social grouping: Examples from the New World. American Anthropologist 60(2):298–334.
Chenhall, Robert C.
  1967   The Silo Site. The Arizona Archaeologist, vol. 2. Arizona Archaeological Society.

Childe, V. Gordon
    1951   Man makes himself. 3rd ed. London: Watts.
Chisolm, Michael
    1979   Rural settlement and land use: An essay on location. 3rd ed. London:
            Hutchinson University Library.
Ciolek-Torrello, Richard S., and David H. Greenwald
    1988   Site structure and domestic organization in the Picacho Mountain area.
            In Recent research on Tucson Basin prehistory: Proceedings of the
            Second Tucson Basin Conference. Ed. W. H. Doelle and P. R. Fish.
            Institute for American Research Anthropological Papers, no. 10,
            pp. 109–144. Tucson.
Ciolek-Torrello, Richard S., and David R. Wilcox, eds.
    1988   Hohokam settlement along the slopes of the Picacho Mountains: Syn-
            thesis and conclusions. Museum of Northern Arizona Research Paper,
            no. 35, vol. 6. Flagstaff.
Ciolek-Torrello, Richard S., Martha M. Callahan, and David H. Greenwald
    1988   Hohokam settlement along the slopes of the Picacho Mountains: The
            Brady Wash sites. Tucson Aqueduct Project, parts 1 and 2. Museum of
            Northern Arizona Research Paper, no. 35, vol. 2. Flagstaff.
Clary, Karen Husum
    1984   Anasazi diet and subsistence as revealed by coprolites from Chaco
            Canyon. *In* Recent research on Chaco prehistory. Ed. W. J. Judge and
            J. D. Schelberg. Reports of the Chaco Center, no. 8, pp. 265–79.
            Albuquerque: Division of Cultural Research, National Park Service.
Cohen, Ronald
    1978   State foundations: A controlled comparison. *In* Origins of the state. Ed.
            R. Cohen and E. R. Service, pp. 141–60. Philadelphia: Institute for the
            Study of Human Issues (ISHI).
Colson, Elizabeth
    1979   In good years and in bad: Food strategies of self-reliant societies. Journal
            of Anthropological Research 35:18–29.
Colton, Harold S.
    1941   Prehistoric trade in the Southwest. The Scientific Monthly 52:308–19.
Cordell, Linda S.
    1979   Cultural resources overview of the Middle Rio Grande Valley, New
            Mexico. Washington, D.C.: U.S. Government Printing Office.
    1982   The Pueblo period in the San Juan Basin: An overview and some
            research problems. *In* The San Juan tomorrow: Planning for the conser-
            vation of cultural resources in the San Juan Basin. Ed. F. Plog and W.
            Wait, pp. 59–83. Santa Fe: National Park Service, Southwest Region, in
            cooperation with the School of American Research.
Cordell, Linda S., and Fred Plog
    1979   Escaping the confines of normative thought: A reevaluation of Puebloan
            prehistory. American Antiquity 44(3):405–29.
Cowgill, George L.
    1975   On causes and consequences of ancient and modern population
            changes. American Anthropologist 77:505–25.

Crabtree, Don E.
1973 Experiments in replicating Hohokam points. Tebiwa 16(1):10–45. Pocatello, Idaho.

Craig, Douglas B., and Henry D. Wallace
1987 Prehistoric settlement in the Cañada del Oro Valley, Arizona: The Rancho Vistoso Survey Project. Institute for American Research Anthropological Papers, no. 8. Tucson.

Crown, Patricia L.
1981 Analysis of the Las Colinas ceramics. In The 1968 excavations at Mound 8, Las Colinas Ruin group, Phoenix, Arizona. Ed. L. C. Hammack and A. P. Sullivan. Arizona State Museum Archaeological Series, no. 154, pp. 87–169. Tucson: University of Arizona.

1983a Classic period ceramic manufacture: Exploring variability in Hohokam vessel production and use. In Hohokam archaeology along the Salt-Gila aqueduct, Central Arizona Project: Material culture. Ed. L. S. Teague and P. L. Crown. Arizona State Museum Archaeological Series, no. 150, vol. 8, pp. 119–204. Tucson: University of Arizona.

1983b Design variability in Salt-Gila aqueduct red-on-buff ceramics. In Hohokam archaeology along the Salt-Gila aqueduct, Central Arizona Project: Material culture. Ed. L. S. Teague and P. L. Crown. Arizona State Museum Archaeological Series, no. 150, vol. 8, pp. 205–48. Tucson: University of Arizona.

1983c Introduction: Field houses and farmsteads in south-central Arizona. In Hohokam archaeology along the Salt-Gila aqueduct, Central Arizona Project: Small habitation sites along Queen Creek. Ed. L. S. Teague and P. L. Crown. Arizona State Museum Archaeological Series, no. 150, vol. 5, pp. 3–22. Tucson: University of Arizona.

1984a Ceramic vessel exchange in southern Arizona. In Hohokam archaeology along the Salt-Gila aqueduct, Central Arizona Project: Synthesis and conclusions. Ed. L. S. Teague and P. L. Crown. Arizona State Museum Archaeological Series, no. 150, vol. 9, pp. 251–304. Tucson: University of Arizona.

1984b Hohokam subsistence and settlement in the Salt-Gila Basin. In Hohokam archaeology along the Salt-Gila aqueduct, Central Arizona Project: Synthesis and conclusions. Ed. L. S. Teague and P. L. Crown. Arizona State Museum Archaeological Series, no. 150, vol. 9, pp. 87–114. Tucson: University of Arizona.

1984c Prehistoric agricultural technology in the Salt-Gila Basin. In Hohokam archaeology along the Salt-Gila aqueduct, Central Arizona Project: Environment and subsistence. Ed. L. S. Teague and P. L. Crown. Arizona State Museum Archaeological Series, no. 150, vol. 7, pp. 207–60. Tucson: University of Arizona.

1985a Intrusive ceramics and the identification of Hohokam exchange networks. In Proceedings of the 1983 Hohokam Conference. Ed. A. E. Dittert Jr. and D. E. Dove. Occasional Paper, no. 2, part 2, pp. 439–58. Arizona Archaeological Society, Phoenix Chapter.

1985b Morphology and function of Hohokam small structures. The Kiva 50(2–3):75–94.

1987a Classic period Hohokam settlement and land use in the Casa Grande Ruins area, Arizona. Journal of Field Archaeology 14:147–62.

1987b Water storage in the prehistoric Southwest. The Kiva 52(3):209–28.

Crown, Patricia L., and Ronald L. Bishop

1987 Convergence in ceramic manufacturing traditions in the late prehistoric Southwest. Paper presented at 52nd annual meeting, Society for American Archaeology, Toronto.

Crown, Patricia L., and Earl W. Sires, Jr.

1984 The Hohokam chronology and Salt-Gila aqueduct research. In Hohokam archaeology along the Salt-Gila aqueduct, Central Arizona Project: Synthesis and conclusions. Ed. L. S. Teague and P. L. Crown. Arizona State Museum Archaeological Series, no. 150, vol. 9, pp. 73–86. Tucson: University of Arizona.

Cummings, Byron

1926 Ancient canals of the Casa Grande. Progressive Arizona 3(5):9–10.

Cushing, Frank Hamilton

1890 Preliminary notes on the origin, working hypothesis, and primary researches of the Hemenway Southwestern Archaeological Expedition. Congrès International des Américanistes, Compte-Rendu de la Septième Session, pp. 151–94. Berlin.

1892 Journal of the Hemenway Southwestern Archaeological Expedition. Peabody Museum Archives, Harvard University, Cambridge.

1893 Itinerary of the initial work at the ruin cluster of Los Muertos. Manuscript, Southwestern Museum, Los Angeles.

Czaplicki, Jon S., compiler

1984 Class III survey of the Tucson aqueduct Phase A corridor, Central Arizona Project. Arizona State Museum Archaeological Series, no. 165. Tucson: University of Arizona.

Dart, Allen

1983 Investigations at the Chiadag site (AZ U:15:99), a field house on Queen Creek. In Hohokam archaeology along the Salt-Gila aqueduct, Central Arizona Project: Small habitation sites along Queen Creek. Ed. L. S. Teague and P. L. Crown. Arizona State Museum Archaeological Series, no. 150, vol. 5, pp. 325–52. Tucson: University of Arizona.

1987 Archaeological studies of Avra Valley, Arizona, for the Papago water supply project. Institute for American Research Anthropological Papers, no. 9. Tucson.

Dart, Allen, and William R. Gibson

1988 The western extent of the Tucson Basin Hohokam: Evidence from recent surveys in the Avra Valley. In Recent research on Tucson Basin prehistory: Proceedings of the Second Tucson Basin Conference. Ed. W. H. Doelle and P. R. Fish. Institute for American Research Anthropological Papers, no. 10, pp. 253–76. Tucson.

Davis, Whitney

1984 Representation, knowledge, and legitimation in the early Egyptian state. Paper presented at the advanced seminar, Early complex societies of Africa. School of American Research, Santa Fe. Manuscript, Northwestern University, Evanston, Illinois.

Dean, Jeffrey S.
  1969 Chronological analysis of Tsegi phase sites in northeastern Arizona.
        Papers of the Laboratory of Tree-Ring Research, no. 3. Tucson: Univer-
        sity of Arizona.
  1987 Thoughts on Hohokam settlement behavior: Comments on "The Hoho-
        kam village." In The Hohokam village: Site structure and organization.
        Ed. D. E. Doyel, pp. 253–62. Glenwood Springs, Colorado: South-
        western and Rocky Mountain Division of the American Association for
        the Advancement of Science.
  1988 Thoughts on Hohokam chronology. Paper presented at conference,
        Changing views on Hohokam archaeology. Amerind Foundation, Dra-
        goon, Arizona. In Exploring the Hohokam: Prehistoric dwellers of the
        American desert. Ed. G. J. Gumerman. Albuquerque: University of New
        Mexico Press. In press.
Dean, Jeffrey S., and Richard L. Warren
  1983 Dendrochronology. In The architecture and dendrochronology of
        Chetro Ketl. Ed. S. H. Lekson. Reports of the Chaco Center, no. 6,
        pp. 105–240. Albuquerque: Division of Cultural Research, National
        Park Service.
Dean, Jeffrey S., Robert C. Euler, George J. Gumerman, Fred Plog, Richard H.
Hevley, and Thor N. V. Karlstrom
  1985 Human behavior, demography, and paleoenvironment on the Colorado
        Plateaus. American Antiquity 50:537–54.
Deaver, William L.
  1983 Excavations at the Ellsworth site (AZ U:15:57), a Hohokam field house
        on Queen Creek. In Hohokam archaeology along the Salt-Gila aque-
        duct, Central Arizona Project: Small habitation sites along Queen Creek.
        Ed. L. S. Teague and P. L. Crown. Arizona State Museum Archaeological
        Series, no. 150, vol. 5, pp. 225–310. Tucson: University of Arizona.
Debowski, Sharon S.
  1974 Appendix K: Provenience and description of shell and miscellaneous
        artifacts from the Escalante Ruin group. In Excavations in the Escalante
        Ruin group, southern Arizona. By D. E. Doyel. Arizona State Museum
        Archaeological Series, no. 37, pp. 276–98. Tucson: University of Ari-
        zona.
  1982 Shell artifacts from the Bis sa'ani Community. In Bis sa'ani: A late Bonito
        phase community on Escavada Wash, northwest New Mexico. Ed. C. D.
        Breternitz, D. E. Doyel, and M. P. Marshall. Navajo Nation Papers in
        Anthropology, no. 14, pp. 1093–98. Window Rock, Arizona.
Debowski, Sharon S., Anique George, Richard Goddard, and Deborah Mullon
  1976 An archaeological survey of the Buttes Dam Reservoir. Arizona State
        Museum Archaeological Series, no. 93. Tucson: University of Arizona.
Di Peso, Charles C.
  1956 The Upper Pima of San Cayetano del Tumacacori: An archaeo-historical
        reconstruction of the Ootam of Pimeria Alta. The Amerind Foundation,
        no. 7. Dragoon, Arizona.
  1974 The Medio period. Casas Grandes: A fallen trading center of the Gran
        Chichimeca, vol. 2. The Amerind Foundation, no. 9. Flagstaff: North-
        land Press.

1984   The structure of the eleventh-century Casas Grandes agricultural system. *In* Prehistoric agricultural strategies in the Southwest. Ed. S. K. Fish and P. R. Fish. Arizona State University Anthropological Research Papers, no. 33, pp. 261–69. Tempe.

Di Peso, Charles C., John B. Rinaldo, and Gloria Fenner

1974a   Casas Grandes: A fallen trading center of the Gran Chichimeca, vols. 4–8. The Amerind Foundation, no. 9. Dragoon, Arizona.

1974b   Ceramics and shell. Casas Grandes: A fallen trading center of the Gran Chichimeca, vol. 6. The Amerind Foundation, no. 9. Dragoon, Arizona.

Doelle, William H.

1976   Desert resources and Hohokam subsistence: The Conoco Florence Project. Arizona State Museum Archaeological Series, no. 103. Tucson: University of Arizona.

1980   Comments on papers by Di Peso and Masse. *In* Current issues in Hohokam prehistory: Proceedings of a symposium. Ed. D. E. Doyel and F. Plog. Arizona State University Anthropological Research Papers, no. 23, pp. 231–35. Tempe.

1985   The southern Tucson Basin Rillito-Rincon subsistence, settlement, and community structure. *In* Proceedings of the 1983 Hohokam Conference. Ed. A. E. Dittert Jr. and D. E. Dove. Occasional Paper, no. 2, part 1, pp. 183–98. Arizona Archaeological Society, Phoenix Chapter.

1988   Preclassic community patterns in the Tucson Basin. *In* Recent research on Tucson Basin prehistory: Proceedings of the Second Tucson Basin Conference. Ed. W. H. Doelle and P. R. Fish. Institute for American Research Anthropological Papers, no. 10, pp. 277–312. Tucson.

Doelle, William H., and Mark D. Elson

1986   The Valencia Site testing project. Institute for American Research Technical Report, no. 86–6. Tucson.

Doelle, William H., and Henry D. Wallace

1986   Hohokam settlement patterns in the San Xavier project area, southern Tucson Basin. Institute for American Research Technical Report, no. 84–6. Tucson.

1988a   The transition to history in Pimería Alta. Paper presented at the Southwest Symposium. January 15–16, Arizona State University, Tempe.

1988b   The changing role of the Tucson Basin in the Hohokam regional system. *In* Exploring the Hohokam: Prehistoric dwellers of the Arizona desert. Ed. G. J. Gumerman. Albuquerque: University of New Mexico Press. In press.

Doelle, William H., Allen Dart, and Henry D. Wallace

1985   The southern Tucson Basin survey: Intensive survey along the Santa Cruz River. Institute for American Research Technical Report, no. 85–3. Tucson.

Doelle, William H., Frederick W. Huntington, and Henry D. Wallace

1987   Rincon phase reorganization in the Tucson Basin. *In* The Hohokam village: Site structure and organization. Ed. D. E. Doyel, pp. 71–96. Glenwood Springs, Colorado: American Association for the Advancement of Science.

Doolittle, William E.
1984 Agricultural change as an incremental process. Annals of the Association of American Geographers 74:124–37.
1985 The use of check dams for protecting downstream agricultural lands in the prehistoric Southwest: A contextual analysis. Journal of Anthropological Research 41:279–305.

Downum, Christian E.
1986 The occupational use of hill space in the Tucson Basin: Evidence from Linda Vista Hill. The Kiva 51(4):219–32.

Doyel, David E.
1974 Excavations in the Escalante Ruin group, southern Arizona. Arizona State Museum Archaeological Series, no. 37. Tucson: University of Arizona.
1976 Classic period Hohokam in the Gila River Basin, Arizona. The Kiva 42(1):27–38.
1977a Classic period Hohokam in the Escalante Ruin group. Ph.D. dissertation, University of Arizona. Ann Arbor: University Microfilms.
1977b Excavations in the middle Santa Cruz River valley, southeastern Arizona. Contribution to Highway Salvage Archaeology in Arizona, no. 44. Tucson: Arizona State Museum.
1979 The prehistoric Hohokam of the Arizona desert. American Scientist 67:544–54.
1980 Hohokam social organization and the Sedentary to Classic transition. In Current issues in Hohokam prehistory: Proceedings of a symposium. Ed. D. E. Doyel and F. Plog. Anthropological Research Papers, no. 23, pp. 23–40. Tempe: Arizona State University.
1981 Late Hohokam prehistory in southern Arizona. Contributions to Archaeology, no. 2. Scottsdale, Arizona: Gila Press.
1983 The evolution of regional diversity in the prehistoric Southwest: Hohokam and Anasazi Pueblo. In Proceedings of the 1981 Anasazi Conference. Ed. J. Smith, pp. 43–48. Mesa Verde National Park, Colorado: Mesa Verde Museum Association.
1984a Sedentary period Hohokam paleo-economy in the New River drainage, central Arizona. In Prehistoric agricultural strategies in the Southwest. Ed. S. K. Fish and P. R. Fish. Arizona State University Anthropological Research Papers, no. 33, pp. 35–52. Tempe.
1984b From foraging to farming: An overview of Tucson Basin prehistory. The Kiva 49(3–4):147–65.
1985a Current directions in Hohokam research. In Proceedings of the 1983 Hohokam Conference. Ed. A. E. Dittert Jr. and D. E. Dove. Occasional Paper, no. 2, part 1, pp. 3–26. Arizona Archaeological Society, Phoenix Chapter.
1985b Exchange and interaction. In Hohokam settlement and economic systems in the central New River drainage, Arizona. Ed. D. E. Doyel and M. D. Elson. Soil Systems Publications in Archaeology, no. 4, pp. 715–26. Phoenix.
1987 The role of commerce in Hohokam society. Paper presented at the advanced seminar, Cultural complexity in the arid Southwest. School of

American Research, Santa Fe. Manuscript, Pueblo Grande Museum, Phoenix.

1988   Hohokam cultural evolution in the Phoenix Basin. *In* Exploring the Hohokam: Prehistoric dwellers of the Arizona desert. Ed. G. J. Gumerman. Albuquerque: University of New Mexico Press. In press.

1989   Prehistoric inter-regional ceramic exchange in the Phoenix Basin. Paper presented at 54th annual meeting, Society for American Archaeology, April, Atlanta.

Doyel, David E., ed.
1987   The Hohokam village: Site structure and organization. Glenwood Springs, Colorado: American Association for the Advancement of Science.

Doyel, David E., and Mark D. Elson, eds.
1985   Hohokam settlement and economic systems in the central New River drainage, Arizona. Soil Systems Publications in Archaeology, no. 4. Phoenix.

Doyel, David E., and Emil W. Haury, eds.
1976   The 1976 Salado conference. The Kiva 42(1).

Doyel, David E., Cory D. Breternitz, and Michael P. Marshall
1984   Chacoan community structure: Bis sa'ani Pueblo and the Chaco halo. *In* Recent research on Chaco prehistory. Ed. W. J. Judge and J. D. Schelberg. Reports of the Chaco Center, no. 8, pp. 37–54. Albuquerque: Division of Cultural Research, National Park Service.

Dozier, Edward P.
1970   The Pueblo Indians of North America. New York: Holt, Rinehart and Winston.

Drager, Dwight L.
1976   Anasazi population estimates with the aid of data derived from photogrammetric maps. *In* Remote sensing experiments in cultural resource studies. Assembled by T. R. Lyons. Reports of the Chaco Center, no. 1, pp. 157–71. Albuquerque: Division of Cultural Research, National Park Service.

Drennan, Robert D.
1984a   Long-distance movement of goods in the Mesoamerican Formative and Classic. American Antiquity 49:27–43.

1984b   Long-distance transport costs in prehispanic Mesoamerica. American Anthropologist 86:105–12.

Earle, Timothy K.
1977   A reappraisal of redistribution: Complex Hawaiian chiefdoms. *In* Exchange systems in prehistory. Ed. T. K. Earle and J. Erickson, pp. 213–29. New York: Academic Press.

1978   Economic and social organization of a complex chiefdom: The Halelea district, Kaua'i, Hawaii. University of Michigan, Museum of Anthropology, Anthropology Paper, no. 63. Ann Arbor.

Ebert, James I., and Robert K. Hitchcock
1973   Spatial inference and the archeology of complex societies. Paper presented at conference, Formal methods for the analysis of regional social structure. Mathematics in Social Sciences Board, Santa Fe.

Eddy, Frank W.
1977 Archaeological investigations at Chimney Rock Mesa: 1970–1972. Memoirs of the Colorado Archaeological Societies 1. Boulder.

Effland, Richard W., Jr.
1985 The middle Gila Basin revisited: An examination of settlement-subsistence patterns and change. In Proceedings of the 1983 Hohokam Conference. Ed. A. E. Dittert Jr. and D. E. Dove. Occasional Paper, no. 2, part 1, pp. 353–72. Arizona Archaeological Society, Phoenix Chapter.

Effland, Richard W., Jr., and Adrianne G. Rankin
1988 Adaptation with the Santa Cruz River floodplain near Mission San Xavier: Response to changing environments. In Recent research on Tucson Basin prehistory: Proceedings of the Second Tucson Basin Conference. Ed. W. H. Doelle and P. R. Fish. Institute for American Research Anthropological Papers, no. 10, pp. 183–206. Tucson.

Eggan, Fred
1950 Social organization of the Western Pueblos. Chicago: University of Chicago Press.

Eighmy, Jeffrey L., and David E. Doyel
1987 A re-analysis of first-reported archaeomagnetic dates from the Hohokam area, southern Arizona. Journal of Field Archaeology 14:331–42.

Eighmy, Jeffrey L., and Randall H. McGuire
1988 Archaeomagnetic dates and the Hohokam phase sequence. Technical Series, no. 3. Boulder: Archaeometric Lab, Department of Anthropology, Colorado State University.

Elson, Mark D.
1986 Archaeological investigations at the Tanque Verde Wash site, a middle Rincon settlement in the eastern Tucson Basin. Institute for American Research Anthropological Papers, no. 7. Tucson.

Elson, Mark D., and William Doelle
1987 Archaeological survey in Catalina State Park with a focus on the Romero Ruin. Institute for American Research Technical Report, no. 87–4. Tucson.

Emory, W. H.
1848 Notes of a military reconnaissance from Fort Leavenworth, in Missouri, to San Diego, in California, including part of the Arkansas, Del Norte, and Gila rivers. 30th Congress, 1st Session (House), Executive Document 41. Washington, D.C.

Eschman, Peter N.
1983 Archaic site typology and chronology. In Economy and interaction along the lower Chaco River. Ed. P. Hogan and J. C. Winter, pp. 375–84. Albuquerque: Office of Contract Archaeology and Maxwell Museum of Anthropology, University of New Mexico.

Euler, Robert C., George J. Gumerman, Thor N. V. Karlstrom, Jeffrey S. Dean, and Richard H. Hevly
1979 The Colorado Plateaus: Cultural dynamics and paleoenvironment. Science 205:1089–1101.

Evans, John, and Harry F. Hillman
  1981 Casa Grande, an ancient astronomical observatory. Arizona Highways 57(10):32.

Evenari, M., L. Shanan, and N. Tadmor
  1971 The Negev: The challenge of a desert. Cambridge: Harvard University Press.

Feinman, Gary, and Jill Neitzel
  1984 Too many types: An overview of sedentary pre-state societies in the Americas. In Advances in archaeological method and theory, vol. 7. Ed. M. B. Schiffer, pp. 39–102. New York: Academic Press.

Ferdon, Edwin N., Jr.
  1955 A trial survey of Mexican-Southwestern architectural parallels. Monographs of the School of American Research, no. 21. Santa Fe.
  1967 The Hohokam "ball court": An alternative view of its function. The Kiva 33(1):1–14.

Ferg, Alan, and Amadeo M. Rea
  1983 Prehistoric bird bone from the Big Ditch site, Arizona. Journal of Ethnobiology 3:99–108.

Ferg, Alan, Kenneth C. Rozen, William L. Deaver, Martyn A. Tagg, David A. Phillips, and David A. Gregory
  1984 Hohokam habitation sites in the northern Santa Rita Mountains. Arizona State Museum Archaeological Series, no. 147, vol. 2. Tucson: University of Arizona.

Ferguson, T. J., and E. Richard Hart
  1985 A Zuni atlas. Norman: University of Oklahoma Press.

Fewkes, Jesse Walter
  1892 A report on the present condition of a ruin in Arizona called Casa Grande. Journal of American Ethnology and Archaeology 2:177–93.
  1908 Excavations at Casa Grande, Arizona, in 1906–1907. Smithsonian Miscellaneous Collections, vol. 50, pp. 289–329. Washington, D.C.: U.S. Government Printing Office.
  1910 Prehistoric ruins of the Gila Valley. Smithsonian Miscellaneous Collections, vol. 52, pp. 403–36. Washington, D.C.: U.S. Government Printing Office.
  1912 Casa Grande, Arizona. In Twenty-eighth annual report of the Bureau of American Ethnology, pp. 25–179. Washington, D.C.: U.S. Government Printing Office.

Firth, Raymond
  1936 We, the Tikopia. London: Allen and Unwin.
  1959 Social change in Tikopia. New York: MacMillan.

Fish, Paul R.
  1983 Hohokam prehistory. Manuscript, Arizona State Museum, University of Arizona, Tucson.

Fish, Paul R., and Suzanne K. Fish
  1977 Verde Valley archaeology: Review and perspective. Museum of Northern Arizona Research Paper, no. 8. Flagstaff.
  1988 Hohokam political and social organization. In Exploring the Hohokam:

Prehistoric dwellers of the Arizona desert. Ed. G. J. Gumerman. Albuquerque: University of New Mexico Press. In press.

Fish, Paul R., Suzanne K. Fish, and John H. Madsen
1988 Differentiation in bajada portions of a Tucson Basin Classic community. *In* Recent research on Tucson Basin prehistory: Proceedings of the Second Tucson Basin Conference. Ed. W. H. Doelle and P. R. Fish. Institute for American Research Anthropological Papers, no. 10, pp. 225–40. Tucson.

Fish, Paul R., Peter J. Pilles, Jr., and Suzanne K. Fish
1980 Colonies, traders and traits: The Hohokam in the north. *In* Current issues in Hohokam prehistory: Proceedings of a symposium. Ed. D. E. Doyel and F. Plog. Anthropological Research Papers, no. 23, pp. 151–75. Tempe: Arizona State University.

Fish, Paul R., Suzanne K. Fish, John Madsen, Charles Miksicek, Christine Szuter, and John Field
1987 A long-term Pioneer adaptation in the northern Tucson Basin. Paper presented at the 1987 Hohokam Symposium, The Archaic-Hohokam transition. January 30–31, Tempe, Arizona.

Fish, Suzanne K.
1984 The modified environment of the Salt-Gila aqueduct sites: A palynological perspective. *In* Hohokam archaeology along the Salt-Gila aqueduct, Central Arizona Project: Environment and subsistence. Ed. L. S. Teague and P. L. Crown. Arizona State Museum Archaeological Series, no. 150, vol. 7, pp. 39–52. Tucson: University of Arizona.

Fish, Suzanne K., and Paul R. Fish, eds.
1984 Prehistoric agricultural strategies in the Southwest. Anthropological Research Papers, no. 33. Tempe: Arizona State University.

Fish, Suzanne K., and William B. Gillespie
1987 Prehistoric use of riparian resources at the San Xavier Bridge site. *In* The archaeology of the San Xavier Bridge site (AZ BB:13:14), Tucson Basin, southern Arizona. Ed. J. C. Ravesloot. Arizona State Museum Archaeological Series, no. 171, pp. 71–80. Tucson: University of Arizona.

Fish, Suzanne K., Paul R. Fish, and John H. Madsen
1985 A preliminary analysis of Hohokam settlement and agriculture in the northern Tucson Basin. *In* Proceedings of the 1983 Hohokam Conference. Ed. A. E. Dittert Jr. and D. E. Dove. Occasional Paper, no. 2, part 1, pp. 75–100. Arizona Archaeological Society, Phoenix Chapter.
1989 Classic period Hohokam community integration in the Tucson Basin. *In* The sociopolitical structure of prehistoric Southwestern societies. Ed. S. Upham, K. Lightfoot, and R. Jewett, pp. 237–67. New York: Westview Press.

Fish, Suzanne K., Paul R. Fish, Charles H. Miksicek, and John Madsen
1985 Prehistoric agave cultivation in southern Arizona. Desert Plants 7:102–12.

Flannery, Kent V.
1968 The Olmec and the Valley of Oaxaca: A model for inter-regional interaction in Formative times. *In* Dumbarton Oaks Conference on the Olmec.

Ed. E. P. Benson, pp. 79–110. Washington, D.C.: Dumbarton Oaks Research Library.

1972 The cultural evolution of civilizations. Annual Review of Ecology and Systematics 3:399–426.

1976 Linear stream patterns and riverside settlement rules. In The early Mesoamerican village. Ed. K. V. Flannery, pp. 173–80. New York: Academic Press.

Flannery, Kent V., ed.
1976 The early Mesoamerican village. New York: Academic Press.

Ford, Richard I.
1968 An ecological analysis involving the population of San Juan Pueblo, New Mexico. Ph.D. dissertation, University of Michigan, Ann Arbor.

1972a Barter, gift, or violence: An analysis of Tewa intertribal exchange. In Social exchange and interaction. Ed. E. Wilmsen. University of Michigan Museum Memoirs, no. 46, pp. 21–45. Ann Arbor.

1972b An ecological perspective on the Eastern Pueblos. In New perspectives on the Pueblos. Ed. A. Ortiz, pp. 1–17. Albuquerque: University of New Mexico Press.

1985 Patterns of prehistoric food production in North America. In Prehistoric food production in North America. Ed. R. I. Ford. Anthropological Papers of the Museum of Anthropology, no. 75, pp. 341–64. Ann Arbor: University of Michigan.

Fowler, Andrew P., John R. Stein, and Roger Anyon
1987 An archaeological reconnaissance of west-central New Mexico: The Anasazi Monuments Project. Draft report, New Mexico Historic Preservation Division, Office of Cultural Affairs, Santa Fe.

Fried, Morton H.
1967 The evolution of political society: An essay in political anthropology. New York: Random House.

Frisbie, Theodore R.
1975 Hishi as money in the Puebloan Southwest. In Collected papers in honor of Florence Hawley Ellis. Ed. T. R. Frisbie. Papers of the Archaeological Society of New Mexico, no. 2, pp. 120–42.

1980 Social ranking in Chaco Canyon, New Mexico: A Mesoamerican reconstruction. Transactions of the Illinois Academy of Science 72(4):60–69.

1983 Anasazi-Mesoamerican relationships: From the bowels of the earth and beyond. In Proceedings of the 1981 Anasazi Symposium. Ed. J. E. Smith, pp. 214–26. Cortez, Colorado: Mesa Verde Museum Association.

Fritz, John M.
1978 Paleopsychology today: Ideational systems and human adaptation in prehistory. In Social archaeology: Beyond subsistence and dating. Ed. C. L. Redman, M. J. Berman, E. V. Curtin, W. T. Langhorne, Jr., N. M. Versaggi, and J. C. Wanser, pp. 37–59. New York: Academic Press.

1986 Vijayanagara: Authority and meaning of a South Indian imperial capital. American Anthropologist 88:44–55.

Fuller, S. L., A. E. Rogge, and L. M. Gregonis
1976 Orme alternatives: The archaeological resources of Roosevelt Lake and

Horseshoe Reservoir. Arizona State Museum Archaeological Series, no. 98. Tucson: University of Arizona.

Gasser, Robert E.

1979 Seeds, seasons, and ecosystems: Sedentary Hohokam groups in the Papaguería. The Kiva 44(2–3):101–12.

1980 Exchange and the Hohokam archaeobotanical record. *In* Current issues in Hohokam prehistory: Proceedings of a symposium. Ed. D. E. Doyel and F. Plog. Anthropological Research Papers, no. 23, pp. 72–77. Tempe: Arizona State University.

1981 The plant remains from the Escalante Ruin group. *In* Late Hohokam prehistory in southern Arizona. By D. E. Doyel. Contributions to Archaeology, no. 2, pp. 84–89. Scottsdale, Arizona: Gila Press.

1988 Modeling Hohokam subsistence. *In* Exploring the Hohokam: Prehistoric dwellers of the Arizona desert. Ed. G. J. Gumerman. Albuquerque: University of New Mexico Press. In press.

Gasser, Robert E., and S. Kwiatkowski

1988 Modeling Hohokam subsistence. Paper presented at the conference, Changing views on Hohokam archaeology. Amerind Foundation, Dragoon, Arizona.

Gasser, Robert E., and Charles Miksicek

1985 The specialists: A reappraisal of Hohokam exchange and the archaeobotanical record. *In* Proceedings of the 1983 Hohokam Conference. Ed. A. E. Dittert Jr. and D. E. Dove. Occasional Paper, no. 2, part 2, pp. 483–98. Arizona Archaeological Society, Phoenix Chapter.

Geib, Phil R., and Martha M. Callahan

1987 Ceramic exchange within the Kayenta Anasazi region: Volcanic ash-tempered Tusayan Whiteware. The Kiva 52(2):95–112.

Gillespie, William B.

1984 Una Vida. *In* Great Pueblo architecture of Chaco Canyon. By S. H. Lekson. Publications in Archeology 18B, Chaco Canyon Studies, pp. 79–94. Albuquerque: Division of Cultural Research, National Park Service.

1985 Holocene climate and environment of Chaco Canyon. *In* Environment and subsistence of Chaco Canyon, New Mexico. Ed. F. J. Mathien. Publications in Archeology, no. 18E, Chaco Canyon Studies, pp. 13–45. Albuquerque: National Park Service.

Gillespie, William B., and Robert P. Powers

1983 Regional settlement changes and past environment in the San Juan Basin. Paper presented at 2nd Anasazi Symposium, Salmon Ruins, Bloomfield, New Mexico.

Gladwin, Harold S.

1928 Excavations at Casa Grande, Arizona. Southwest Museum Papers, no. 2. Los Angeles.

1930 An outline of the Southwestern prehistoric. Arizona Historical Review 3(1).

1942 Excavations at Snaketown III: Revisions. Medallion Papers, no. 30. Globe, Arizona: Gila Pueblo.

1945   The Chaco branch. Medallion Papers, no. 33. Globe, Arizona: Gila Pueblo.

1948   Excavations at Snaketown IV: Review and conclusions. Medallion Papers, no. 38. Globe, Arizona: Gila Pueblo.

Gladwin, Harold S., Emil W. Haury, Edwin B. Sayles, and Nora Gladwin

1937   Excavations at Snaketown I: Material culture. Medallion Papers, no. 25. Globe, Arizona: Gila Pueblo.

Gladwin, Winifred, and Harold S. Gladwin

1933   Some Southwestern pottery types, series III. Medallion Papers, no. 13. Globe, Arizona: Gila Pueblo.

1935   The eastern range of the red-on-buff culture. Medallion Papers, no. 16. Globe, Arizona: Gila Pueblo.

Glassow, Michael A.

1980   Prehistoric agricultural development in the northern Southwest. Ballena Press Anthropological Papers, no. 16. Socorro, New Mexico.

Goody, Jack

1972   Domestic groups. Addison-Wesley Modular Publication, no. 28.

Goodyear, Albert C., III

1975   Hecla II and III: An interpretive study of archaeological remains from the Lakeshore Project, Papago Indian Reservation, south-central Arizona. Anthropological Research Papers, no. 4. Tempe: Arizona State University.

Gorman, Frederick J. E., and S. Terry Childs

1981   Is Prudden's unit type of Anasazi settlement valid and reliable? North American Archaeologist 2:153–92.

Grady, Mark A.

1976   Aboriginal agrarian adaptation to the Sonoran desert: A regional synthesis and research design. Ph.D. dissertation, Department of Anthropology, University of Arizona, Tucson.

Graves, Michael W.

1987   Rending reality in archaeological analysis: A reply to Upham and Plog. Journal of Field Archaeology 14:243–49.

Graybill, Donald A.

1989   The reconstruction of prehistoric Salt River streamflow. In The 1982–1984 excavations at Las Colinas: Environment and subsistence. By D. A. Graybill, D. A. Gregory, F. L. Nials, S. K. Fish, R. Gasser, C. Miksicek, and C. Szuter, pp. 25–38. Arizona State Museum Archaeological Series, no. 162, vol. 5. University of Arizona, Tucson.

Graybill, Donald A. , and Fred L. Nials

1989   Aspects of climate, steamflow, and geomorphology affecting irrigation patterns in the Salt River valley. In The 1982–1984 excavations at Las Colinas: Environment and subsistence. By D. A. Graybill, D. A. Gregory, F. L. Nials, S. K. Fish, R. Gasser, C. Miksicek, and C. Szuter, pp. 5–23. Arizona State Museum Archaeological Series, no. 162, vol. 5. University of Arizona, Tucson.

Grayson, Donald K.

1984   Quantitative zooarchaeology. New York: Academic Press.

Grebinger, Paul
    1971   Hohokam cultural development in the middle Santa Cruz River valley,
            Arizona. Ph.D. dissertation, Department of Anthropology, University of
            Arizona, Tucson.
    1973   Prehistoric social organization in Chaco Canyon, New Mexico: An
            alternative reconstruction. The Kiva 39(1):3–23.
    1978   Prehistoric social organization in Chaco Canyon, New Mexico: An
            evolutionary perspective. In Discovering past behavior: Experiments in
            the archaeology of the American Southwest. Ed. P. Grebinger, pp. 73–
            99. New York: Gordon and Breach.
Greene, Jerry L., and Thomas W. Mathews
    1976   Faunal study of unworked mammalian bones. In The Hohokam: Desert
            farmers and craftsmen. By E. W. Haury, pp. 367–73. Tucson: University
            of Arizona Press.
Greenwald, David H.
    1988 · Investigations of the Baccharis site and extension Arizona Canal: His-
            toric and prehistoric land use patterns in the northern Salt River valley.
            Museum of Northern Arizona Research Paper, no. 40. Flagstaff.
Greenwald, David H., and Richard Ciolek-Torrello, eds.
    1988   Archaeological investigations at the Dutch Canal ruin, Phoenix, Ari-
            zona. Museum of Northern Arizona Research Paper, no. 38. Flagstaff.
Gregory, David A.
    1982   The morphology of platform mounds and the structure of Classic period
            Hohokam sites. Paper presented at 47th annual meeting of the Society
            for American Archaeology, Minneapolis. Manuscript, Arizona State Mu-
            seum Library, University of Arizona, Tucson.
    1984   Excavations at the Siphon Draw site. In Hohokam archaeology along the
            Salt-Gila aqueduct, Central Arizona Project: Prehistoric occupation of
            the Queen Creek delta. Ed. L. S. Teague and P. L. Crown. Arizona State
            Museum Archaeological Series, no. 150, vol. 4, pp. 15–218. Tucson:
            University of Arizona.
    1987   The morphology of platform mounds and the structure of Classic period
            Hohokam sites. In The Hohokam village: Site structure and organiza-
            tion. Ed. D. E. Doyel, pp. 183–210. Glenwood Springs, Colorado:
            American Association for the Advancement of Science.
Gregory, David A., and Thomas R. McGuire
    1982   Research design for the testing of Interstate 10 corridor prehistoric and
            historic remains between Interstate 17 and 30th Drive (Group II, Las
            Colinas). Arizona State Museum Archaeological Series, no. 157. Tucson:
            University of Arizona.
Gregory, David A., and Fred L. Nials
    1985   Observations concerning the distribution of Classic period Hohokam
            platform mounds. In Proceedings of the 1983 Hohokam Conference.
            Ed. A. E. Dittert Jr. and D. E. Dove. Occasional Paper, no. 2, part 1,
            pp. 373–88. Arizona Archaeological Society, Phoenix Chapter.
Gregory, David A., David R. Abbott, Deni J. Seymour, and Nancy M. Bannister
    1988   The 1982–1984 excavations at Las Colinas: The mound 8 precinct.

Arizona State Museum Archaeological Series, no. 162, vol. 3. Tucson: University of Arizona.

Gregory, David A., William L. Deaver, Suzanne K. Fish, Ronald Gardiner, Robert W. Layhe, Fred L. Nials, and Lynn S. Teague

1988   The 1982–1984 excavations at Las Colinas: The site and its features. Arizona State Museum Archaeological Series, no. 162, vol. 2. Tucson: University of Arizona.

Gregory, David A., Fred L. Nials, Patricia L. Crown, Lynn S. Teague, and David A. Phillips Jr.

1985   The 1982–1984 excavations at Las Colinas: Research design. Arizona State Museum Archaeological Series, no. 162, vol. 1. Tucson: University of Arizona.

Gumerman, George J., and Emil W. Haury

1979   Prehistory: Hohokam. In Southwest. Ed. A. Ortiz. Handbook of North American Indians, vol. 9, pp. 75–90. Washington, D.C.: Smithsonian Institution.

Haas, Jonathan

1971   The Ushklish Ruin: A preliminary report on excavations of a Colonial period Hohokam site in the lower Tonto Basin, central Arizona. Manuscript, Arizona State Museum, University of Arizona, Tucson.

1982   The evolution of the prehistoric state. New York: Columbia University Press.

Hack, John T.

1942   The changing physical environment of the Hopi Indians of Arizona. Reports of the Awatovi Expedition, no. 1. Papers of the Peabody Museum of American Archaeology, vol. 35, no. 1. Cambridge: Harvard University.

Hackenberg, Robert A.

1964   Aboriginal land use and occupancy of the Papago Indians. Manuscript, Arizona State Museum, University of Arizona, Tucson.

Hage, Per, and Frank Harary

1983   Structural models in anthropology. Cambridge: Cambridge University Press.

Halbirt, Carl D., and Richard S. Ciolek-Torrello

1985   Changing interactions in the northern Mogollon regions prior to A.D. 1000. Paper presented at 50th annual meeting, Society for American Archaeology, Denver.

Halbirt, Carl D., and Steven G. Dosh

1986   Archaeological investigations: White Mountain Apache Indian Tribe, Tribal Development Office, Canyon Day Wastewater Treatment Facility, Fort Apache Indian Reservation, Gila and Navajo counties, Arizona. Manuscript, Museum of Northern Arizona, Flagstaff.

Hallasi, Judith A.

1979   Archaeological excavation at the Escalante Site, Dolores, Colorado, 1975 and 1976. Cultural Resources Series, no. 7, part 2. Denver: Colorado State Office, Bureau of Land Management.

Halseth, Odd S.

1936   Prehistoric irrigation in the Salt River valley. In Symposium on prehistoric agriculture. University of New Mexico Bulletin, Anthropological Series, vol. 1, no. 5, pp. 42–47. Albuquerque.

Hammack, Laurens C., and Alan P. Sullivan, eds.

1981   The 1968 excavations at Mound 8, Las Colinas Ruins group, Phoenix, Arizona. Arizona State Museum Archaeological Series, no. 154. Tucson: University of Arizona.

Hargrave, Lyndon L.

1970   Mexican macaws: Comparative osteology and survey of remains from the Southwest. Anthropological Papers, no. 20. University of Arizona, Tucson.

Harris, Myra

1974   An investigation into trade and contact at Vosberg, Arizona. M.A. thesis, Department of Anthropology, Arizona State University, Tempe.

Hassan, Fekri

1981   Demographic archaeology. New York: Academic Press.

Hastings, Russell

1934   Report of archaeological excavations at Casa Grande National Monument under C.W.A. Program 1934. Monthly Report of the Southwestern Monuments Association, March 1934, Supplement. Globe, Arizona: Gila Pueblo.

Hastorf, Christine A.

1980   Changing resource use in subsistence agricultural groups of the prehistoric Mimbres River valley, New Mexico. *In* Modeling change in prehistoric subsistence economies. Ed. T. K. Earle and A. L. Christenson, pp. 79–120. New York: Academic Press.

Haury, Emil W.

1932   Roosevelt:9:6, a Hohokam site of the Colonial period. Medallion Papers, no. 11. Globe, Arizona: Gila Pueblo.

1945   The excavation of Los Muertos and neighboring ruins in the Salt River valley, southern Arizona. Papers of the Peabody Museum of American Archaeology and Ethnology, vol. 24, no. 1. Cambridge: Harvard University.

1950   The stratigraphy and archaeology of Ventana Cave. Tucson: University of Arizona Press.

1967   The Hohokam, first masters of the American desert. National Geographic 131:670–95.

1975   The stratigraphy and archaeology of Ventana Cave. 2nd ed. Tucson: University of Arizona Press.

1976   The Hohokam: Desert farmers and craftsmen. Tucson: University of Arizona Press.

1980   Comments on the Hohokam symposium. *In* Current issues in Hohokam prehistory: Proceedings of a symposium. Ed. D. E. Doyel and F. Plog. Anthropological Research Papers, no. 23, pp. 113–20. Tempe: Arizona State University.

Hawley, Florence M.

1934   The significance of the dated prehistory of Chetro Ketl, Chaco Canyon, New Mexico. Monographs of the School of American Research, no. 2, Santa Fe.

Hayden, Irwin
1931   Field report on major antiquities, Grewe Site, Coolidge, Arizona. Manuscript, National Park Service Library, Casa Grande Ruins National Monument, Coolidge, Arizona.
Hayden, Julian D.
1945   Salt erosion. American Antiquity 10:373–78.
1957   Excavations, 1940, at University Indian Ruin, Tucson, Arizona. Southwestern Monuments Association, Technical Series, no. 5. Globe, Arizona: Gila Pueblo.
1970   On Hohokam origins and other matters. American Antiquity 35:87–93.
1972   Hohokam petroglyphs of the Sierra Pinacate, Sonora, and the Hohokam shell expeditions. The Kiva 37(2):74–83.
Hayes, Alden C.
1981   A survey of Chaco Canyon archeology. In Archeological surveys of Chaco Canyon, New Mexico. By A. C. Hayes, D. M. Brugge, and W. J. Judge. National Park Service Archeological Series, no. 17A, Chaco Canyon Studies, pp. 1–68. Washington, D.C.
Hayes, Alden C., and Thomas C. Windes
1975   An Anasazi shrine in Chaco Canyon. In Collected papers in honor of Florence Hawley Ellis. Ed. T. R. Frisbie. Papers of the Archaeological Society of New Mexico, no. 2, pp. 143–56. Santa Fe.
Henderson, T. Kathleen
1987a The growth of a Hohokam village. In The Hohokam village: Site structure and organization. Ed. D. E. Doyel, pp. 97–126. Glenwood Springs, Colorado: American Association for the Advancement of Science.
1987b Ceramics, dates, and the growth of the Marana Community. In Studies in the Hohokam community of Marana. Ed. G. Rice. Anthropological Field Studies, no. 15, pp. 49–78. Tempe: Arizona State University.
1987c Field investigations at the Marana Community complex. Anthropological Field Studies, no. 14. Tempe: Department of Anthropology, Arizona State University.
Henderson, T. Kathleen, ed.
1987   Structure and organization at La Ciudad. Anthropological Field Studies, no. 18. Tempe: Department of Anthropology, Arizona State University.
Hendrickson, Dean A., and W. L. Minckley
1984   Cienegas: Vanishing climax communities of the American Southwest. Desert Plants 6:131–75.
Herskovitz, Robert M.
1974   The Superstition Freeway Project: A preliminary report on the salvage excavation of a dual component Hohokam site in Tempe, Arizona. Tucson: Arizona State Museum, in cooperation with the Arizona Highway Department.
1981   AZ U:9:46: A dual component Hohokam site in Tempe, Arizona. The Kiva 47(1–2).
Hill, James N.
1970   Broken K Pueblo. Anthropological Papers of the University of Arizona, no. 18. Tucson.

Hoffman, Teresa L., David E. Doyel, and Mark D. Elson
1985   Ground stone tool production in the New River Basin. *In* Proceedings of the 1983 Hohokam Conference. Ed. A. E. Dittert Jr. and D. E. Dove. Occasional Paper, no. 2, part 2, pp. 655–86. Arizona Archaeological Society, Phoenix Chapter.

Hogan, Patrick F.
1983   Paleoenvironmental reconstruction. *In* Economy and interaction along the lower Chaco River: The Navajo Mine Archeology Program. Ed. P. F. Hogan and J. C. Winter, pp. 49–62. Albuquerque: Office of Contract Archeology and Maxwell Museum of Anthropology, University of New Mexico.

Howard, Ann Valdo
1983   The organization of inter-regional shell production and exchange within southwestern Arizona. M.A. thesis, Department of Anthropology, Arizona State University, Tempe.
1985   A reconstruction of Hohokam inter-regional shell production and exchange within southwestern Arizona. *In* Proceedings of the 1983 Hohokam Conference. Ed. A. E. Dittert Jr. and D. E. Dove. Occasional Paper, no. 2, part 2, pp. 459–72. Arizona Archaeological Society, Phoenix Chapter.
1987   Late Archaic and Pioneer period shell utilization: An examination of early shell production and exchange within Arizona. Paper presented at 1987 Hohokam Symposium, The Archaic-Hohokam transition. January 30–31, Tempe, Arizona.

Howard, Jerry B.
1985   Courtyard groups and domestic cycling: A hypothetical model of growth. *In* Proceedings of the 1983 Hohokam Conference. Ed. A. E. Dittert Jr. and D. E. Dove. Occasional Paper, no. 2, part 1, pp. 311–26. Arizona Archaeological Society, Phoenix Chapter.
1987   The Lehi canal system: Organization of a Classic period community. *In* The Hohokam village: Site structure and organization. Ed. D. E. Doyel, pp. 211–22. Glenwood Springs, Colorado: American Association for the Advancement of Science.

Huckell, Bruce B.
1979   The Coronet Real Project: Archaeological investigations on the Luke Range, southwestern Arizona. Arizona State Museum Archaeological Series, no. 129. Tucson: University of Arizona.
1987   Agriculture and Late Archaic settlements in the river valleys of southeastern Arizona. Paper presented at 1987 Hohokam Symposium, The Archaic-Hohokam transition. January 30–31, Tempe, Arizona.
1988   Late Archaic archaeology of the Tucson Basin: A status report. *In* Recent research on Tucson Basin prehistory: Proceedings of the Second Tucson Basin Conference. Ed. W. H. Doelle and P. R. Fish. Institute for American Research Anthropological Papers, no. 10, pp. 57–80. Tucson.

Hughes, Richard E.
1984   Obsidian sourcing studies in the Great Basin: Problems and prospects. *In* Obsidian sources in the Great Basin. Ed. R. E. Hughes. Contributions

of the University of California Archaeological Research Facility, no. 15, pp. 1–19. Berkeley.

Hunter-Anderson, Rosalind L.
1981   Comments on Cordell and Plog's "Escaping the confines of normative thought." American Antiquity 46:194–97.

Huntington, Ellsworth
1914   The climatic factor in arid America. Carnegie Institution Publication, no. 192. Washington, D.C.

Huntington, Frederick W.
1985   Archaeological investigations at the West Branch Site: Early and middle Rincon occupation in the southern Tucson Basin. Institute for American Research Anthropological Papers, no. 5. Tucson.

Ibn Khaldun
1967   The Muqaddimah: An introduction to history. Trans. F. Rosenthal. Princeton: Princeton University Press.

Irwin-Williams, Cynthia
1983   Socio-economic order and authority structure in the Chacoan community at Salmon Ruin. Paper presented at 1983 Anasazi Symposium, Salmon Ruins, Farmington, New Mexico.

Irwin-Williams, Cynthia, and Philip H. Shelley, eds.
1980   Investigations at the Salmon Site: The structure of Chacoan society in the northern Southwest, 4 vols. Portales: Eastern New Mexico University.

Israelsen, O. W., and V. E. Hansen
1967   Irrigation principles and practices. 3rd ed. New York: John Wiley & Sons.

Ives, John C., and Dan J. Opfenring
1966   Some investigations into the nature of the early phases of the Hohokam culture, central Arizona. Preliminary report submitted to the National Science Foundation. Manuscript, Department of Anthropology, Arizona State University, Tempe.

Jeançon, Jean A., and Frank H. H. Roberts Jr.
1923   Further archaeological research in the northeastern San Juan Basin of Colorado, during the summer of 1922. The Colorado Magazine 1(1): 11–28.
1924   Further archaeological research in the northeastern San Juan Basin of Colorado, during the summer of 1922. The Colorado Magazine 1(2): 65–70; 1(3):108–18; 1(4):163–73; 1(5):213–24; 1(6):260–76; 1(7): 301–307.

Jernigan, E. Wesley
1978   Jewelry of the prehistoric Southwest. Albuquerque: University of New Mexico Press.

Jett, Stephen C., and Peter B. Moyle
1986   The exotic origins of fishes depicted on prehistoric Mimbres pottery from New Mexico. American Antiquity 51:688–720.

Jewett, Roberta A.
1989   Distance, integration, and complexity: The spatial organization of pan-regional settlement clusters in the American Southwest. In The socio-

political structure of prehistoric Southwestern societies. Ed. S. Upham, K. G. Lightfoot, and R. A. Jewett, pp. 363–88. Boulder: Westview Press.

Johnson, Alfred E.
1964   Archaeological excavations in Hohokam sites of southern Arizona. American Antiquity 30:145–61.

Johnson, Gregory A.
1978   Information sources and the development of decision-making organizations. *In* Social archaeology: Beyond subsistence and dating. Ed. C. L. Redman, M. J. Berman, E. V. Curtin, W. T. Langhorne Jr., N. M. Versaggi, and J. C. Wanser, pp. 87–112. New York: Academic Press.

Johnson, Paul C.
1978   An analysis of the faunal remains from Alder Wash (AZ BB:6:9) and the Dos Bisnagas site (AZ BB:6:6). *In* The Peppersauce Wash Project: Excavations at three multicomponent sites in the lower San Pedro Valley, Arizona. Ed. W. B. Masse. Manuscript, Arizona State Museum, University of Arizona, Tucson.

Jorde, Lynn B.
1977   Precipitation cycles and cultural buffering in the prehistoric Southwest. *In* For theory building in archaeology. Ed. L. R. Binford, pp. 385–96. New York: Academic Press.

Joseph, Alice, Rosamund B. Spicer, and Jane Chesky
1949   The desert people: A study of the Papago Indians. Chicago: University of Chicago Press.

Judd, Neil M.
1930   Arizona sacrifices her prehistoric canals. Explorations and field-work of the Smithsonian Institution in 1929. Smithsonian Institution Publication, no. 3060. Washington, D.C.

1931   Arizona's prehistoric canals from the air. Explorations and field-work of the Smithsonian Institution in 1930. Smithsonian Institution Publication, no. 3111, pp. 157–66. Washington, D.C.

1954   The material culture of Pueblo Bonito. Smithsonian Miscellaneous Collections, vol. 124. Washington, D.C.: U.S. Government Printing Office.

1959   Pueblo del Arroyo, Chaco Canyon, New Mexico. Smithsonian Miscellaneous Collections, vol. 138, no. 1. Washington, D.C.: U.S. Government Printing Office.

1964   The architecture of Pueblo Bonito. Smithsonian Miscellaneous Collections, vol. 147, no. 1. Washington, D.C.: U.S. Government Printing Office.

Judge, W. James
1972   Archaeological survey of the Chaco Canyon area: 1971. Report submitted to the Chaco Center, National Park Service, University of New Mexico

1976   Archaeological field procedural manual. On file, Chaco Project, National Park Service, University of New Mexico.

1977   The emergence of complexity in Chaco Canyon, New Mexico. Paper presented at symposium, Mechanisms in the evolution of formative societies, 76th annual meeting of the American Anthropological Association, Houston.

1979   The development of a complex cultural ecosystem in the Chaco Basin, New Mexico. *In* Proceedings of the first conference on scientific research in the national parks, part 3. Ed. R. M. Linn, pp. 901–6. National Park Service Transactions and Proceedings Series, no. 5.

1982   The Paleo-Indian and Basketmaker periods: An overview and some research problems. *In* The San Juan tomorrow: Planning for the conservation of cultural resources in the San Juan Basin. Ed. F. Plog and W. Wait, pp. 5–57. Santa Fe: National Park Service, Southwest Region, in cooperation with the School of American Research.

1983   Chaco Canyon—San Juan Basin. Paper presented at advanced seminar, Dynamics of Southwestern prehistory. School of American Research, September 1983, Santa Fe.

1984   New light on Chaco Canyon. *In* New light on Chaco Canyon. Ed. D. G. Noble, pp. 1–12. Santa Fe: School of American Research Press.

1989   Chaco Canyon—San Juan Basin. *In* Dynamics of Southwestern prehistory. Ed. L. Cordell and G. Gumerman, pp. 209–62. Washington, D.C.: Smithsonian Institution.

Judge, W. James, and John D. Schelberg, eds.
1984   Recent research on Chaco prehistory. Reports of the Chaco Center, no. 8. Albuquerque: Division of Cultural Research, National Park Service.

Judge, W. James, William B. Gillespie, Stephen H. Lekson, and H. Wolcott Toll
1981   Tenth-century developments in Chaco Canyon. *In* Collected papers in honor of Erik Kellerman Reed. Ed. A. H. Schroeder. Papers of the Archaeological Society of New Mexico, no. 6, pp. 65–98. Albuquerque.

Kane, Allen E.
1989   Did the sheep look up? Sociopolitical complexity in ninth-century Dolores society. *In* The sociopolitical structure of prehistoric Southwestern societies. Ed. S. Upham, K. G. Lightfoot, and R. A. Jewett, pp. 307–62. Boulder: Westview Press.

Kelley, J. Charles
1971   Archaeology of the northern frontier: Pochtecas and Durango. *In* Archaeology of northern Mesoamerica. Ed. I. Bernal and G. F. Ekholm. Handbook of Middle American Indians, vol. 11, pp. 768–801. Austin: University of Texas Press.

1980   Comments on the papers by Plog, Doyel, and Riley. *In* Current issues in Hohokam prehistory: Proceedings of a symposium. Ed. D. E. Doyel and F. Plog. Anthropological Research Papers, no. 23, pp. 49–66. Tempe: Arizona State University.

Kelley, J. Charles, and Ellen Abbott Kelley
1975   An alternative hypothesis for the explanation of Anasazi culture history. *In* Collected papers in honor of Florence Hawley Ellis. Ed. T. R. Frisbie. Papers of the Archaeological Society of New Mexico, no. 2, pp. 178–223. Albuquerque.

Kent, Kate Peck
1957   The cultivation and weaving of cotton in the prehistoric southwestern United States. Transactions of the American Philosophical Society, vol. 47, no. 3. Washington, D.C.

Kerley, Janet M., and Patrick F. Hogan
  1983 Preliminary debitage analysis. *In* Economy and interaction along the lower Chaco River: The Navajo Mine Archeology Program. Ed. P. F. Hogan and J. C. Winter, pp. 255–61. Albuquerque: Office of Contract Archeology and Maxwell Museum of Anthropology, University of New Mexico.

Kidder, Alfred V.
  1924 An introduction to the study of Southwestern archaeology, with a preliminary account of the excavations at Pecos. Papers of the Phillips Academy Southwestern Expedition, no. 1. New Haven: Phillips Academy.
  1927 Southwestern archaeological conference. Science 68:489–91.

Kidder, Alfred V., Harriet S. Cosgrove, and Cornelieus B. Cosgrove
  1949 The Pendleton ruins, Hidalgo County, New Mexico. Carnegie Institute of Washington Publications, no. 585. Contributions to American Anthropology and History, vol. 10, no. 50.

Kincaid, Chris, ed.
  1983 Chaco Roads Project Phase I: A reappraisal of prehistoric roads in the San Juan Basin, 1983. Santa Fe and Albuquerque: New Mexico State Office and Albuquerque District Office, Bureau of Land Management.

Kirkby, Anne V. T.
  1973 The use of land and water resources in the past and present valley of Oaxaca, Mexico. Memoirs of the Museum of Anthropology, University of Michigan, no. 5. Ann Arbor.

Kisselburg, JoAnn
  1987 Specialization and differentiation: Non-subsistence economic pursuits in courtyard systems at La Ciudad. *In* The Hohokam village: Site structure and organization. Ed. D. E. Doyel, pp. 159–70. Glenwood Springs, Colorado: American Association for the Advancement of Science.

Kokalis, Peter G.
  1971 Terraces of the lower Salt River valley, Arizona. M.A. thesis, Department of Anthropology, Arizona State University, Tempe.

Kowalewski, Stephen A., Richard E. Blanton, Gary Feinman, and Laura Finsten
  1983 Boundaries, scale, and internal organization. Journal of Anthropological Archaeology 2:32–56.

Kroeber, Alfred
  1917 Zuñi kin and clan. Anthropological Papers of the American Museum of Natural History 18(2)37–205. New York.

Kus, Susan M.
  1983 The social representation of space: Dimensioning the cosmological and the quotidian. *In* Archaeological hammers and theories. Ed. J. A. Moore and A. S. Keene, pp. 277–98. New York: Academic Press.

Lagasse, Peter F., William B. Gillespie, and Kenneth G. Eggert
  1984 Hydraulic engineering analysis of prehistoric water-control systems at Chaco Canyon. *In* Recent research on Chaco prehistory. Ed. W. J. Judge and J. D. Schelberg. Reports of the Chaco Center, no. 8, pp. 187–211. Albuquerque: Division of Cultural Research, National Park Service.

Landis, Daniel G.
   1988   Chipped stone assemblages of the Grand Canal Ruins. *In* Archaeological
          investigations at the Grand Canal Ruins: A Classic period site in Phoe-
          nix, Arizona. Ed. D. R. Mitchell, pp. 385–441. Soil Systems Publications
          in Archaeology, no. 12. Phoenix.
Lange, Richard C.
   1982   Steatite: An analysis and assessment of form and distribution. *In* Cholla
          Project archaeology. Ed. J. J. Reid. Arizona State Museum Archaeological
          Series, no. 161, vol. 1, pp. 167–92. Tucson: University of Arizona.
LeBlanc, Steven A.
   1982   Temporal change in Mogollon ceramics. *In* Southwestern ceramics: A
          comparative review. Ed. A. H. Schroeder. The Arizona Archaeologist,
          vol. 15, pp. 107–28. Phoenix: Arizona Archaeological Society.
   1983   Aspects of Southwestern prehistory, A.D. 700–1450. Paper presented at
          48th annual meeting, Society for American Archaeology, Pittsburgh.
   1986   Aspects of Southwestern prehistory, A.D. 900–1400. *In* Ripples in the
          Chichimec Sea: New considerations of Southwestern-Mesoamerican
          interactions. Ed. F. J. Mathien and R. H. McGuire, pp. 105–34. Carbon-
          dale: Southern Illinois University Press.
Lekson, Stephen H.
   1984   Largest settlement size as an index of socio-political complexity. Paper
          presented at 49th annual meeting, Society for American Archaeology,
          Portland, Oregon. Published in 1985 in Haliksai: UNM Contributions
          to Anthropology 4:68–75. Albuquerque: University of New Mexico.
   1985   Review of Breternitz et al. (eds.), Bis sa'ani: A late Bonito phase commu-
          nity on Escavada Wash, northwest New Mexico. The Kiva 50(2–3):
          164–67.
   1986   Great Pueblo architecture of Chaco Canyon, New Mexico. Albuquer-
          que: University of New Mexico Press. Originally published in 1984 as
          Publications in Archeology, no. 18B, Chaco Canyon Studies. Albuquer-
          que: National Park Service.
   1988   The Mangas phase in Mimbres archaeology. The Kiva 53(2):129–46.
Lekson, Stephen H., ed.
   1984   The architecture and dendrochronology of Chetro Ketl, Chaco Canyon,
          New Mexico. Reports of the Chaco Center, no. 6. Albuquerque: Division
          of Cultural Research, National Park Service.
Lekson, Stephen H., Thomas C. Windes, John R. Stein, and W. James Judge
   1988   The Chaco Canyon community. Scientific American 256(7):100–109.
Lightfoot, Kent G.
   1979   Food redistribution among prehistoric Pueblo groups. The Kiva 44(4):
          319–39.
   1984   Prehistoric political dynamics: A case study from the American South-
          west. Dekalb: Northern Illinois University Press.
Lister, Robert H.
   1978   Mesoamerican influences at Chaco Canyon, New Mexico. *In* Across the
          Chichimec Sea: Papers in honor of J. Charles Kelley. Ed. C. Riley and B.
          Hedrick, pp. 233–41. Carbondale: Southern Illinois University Press.

Lister, Robert H., and Florence C. Lister
  1981 Chaco Canyon: Archaeology and archaeologists. Albuquerque: University of New Mexico Press.
Loose, Richard W., and Thomas R. Lyons
  1976 The Chetro Ketl field: A planned water control system in Chaco Canyon. *In* Remote sensing experiments in cultural resource studies: Nondestructive methods of archeological exploration, survey and analysis, assembled by Thomas R. Lyons. Reports of the Chaco Center, no. 1, pp. 133–56. Albuquerque: Division of Cultural Research, National Park Service.
Love, David W.
  1977 Dynamics of sedimentation and geomorphic history of Chaco Canyon National Monument, New Mexico. *In* New Mexico Geological Society guidebook, 28th field conference, San Juan Basin III. Ed. J. E. Fassett, pp. 291–300. Socorro: New Mexico Bureau of Mines and Minerals.
Lowe, Charles H., ed.
  1964 The vertebrates of Arizona. Tucson: University of Arizona Press.
Lucius, William
  1984 The ceramic data base. *In* Dolores Archaeological Program: Synthetic report, 1978–1981, submitted by D. A. Breternitz, pp. 215–23. Denver: Engineering and Research Center, Bureau of Reclamation.
Mann, Michael
  1986 The sources of social power, vol. 1: A history of power from the beginning to A.D. 1760. Cambridge: Cambridge University Press.
Marmaduke, William S., and Richard J. Martynec
  1986 Productive specialization and the Hohokam shell trade. Paper presented at the Arizona Archaeological Society meetings, Pueblo Grande Museum, Phoenix.
Marshall, Michael P., David E. Doyel, and Cory D. Breternitz
  1982 A regional perspective on the late Bonito phase. *In* Bis sa'ani: A late Bonito phase community on Escavada Wash, northwest New Mexico. Ed. C. D. Breternitz, D. E. Doyel, and M. P. Marshall. Navajo Nation Papers in Anthropology, no. 14, pp. 1227–40. Window Rock, Arizona.
Marshall, Michael P., John R. Stein, Richard W. Loose, and Judith E. Novotny
  1979 Anasazi communities in the San Juan Basin. Albuquerque and Santa Fe: Public Service Company of New Mexico and New Mexico Historic Preservation Bureau.
Martin, Paul S.
  1936 Lowry Ruin in southwestern Colorado. Field Museum of Natural History Anthropological Series, no. 23, vol. 1. Chicago.
Martin, Paul S., and Fred Plog
  1973 Archaeology of Arizona. New York: Natural History Press/Doubleday.
Masse, W. Bruce
  1976 The Hohokam Expressway Project: A study of prehistoric irrigation in the Salt River valley, Arizona. Contribution to Highway Salvage Archaeology in Arizona, no. 43. Tucson: Arizona State Museum.
  1979 An intensive survey of prehistoric dry farming systems near Tumamoc Hill in Tucson, Arizona. The Kiva 45(1–2):141–86.

1980a The Hohokam of the lower San Pedro Valley and the northern Papagueria: Continuity and variability in two regional populations. *In* Current issues in Hohokam prehistory: Proceedings of a symposium. Ed. D. E. Doyel and F. Plog. Anthropological Research Papers, no. 23, pp. 205–23. Tempe: Arizona State University.

1980b Excavations at Gu Achi: A reappraisal of Hohokam settlement and subsistence in the Arizona Papagueria. Western Archaeological Center Publications in Anthropology, no. 12. Tucson: National Park Service.

1981a Prehistoric irrigation systems in the Salt River valley, Arizona. Science 214:408–15.

1981b A reappraisal of the protohistoric Sobaipuri Indians of southeastern Arizona. *In* the protohistoric period in the North American Southwest, A.D. 1450–1700. Ed. D. R. Wilcox and W. B. Masse. Arizona State University Anthropological Research Papers, no. 24, pp. 28–56. Tempe.

1982 Hohokam ceramic art: Regionalism and the imprint of societal change. *In* Southwestern ceramics: A comparative review. Ed. A. H. Schroeder. The Arizona Archaeologist, vol. 15, pp. 71–105. Phoenix: Arizona Archaeological Society.

1986 Archaeological sediments of the Hohokam Expressway canals. *In* The 1982–1984 excavations at Las Colinas: The site and its features. Ed. D. A. Gregory and C. A. Heatherington. Manuscript, Cultural Resource Management Division, Arizona State Museum, University of Arizona, Tucson.

1988 Systems and systematics: A critique of the interdisciplinary study of Hohokam irrigation. Paper presented at Arizona Archaeological Council symposium, Prehistoric irrigation in Arizona. Pueblo Grande Museum, Phoenix.

1989 The archaeology and ecology of fishing in the Belau Islands, Micronesia. Ph.D. dissertation, Department of Anthropology, Southern Illinois University, Carbondale.

Masse, W. Bruce, ed.

1987 Archaeological investigations of portions of the Las Acequias–Los Muertos irrigation system: Testing and partial data recovery within the Tempe section of the outer loop freeway system, Maricopa County, Arizona. Arizona State Museum Archaeological Series, no. 176. Tucson: University of Arizona.

Mathien, Frances Joan

1984 Social and economic implications of jewelry items of the Chaco Anasazi. *In* Recent research on Chaco prehistory. Ed. W. J. Judge and J. D. Schelberg. Reports of the Chaco Center, no. 8, pp. 173–86. Albuquerque: Division of Cultural Research, National Park Service.

1985 Ornaments and minerals from Chaco Canyon National Park Service Project, 1971–1978. Manuscript, Division of Cultural Research, National Park Service, Santa Fe.

1986 External contact and the Chaco Anasazi. *In* Ripples in the Chichimec Sea: New considerations of Southwestern-Mesoamerican interactions. Ed. F. J. Mathien and R. H. McGuire, pp. 220–42. Carbondale: Southern Illinois University Press.

Mathien, Frances Joan, and Randall H. McGuire, eds.
  1986   Ripples in the Chichimec Sea: New considerations of Southwestern-Mesoamerican interactions. Carbondale: Southern Illinois University Press.
Mathien, Frances Joan, and Thomas C. Windes, eds.
  1987   Artifactual and biological analyses. Investigations at the Pueblo Alto complex, Chaco Canyon, New Mexico, vol. 3. Publications in Archeology 18F. Santa Fe: National Park Service.
Mayo, Ernst
  1949   Systematics and the origin of species. New York: Columbia University Press.
McGregor, John C.
  1941   Winona and Ridge ruins: Architecture and material culture. Museum of Northern Arizona Bulletin, no. 18. Flagstaff.
  1965   Southwestern archaeology. 2nd ed. Urbana: University of Illinois Press.
McGuire, Randall H.
  1980   The Mesoamerican connection in the Southwest. The Kiva 46(1–2):3–38.
  1983   Breaking down cultural complexity: inequality and heterogeneity. In Advances in archaeological method and theory. Ed. M. B. Schiffer, vol. 6, pp. 91–142. New York: Academic Press.
  1988   On the outside looking in: The concept of periphery in Hohokam archaeology. In Exploring the Hohokam: Prehistoric desert dwellers of the Arizona desert. Ed. G. J. Gumerman. Albuquerque: University of New Mexico Press. In press.
McGuire, Randall H., and Christopher E. Downum
  1982   A preliminary consideration of desert-mountain trade. In Mogollon archaeology. Ed. P. H. Beckett, pp. 205–25. Santa Fe: Acoma Books.
McGuire, Randall H., and A. V. Howard
  1987   The structure and organization of Hohokam shell exchange. The Kiva 52(2):113–46.
McGuire, Randall H., and Michael B. Schiffer, eds.
  1982   Hohokam and Patayan: Prehistory of southwestern Arizona. New York: Academic Press.
McIntosh, Susan K.
  1984   Blacksmiths and the evolution of political complexity in Mande society: An hypothesis. Paper presented at advanced seminar, The emergence of complex societies in Africa. School of American Research, Santa Fe.
McKenna, Peter J.
  1984   The architecture and material culture of 29SJ1360. Reports of the Chaco Center, no. 7. Albuquerque: Division of Cultural Research, National Park Service.
  n.d.   Chaco Project ceramics overview: Typology and form section. Manuscript in preparation, Division of Cultural Research, National Park Service, Santa Fe.
McKenna, Peter J., and Marcia Truell
  1986   Small site architecture of Chaco Canyon. Publication in Archaeology, no. 18D. Santa Fe: Division of Cultural Research, National Park Service.

McLellen, George
  1969   The origin, development and typology of Anasazi kivas and great kivas. Ph.D. dissertation, Department of Anthropology, University of Colorado, Boulder.
Merbs, Charles F.
  1985   Paleopathology of the Hohokam. *In* Proceedings of the 1983 Hohokam Conference. Ed. A. E. Dittert Jr. and D. E. Dove. Occasional Paper, no. 2, part 1, pp. 127–42. Arizona Archaeological Society, Phoenix Chapter.
Midvale, Frank
  1965   Prehistoric irrigation of the Casa Grande Ruins area. The Kiva 30: 82–86.
  1968   Prehistoric irrigation in the Salt River valley. The Kiva 34(1):28–32.
  1970   Prehistoric canal-irrigation in the Buckeye Valley and Gila Bend areas in western Maricopa County, Arizona. Paper presented at symposium on water control, 43rd Annual Pecos Conference, Santa Fe.
  1974   Prehistoric ruins and irrigation in the eastern Buckeye Valley. The Arizona Archaeologist 8:37–39.
Miksicek, Charles H.
  1984   Historic desertification, prehistoric vegetation change, and Hohokam subsistence in the Salt-Gila Basin. *In* Hohokam archaeology along the Salt-Gila aqueduct, Central Arizona Project: Environment and subsistence. Ed. L. S. Teague and P. L. Crown. Arizona State Museum Archaeological Series, no. 150, vol. 7, pp. 53–80. Tucson: University of Arizona.
Mills, Barbara J.
  1986   Regional patterns of ceramic variability in the San Juan Basin: The ceramics from the Chaco Inventory Survey. *In* Archaeological survey at Chaco Culture National Historic Park. Ed. R. B. Powers. Reports of the Chaco Center. Santa Fe: Division of Cultural Research, National Park Service. In preparation.
Mindeleff, Cosmos
  1896   Casa Grande Ruin. Thirteenth Annual Report of the Bureau of American Ethnology, 1891–1892. Washington, D.C.: U.S. Government Printing Office.
  1897   The repair of Casa Grande Ruin, Arizona, in 1891. *In* Fifteenth Annual Report of the Bureau of American Ethnology, pp. 315–19. Washington, D.C.: U.S. Government Printing Office.
Minnis, Paul E.
  1985   Social adaptation to food stress. Chicago: University of Chicago Press.
Mitchell, Douglas R., ed.
  1988   Excavations at La Lomita Pequeña. Soil Systems Publications in Archaeology, no. 10. Phoenix.
Molloy, John
  1969   The Casa Grande archeological zone: Precolumbian astronomical observation. Manuscript, Western Archeological Center, National Park Service, Tucson.
Morgan, Lewis Henry
  1877   Ancient society. New York: Holt.

Morris, Donald H.
1969   Red Mountain: An early Pioneer period Hohokam site in the Salt River valley of central Arizona. American Antiquity 34:40–53.
1970   Walnut Creek Village: A ninth-century Hohokam-Anasazi settlement in the mountains of central Arizona. American Antiquity 35:49–61.
Morris, Donald H., and Dan Brooks
1987   Cremations at the Marana sites. In Studies in the Hohokam community of Marana. Ed. G. E. Rice, pp. 223–34. Arizona State University Anthropological Field Studies, no. 15. Tempe.
Morris, Earl H.
1919   The Aztec Ruin. Anthropological Papers of the American Museum of Natural History, no. 25(1). New York.
1921   The house of the great kiva at the Aztec Ruin. Anthropological Papers of the American Museum of Natural History, no. 26(2). New York.
1939   Archaeological studies in the La Plata district. Carnegie Institution of Washington Publication, no. 519. Washington, D.C.
Nabhan, Gary P.
1982   The desert smells like rain: A naturalist in Papago Indian country. San Francisco: North Point Press.
1983   Papago fields: Arid lands ethnobotany and agricultural ecology. Ph.D. dissertation, University of Arizona, Tucson.
1986   Ak-cin "arroyo mouth" and the environmental setting of the Papago Indian fields in the Sonoran desert. Applied Geography 6:61–75.
Nabhan, Gary P., and W. Bruce Masse
1986   Floodwater agriculture in the Sonoran desert: Ethnographic and archaeological perspectives. Paper presented at 51st annual meeting, Society for American Archaeology, New Orleans.
Naroll, Raoul
1962   Floor area and settlement pattern. American Antiquity 27:587–89.
Needham, Rodney
1975   Polythetic classification: Convergence and consequences. Man 10(3): 349–69.
Neely, James A.
1974   The prehistoric Lunt and Stove Canyon sites, Point of Pines, Arizona. Ph.D. dissertation, Department of Anthropology, University of Arizona, Tucson.
Neitzel, Jill
1984   The regional organization of the Hohokam in the American Southwest: A stylistic analysis of red-on-buff pottery. Ph.D. dissertation, Department of Anthropology, Arizona State University, Tempe.
Nelson, Richard S.
1981   The role of a Puchteca system in Hohokam Exchange. Ph.D. dissertation, Department of Anthropology, New York University, New York.
1986   Pochtecas and prestige: Mesoamerican artifacts in Hohokam sites. In Ripples in the Chichimec Sea: New considerations of Southwestern-Mesoamerican interactions. Ed. F. J. Mathien and R. H. McGuire, pp. 154–82. Carbondale: Southern Illinois University Press.

Netting, Robert McC., Richard W. Wilk, and Eric J. Arnould, eds.
  1984   Households: comparative and historical studies of the domestic group.
          Berkeley: University of California Press.
Nials, Fred L., and David A. Gregory
  1989   Irrigation systems in the lower Salt River valley. *In* The 1982–1984
          excavations at Las Colinas: Environment and subsistence. By D. A.
          Graybill, D. A. Gregory, F. L. Nials, S. K. Fish, R. Gasser, C. Miksicek,
          and C. Szuter. Arizona State Museum Archaeological Series, no. 162,
          vol. 5, pp. 39–58. Tucson: University of Arizona.
Nials, Fred L., David A. Gregory, and Donald A. Graybill
  1989   Salt River streamflow and Hohokam irrigation systems. *In* The 1982–
          1984 excavations at Las Colinas: Environment and subsistence. By D. A.
          Graybill, D. A. Gregory, F. L. Nials, S. K. Fish, R. Gasser, C. Miksicek,
          and C. Szuter. Arizona State Museum Archaeological Series, no. 162,
          vol. 5, pp. 59–78. Tucson: University of Arizona.
Nials, Fred L., John Stein, and John Roney
  1987   Chacoan roads in the southern periphery: Results of Phase II of the BLM
          Chaco Roads Project. Cultural Resource Series, no. 1. Albuquerque:
          Albuquerque District Office, Bureau of Land Management.
Nicholas, Linda M.
  1981   Irrigation and sociopolitical development in the Salt River valley, Ari-
          zona: An examination of three prehistoric canal systems. M.A. thesis,
          Department of Anthropology, Arizona State University, Tempe.
Nicholas, Linda M., and Gary M. Feinman
  1989   A regional perspective on Hohokam irrigation in the lower Salt River
          valley, Arizona. *In* The Sociopolitical structure of prehistoric South-
          western societies. Ed. S. Upham, K. G. Lightfoot, and R. A. Jewett,
          pp. 199–235. Boulder, Colorado: Westview Press.
Nicholas, Linda M., and Jill Neitzel
  1984   Canal irrigation and sociopolitical organization in the lower Salt River
          valley: A diachronic analysis. *In* Prehistoric agricultural strategies in the
          Southwest. Ed. S. K. Fish and P. R. Fish. Arizona State University
          Anthropological Research Papers, no. 33, pp. 161–78. Tempe.
Obenauf, Margaret Senter
  1980   The Chacoan roadway system. M.A. thesis, Department of Anthropol-
          ogy, University of New Mexico, Albuquerque.
Orcutt, Janet D., Eric Blinman, and Timothy A. Kohler
  1988   Explanations of population aggregation in the Mesa Verde region prior
          to A.D. 900. Paper presented at Southwest Symposium, January 15–16,
          Arizona State University, Tempe.
Ortiz, Alfonso
  1969   The Tewa world. Chicago: University of Chicago Press.
Pailes, Richard A.
  1963   An analysis of the Fitch Site and its relationship to the Hohokam Classic
          period. M.A. thesis, Department of Anthropology, Arizona State Univer-
          sity, Tempe.
Palkovich, Ann M.
  1984   Disease and mortality patterns in the burial rooms of Pueblo Bonito:

Preliminary considerations. *In* Recent research on Chaco prehistory. Ed. W. J. Judge and J. D. Schelberg. Reports of the Chaco Center, no. 8, pp. 103–13. Albuquerque: Division of Cultural Research, National Park Service.

Patrick, H. R.
1903 The ancient canal systems and pueblos of the Salt River valley. Phoenix Free Museum Bulletin, no. 1.

Paynter, Robert W.
1983 Expanding the scope of settlement analysis. *In* Archaeological hammers and theories. Ed. J. A. Moore and A. S. Keene, pp. 233–75. New York: Academic Press.

Peckham, Stewart
1979 When is a Rio Grande kiva? *In* Collected papers in honor of Bertha Pauline Dutton. Ed. A. H. Schroeder. Papers of the Archaeological Society of New Mexico, no. 4, pp. 55–86. Albuquerque.

Peebles, Christopher S., and Susan M. Kus
1977 Some archaeological correlates of ranked societies. American Antiquity 42:421–48.

Pepper, George H.
1920 Pueblo Bonito. Anthropological Papers of the American Museum of Natural History, no. 27. New York.

Péwé, Troy L.
1978 Terraces of the lower Salt River valley in relation to the late Cenozoic history of the Phoenix Basin, Arizona. *In* Guidebook to the geology of central Arizona. Ed. D. M. Burt and T. L. Péwé. State of Arizona Bureau of Geology and Mineral Technology Special Paper, no. 2, pp. 1–46.

Pierson, Lloyd M.
1956 A history of Chaco Canyon National Monument. Manuscript, Chaco Culture National Historic Monument, National Park Service.

Pilles, Peter J., Jr.
1967 Construction salvage archaeology at La Ciudad, Arizona (T:12: 2[PGM]), August 15 to September 15, 1967. Manuscript, Pueblo Grande Museum, Phoenix.

Pinkley, Frank
1935 Seventeen years ago. Southwestern Monuments Report for 1935, Supplement for November and December, pp. 383–89, 455–62. Globe, Arizona: Gila Pueblo.

Pippin, Lonnie C.
1979 The prehistory and paleoecology of Guadalupe Ruin, Sandoval County, New Mexico. Ph.D. dissertation, Department of Anthropology, Washington State University, Pullman.

Plog, Fred
1980 Explaining culture change in the Hohokam Preclassic. *In* Current issues in Hohokam prehistory: Proceedings of a symposium. Ed. D. E. Doyel and F. Plog. Arizona State University Anthropological Research Papers, no. 23, pp. 4–22. Tempe.

Plog, Fred, and Walter Wait, eds.
1982 The San Juan tomorrow: Planning for the conservation of cultural

resources in the San Juan Basin. Santa Fe: National Park Service, Southwest Region, in cooperation with the School of American Research.

Plog, Fred, Steadman Upham, and Phil C. Weigand
1982   A perspective on Mogollon-Mesoamerican interaction. *In* Mogollon archaeology: Proceedings of the 1980 Mogollon Conference. Ed. P. H. Beckett and K. Silverbird, pp. 227–38. Ramona, California: Acoma Books.

Plog, Stephen
1980a   Village autonomy in the American Southwest. *In* Models and methods in regional exchange. Ed. R. E. Fry. Society for American Archaeology Papers, no. 1, pp. 135–46.
1980b   Stylistic variation in prehistoric ceramics: Design analysis in the American Southwest. New York and Cambridge: Cambridge University Press.

Powell, Shirley
1983   Mobility and adaptation: The Anasazi of Black Mesa, Arizona. Carbondale: Southern Illinois University Press.

Powers, Robert P., William B. Gillespie, and Stephen H. Lekson
1983   The outlier survey: A regional view of settlement in the San Juan Basin. Reports of the Chaco Center, no. 3. Albuquerque: Division of Cultural Research, National Park Service.

Prudden, T. Mitchell
1918   A further study of prehistoric small house ruins in the San Juan watershed. *In* Memoirs of the American Anthropological Association, vol. 5, no. 1, pp. 3–50.

Rafferty, Kevin
1982   Hohokam micaceous schist mining and craft specialization: An example from Gila Butte, Arizona. Anthropology 6(1–2):199–222.

Rappaport, Roy A.
1968   Pigs for the ancestors. New Haven: Yale University Press.

Ravesloot, John C.
1987   Summary and conclusions. *In* The archaeology of the San Xavier Bridge site (AZ BB:13:14), Tucson Basin, Arizona. Arizona State Museum Archaeological Series, no. 171, pp. 149–51. Tucson: University of Arizona.

Ravesloot, John C., Jeffrey S. Dean, and Michael S. Foster
1986   A new perspective on the Casas Grandes tree-ring dates. Paper presented at 4th Mogollon Conference, October 16–17, University of Arizona, Tucson.

Rea, Amadeo M.
1979   The ecology of Pima fields. Environment Southwest 484:1–6.
1983   Once a river: Bird life and habitat changes on the middle Gila. Tucson: University of Arizona Press.

Redman, Charles L.
1978a   The rise of civilization. San Francisco: W. H. Freeman.
1978b   Mesopotamian urban ecology: The systemic context of the emergence of urbanism. *In* Social archaeology: Beyond subsistence and dating. Ed. C. L. Redman, M. J. Berman, E. V. Curtin, W. T. Langhorne Jr., N. M. Versaggi, and J. C. Wasner, pp. 329–47. New York: Academic Press.

1986 Qsar es-Seghir: An archaeological view of medieval life. New York: Academic Press.

Reed, Alan D.
1979 The Dominguez Ruin: A McElmo phase pueblo in southwestern Colorado. *In* The archaeology and stabilization of the Dominguez and Escalante ruins. By A. Reed, J. Hallasi, A. White, and D. Breternitz, pp. 1–196. Cultural Resource Series 7. Denver: Bureau of Land Management, Colorado State Office.

Renfrew, Colin
1974 Beyond a subsistence economy: The evolution of social organization in prehistoric Europe. *In* Reconstructing complex societies. Ed. C. B. Moore. Bulletin of the American School of Oriental Research, no. 20, pp. 69–85. Baltimore.

Reyman, Jonathan E.
1971 Mexican influence on Southwestern ceremonialism. Ph.D. dissertation, Southern Illinois University, Carbondale. Ann Arbor: University Microfilms.
1980 The predictive dimension of priestly power. Transactions of the Illinois Academy of Science 72(4):40–59.
1987 Review of "Recent Research on Chaco Prehistory," edited by W. James Judge and John D. Schelberg. The Kiva 52(2):147–51.

Rice, Glen E.
1987a La Ciudad: A perspective on Hohokam community systems. *In* The Hohokam village: Site structure and organization. Ed. D. E. Doyel, pp. 127–58. Glenwood Springs, Colorado: American Association for the Advancement of Science.
1987b The Marana Community complex: A twelfth-century Hohokam chiefdom. *In* Studies in the Hohokam community of Marana. Ed. G. E. Rice. Anthropological Field Studies, no. 15, pp. 249–53. Tempe: Office of Cultural Resource Management, Arizona State University.

Rice, Glen E., ed.
1987a The Hohokam community of La Ciudad. Office of Cultural Resource Management Report, no. 69. Tempe: Arizona State University.
1987b Studies in the Hohokam community of Marana. Anthropological Field Studies, no. 15. Tempe: Office of Cultural Resource Management, Arizona State University.

Rice, Glen E., David Wilcox, K. Rafferty, and James Schoenwetter
1979 An archaeological test of sites in the Gila Butte-Santan region, south-central Arizona. Arizona State University Anthropological Research Papers, no. 18. Tempe.

Riley, Carroll L.
1982 The frontier people: The greater Southwest in the protohistoric period. Southern Illinois University at Carbondale Center for Archaeological Investigations Occasional Paper, no. 1.
1987 The frontier people: The greater Southwest in the protohistoric period. Albuquerque: University of New Mexico Press.

Roberts, Frank H. H.
1927 The ceramic sequence in the Chaco Canyon, New Mexico, and its

relation to the cultures of the San Juan Basin. Ph.D. dissertation, Department of Anthropology, Harvard University.

1929   Shabik'eshchee Village: A late Basketmaker site in the Chaco Canyon, New Mexico. Bureau of American Ethnology Bulletin, no. 92. Washington, D.C.

1931   The ruins at Kiatuthlanna, eastern Arizona. Bureau of American Ethnology Bulletin, no. 100. Washington, D.C.

1932   The Village of the Great Kivas on the Zuni reservation, New Mexico. Bureau of American Ethnology Bulletin, no. 111. Washington, D.C.

1935   A survey of Southwestern archaeology. American Anthropologist 37: 1–33.

Rodgers, James B.
1978   The Fort Mountain archaeological complex, Cave Buttes, Arizona. In Limited activity and occupation sites: A collection of conference papers. Ed. A. E. Ward. Contributions to Anthropological Studies, no. 1, pp. 147–63. Albuquerque: Center for Anthropological Studies.

Rohn, Arthur H.
1965   Postulation of socio-economic groups from archaeological evidence. In Contributions to the Wetherill Mesa archaeological project. Compiled by D. Osborne, pp. 65–69. Memoirs of the Society for American Archaeology, no. 19.

1977   Cultural change and continuity on Chapin Mesa. Lawrence: Regents Press of Kansas.

Roper, Donna C.
1979   The method and theory of site catchment analysis: A critical review. In Advances in archaeological method and theory, vol. 2. Ed. M. B. Schiffer, pp. 119–40. New York: Academic Press.

Rose, Martin R.
1979   Preliminary annual and seasonal dendroclimatic reconstructions for the northwest plateau, southwest Colorado, southwest mountains, and northern mountain climatic regions, A.D. 900–1969. Manuscript, Division of Cultural Research, National Park Service, Santa Fe.

Rose, Martin R., William J. Robinson, and Jeffrey S. Dean
1982   Dendroclimatic reconstruction for the southeastern Colorado Plateau. Final report submitted to the Division of Cultural Research, National Park Service, Albuquerque.

Ruppé, Reynold J.
1966   A survey of the Hohokam remains in the Salt drainage. Final report submitted to the National Science Foundation. Manuscript, Department of Anthropology, Arizona State University, Tempe.

Russell, Frank
1908   The Pima Indians. Twenty-sixth Annual Report of the Bureau of American Ethnology. Washington, D.C.

Sanders, William T., and Barbara J. Price
1968   Mesoamerica: The evolution of a civilization. New York: Random House.

Sanders, William T., Jeffrey R. Parsons, and Robert S. Santley
1979   The Basin of Mexico. New York: Academic Press.

Schaller, David M.
1985   Petrographic analysis of ground stone artifacts. *In* Hohokam settlement and economic systems in the central New River drainage, Arizona. Ed. D. E. Doyel and M. D. Elson. Soil Systems Publications in Archaeology, no. 4, pp. 779–82. Phoenix.
1987   Mineralogy and petrology of lithic artifacts, Liberty to Coolidge Rebuild Project. Manuscript, Pueblo Grande Museum, Phoenix.
Schelberg, John D.
1982   Economic and social development as an adaptation to a marginal environment in Chaco Canyon, New Mexico. Ph.D. dissertation, Department of Anthropology, Northwestern University, Evanston, Illinois.
1983   The Chacoan Anasazi: A stratified society in the San Juan Basin. Paper presented at 2nd Anasazi Symposium, Salmon Ruins, Bloomfield, New Mexico.
Schiffer, Michael B.
1982   Hohokam chronology: An essay on history and method. *In* Hohokam and Patayan: Prehistory of southwestern Arizona. Ed. R. H. McGuire and M. B. Schiffer, pp. 299–344. New York: Academic Press.
1985   Radiocarbon dating and the "old wood" problem: The case of the Hohokam chronology. Journal of Archaeological Science 13(1):13–30.
Schmidt, Erich F.
1928   Time-relations of prehistoric pottery types in southern Arizona. Anthropological Papers 30(5). New York: American Museum of Natural History.
Schroeder, Albert H.
1940   A stratigraphic survey of pre-Spanish trash mounds of the Salt River valley, Arizona. M.A. thesis, Department of Anthropology, University of Arizona, Tucson.
1947   Did the Sinagua of the Verde Valley settle in the Salt River valley? Southwestern Journal of Anthropology 3(3):230–46.
1948   Montezuma Well. Plateau 20(3):37–40.
1960   The Hohokam, Sinagua, and the Hakataya. Archives of Archaeology, no. 5. Menasha, Wisconsin: Society for American Archaeology.
1966   Pattern diffusion from Mexico into the Southwest after A.D. 600. American Antiquity 31:683–704.
1981   How far can a Pochteca leap without leaving footprints? *In* Collected papers in honor of Erik Kellerman Reed. Ed. A. H. Schroeder. Papers of the Archaeological Society of New Mexico, no. 6, pp. 43–64. Albuquerque.
Sebastian, Lynne
1983   Regional interaction: The Puebloan adaptation. *In* Economy and interaction along the lower Chaco River: The Navajo Mine Archeology Program. Ed. P. F. Hogan and J. C. Winter, pp. 445–52. Albuquerque: Office of Contract Archeology and Maxwell Museum of Anthropology, University of New Mexico.
1988   Leadership, power, and productive potential: A political model of the Chaco system. Ph.D. dissertation, University of New Mexico. Ann Arbor: University Microfilms.

Sebastian, Lynne, and Jeffrey H. Altschul
1986 Settlement pattern, site typology, and demographic analyses: The Anasazi, Archaic, and unknown sites. *In* Archaeological Survey at Chaco Culture National Historic Park. Ed. R. B. Powers. Reports of the Chaco Center. Santa Fe: Division of Cultural Research, National Park Service. In preparation.

Service, Elman R.
1962 Primitive social organization. New York: Random House.
1975 Origins of the state and civilization: The process of cultural evolution. New York: W. W. Norton.

Seymour, Deni J.
1988 An alternative view of Sedentary period Hohokam shell ornament production. American Antiquity 53:812–29.
1989 The dynamics of Sobaipuri settlement in the eastern Pimeria Alta. Journal of the Southwest 31(2):205–22.

Seymour, Deni, and Michael B. Schiffer
1987 A preliminary analysis of pithouse assemblages from Snaketown, Arizona. *In* Method and theory for activity area research: An ethnoarchaeological approach. Ed. S. Kent, pp. 549–602. New York: Columbia University Press.

Shackley, M. Steven
1988 Sources of archaeological obsidian in the Southwest: An archaeological and geochemical study. American Antiquity 53:752–72.

Shepard, Anna O.
1963 The beginnings of ceramic industrialization: An example from the Oaxaca Valley. Notes from the Ceramic Laboratory, no. 2. Washington, D.C.: Carnegie Institution of Washington.

Simmons, Alan H.
1982 Technological and typological variability of lithic assemblages in the Bis sa'ani Community. *In* Bis sa'ani: A late Bonito phase community on Escavada Wash, northwest New Mexico. Ed. C. D. Breternitz, D. E. Doyel, and M. P. Marshall. Navajo Nation Papers in Anthropology, no. 14, pp. 955–1013. Window Rock, Arizona.

Sires, Earl W., Jr.
1983 Archaeological investigations at Las Fosas (AZ U:15:19): A Classic period settlement on the Gila River. *In* Hohokam archaeology along the Salt-Gila aqueduct, Central Arizona Project: Habitation sites on the Gila River. Ed. L. S. Teague and P. L. Crown. Arizona State Museum Archaeological Series, no. 150, vol. 6, pp. 493–658. Tucson: University of Arizona.
1984a Hohokam architecture and site structure. *In* Hohokam archaeology along the Salt-Gila aqueduct, Central Arizona Project: Synthesis and conclusions. Ed. L. S. Teague and P. L. Crown. Arizona State Museum Archaeological Series, no. 150, vol. 9, pp. 115–40. Tucson: University of Arizona.
1984b Excavations at Frogtown (AZ U:15:61). *In* Hohokam archaeology along the Salt-Gila aqueduct, Central Arizona Project: Prehistoric occupation of the Queen Creek delta. Ed. L. S. Teague and P. L. Crown. Arizona

State Museum Archaeological Series, no. 150, vol. 4, pp. 357–542. Tucson: University of Arizona.

1984c   Smiley's Well (AZ U:14:73, Locus A), a transitional (Sedentary-Classic period) Hohokam farmstead along the lower Queen Creek drainage. *In* Hohokam archaeology along the Salt-Gila aqueduct, Central Arizona Project: Small habitation sites on Queen Creek. Ed. L. S. Teague and P. L. Crown. Arizona State Museum Archaeological Series, no. 150, vol. 5, pp. 23–82. Tucson: University of Arizona.

1984d   Excavations at El Polvoron (AZ U:15:59). *In* Hohokam archaeology along the Salt-Gila aqueduct, Central Arizona Project: Prehistoric occupation of the Queen Creek delta. Ed. L. S. Teague and P. L. Crown. Arizona State Museum Archaeological Series, no. 150, vol. 4, pp. 221–326. Tucson: University of Arizona.

1987   Hohokam architectural variability and site structure during the Sedentary-Classic transition. *In* The Hohokam village: Site structure and organization. Ed. D. E. Doyel, pp. 171–82. Glenwood Springs, Colorado: American Association for the Advancement of Science.

Sofaer, Anna, Michael C. Marshall, and Rolf M. Sinclair

1989   The Great North Road: The cosmographic expression of the Chaco culture of New Mexico. *In* World archaeoastronomy. Ed. A. Aveni, pp. 365–76. Cambridge: Cambridge University Press.

Spicer, Edward H.

1962   Cycles of conquest. Tucson: University of Arizona Press.

Sprague, Roderick

1964   Inventory of prehistoric Southwestern copper bells: Additions and corrections. The Kiva 30(1):18–24.

Stafford, C. Russell

1978   Archaeological investigations at Seneca Lake, San Carlos Indian Reservation, Arizona. Anthropological Research Paper, no. 14. Tempe: Arizona State University.

Stark, Barbara L.

1986   Perspectives on the peripheries of Mesoamerica. *In* Ripples in the Chichimec Sea: New considerations of Southwestern-Mesoamerican interactions. Ed. F. J. Mathien and R. H. McGuire, pp. 270–90. Carbondale: Southern Illinois University Press.

Steen, Charlie

1965   Excavations in Compound A, Casa Grande National Monument, 1963. The Kiva 31(2):59–82.

Stein, John R.

1989   The Chaco roads: Clues to an ancient riddle? El Palacio 94(3):4–17.

Stein, John R., and Peter J. McKenna

1988   An archaeological reconnaissance of a late Bonito phase occupation near Aztec Ruins National Monument, New Mexico. Santa Fe: Southwest Cultural Resources Center, National Park Service.

Stubbs, Stanley

1950   Bird's eye view of the pueblos. Norman: University of Oklahoma Press.

Sullivan, Alan P., III

1983   Storage, nonedible resource processing, and the interpretation of sherd and lithic scatters in the Sonoran desert lowlands. Journal of Field Archaeology 10:309–23.

1988   Prehistoric Southwestern ceramic manufacture: The limitations of current evidence. American Antiquity 53:23–35.

Szuter, Christine R.

1984   Faunal exploitation and the reliance on small game animals among the Hohokam. In Hohokam archaeology along the Salt-Gila aqueduct, Central Arizona Project: Environment and subsistence. Ed. L. S. Teague and P. L. Crown. Arizona State Museum Archaeological Series, no. 150, vol. 7, pp. 139–69. Tucson: University of Arizona.

Szuter, Christine R., and Frank E. Bayham

1989   Sedentism and prehistoric animal procurement among desert horticulturalists of the North American Southwest. In Farmers as hunters: The implications of sedentism. Ed. S. Kent, pp. 80–95. Cambridge: Cambridge University Press.

Tainter, Joseph A., and David "A" Gillio

1980   Cultural resources overview: Mt. Taylor area, New Mexico. Albuquerque and Santa Fe: USDA Forest Service and USDI Bureau of Land Management.

Teague, Lynn S.

1984   Settlement and population. In Hohokam archaeology along the Salt-Gila aqueduct, Central Arizona Project: Synthesis and conclusions. Ed. L. S. Teague and P. L. Crown. Arizona State Museum Archaeological Series, no. 150, vol. 9, pp. 141–54. Tucson: University of Arizona.

1985   The organization of Hohokam exchange. In Proceedings of the 1983 Hohokam Symposium, part 2. Ed. A. E. Dittert Jr. and D. E. Dove. Occasional Paper, no. 2, pp. 397–418. Arizona Archaeological Society, Phoenix Chapter.

Teague, Lynn S., and Patricia L. Crown, eds.

1982– Hohokam archaeology along the Salt-Gila aqueduct, Central Arizona
1984   Project, vols. 1–9. Arizona State Museum Archaeological Series, no. 150. Tucson: University of Arizona.

1984   Hohokam archaeology along the Salt-Gila aqueduct, Central Arizona Project: Synthesis and conclusions. Arizona State Museum Archaeological Series, no. 150, vol. 9. Tucson: University of Arizona.

Toll, H. Wolcott

1981   Ceramic comparisons concerning redistribution in Chaco Canyon, New Mexico. In Production and distribution: A ceramic viewpoint. Ed. H. Howard and E. Morris. British Archaeological Reports, no. 120, pp. 83–121. Oxford.

1984   Trends in ceramic import and distribution in Chaco Canyon. In Recent research on Chaco prehistory. Ed. W. J. Judge and J. D. Schelberg. Reports of the Chaco Center, no. 8, pp. 115–36. Albuquerque: Division of Cultural Research, National Park Service.

1985   Pottery, production, public architecture, and the Chaco Anasazi system. Ph.D. dissertation, University of Colorado. Ann Arbor: University Microfilms.

1986   Chaco project ceramic overview: Technology and temper. Manuscript, Division of Cultural Research, National Park Service, Santa Fe.

1990   A reassessment of Chaco cylinder jars. *In* Clues to the past: Papers in honor of William Sundt. Ed. M. S. Duran and D. T. Kirkpatrick, pp. 273–305. Papers of the Archaeological Society of New Mexico, no. 16. Albuquerque: Albuquerque Archaeological Society Press.

Toll, H. Wolcott, and Peter J. McKenna

1987   The ceramography of Pueblo Alto. *In* Artifactual and biological analyses. Investigations at the Pueblo Alto complex, Chaco Canyon, New Mexico, 1975–1979, vol. 3, no. 1. Ed. F. J. Mathien and T. C. Windes, pp. 19–230. Publications in Archeology 18F. Santa Fe: National Park Service.

Toll, H. Wolcott, Thomas C. Windes, and Peter J. McKenna

1980   Late ceramic patterns in Chaco Canyon: The pragmatics of modeling ceramic exchange. *In* Models and methods in regional exchange. Ed. R. E. Fry. Society for American Archaeology Papers, no. 1, pp. 95–117.

Toll, Mollie S.

1984   Taxonomic diversity in flotation and macrobotanical assemblages from Chaco Canyon. *In* Recent research on Chaco prehistory. Ed. W. J. Judge and J. D. Schelberg. Reports of the Chaco Center, no. 8, pp. 241–50. Albuquerque: Division of Cultural Research, National Park Service.

1985   An overview of Chaco Canyon macrobotanical materials and analyses to date. *In* Environment and subsistence of Chaco Canyon, New Mexico. Ed. F. J. Mathien. Publications in Archeology, no. 18E, Chaco Canyon Studies, pp. 247–77. Albuquerque: National Park Service.

Tower, Donald B.

1945   The use of marine mollusca and their value in reconstructing prehistoric trade routes in the American Southwest. Papers of the Excavators Club 2:1–56. Cambridge.

Truell, Marcia L.

1986   A summary of small site architecture in Chaco Canyon, New Mexico. *In* Small site architecture of Chaco Canyon. By P. J. McKenna and M. L. Truell. Publications in Archeology, no. 18D, Chaco Canyon Studies, pp. 115–502. Santa Fe: National Park Service.

Truell, Marcia L., Frances J. Mathien, Peter J. McKenna, H. Wolcott Toll, William B. Gillespie, Catherine M. Cameron, Louann Jacobson, and Judith L. Miles

1990   Excavations at 29SJ633: The eleventh hour site. Reports of the Chaco Center, no. 10. National Park Service, Santa Fe. In preparation.

Turner, Raymond M., and David E. Brown

1982   Sonoran desertscrub. *In* Biotic communities of the American Southwest: United States and Mexico. Ed. D. E. Brown. Desert Plants 4(1–4): 181–221.

Turney, Omar A.

1929   Prehistoric irrigation in Arizona. Phoenix: Office of Arizona State Historian.

Tyler, H. A.

1964   Pueblo gods and myths. Norman: University of Oklahoma Press.

Underhill, Ruth M.
  1939   Social organization of the Papago Indians. New York: Columbia University Press.
U.S. Department of the Interior
  1962   Appraisal report: Central Arizona Project. Boulder City, Nevada: Bureau of Reclamation Regional Office.
Upham, Steadman
  1982   Polities and power: An economic and political history of the Western Pueblo. New York: Academic Press.
Upham, Steadman, and Paul F. Reed
  1989   Inferring the structure of Anasazi warfare. In Cultures in conflict: Current archaeological perspectives. Ed. D. C. Tkaczuk and B. C. Vivian, pp. 153–62. Calgary: Chacmool, The Archaeological Association of the University of Calgary.
Upham, Steadman, and Glen Rice
  1980   Up the canal without a pattern: Modelling Hohokam interaction and exchange. In Current issues in Hohokam prehistory: Proceedings of a symposium. Ed. D. E. Doyel and F. Plog. Arizona State University Anthropological Research Papers, no. 23, pp. 78–105. Tempe.
Valcarce, J. P., and D. W. Kayser
  1969   Recently discovered compounds at Casa Grande Ruins National Monument. The Kiva 35(1):55–56.
Vierra, Bradley J.
  1980   A summary and comparison of the excavated Archaic and Anasazi sites. In Human adaptation in a marginal environment: The UII mitigation project. Ed. J. L. Moore and J. C. Winter, pp. 382–89. Albuquerque: Office of Contract Archeology, University of New Mexico.
Vink, A. P. A.
  1983   Landscape ecology and land use. New York: Longman.
Vita-Finzi, Claudio, and Eric S. Higgs
  1970   Prehistoric economy in the Mount Carmel area of Palestine: Site catchment analysis. Proceedings of the Prehistoric Society 36:1–37.
Vivian, Gordon
  1959   The Hubbard Site and other tri-wall structures in New Mexico and Colorado. Archaeological Series, no. 5. Washington, D.C.: National Park Service.
Vivian, Gordon, and Tom W. Mathews
  1965   Kin Kletso: A Pueblo III community in Chaco Canyon, New Mexico. Southwestern Monuments Association Technical Series, no. 6(1). Globe, Arizona.
Vivian, Gordon, and Paul Reiter
  1960   The great kivas of Chaco Canyon and their relationships. School of American Research Monograph, no. 22. Santa Fe.
Vivian, R. Gwinn
  1970a   An inquiry into prehistoric social organization in Chaco Canyon, New Mexico. In Reconstructing prehistoric Pueblo society. Ed. W. A. Longacre, pp. 59–83. Albuquerque: University of New Mexico Press.
  1970b   Aspects of prehistoric society in Chaco Canyon, New Mexico. Ph.D.

dissertation, Department of Anthropology, University of Arizona, Tucson.

1974   Conservation and diversion: Water-control systems in the Anasazi Southwest. *In* Irrigation's impact on society. Ed. T. Downing and McG. Gibson. Anthropological Papers of the University of Arizona, no. 25, pp. 95–112. Tucson.

1981   Agricultural and social adjustments to changing environments in the Chaco Basin. Paper presented at 80th annual meeting, American Anthropological Association, Los Angeles.

1983a   Identifying and interpreting Chacoan roads: An historical perspective. *In* Chaco Roads Project: Phase 1. Ed. C. Kincaid, pp. 3.1–3.20. Albuquerque: Bureau of Land Management.

1983b   The Chacoan phenomenon: Culture growth in the San Juan Basin. Paper presented at 1983 Anasazi Symposium, Salmon Ruins, Farmington, New Mexico.

1984   Agricultural and social adjustments to changing environments in the Chaco Basin. *In* Prehistoric agricultural strategies in the Southwest. Ed. S. K. Fish and P. R. Fish. Arizona State University Anthropological Research Papers, no. 33, pp. 243–57. Tempe.

1989   Kluckhohn reappraised: The Chacoan system as an egalitarian enterprise. Journal of Anthropological Research 45:101–13.

Vivian, R. Gwinn, Dulce N. Dodgen, and Gayle H. Hartmann
1978   Wooden ritual artifacts from Chaco Canyon, New Mexico. Anthropological Papers of the University of Arizona, no. 32. Tucson.

Vokes, Arthur
1983   The shell assemblages of the Salt-Gila aqueduct sites. *In* Hohokam archaeology along the Salt-Gila aqueduct, Central Arizona Project: Material culture. Ed. L. S. Teague and P. L. Crown. Arizona State Museum Archaeological Series, no. 150, vol. 8, pp. 463–574. Tucson: University of Arizona.

Wallace, Henry D.
1988   Ceramic boundaries and interregional interaction: New perspectives on the Tucson Basin Hohokam. *In* Recent research on Tucson Basin prehistory: Proceedings of the Second Tucson Basin Conference. Ed. W. H. Doelle and P. R. Fish. Institute for American Research Anthropological Papers, no. 10, pp. 313–48. Tucson.

Wallace, Henry D., and James Heidke
1986   Ceramic production and exchange. *In* Archaeological investigations at the Tanque Verde Wash site: A middle Rincon settlement in the eastern Tucson Basin. Ed. M. D. Elson. Institute for American Research Anthropological Papers, no. 7, pp. 233–70. Tucson.

Wallace, Henry D., and James P. Holmlund
1984   The Classic period in the Tucson Basin. The Kiva 49(3–4):167–94.

Ward, Albert E., ed.
1978   Limited activity and occupation sites: A collection of conference papers. Contributions to Anthropological Studies, no. 1. Albuquerque: Center for Anthropological Studies.

Warren, A. Helene
1977 Source area studies of Pueblo I–III pottery of Chaco Canyon. Manuscript, Division of Cultural Research, National Park Service, Santa Fe.

Washburn, Dorothy K.
1980 The Mexican connection: Cylinder jars from the Valley of Oaxaca. Transactions of the Illinois Academy of Science 72(4):70–85.

Wasley, William W.
1960 A Hohokam platform mound at the Gatlin Site, Gila Bend, Arizona. American Antiquity 26:244–62.

1966 Classic period Hohokam. Paper presented at 31st annual meeting, Society for American Archaeology, Reno.

Wasley, William W., and Blake Benham
1968 Salvage excavation on the Buttes Dam site, southern Arizona. The Kiva 33(4):244–79.

Wasley, William W., and Alfred E. Johnson
1965 Salvage archaeology in Painted Rocks Reservoir, western Arizona. Anthropological Papers of the University of Arizona, no. 9. Tucson.

Waters, Michael R.
1987 Holocene alluvial geology and geoarchaeology of AZ BB:13:14 and the San Xavier reach of the Santa Cruz River, Arizona. In The archaeology of the San Xavier Bridge site (AZ BB:13:14), Tucson Basin, Arizona. Ed. J. C. Ravesloot. Arizona State Museum Archaeological Series, no. 171, pp. 39–60. Tucson: University of Arizona.

1988 Holocene alluvial geology and geoarchaeology of AZ BB:13:14 and the San Xavier reach of the Santa Cruz River, Arizona. Geological Society of America Bulletin 100:479–91.

Waters, Michael R., and John J. Field
1986 Geomorphic analysis of Hohokam settlement patterns on alluvial fans along the western flank of the Tortolita Mountains, Arizona. Geoarchaeology 1:324–45.

Watson, Patty Jo, Steven LeBlanc, and Charles Redman
1980 Aspects of Zuni prehistory: Preliminary report on excavations and survey in the El Morro Valley of New Mexico. Journal of Field Archaeology 7:201–17.

Weaver, Donald E., Jr.
1972a Investigations concerning the Hohokam Classic period in the lower Salt River valley. M.A. thesis, Department of Anthropology, Arizona State University, Tempe.

1972b A cultural-ecological model for the Classic Hohokam period in the lower Salt River valley, Arizona. The Kiva 38(1):43–52.

Weed, Carol S.
1972 The Beardsley Canal site. The Kiva 38(2):57–94.

Weed, Carol S., and Albert E. Ward
1970 The Henderson site: Colonial Hohokam in north-central Arizona. The Kiva 35(2):1–12.

Weigand, Phil C.
1978 The Prehistoric of the state of Zacatecas: An interpretation, part 1. Anthropology 2(1):67–87.

1979 The Prehistoric of the state of Zacatecas: An interpretation, part 2. Anthropology 2(2):22–41.

Weigand, Phil C., and Garman Harbottle
1987 The role of turquoise in the ancient Mesoamerican trade structure. Paper presented at 52nd annual meeting, Society for American Archaeology, Toronto.

Weigand, Phil C., Garman Harbottle, and Edward V. Sayre
1977 Turquoise sources and source analysis: Mesoamerica and the southwestern U.S.A. *In* Exchange systems in prehistory. Ed. T. K. Earle and J. E. Ericson, pp. 15–24. New York: Academic Press.

Wheat, Joe Ben
1955 Mogollon culture prior to A.D. 1000. Memoirs of the Society for American Archaeology, no. 10. Menasha, Wisconsin.
1983 Anasazi who? *In* Proceedings of the 1981 Anasazi symposium. Ed. J. E. Smith, pp. 11–15. Mesa Verde National Park, Colorado: Mesa Verde Museum Association.

White, Leslie A.
1962 The Pueblo of Sia, New Mexico. Bureau of American Ethnology Bulletin 184. Washington, D.C.

Whiteley, Peter M.
1988 Deliberate acts: Changing Hopi culture through the Oraibi split. Tucson: University of Arizona Press.

Whittlesey, Stephanie M.
1978 Status and death at Grasshopper Pueblo: Experiments toward an archaeological theory of correlates. Ph.D. dissertation, University of Arizona, Tucson. Ann Arbor: University Microfilms.
1982 Uses and abuses of Mogollon mortuary data. *In* Recent research in Mogollon archaeology. Ed. S. Upham, F. Plog, D. Batcho, and B. Kauffman, pp. 276–84. Las Cruces: University Museum, New Mexico State University.

Wilcox, David R.
1975 A strategy for perceiving social groups in Puebloan sites. *In* Chapters in the prehistory of eastern Arizona. By P. S. Martin, E. Zubrow, D. Bowman, D. Gregory, J. Hanson, M. Schiffer, and D. Wilcox, vol. 4, pp. 120–65. Fieldiana: Anthropology, no. 65. Chicago: Field Museum of Natural History.
1979a The Hohokam regional system. *In* An archaeological test of sites in the Gila Butte-Santan region, south-central Arizona. By G. E. Rice, D. Wilcox, K. Rafferty, and J. Schoenwetter. Arizona State University Anthropological Research Papers, no. 18, pp. 77–116. Tempe.
1979b Warfare implications of dry-laid masonry walls on Tumamoc Hill. The Kiva 45(1–2):15–38.
1980 The current status of the Hohokam concept. *In* Current issues in Hohokam prehistory: Proceedings of a symposium. Ed. D. E. Doyel and F. Plog. Arizona State University Anthropological Research Papers, no. 23, pp. 236–42. Tempe.
1981 Changing perspectives on the protohistoric Pueblos. *In* The protohistoric period in the North American Southwest, A.D. 1450–1700. Ed.

D. R. Wilcox and W. B. Masse. Arizona State University Anthropological Research Papers, no. 24, pp. 378–409. Tempe.

1982 A set-theory approach to sampling pueblos: The implications of room-set additions at Grasshopper Pueblo. *In* Multidisciplinary research at Grasshopper Pueblo, Arizona. Ed. W. A. Longacre, S. J. Holbrook, and M. W. Graves. Anthropological Papers of the University of Arizona, no. 40, pp. 19–27. Tucson.

1984 One hundred years of archaeology at Pueblo Grande. Manuscript, Pueblo Grande Museum, Phoenix.

1985 Preliminary report on new data on Hohokam ballcourts. *In* Proceedings of the 1983 Hohokam Symposium, part 2. Ed. A. E. Dittert Jr. and D. E. Dove. Occasional Paper, no. 2, pp. 641–54. Arizona Archaeological Society, Phoenix Chapter.

1986a The Tepiman connection: A model of Mesoamerican-Southwestern interaction. *In* Ripples in the Chichimec Sea: New considerations of Southwestern-Mesoamerican interactions. Ed. F. J. Mathien and R. H. McGuire, pp. 135–53. Carbondale: Southern Illinois University Press.

1986b A history of research on the question of Mesoamerican-Southwestern connections. *In* Ripples in the Chichimec Sea: New considerations of Southwestern-Mesoamerican interactions. Ed. F. J. Mathien and R. H. McGuire, pp. 9–44. Carbondale: Southern Illinois University Press.

1986c Excavations of three sites on Bottomless Pits Mesa, Flagstaff, Arizona. Interim report submitted to Coconino National Forest, Flagstaff.

1987a Frank Midvale's investigation of the site of La Ciudad. Arizona State University Anthropological Field Studies, no. 19. Tempe.

1987b The evolution of Hohokam ceremonial systems. *In* Astronomy and ceremony in the prehistoric Southwest. Ed. J. Carlson and W. J. Judge. Papers of the Maxwell Museum of Anthropology, no. 2, pp. 149–68. Albuquerque.

1988a The Mesoamerican ballgame in the American Southwest. *In* The Mesoamerican ballgame. Ed. V. L. Scarborough and D. R. Wilcox. Tucson: University of Arizona Press. In press.

1988b Changing contexts of Pueblo adaptations, A.D. 1250–1600. Paper presented at Conference on Plains and Pueblo Interaction. Fort Burgwin Research Center, September 17–20, 1987, Ranchos de Taos, New Mexico. Revised manuscript in author's possession.

1988c The regional context of the Brady Wash and Picacho area sites. *In* Hohokam settlement along the slopes of the Picacho Mountains: Synthesis and conclusions. Ed. R. Ciolek-Torrello and D. R. Wilcox, pp. 244–67. Museum of Northern Arizona Research Paper 35. Flagstaff.

1988d A processual model of Charles C. Di Peso's Babocomari site and related systems. Manuscript, Museum of Northern Arizona, Flagstaff.

1989 Hohokam warfare. *In* Cultures in conflict: Current archaeological perspectives. Ed. D. C. Tkaczuk and B. C. Vivian, pp. 163–72. Calgary: Chacmool, the Archaeological Association of the University of Calgary.

Wilcox, David R., and Lynette O. Shenk

1977 The architecture of the Casa Grande and its interpretation. Arizona State Museum Archaeological Series, no. 115. Tucson: University of Arizona.

Wilcox, David R., and Charles Sternberg
  1981   Additional studies of the architecture of the Casa Grande and its inter-
          pretation. Arizona State Museum Archaeological Series, no. 146. Tuc-
          son: University of Arizona.
  1983   Hohokam ballcourts and their interpretation. Arizona State Museum
          Archaeological Series, no. 160. Tucson: University of Arizona.
Wilcox, David R., Thomas R. McGuire, and Charles Sternberg
  1981   Snaketown revisited. Arizona State Museum Archaeological Series,
          no. 155. Tucson: University of Arizona.
Wilk, Richard R., and William L. Rathje, eds.
  1982   Archaeology of the household: Building a prehistory of domestic life.
          American Behavioral Scientist 25(6).
Wilson, Eldred D.
  1962   A resume of the geology of Arizona. Arizona Bureau of Mines Bulletin,
          no. 171. Tucson: University of Arizona Press.
Wilson, John P.
  1979   Cultural resources of the Alamito Coal Lease Area, northwestern New
          Mexico. Tucson: Alamito Coal Company.
Windes, Thomas C.
  1978   Stone circles of Chaco Canyon, northwestern New Mexico. Reports of
          the Chaco Center, no. 5. Albuquerque: Division of Cultural Research,
          National Park Service.
  1981   A new look at population in Chaco Canyon. Paper presented at 46th
          annual meeting, Society for American Archaeology, San Diego.
  1982a A second look at population in Chaco Canyon. Paper presented at 47th
          annual meeting, Society for American Archaeology, Minneapolis.
  1982b Lessons from the Chacoan Survey: The pattern of Chacoan trash dis-
          posal. The New Mexico Archeological Council Newsletter 4(5–6):
          5–14.
  1984a A view of Cibola Whiteware from Chaco Canyon. In Regional analysis of
          prehistoric ceramic variation: Contemporary studies of the Cibola
          Whiteware. Ed. A. P. Sullivan and J. L. Hantman, pp. 94–119. Arizona
          State University Anthropological Research Papers, no. 31, Tempe.
  1984b A new look at population in Chaco Canyon. In Recent research on
          Chaco prehistory. Ed. W. J. Judge and J. D. Schelberg. Reports of the
          Chaco Center, no. 8, pp. 75–87. Albuquerque: Division of Cultural
          Research, National Park Service.
  1987a Investigations at the Pueblo Alto complex, Chaco Canyon, New Mexico,
          1975–1979, vols. 1 and 2. Publications in Archeology, no. 18F. Santa
          Fe: National Park Service.
  1987b Population Estimates. In Summary of tests and excavations at the Pueblo
          Alto community. Investigations at the Pueblo Alto complex, Chaco
          Canyon, New Mexico, 1975–1979, vol. 1. By T. C. Windes, pp. 383–
          406. Publications in Archeology, no. 18F. Santa Fe: National Park
          Service.
Windes, Thomas C., and William H. Doleman
  1985   Small house population dynamics during the Bonito phase in Chaco

Canyon. Paper presented at 50th annual meeting, Society for American Archaeology, Denver.

Winter, Joseph C.
1980 Human adaptation in a marginal environment. *In* Human adaptation in a marginal environment: The UII mitigation project. Ed. J. L. Moore and J. C. Winter, pp. 483–520. Albuquerque: Office of Contract Archeology, University of New Mexico.

Wiseman, Regge
1982 Climatic changes and population shifts in the Chuska Valley: A trial correlation. *In* Collected papers in honor of John W. Runyon. Ed. G. X. Fitzgerald. Papers of the Archaeological Society of New Mexico, no. 7, pp. 111–25. Albuquerque.

Wiseman, Regge N., and J. Andrew Darling
1986 The Bronze Trail Site group. *In* By hands unknown: Papers on rock art and archaeology in honor of James G. Bain. Ed. A. Poore, pp. 115–43. Papers of the Archaeological Society of New Mexico, no. 12. Albuquerque.

Wood, J. Scott
1985 The northeastern periphery. *In* Proceedings of the 1983 Hohokam Symposium, part 1. Ed. A. E. Dittert Jr. and D. E. Dove. Occasional Paper, no. 2, pp. 239–62. Arizona Archaeological Society, Phoenix Chapter.

Woodbury, Richard B.
1960 The Hohokam canals at Pueblo Grande, Arizona. American Antiquity 26:267–70.
1961a A reappraisal of Hohokam irrigation. American Anthropologist 63: 550–60.
1961b Prehistoric agriculture at Point of Pines, Arizona. Memoirs of the Society for American Archaeology, no. 17. Menasha, Wisconsin.

Woodward, Arthur
1931 The Grewe Site. Occasional Papers, no. 1. Los Angeles: The Los Angeles Museum of History, Science, and Art.
1936 A shell bracelet manufactory. American Antiquity 2:117–25.
1941 Hohokam mosaic mirrors. Quarterly 4:7–11. Los Angeles: Museum Patrons Association of the Los Angeles City Museum.

Woosley, Anne I.
1980 Agricultural diversity in the prehistoric Southwest. The Kiva 45:317–36.

Wormington, H. Marie
1947 Prehistoric Indians of the Southwest. Denver Museum of Natural History Popular Series, no. 7.

Zazlow, Bert, and Alfred E. Dittert Jr.
1977 Pattern technology of the Hohokam. Anthropological Research Papers, no. 2. Tempe: Arizona State University.

Index

School of American Research Advanced Seminar Series

PUBLISHED BY SAR PRESS

CHACO & HOHOKAM: PREHISTORIC REGIONAL SYSTEMS IN THE AMERICAN SOUTHWEST
Patricia L. Crown &
W. James Judge, eds.

RECAPTURING ANTHROPOLOGY: WORKING IN THE PRESENT
Richard G. Fox, ed.

WAR IN THE TRIBAL ZONE: EXPANDING STATES AND INDIGENOUS WARFARE
R. Brian Ferguson &
Neil L. Whitehead, eds.

IDEOLOGY AND PRE-COLUMBIAN CIVILIZATIONS
Arthur A. Demarest &
Geoffrey W. Conrad, eds.

DREAMING: ANTHROPOLOGICAL AND PSYCHOLOGICAL INTERPRETATIONS
Barbara Tedlock, ed.

HISTORICAL ECOLOGY: CULTURAL KNOWLEDGE AND CHANGING LANDSCAPES
Carole L. Crumley, ed.

THEMES IN SOUTHWEST PREHISTORY
George J. Gumerman, ed.

MEMORY, HISTORY, AND OPPOSITION UNDER STATE SOCIALISM
Rubie S. Watson, ed.

OTHER INTENTIONS: CULTURAL CONTEXTS AND THE ATTRIBUTION OF INNER STATES
Lawrence Rosen, ed.

LAST HUNTERS–FIRST FARMERS: NEW PERSPECTIVES ON THE PREHISTORIC TRANSITION TO AGRICULTURE
T. Douglas Price &
Anne Birgitte Gebauer, eds.

MAKING ALTERNATIVE HISTORIES: THE PRACTICE OF ARCHAEOLOGY AND HISTORY IN NON-WESTERN SETTINGS
Peter R. Schmidt &
Thomas C. Patterson, eds.

SENSES OF PLACE
Steven Feld & Keith H. Basso, eds.

CYBORGS & CITADELS: ANTHROPOLOGICAL INTERVENTIONS IN EMERGING SCIENCES AND TECHNOLOGIES
Gary Lee Downey & Joseph Dumit, eds.

ARCHAIC STATES
Gary M. Feinman & Joyce Marcus, eds.

CRITICAL ANTHROPOLOGY NOW: UNEXPECTED CONTEXTS, SHIFTING CONSTITUENCIES, CHANGING AGENDAS
George E. Marcus, ed.

THE ORIGINS OF LANGUAGE: WHAT NONHUMAN PRIMATES CAN TELL US
Barbara J. King, ed.

REGIMES OF LANGUAGE: IDEOLOGIES, POLITIES, AND IDENTITIES
Paul V. Kroskrity, ed.

BIOLOGY, BRAINS, AND BEHAVIOR: THE EVOLUTION OF HUMAN DEVELOPMENT
Sue Taylor Parker, Jonas Langer, &
Michael L. McKinney, eds.

WOMEN & MEN IN THE PREHISPANIC SOUTHWEST: LABOR, POWER, & PRESTIGE
Patricia L. Crown, ed.

HISTORY IN PERSON: ENDURING STRUGGLES, CONTENTIOUS PRACTICE, INTIMATE IDENTITIES
Dorothy Holland & Jean Lave, eds.

THE EMPIRE OF THINGS: REGIMES OF VALUE AND MATERIAL CULTURE
Fred R. Myers, ed.

URUK MESOPOTAMIA & ITS NEIGHBORS: CROSS-CULTURAL INTERACTIONS IN THE ERA OF STATE FORMATION
Mitchell S. Rothman, ed.

CATASTROPHE & CULTURE: THE ANTHROPOLOGY OF DISASTER
Susanna M. Hoffman &
Anthony Oliver-Smith, eds.

PUBLISHED BY UNIVERSITY OF ARIZONA PRESS

THE COLLAPSE OF ANCIENT STATES AND
CIVILIZATIONS
Norman Yoffee &
George L. Cowgill, eds.

PUBLISHED BY UNIVERSITY OF NEW MEXICO PRESS

RECONSTRUCTING PREHISTORIC PUEBLO
SOCIETIES
William A. Longacre, ed.

NEW PERSPECTIVES ON THE PUEBLOS
Alfonso Ortiz, ed.

STRUCTURE AND PROCESS IN LATIN
AMERICA
Arnold Strickon &
Sidney M. Greenfield, eds.

THE CLASSIC MAYA COLLAPSE
T. Patrick Culbert, ed.

METHODS AND THEORIES OF
ANTHROPOLOGICAL GENETICS
M. H. Crawford & P. L. Workman, eds.

SIXTEENTH-CENTURY MEXICO:
THE WORK OF SAHAGUN
Munro S. Edmonson, ed.

ANCIENT CIVILIZATION AND TRADE
Jeremy A. Sabloff &
C. C. Lamberg-Karlovsky, eds.

PHOTOGRAPHY IN ARCHAEOLOGICAL
RESEARCH
Elmer Harp, Jr., ed.

MEANING IN ANTHROPOLOGY
Keith H. Basso & Henry A. Selby, eds.

THE VALLEY OF MEXICO: STUDIES IN
PRE-HISPANIC ECOLOGY AND SOCIETY
Eric R. Wolf, ed.

DEMOGRAPHIC ANTHROPOLOGY:
QUANTITATIVE APPROACHES
Ezra B. W. Zubrow, ed.

THE ORIGINS OF MAYA CIVILIZATION
Richard E. W. Adams, ed.

EXPLANATION OF PREHISTORIC CHANGE
James N. Hill, ed.

EXPLORATIONS IN ETHNOARCHAEOLOGY
Richard A. Gould, ed.

ENTREPRENEURS IN CULTURAL CONTEXT
Sidney M. Greenfield, Arnold Strickon,
& Robert T. Aubey, eds.

THE DYING COMMUNITY
Art Gallaher, Jr. &
Harlan Padfield, eds.

SOUTHWESTERN INDIAN RITUAL DRAMA
Charlotte J. Frisbie, ed.

LOWLAND MAYA SETTLEMENT PATTERNS
Wendy Ashmore, ed.

SIMULATIONS IN ARCHAEOLOGY
Jeremy A. Sabloff, ed.

CHAN CHAN: ANDEAN DESERT CITY
Michael E. Moseley & Kent C. Day, eds.

SHIPWRECK ANTHROPOLOGY
Richard A. Gould, ed.

ELITES: ETHNOGRAPHIC ISSUES
George E. Marcus, ed.

THE ARCHAEOLOGY OF LOWER CENTRAL
AMERICA
Frederick W. Lange &
Doris Z. Stone, eds.

LATE LOWLAND MAYA CIVILIZATION:
CLASSIC TO POSTCLASSIC
Jeremy A. Sabloff &
E. Wyllys Andrews V, eds.

Participants in the advanced seminar "Cultural Complexity in the Arid Southwest: The Hohokam and Chacoan Regional Systems." School of American Research, Santa Fe, October 1987.

Front row, left to right: David E. Doyel, Lynne Sebastian, W. James Judge, Patricia L. Crown, David A. Gregory.

Back row, left to right: Stephen H. Lekson, H. Wolcott Toll, R. Gwinn Vivian, W. Bruce Masse, Charles L. Redman, David R. Wilcox.